ART FOR
PREADOLESCENTS

ART FOR PREADOLESCENTS

Angiola R. Churchill

Associate Professor of Art Education
New York University

McGraw-Hill Book Company

New York   St. Louis   San Francisco   Düsseldorf
Johannesburg   Kuala Lumpur   London   Mexico
Montreal   New Delhi   Panama
Rio de Janeiro   Singapore
Sydney   Toronto

Art for Preadolescents

Library of Congress Catalog Card Number 70-144767

07-010857-9

1234567890 HDMA 7987654321

*This book was set in Optima by John C. Meyer & Son, printed on
permanent paper by Halliday Lithograph Corporation, and bound
by The Maple Press Co. The designer was Elliot Epstein; the
drawings were done by John Cordes, J. & R. Technical Services,
Inc. The editors were Samuel B. Bossard and Helen Greenberg.
John F. Harte supervised production.*

Contents

10. Our Assemblage Environment, 317

11. The Collaborative Arts, 341

Summary: A Time for Liberation, 397

Preface

This book is an attempt to explore preadolescents' artistic interests and responses, to identify various special problems they face in growing up in our society, and to suggest how we might help them apply creative attitudes to living. Unfortunately, preadolescents, because of their own growth patterns and the low status of the arts in education and society, frequently lose interest in the arts permanently. However, if suitable art experiences are consistently available, the basic nature of the arts will be seen as being compatible with the basic impetus of preadolescence. The arts present the preadolescent with opportunities to solve problems, make choices, and pursue self-investigation leading to self-knowledge—all of which encourage personality development and help the child to define his role in society.

I became interested in preadolescents twenty-five years ago when I left college teaching and began to work with the elementary grades at the Ethical Culture Schools in New York. Children from ten to thirteen years of age make special demands upon their teachers. Though still children, they are already coping with imminent physical maturity. They are dependent, yet seeking independence; brimming with ideas and energy, yet incapable of prolonged interests. They are brash and sassy, yet they long for approbation, acceptance, and respect.

Early in my experience at the elementary level, I realized that while very young children were easy and rewarding to work with, because of their spontaneity and warmth and the quality of their art expression, the joys of teaching preadolescents were harder won. My greatest efforts were directed at solving one problem: how to reach this special age group. It became a matter of trying to extricate myself as well as I could from the fractious binds the children and I found ourselves in so often. All my ingenuity was demanded. Like many other teachers, I had come, almost without preparation and almost unaware, upon a special region of continuing interest and challenge in my life's work.

When, after twelve years, I returned to college to teach prospective teachers, my involvement with preadolescents continued. All too often, too many first-year teachers, regardless of preference, find that the only available appointments are in the first year of junior high schools—scarcely a satisfactory first teaching experience and hardly beneficial to preadolescent pupils. Undergraduates in teachers' colleges therefore need a curriculum that incorporates theory and practice in the teaching of preadolescents. There is, however, very little source material, apart from the records of personal successes of a few art teachers. Even psychologists have neglected this segment of child development; library shelves are filled with studies of adolescents and of children under the age of nine or so, but few of preadolescents. The lack of research and of published material became apparent, and I chose this no-man's-land of child development as an area of special research.

During the last six years, changes in education have focused some attention on the problems of preadolescents. Urban underprivileged minorities have begun to insist upon more community control and that educators meet more realistically the special needs of this age group. The push to investigate and reevaluate methods and curricula has been salubrious. Administrators, parents, teachers, and minority-group committees have become more willing to deal with the fact that preadolescents must be considered as not necessarily isolated from younger or older pupils but as constituting a group with characteristics of its own.

Although this book is devoted to the art curriculum for grades five, six, and seven, one of my purposes is to involve *all* teachers of preadolescents in the promulgation of aesthetic activities that channel preadolescents' energies and talents so that they may find art a meaningful resource for the rest of their lives. It seems reasonable to show that children, as people and as artists, express themselves in themes common to man in every epoch of history. They create people, in order to know themselves; animals, to express their affinity with them; supernatural creatures, to control their fear of the unknown; and environments, to create and embellish a place of their own. Their symbolic abstractions express their joy in the phenomena of color, texture, and other optical experiences; they are also a way of communicating many things otherwise difficult to express. The alert teacher recognizes these elemental reactions *as they emerge* with the particular slant preadolescents give to them. Pictures of their work are coordinated with the text throughout. Résumés of art history and criticism are included to enrich the teacher's perceptions of what these children are doing.

Theory and practice are interwoven in this book. Teaching methods and strategies are related to the psychological traits of preadolescents: their urge to act in groups, and their desire to emerge from the fantasied ambience of childhood into the realities, however disturbing, of the adult world. They are particularly susceptible to the influence of what is going on *right now* in *their* life. Therefore, I have tried to give emphasis to the contemporary art scene, the intricate interrelationships of mixed media and the transitory modes which reflect the turmoil and changes in modern life while at the same time showing the relationship of preadolescents' art to both their daily lives and contemporary art forms.

Equally important, attention has been given to the techniques and atmosphere necessary to the creation of art: in other words, how learning takes place in this field and how it can best be nurtured by the teacher. Surveys and anecdotes provide resources for the teacher to develop individual patterns of work and plans for explanations. An extensive bibliography is included for further investigation.

A slide collection containing examples, in color, of preadolescent two- and three-dimensional works accompanies the book, deepening the salient points made in the text. The collection is meant to be used by student teachers and teachers to supplement the text in class discussions and as a resource for independent study.

Last devices, insights, and conditions have been identified which have made programs, activities, and projects memorable moments in living and learning for myself, my students, and fellow teachers. Anecdotes of teachers' efforts to build upon preadolescents' desire to work in groups will, I hope, help teachers use fully such collaborative arts as drama, puppetry, happenings, and film making. I believe that this book may provide more understanding of today's preadolescents and the need for teachers to orient themselves to the changing concepts of education. The problem of the inner city and its children comes into focus frequently throughout these pages. I have tried to persuade others that experience in art brings additional fulfillment; that the substance of art expands the means by which to share with others; and that awareness must be nurtured seriously and consistently. Perhaps teachers and prospective teachers will, through this book, become involved and fascinated by the preadolescent and will appreciate his drive to create art.

Angiola R. Churchill

Acknowledgments

I am grateful to Lucile F. Young, who trained me as a beginning teacher, and Lera Beth Lumbley, a colleague in my years of teaching at the Ethical Culture School.

My thanks to Viktor d'Amico for providing a consistently important influence through all my years of teaching.

Mildred Fairchild and Edwin Ziegfeld offered dependable support and guidance during my college years. Justin Schorr gave sustained cooperation and invaluable assistance in my doctoral work. Howard Conant, chairman, and the art staff at New York University have provided a congenial atmosphere for discussion and constructive testing of ideas.

Readers will recognize the influence of such philosophers as Dewey and such historians as Haftmann, as well as the innovative programs and methods of specialists in the traditional and collaborative arts. Hopefully, all will have received proper mention in text, references or bibliography. Regrettably, a few will have been overlooked. To all I owe my thanks for the richness they have provided in my work with students and in this volume.

My appreciation is also due to the many school administrators, teachers and student teachers who aided so much in the development of this work by making available their resources and services; special thanks to Marion Quinn Dix, Olive L. Riley, Victoria Wagner, Temina Gezari, and George Kay.

This book owes much to Gerta Prosser. Not only has her scrutiny improved the structure, flow, logic, readability and style of the text, but she has maintained my morale throughout this effort.

My thanks also to the staff of McGraw-Hill: to Bernard Myers and Sam Bossard, who gave me generous support and held to the highest standards of publishing; to Helen Greenberg for judicious cutting and meticulous attention to detail involved in producing a book with so many illustrations; and to Elliot Epstein for a design of fine quality and taste and for his genuine delight in the children's work.

To Nancy Copeland, who labored through numerous and tedious readings of galleys, I owe my thanks.

Finally, the writer wishes to express profound indebtedness to her immediate family: her mother, Ester Riva, and her husband, Walter F. Churchill, for their confidence, encouragement, tolerance and forebearance during the several years in which this book came into being.

Angiola R. Churchill

Photographic Credits

I am most grateful to administrators, teachers, student teachers, and photographers who have made available the many photographs contained in this book. It would have been desirable to place credits for each picture on the page where it appears, but the number of reproductions and the requirements of design made this impossible. I hope that the following plan will prove satisfactory. Each source will be cited, followed by the page numbers on which its photographs appear. If more than one photograph appears on a given page, the method of identification will be as follows: reading (from top to bottom on the left). *a, b, c;* (from top to bottom on the right) *a, b, c* (letters read from top to bottom of page).

Bentley School   *Art instructor:* Betty Thompson. *Photographer:* Michael Sullivan—377.

Board of Jewish Education   *Art director:* Temima Gezari; *Photographer:* Herbert Sonnenfeld—36, 259.

Bureau of Art, Board of Education, City of New York   *Art directors:* Olive L. Riley (former), George Kay (present). All photographs by Michael Sullivan and Angiola Churchill, except where indicated—23, 28, 29 left *b,* 38 left *b,* 49 (mural by John Hendericks—*Art supervisor:* Cecille Davis, District 6), 68, 71 *c,* 72 (Lillian Stienmuller, *Instructor*), 74 *a,* 75 *a, b,* 76, 84 left *a,* 96 (four), 159, 163, 171 (*Photographer:* Judith Riesner; *Art supervisor:* Marjorie Doe, District 10), 218 *a,* 221 right *a,* 222, 223 (two), 246, 258, 259 *b,* 300 (Jr. H. 71: Sharon Hausman, *student teacher;* Mora Irael, *Instructor*), 368 (five) Mel Hans *Photographer,* 386 (four).

Children's Art Studio (a diagnostic study), New York University, 1959   Sponsored by Minn. Mining & Manufacturing Co. *Director:* Howard Conant. *Art instructor:* Angiola Churchill. *Photographers:* Michael Sullivan—91 (two), 152, 213 (three); William R. Simmons—313, 320.

Howard Conant—*Photographer and instructor*—298.

Tom Cresap—*Photographer*—380.

Elizabeth, N. J., Public Schools, Art Education Department   *Director of art education:* Marion Quin Dix. *Photographers:* Daily Journal Photographers—319; Richard Koles—336; David Kidwell—339; Linda A. Shulsky—325, 335 left *c,* 338; Michael Sullivan—10, 332, 323, 329 (two), 333, 336 (two), 367. (Instructors connected with these photographs—Henrietta Rontino, Lee Andeson, Anne Dobek, Mildred Wolf, Ronald Gaschke, Mary Jane Austin, Jerry Hochberg.)

Ethical Culture Schools (Fieldston)   *Art chairman:* Philip Held. *Photographers:* Ada Landis—151, 260; Victor Consiglio—335, 337 right *c.*

Ethical Culture Schools (Midtown)   Former art instructors under whose supervision the work shown was produced: Angiola R. Churchill, Lera Beth Lumbley, Lucile F. Young.
Photographers: Angiola R. Churchill—20, 21, 22, 24, 25, 29 left and right *a*, 30 (three), 32 (two), 34 (two), 35, 36 left and right *a*, 37, 38 *a*, 68 left, 69 (two), 71 left and right *a*, 72 *c*, 73 *a*, 74 *b*, 75 *c*, 77 (two), 79 (four), 80 *b*, 81, 82, 95 (two), 115 (three), 117 (four), 120 (two), 122 (two), 123, 124, 130, 131, 132, 133 (three), 135, 136 (two), 137, 138, 139, 140, 141, 142 (two), 153, 154 left *c*, 172 right *c*, 180, 181 (two), 182, 185, 220, 221 right *b*, 232, 235, 245 *b*, 267, 268 left *b*, 282, 306, 331, 388, 389, 390 (three), 391 (three); Margot Kaiser—*Photographer*— 292, 293 *c*; Joan la Rocca—*Photographer*—309; Morris Rosenfeld—*Photographer* —334; Mr. and Mrs. S. Z. Rosenfeld—27 *c*, 247, 268 right *b*, 293 *c*, 334; Michael Sullivan—27 *a*, 73 *b*, 83 (two) 84 left *a*, right *b*, 155, 162 (two), 164, 165 (three), 167 (two), 169 (two), 170, 172 left *c*, 183 (three), 211, 218 *b*, 221 left *b*, 223 left *b*, 234, 245 *a*, 248, 252, 256, 261, 286, 293 left and right *b*, 357; Soichi Sunami— *Photographer*—314.

Steven Greenbaum—*Instructor and photographer*—386 (two).

Pecky Kaupelis—*Photographer*—326.

Tad Krumeich—*Instructor* (Michael Sullivan *Photographer*)—70.

Little Red School House   Art directors: Walter Kendra (former); Marcia Wallace (present). *Photographers:* Raimondo Borea (Marcie Wallace *Instructor*)—Introduction page 9; *Photographers:* Michael Sullivan (Elizabeth Weiner *Instructor*)— 233; *Photographers:* Gail Miller *Photographer and Student Teacher* under Walter Kendra—378 (two).

Museum of Modern Art   *Educational director:* Viktor d'Amico. *Photographer:* Soichi Sunami—265, 280, 299, 301, 304, 310 left *b*, 312, 332.

New Lincoln School   *Art director:* Lois Lord (former); Doris Staal (present). *Photographers:* Elizabeth Barbrove—237; Lois Lord—92 (two), 236, 310, 311; Phyllis Stepper—80 *a*.

Phillips M. Simkin   *Photographer:* Introduction page 7, 328 (two).

Westport, Conn., Public Schools   *Art instructor:* Burt Chernow; *Photographer:* Michael Sullivan—159 right *c*, 161.

White Plains Storefront Studio   *Directors:* Jam McEvoy and Joy Moser. *Photographer:* Joy Moser—Introduction page 6, 327, 353.

Whitney American Museum of Art, The Art Resources Center   *Head, education department:* David Hupert. Introduction page 11, 13.

Introduction:
A New Environment
for Learning

Now that repressive teaching methods and old-fashioned school housing are being challenged by so many at all levels of American society, will the pied pipers of art education at last be given the support that will enable them to work more significantly with children in our public schools?

In the elementary grades, the art teacher still pushes her cart of colors and stuffs up and down many corridors. On her way to school, she has scavenged bits of string and odds and ends from the friendly grocer, who considers her a nice lady who really likes kids. She goes from room to room. The children prick up their ears and reach out for the materials and experiences she brings. When they enter secondary school they find her in her art room—a haven for them in spite of its limitations, a place of fantasy and pleasure.

In the past, only the children could hear the summoning tune. Nowadays there are signs that it has reached other ears and that the philosophy and methods of art education, which have made their way slowly into the schools, are beginning to receive the attention they deserve. Art educators have long advocated flexible scheduling, open studios, mixed age levels, free experimentation, free choice of activities, more individual attention and better correlated studies in the humanities. They have had little faith in IQ tests and have persistently refused to accept the standard competitive marking system. They have believed in a multisensory approach to learning and have been adamant in their refusal to use those two killjoys, humiliation and coercion, establishing in their stead experimentation and play as essential tools of learning.

Enlightened educators in all fields are now saying what the artist-teacher has been saying for years:

We can take that extra two-thirds of the present school time available right now (as a few experimental schools are doing) and get on with the most exhilarating experiment in man's history: to help every child become, in his own way, an artist: to help every child become, in his

1

own way, a genius: to see how far toward ecstasy and accomplishment every human being can go. [1: pp. 116–117]

In keeping with our original, now fading, pioneer mores, American educators have traditionally had a bias against the arts. In a utilitarian culture, art is play, and play is sinful and weakening. What Leonard (1) calls the "Dionysian spirit" has been kept out of learning except in a few progressive schools, which were spurred on by Dewey and other reformers and organized on the principle that children learn best when self-motivated, curiosity-motivated, and solving problems in ways that give them personal joy and ego satisfaction.

Now scientists, politicians, businessmen, intellectuals, leaders of minority groups, parents, enlightened school superintendents, and professors are at last realizing that what is learned in public schools is only a fraction of what children could learn during the same period of time. Spelling, reading, and mathematics are basic tools that can be taught by new efficient methods developed by our technology. Experimenters are searching for new environments to house new methods and media that may keep our young willingly in school and also equip them more rationally for existence in the modern world. Worse evils than play and addiction to art have cropped up in the last decade. Even our most conservative academicians sense that survival depends in part on our ability to push out obsolete curricula, to relax schedules, to remodel and adjust the teaching hierarchy, to hook in some technological aids, to open the windows a few inches for fresh air.

There are reformers who say that the educational establishment cannot merely be patched up, but must be torn down and built anew. Changes are certainly needed in both principles and practices; the reform must be physical as well as academic. What is needed is a whole new school environment to serve the child growing up in the middle of the debris and the excitement of the techno-humanistic revolution.

A crippling assumption underlying our public schools is that all children should be treated uniformly, and that they, in turn, must conform to certain learning and behavior patterns. This is a pragmatic attitude stemming from the nineteenth-century belief that a factory assembly line technique is the most efficient way of educating the "masses." In spite of talk about differences in personality, intellect and culture, our schools still teach according to mass-oriented curricula; any deviation from so-called normal middle-class American values is still penalized. The revolt of a segment (not inconsiderable) of our middle- and lower-class youth, who now comprise over half of our active population, can be taken as a warning and a sign.

Another obsolete belief is that children learn best in a situation of aggressive competition and that fundamentally we all work for material rewards. It will be hard to convince many educators that we are passing out of an era of dog-eat-dog competition and that the children of today may be motivated by a whole different set of rewards involving communication and creativity. The out-of-date marking system in our schools seems barbaric to the younger generation. They want us to move away from the compartmentalized education of the nineteenth century as well, in which each subject area was treated as a separate entity. Children react best to learning in which disciplines and arts are considered in combination or as having relation to each other.

In great part, youth is turning away from congested, inadequate school buildings and a system by which learning is presented in packages. They want and need a more natural and direct learning experience related to their personal lives and the times they live in. They find it impossible to adjust to two segregated and warring worlds: the outside environment with its electronic speed and violently new popular culture, and the confined structure and static curriculum in which the twentieth century has barely been recognized. Most of the children spend their school days occupied with daydreams, petty cheating, learning to take tests, playing it cool and getting ahead by producing neat notebooks and simulating the "right" attitudes. The rest of the students, including the racial and ethnic minorities, simply "turn off" and refuse to play the game. The dropout is the significant educational phenomenon of our day.

Children are born now into a chaotic and ambivalent world. A stable identity is hard to come by, especially in the cities. Moments of exhilaration, pleasure, confidence, and intellectual discovery mean more to the child who is trying to find out who he is than endlessly forcing himself to meet standards which will some day turn him into a certain kind of ideal American. For a vast proportion of our public schoolchildren, this middle-class identity seems unattainable. For some it has even become undesirable.

It was Dewey who first insisted that education should be a "process of living" and not merely a preparation for future living. Our schools today provide little process of living. They have become more like detention homes in which the children pass hour after hour waiting for the bell to ring or the siren to sound. The keepers tell them, *Sh-sh,* stop asking questions, *sh-sh,* keep your bodies still. Such physical restraint is exhausting. The fatigued children, whose instinct is to move, are held down by equally fatigued teachers who must maintain control by excessive discipline. This is the deadly product of overcrowding.

Even new schools, as they are planned and built today, are

old-fashioned. The environment for learning remains sterile and constrained. Until new principles involving mobility, play, choice, creativity, and self-activation are understood and technological aids are increasingly adopted, school architecture will continue to be dehumanizing.

Science has discovered that the reaction of a creature to its environment can change its brain chemistry. A group of rats brought up in a communal cage, with toys to play with, in a room full of sun and air, and taken out and handled gently every day produced a higher proportion of an important brain enzyme than a group of their litter mates living in isolated cages in a dark, silent room and deprived of any affection or entertainment. The cortex area (associated with higher learning) proved to be noticeably larger and heavier in the brains of the privileged rats (1: pp. 36–37).

When one recalls the environmental poverty of many schoolrooms, especially in the city ghettos—the high, antiseptic walls, hospitallike, within which the children are held in rigid silence behind their separate barriers of fear and no-English and shame—then the crime we are perpetuating against children seems enormous. The worst victims have been children of parents too poor or ignorant of their rights to demand anything else. Needless to say, the education of the disadvantaged attracted minimum attention in the past, and now the urban overpopulation crisis finds us wanting.

History records numerous instances of the stifling of the human potential by either cruel intention or indifference. Lack of scientific knowledge and man's consuming fear for his individual survival made it easy to accept the notion that certain groups of men, because they were poor or had dissimilar physical or cultural qualities, were therefore intellectually inferior and less initiative and intelligence potential could be expected of them. Though science has debunked this notion, it is still prevalent, often automatic, and children of a large segment of our population are labeled and categorized in ways that hamper their natural growth. It is now known that *every* individual could do infinitely more than is expected of him, regardless of class, race or culture. The key to his development lies in how he is regarded by others, how he is encouraged to try, how he is respected for the things he knows and the person he is, and, finally and realistically, what opportunities society offers him. If society offers him none, why should he make the effort? If he himself is convinced he is inferior, how can he make the effort? The result can be a colossal waste of our most precious resources: human energy and intelligence.

The many experimental centers blossoming in disadvantaged neighborhoods in recent years have been fruitful with innovative ideas. Their programs provide practical inspiration to work toward a reorganization of our school system. They have proved that art education can play a positive role in the total education of poor and alienated children in our affluent society. The child who is encouraged to create in the various art media is often transformed from an unreachable, withdrawn, nonverbal individual into a student ready and able to receive other types of learning. The multisensory experience seems to help these children adjust to a variety of stimuli in the objective world, as well as lifting their spirits to the point where they are able to take on the difficult tasks of reading, spelling, and mathematics.

The White Plains Storefront Studio, directed by Mrs. Joy Moser and Miss Jan McEvoy, is a case in point. It was my part in one summer program to bring African sculpture and fine reproductions of art from other cultures for the children to handle, look at and talk about. The community was mainly Puerto Rican and black; the children were mostly preadolescents, with a sprinkling of younger ones. They came in droves, 150 per day all summer long. The program became part of the neighborhood life, with parents and older siblings dropping in constantly to see what was going on. Many of the older brothers were in the delinquent category, but nothing was stolen. There was no robbery or vandalism. The storefront became a source of pride, racial identity, and personality development.

The children had access to many art media. In the afternoons, films were shown in the basement. There were shorts about Africa—dances, music, customs, wild animals—nature and science films, and art appreciation tapes. The children also made films of their own. Some were TV-influenced stories, such as Indians attacking white settlers or African tribal war. Mostly the children did their filming in the lots surrounding the storefront, where the stones and rubble of torn-down buildings provided exciting locations for the action.

Some of the children worked 3 hours a day or more, for many days in a row, on a single piece of work—an experience in depth. The mood of the studio was free, untrammeled, and noisy. There was, however, a sophisticated structure underlying the fluidity and permissiveness. Important elements were: no humiliation, no coercion, mixed age levels (the older ones proudly advising the younger and each learning from the other), limited peer group or gang problems, the long hours the children were allowed to spend in the building (they were waiting for their teachers in the morning and had to be pushed out at 4 P.M.), and the open house atmosphere that made the whole community welcome.

The progress of work in all media made it clear that these preadolescents, who were coming to the experience for the first time, with little or no art background, could deal with elaborate ideas provided we were courageous enough to let them handle, digest, and assimilate it into their own styles and moods.

The art appreciation program was highly rewarding. The children touched, held, stroked, and took temporary possession of the African sculpture; it was a warm emotional experience. They seemed to associate with the objects as with old friends. There can be no doubt about the psychological, ego-building value for black youngsters of this contact with great works they recognized as coming out of their own cultural heritage.

We recorded the reactions of the children, both in groups and singly, to reproductions of great art. The tape recorder was in a sense the key that opened the doors of their minds. They were eager to hear their voices played back—another way of finding their identity. We noticed that after hearing themselves on tape, they were able to organize their thoughts better the next time and to improve their delivery and choice of words. I could see no fundamental difference between the reactions of privileged preadolescents I had taught in Ethical Culture schools and these ghetto children. They associated the paintings with events in their own lives and with bits of history they knew (Assyrian horsemen became American Indians for one boy) and even were able, after a short exposure, to look at three reproductions of horses from different civilizations and develop related ideas about them. It was exciting, too, when a shy Puerto Rican child who could not speak English ran off to bring back an issue of *Life* magazine and pointed out an illustrated article on Egyptian art after seeing the reproduction of Tutankhamen.

Projects of this kind seem to make headway in meeting the needs and stimulating the creativity of our urban disadvantaged youth. When a child from a racial or ethnic minority has had

nothing but verbal failures in school, such an opportunity to show intelligence, to develop a feeling for relationships, to be *adequate*, may make all the difference in his future development. Similar programs have been developed by settlement houses and community health centers. Professional art teachers will become more and more involved, as will artists and laymen. Melvin Roman sees it as a general movement spreading through small neighborhoods of inner cities all over the country. These centers will be

staffed by indigenous non-professionals and will offer a wide range of services related to health, education and welfare. It is within such dilineated neighborhoods that artists as members of a change-team can help crystallize and bring into full realization that which is healthy amid so much that is pathological. [2: p. 24]

These centers are most valuable. They do not supplant art programs in the schools; they *support* them. Administrators are beginning to give art courses a more important position in the curriculum. Teachers of other subjects are being encouraged to take art education courses.

Even more significant, integrated humanities programs are being considered and organized. This is in reaction to the general feeling that subjects have been taught too much in isolation from each other and have aimed merely at stocking up the student with enough facts to pass his examinations creditably.

The new aim is to correlate fields of learning and give the student a sense of human culture as a whole, interconnected, and connected to himself. Humanistic values are associated with philosophy, the arts and literature, music, social and personal morality, civil rights, political freedom, loyalty, and bravery, as distinguished from mechanical or utilitarian values. The New York State Education Department's Commission on Humanities defines its aim:

Through the humanities we seek intellectual humility, sensitivity to beauty, and emotional discipline. By them we may come to know the excitement of ideas, the power of imagination, and the unsuspected energies of the creative spirit. [3: p. v]

Explicitly, the students will be offered interdisciplinary courses, some with direct experience in the performing and graphic arts, along with study of literature and correlated with social studies. This is a praiseworthy effort to balance the excessive technological and vocational emphasis in the high schools as well as in the middle, junior high, and upper elementary schools. Colleges are already intensifying their humanities programs.

There is general recognition that children's preferences should be considered more seriously than they are now in the formation of the curriculum. In other words, students should pursue what interests them. Through this pursuit they will come upon the related concepts underlying one field of study and discover and master techniques necessary to the activity or task they have chosen.

To organize the course content that is to be offered to the children, and the scheduling that will make their choices possible, becomes a fascinating challenge, albeit a difficult one. Educators are aware of the benefits of this idea for motivating learning. For years I worked in a private school that instituted a system by which students chose certain projects, activities, and courses. For a large portion of the school week, the children were given "optionals." After hearing about the activities and course content of each optional, every child would sign up for one of them for a term, or possibly a shorter period. Some of the optionals were so popular that there were waiting lists for them; others died, or were discontinued after one trial.

There were choices in specific areas of science, poetry writing, weaving, drama, photography, and newspaper work. Children requested certain other optionals. A grandfather taught one in chess. Other nonprofessionals—relatives, artists, friends—were drawn in to teach. One mother taught cooking. This was not a hobby atmosphere, however; the offerings were well and seriously planned. Professional teachers had the major responsi-

bility. It was up to them to bring the optionals into being, crop and revise them, take them out or put them in again according to the children's interest and the abilities and availability of the personnel. One of the teachers' most important tasks was to analyze the course content and find out why certain optionals failed to interest the children. Without constant evaluation, the system could not succeed.

Even in our existing schools, such a curriculum innovation can be tried if teaching machines, in combination with tutorial programs, have been installed to take care of the basic three R's for 3 or 4 hours in the morning, supplemented by individual and small-group learning programs. This would leave the afternoon for the optionals. The self-motivation brought out by *choosing* makes an astounding difference in a child's learning ability. This is true for any age. It is a pity that most of our students cannot experience the stimulation of private creative research until late high school or college years. At the elementary and high school levels, creative learning can be approximated as the teacher, having invented optionals which cut across different areas of learning, then guides and helps the child comprehend the direction of his activity and learn to evaluate his own achievement. The optional system has worked exceptionally well in art education. It might possibly bring a new current of energy into our wilting inner-city schools.

Other ideas and other questions are cropping up everywhere. Should a child be attached to a given school for all his studies, or should he become more mobile? Are we victims of habit and fear of change when we believe that one static building, with the resources of one staff, can provide adequately stimulating experiences? Learning environments could be located at intervals within a city or suburb, providing different disciplines—music, visual arts, science, drama, and other subjects. Students could come and go between them. The neighborhood school building might perhaps be considered a home base where children would go to plan activities. It would be the center of a galaxy of educational environments, not too far apart from each other, providing variety of scene and personnel. A child might spend 3 hours in one building, 2 in another. The buildings would be not elaborate, but appropriate. The art building, for instance, in a city environment, could be a loft or a storefront. In each building a different atmosphere and behavior would be maintained, depending on the nature of the subject.

This scheme, primarily urban and subject to prohibitive land and real estate values, would of course take different shape in a suburb. Rural districts present other possibilities of solving the problem of immobility, boredom and inevitable alienation from learning.

A relatively recent plan to group preadolescents (aged ten through thirteen) in a "middle school" may remedy the faults of the old junior high school. Such regrouping of age levels may give preadolescents who do not belong with the first four grades or with the more mature adolescents a curriculum adapted to their own needs and enthusiasms. One of the great advantages of the middle school is the opportunity to experiment with a freewheeling schedule, thus allowing studies in depth for children ready to pursue independent work in science, languages, the arts or music. In the middle schools that already exist, humanities programs have become very popular.

Each community will find its own ways to incorporate new ideas that can free its children from nineteenth-century education. Young people with children entering school are pushing their demands for new methods and a more stimulating environ-

ment. A big question mark, of course, hangs over the whole situation. Kenneth B. Clark puts it very bluntly:

There remains the disturbing question . . . whether the selective process involved in training and promoting educators and administrators for our public schools emphasizes qualities of possibity, conformity, caution, smoothness, and superficial affability, rather than the boldness, creativity, and ability to demand and obtain those things that are essential for solid and effective education for all children. If this is true, if our system of training and promotion rewards the wrong characteristics—then our hopes for reform are minimal, if not totally futile . . . To save our urban schools, we must first demonstrate to the public that the present level of public school inefficiency has reached a state of public calamity. It must be demonstrated that minority-group children are not the only victims . . . but that white children—privileged white children—also suffer, both potentially and immediately. [4: p. 138]

As art teachers we have firsthand knowledge of what a proper environment can do for children. In our studios we have created it on a small scale and made it function. It is a space that children can restructure from day to day and week to week. Ideally many art experiences should take place in rooms not unlike the gymnasiums of yesterday or the versatile loft studios of painters and sculptors. Old warehouses, barns, empty stores, and even large cleared-out basements make excellent studios in which space can become a cavern of silence and sounds, mystery and wonder, through the manipulation of light, color, music, movement, and materials.

In this space, there are all manner of materials and objects which children can manipulate and through which they can discover the relationships between man's activities: blocks, planks, rods, cardboard, mirrors, echo chambers, prisms, magnifying glass, abacus, graduated sticks, rulers, hyperbolic parabolas, pyramids, spheres, cones, colors, banners, sculptures, clay, paints, sand, plaster, and concrete (5).

There is no fixed furniture. Children sit or lie on the floor to talk and plan their next activities. Partitions and screens are moved around for privacy. No one is forced to be with the group or to be alone. The Art Resources Center, sponsored by the Whitney Museum, has created a studio environment based on children's need for privacy. Each student has his private space. No child is pestered to clean up. There have been astounding results.

In the art room of a school I worked in, we put mats on the floor for children who felt out of sorts. Somehow everyone must be given temporary relief from group life. The learning experience, which is a combination of cognition and creativity, should

take place in an environment of choice and discrimination. The child must be free to go forward and retreat, to take a stand within himself, to act strenuously when he sees fit. He should never be chained to a desk or kept inactive beyond his normal span of concentration. One of my enterprising student teachers provided a huge carton in the corner of her room where a child could creep in and be alone. An equally ingenious youngster strung up an electric cord with a light bulb so that one could work inside.

In the ideal environment, which is a fluid one, a child can develop to the full senses of touch, sound, taste, smell, and sight. He learns to *see*, in its most profound meaning—with all the senses and the mind. Unless children have space in which to move and build and dream, their minds drowse, atrophy, narrow. Without an active sensory life, they can never feel adequate to their times. Such a life is all but impossible in the present stultifying public school environment.

We have now become aware of the possibility of arranging the entire human environment as a work of art, as a teaching machine designed to maximize perception and to make everyday learning a process of discovery. [6: p. 68]

REFERENCES

1. George B. Leonard, *Education and Ecstasy*, Delacorte Press, New York, 1968.

2. Melvin Roman, "The Arts as Agents for Social Change: A Psychologist's Viewpoint," *Art Education*, December, 1968.

3. Gordon E. Van Hooft, Foreword, *The Humanities: A Planning Guide for Teachers*, New York State Education Department, Bureau of Secondary Curriculum, Albany, New York, 1966.

4. Kenneth B. Clark, "Alternatives to Urban Public Schools," *The Schoolhouse in the City*, ed. by Alvin Toffler, Frederick A. Praeger, Inc., New York, 1968.

5. David Lowry Burgess, *Fragments: A Way of Seeing and Seeking*, Newton Public Schools, Cambridge, Mass., 1968.

6. Marshall McLuhan, *The Medium Is the Message*, Bantam Books, New York, 1967.

PART ONE
PORTRAIT OF THE PREADOLESCENT

A General View   1

Children enter the period of preadolescence with verve, inquisitiveness, and marvelous physical stamina. They want to perform, make, move, explore, learn—all under their own direction. They are well equipped for this because at this stage in their lives they are usually at a peak of good health and are expanding their intellectual capacities.

Boys and girls from ages nine to thirteen look back on their childhood years with scorn; they think of them as repressive and confining. They expect and demand a new freedom and explore its potentialities with zest and enthusiasm. They also look forward consciously to their next plateau—adolescence—when they will gain status and privileges accorded the older children whom they now regard with awe and envy.

With heady, newfound power, preadolescents struggle to rid themselves of their dependence on adults who, they feel, are holding them back. Self-reliance and personal identity are their goals. Often this makes for exaggerated rebellion and bravado, which are annoying to adults. Yet looking closely, one can see their defiance diluted with fears, one of which is, paradoxically, the fear of being rejected by parents and teachers. Much to their chagrin, these boys and girls often fall back into the dependent behavior of early childhood which they now abhor.

As Mary Jane Loomis writes in *The Preadolescent,* "Since ventures into independence are frequently evidence of individual growth resulting in immature, often inferior performance by adult standards, it would seem important to modify expectations in many aspects of home and school living" (1: p. 9). Indeed, this dramatic surge out of babyhood causes a good deal of emotional and intellectual frustration, involving parents and teachers as well as the children themselves, and should be approached with forethought and sympathy.

Preadolescents have earned for themselves an infamous reputation. Teachers who have fled after miserable experiences with this age group have described the children as subversive, secretive, resentful, vindictive, rebellious, selfish, fresh, erratic, boisterous, irresponsible, ill-mannered, obnoxious, incorrigible, and unreachable. And in fact, when observed with neither empathy nor an effort to understand him, the preadolescent lives up to this description. He creates a highly charged atmosphere in school and at home, fights against routines, defies and is rude to adults, slams doors—and then regresses into tears. He feels picked on. At the slightest provocation he shouts the battle cry of his age: "Unfair!"

Too few have admitted that on the other side of the coin the preadolescent is enthusiastic, curious, coming quickly into his intelligence, refreshingly active and manipulative, with an entertaining sense of humor, generously capable of hero worship, very affectionate toward animals, and often loyal and courageous. When his shortcomings and volatility are expected and accepted, he can be an amusing and rewarding human being.

Among these boys and girls, all is restless, changeable, explosive. Constant confrontations with adults are matched by fights with each other. They hate and love violently; there is steady bickering. They run in age- and sex-segregated packs, protecting themselves against parents, school authorities and the whole established order. Curiously enough, they are hostile not only to adults but also to any peers whom they feel are not strong enough emotionally or physically to fight the battle for self-reliance. By and large, their good qualities are hidden behind what seems to be compulsive antisocial behavior, making them a notoriously unreasonable group, difficult to live with and taxing to teach.

Why do they behave in this exaggerated way?

Those who decide to teach preadolescents must unearth all possible facts and intuitions that might help to answer this question. We must try to understand these children with objectivity and empathy if we are going to deal with their problems in our present society.

Margaret Mead optimistically predicts that in the twentieth century we can "preserve and increase the mental health of whole populations" through the "conscious application of our new knowledge of human behavior, derived from the findings of psychiatry, clinical psychology, child development, cultural anthropology and sociology to the problems of child-rearing and adult functioning" (2: p. 11). Other students of anthropology point out that the wide variety of forms that human development takes can be explained not in terms of individuals or groups, physical maturation levels or inherent psychological patterns, but rather in terms of the culture (3: p. 113). For instance, differences between preadolescents of varying cultures can often be linked to the length of time they are expected to be dependent on adults; also pertinent are the differing roles taken on by male and female parents with regard to child training.

In our American middle-class culture, the unusually long period of time it takes a child to become an independent member of society has been justified on the grounds that it takes this long to gain the skills necessary for survival in our complex world. This extended education, however, inflicts on young people a postponement of natural responsibilities and satisfactions. It binds them too long within physical and psychic restrictions. We tend to consider childhood as merely a preparation for rewards to be reaped later on. Childhood and adult life have been rigidly separated. Yet the point of crossover is ambiguous, undefined, and not subject to generalization. Too much rigidity on this score often causes frustration, apprehension, and anger.

Another cultural imposition creating resentment is the predominance of women in all phases of child training both at home and in the school. When the child is very young, the mother rules his behavior, with the father entering the picture merely as an occasional agent of punishment for infringement of the mother's rules. In school, more or less the same conditions prevail. Preadolescent and adolescent boys in particular have trouble under a completely female regime, since this is a time when their masculine identity is at stake. This may be one of the reasons they group into gangs and carry a special rancor toward women and girls, why they resist adult standards, which they have learned to equate with female standards.

A third factor, unique to our American condition and adding to the conflicts and fears of preadolescents, is the wide diversity of our social, religious and moral patterns. The numerous nationalities and classes, all with slightly differing standards of feeling and behavior, may well confuse children trying to find their identity. In this connection the formation of gangs, in which appropriate behavior and standards are clearly laid down, may provide them with the security they need when faced with our shifting multiracial and multiethnic society.

SELF-RELIANCE

The struggle for independence is the dominating urge of the nine- to thirteen-year-olds and the key to their sometimes irritating, sometimes inspiring behavior. It is expressed through many acts and attitudes which we can arbitrarily reduce to two basic trends: (1) hostility toward adults and withdrawal from them, and (2) separation into sex and age groups with their particular mores, patterns, and antagonisms.

Hostility toward adults comes to a head when parents or teachers are reluctant to recognize the child's need and natural aspiration to become an autonomous individual. They often fail to understand that brashness and rebellion are merely his awkward, inept way of defining and testing his position vis-à-vis adults, which is changing due to natural growth—both mental and physical. The child who offends with his belligerence is actually full of discomfort and self-doubt. He needs support and guidance during this period and is desperately disappointed when his loved ones turn against him. Any lack of faith in him aggravates his aggressive behavior. Intense parental resentment and withdrawal can warp his growth. Tendencies toward delinquency begin in preadolescence, and failing the child at this time may mean losing him forever as a constructive member of society.

The child's instinctive responses are quite clear about what he must do at this stage of his growth. It is often a matter of fight or perish. Unconsciously he knows he must reject many of the protective, indulgent features of his previous dependence. Often he is forced to regard a parent as someone who loves, coddles and fondles with smothering affection, or as an infuriating adult who bullies, punishes, denies and rejects for reasons not well understood—or as an irrational combination of both. As the child becomes more equipped to take care of himself physically, he begins to understand that his survival depends upon himself, apart from the whims and temperaments of parents and teachers. With determination he struggles to free himself from an oppressive dependence that humiliates him and endangers his identity.

Most middle-class American parents resist the growing up of their children. By continuing to protect them, they keep them completely to themselves. In America, where the pioneering tradition still lingers on, parents often have conflicting desires: to send their darlings out into the wilderness to become strong and tough, or to keep them snug at the household hearth. They leave the house door open to salve their consciences and at the same time weaken the child by coddling or frightening him so that he cannot summon up the energy to enter the outside world. Sensing the true feeling of his parents and his own lack of preparation, the child becomes too timid to leave home without an enormous struggle and shows symptoms of anxiety, self-recrimination, and lack of identity. He may never win independence from these repressive ties, and resentment may fester, damaging his personality. Such an individual is relegated to the sidelines of life, watching others enjoy their full maturity. The dilemma is well expressed in the painting below.

Grade five—girl

The more aggressive child puts up a real battle, hating and scorning the adults who do not understand the importance of his struggle, who treat him like a baby, have no respect for his gang, his friends, his whole new world, and who shame him by dominating and clinging. His artwork often shows rebellion against adults and regulations, such as the painting of unpopular teachers shown below. Children sometimes paint their parents in violent situations. One girl depicted a bank robbery in which her mother was killed. She told the teacher the story as she methodically painted the blood oozing onto a sidewalk.

Grade five—boy

Preadolescent resentment and rudeness could be cut down considerably if parents gave children of this age some leeway, reducing the supervision and bossing at levels where conformity is not essential. As it is, the child is told what to eat because he must be healthy, what to wear in order to be proper, when to sleep, and where he may or may not go. More freedom would give the child a semblance, at least, of self-assertion, and he might feel less need to flaunt his rebellion and openly challenge all manners, customs, conformity. Here is a typical work in which the children are defying restriction by depicting bad men, gambling, smoking, and drinking.

Grade six—boy

Teachers as well as parents must take preadolescents in stride, keeping a loose rein on their rebellious, surging energies. For it is above all now, and perhaps not in adolescence, when their purposes are clouded by sex complications, that they can get their balance, learn eagerly and fast to survive, to find directions, to find some personal success.

GANGS, CLIQUES, EXPANDING LOYALTIES

Gangs give children defended positions from which they can sally out against grown-ups. A gang or clique also provides a transition from babyhood to maturity. One might call them improvised schools, run by the children themselves, in which they prepare for the outer world, experimenting and gradually assimilating the teachings of adults and lessons of their own experiences. The peer group supplants the family as the children's social world—a world of their own generation and their own sex. Gangs are small subcultures within the culture, each with its own customs and standards. Within them boys and girls get the sense of belonging and recognition that they formerly got in the home.

Groups begin to form as soon as children discover that other children are also experimenting with gradual withdrawal from the family circle. They cling to each other for support, information, models, and leadership. Their parents see them less and less; it is an emotional weaning for both sides. One must sympathize with mothers and fathers, whose deep involvement makes this a painful break. But they must try to adjust to the change, and, wherever possible, facilitate the child's efforts to build affectionate relationships outside the immediate family. For it is among their peers that preadolescents must function, achieve, find rewards and establish individuality. It is interesting that at this period they worry a good deal about the possible

death of parents, perhaps because they feel guilty about rejecting them and also a little fearful.

Eventually the preadolescent is able to establish ties beyond
his home and has, in addition to membership in a gang—with
a secure position and some responsibilities—two or three good
friends. Such first friendships are very significant. Finding someone of one's own sex in whom one can confide anxieties and
enthusiasms and who really understands him, and realizing that
someone else can be as important as oneself—this is a step
toward learning to love. Possessive, fearing parents who do not
allow this transfer of the child's affections from themselves to
others wound the child profoundly and earn his hostility.

Grade five—boy   *Friends*

In his new group life, the child learns to interact and to regulate
his own desires for the sake of the group. Cooperation begins to
emerge as a function of personality. To be accepted, he has to
conform to standards. Gangs and cliques inspire great loyalty.
Children begin to understand and accept the limitations that
such loyalty places upon each individual, and this is a constructive step toward socialization: recognizing the needs and rights
of others. Loomis suggests that gang life not be banned from
school life, but accepted, and thus be "susceptible to classroom
influences. This in turn would contribute to constructive group
inter-relationships" (1: p. 104).

Preadolescent gangs are usually small and fairly informal,
arising spontaneously, forming and reforming as personalities
conflict too strongly or diversions occur. Bernard calls them "a
significant aspect of healthy personality integration" (4: p. 240).
They are also an important aid to boys and girls in defining their

sex roles and expectations. And like all manifestations of growing up, they carry their share of anxiety and emotional disturbance. The fear of being rejected by one's gang runs deep. The need for popularity is of course a universal human trait, but it is especially poignant in children of this age, who are breaking away from the close family circle.

In general, the popular children are the ones who seem happy, like to laugh, are active, aggressive, outgoing and enthusiastic, or very good-looking according to accepted standards. Personality counts for more than intelligence. The most popular are average, not exceptional, and weighted on the side of sociability rather than individuality, though there seems to be a healthy respect for anyone gifted in a special field.

Social class modifies popularity standards. In a middle-class clique, boys are apt to be leaders when they are good in sports, daring, aggressive toward adults, boisterous with older children, untidy, and extraverted. Girls, though they value tidiness, also prefer the outgoing type to the introvert. Underprivileged boys admire belligerent, tough behavior; the girls also favor rowdier, verbally and sexually more aggressive behavior than do the middle-class girls.

When children of both groups are present within one school, the problems of acceptance are enormously complicated. Furthermore, parents and teachers have differing standards of behavior. A child who is popular with his group is not usually popular with his teacher, and vice versa. Also, since the teacher is usually from the middle class, he or she is less apt to understand and condone the manners and values of the popular lower-class leader.

Anxieties about acceptance often stem from physical discrepancies or disabilities. Both boys and girls worry about their size and the fact that they are apt to develop disproportionately

Grade six—girl
Self-portrait

—noses too long for the face, arms too long or too short for the body. Variations in size and physical coordination can cause rejection by the clique. Unathletic children who are too large and heavy suffer trials that may color their entire lives.

Of greatest importance for the preadolescent child is his status in the group. Failure to be accepted can seriously handicap his social adjustment later on. The peer group is the testing ground from which a girl or boy emerges into the culture. Here the sex role, skill in getting along with people, cooperation, exchange of opinion, persuasion, and even leadership are practiced. Gangs support children through the difficult time when they are trying out legs, arms and brains to find out who they really are. The child who does not make this break for independence, passing from the orbit of the parents to that of the gang, must do it at a later period in his life when it can be much more disruptive to himself and those around him.

Grade six—girl
Social ostracism

Sexual identification is one of the major concerns of preadolescents. They are actually aware of sex differences and are constantly analyzing them. Our culture has encouraged this; ever since babyhood they have been subtly instructed in the ways of being a boy or a girl. By the time of preadolescence, the masculine-feminine orientation has been deeply inculcated. At this age, also, they seem to need to become strongly associated with their separate sex groups, in order to prove their biological identities and to take on the obligations and roles which our culture has allocated to the two sexes. Boys and girls feel quite segregated from each other, and indeed antagonistic to a degree that will never occur—barring extreme neuroses—in their lives again.

This natural hostility is strengthened by the fact that at this

THE SEX ROLE

age the girls tend to be bigger, more mature, and likely to beat the boys not only scholastically but in sports too. The girls' ability to get better marks may be either the cause or the effect of the boys' general attitude that to be intellectual or studious is to verge on being effeminate. The boys are often fortified in this belief by adult attitudes and values. It is difficult to distinguish here between biological and cultural factors. But certainly the size differential is one important element in the boy-girl strife, taken together with the boys' built-in resentment against being dominated by women and their ideas not only in the home but in school as well.

American culture is full of ambiguity in this regard. On the one hand, the male is accorded greater prestige than the female; men and boys are generally the heroes in public life, taking on the main economic as well as leadership roles. There are notable exceptions, but by and large a mother's status will appear to the preadolescent as inferior to the father's. On the other hand, we still feel the impact of the frontier days when pioneer women, scarce and therefore valued, fought side by side with their men, suffered and persevered and therefore earned a measure of equality. Later, the suffragettes won women the right to vote. Our little girls are reaping the benefits; they have privileges and ambitions not allowed women in many societies (5: pp. 285–325). It is too early to judge what effect the women's liberation movement will have on the psychology and behavior of preadolescents. However, the explorations generated by the attention now given to this movement may help resolve some of these ambiguities.

The preadolescent boy is faced with this complication as he assumes his male role. History, since it has been recorded, supports male superiority, and the boy, following as best he can in the footsteps of his father and encouraged to do so by countless attitudes of his mother and other women, acts upon his prerogatives, rejecting and belittling the young girl and putting her in her place. She, quite naturally resentful of this treatment, and encouraged in this resentment by her new freedom and equal education, fights the boy in ways that may hurt his sense of maleness.

Because girls mature earlier sexually, they usually hide (sometimes relinquish) their resentment of male superiority during most of preadolescence. Boys cling to their hostility longer, but after the age of eleven or so they begin to tease and bother girls in a way that indicates they are becoming interested in them. Most girls are always interested, and, given a chance, will seek to establish friendly relationships with boys, though when they are rejected they fight back fiercely, with fair or foul play. The pictures that follow are evidence that girls are apt to favor boys more than they are favored by them. When boys depict women, they make comic or grotesque portraits; on the whole they avoid painting pictures or making sculptures of girls of their own age altogether (6: pp. 113–14).

Grade six—girl

Sex roles differ, of course, in the various socioeconomic groups. Often the underprivileged boys are expected to be more physically aggressive, and the girls may be more sexually aware. Boys in all classes run the risk of peer as well as adult censure if they deviate from the accepted "masculine" norm of self-expression. The following paintings, emotionally sensitive, might be considered "mushy" or "sissy" by the gang or labeled "feminine" by watchful parents. According to this system of values, sentiment, emotion, suggestive color and useless designs belong in the girls' realm, while the more factual, precise and accurate expression belongs to the "real boy."

Grade six—boy

Grade seven—
boy *War*

Physical fitness and ability in sports are important male sex symbols to preadolescents, as they are throughout our culture. Boys must show a strong interest in sports and have some proficiency in at least one. This enthusiasm shows up in preadolescent artwork. Even girls are expected to be sports-minded and to take part in appropriate games. They go back and forth between two worlds without censure, but the talented artistic or intellectual boy must make a different sort of adjustment to the physical preoccupation of his peers or be ostracized by the group.

As girls move gradually into their feminine roles, the concept of the "pretty" face and figure becomes a preoccupation; the most popular girls are those who are pleasant, sociable, tidy, and, above all, pretty. One reason may be that these incipient women are setting standards that have to do with femininity and the ability to attract the male, and thereby fulfill an important aspect of the role.

Hero worship plays an important part for both boys and girls in the development of sexual identity and of the ego in general. It is also a function of the child's ambiguous but still strong dependence on the adult world. A child identifies with some adult whom he or she can imitate. Goals and ambitions are often established at this age which influence a person for the rest of his life. Preadolescents fill their artwork with heroes and heroines. The girl imagines herself a dancer; a boy becomes a great football player. Girls want to be singers, actresses, secretaries or nurses; boys take the roles of cowboy, airplane pilot, baseball player, farmer, or truck driver. A boy's choice is influenced not only by his sex but also, of course, by his father's profession, the heroes of his time, his general personality, and the cultural level from which he comes. The girl, on the other hand, is apt to choose a vocation (nurse, teacher, secretary, ballet dancer) regardless of her parents' position in life.

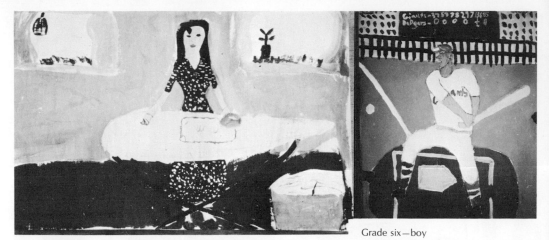

Grade six—boy

Grade five—girl

Grade six—boy

The physical manifestations of sex do not loom as a matter of concern to children of this age to the extent that they will disturb them after puberty. However, confusion and uncertainty on this score may, for various reasons, plague a number of them. Only intelligent counseling can forestall misinformation, worry and guilt. It seems sensible to create an atmosphere in which children feel free to talk about and create art about their developing interest in body changes and functions before fears reach their peak in adolescence. Some art (p. 30, top) shows spontaneous expressions of interest in sex. If it is regarded as normal, the painful self-consciousness suffered during puberty may be reduced.

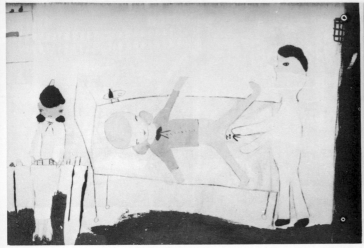

Grade five—three girls *A child is born*   Grade six—boy

ANXIETY   Preadolescent anxiety and disturbances, as we have seen, may arise from many sources: withdrawal of parental love, clashes with other adults and peers about proper behavior, rejection by the gang or clique, worry over the sex role, or conflicts with the opposite sex. Another very important irritant is lack of the competence and skills that the school demands. Insecurity, bravado, and destructiveness often result. A great many of these problems can be traced to the fact that preadolescents are maturing at different rates on different physical and intellectual levels. In a group of eleven-year-olds, for instance, one individual may still be on a plateau of childhood, while another is close to puberty and still another is already into puberty. Parents' recognition of

Grade six—girl

their child's position on this bridge to adolescence can go far to diminish conflict, suffering, and belligerence. Teachers also must be trained to spot the different levels of maturity within one class and to adjust their demands accordingly.

A child's choice of companions, as well as his skill in the classroom, depends on how much he has grown up in mind and body, or, as is so often the case, on how much he has grown up in one and how little in the other. Adult flexibility on this score is important. A mother may become unreasonably worried, for instance, about her daughter's playing with Mary, who is already physically developed, or Mary herself may be made to feel that there is something wrong with her because she is unlike the other girls. Her parents may be upset by her early maturation and frighten her with restrictions and cautionary tales. A boy may develop guilt feelings because of his interest in sex, a subject made taboo by his parents and other adults in charge of his life. A girl often feels painfully tall, broods about her growing breasts, stoops to hide them and appears shorter. Or she may feel she is lacking in some way when she cannot attract or interest a boy who is in fact still too immature to be attracted to any female. All these physical discrepancies take their toll on the efficiency and spirit of the group. If preadolescents are to be spared unnecessary bewilderment and fear, such inequities should be explained to them as perfectly normal effects of growth. They will then be better prepared to anticipate the body changes and emotional storms of adolescence.

INTELLECTUAL CURIOSITY

The most rewarding trait of preadolescents is that they are so eager to learn. They are alert, curious, interested in everything in their environment, and have the drive to pursue a wide range of interests. The scope of their curiosity is indeed phenomenal. They delve into all information available. Even commonplace events seem to take on new meaning, and they are happy to explore with as much depth and enthusiasm as opportunity permits, until distracted by the next fascinating item.

This interest span is short and fitful, varying of course with the individual. The anxiety endemic to this age group makes itself felt in the form of wavering confidence, great sensitivity to competition, and too easy discouragement. These children still look to adults to help them assess their progress and to reassure them. They want to grow up so impatiently that they often take on greater challenges than they can handle. The teacher must guard against unrealistic goals that put too much pressure on the child and cause failure. As every teacher knows, one builds on successes. These lively, active youngsters have a very low frustration threshold, and when the sense of failure permeates the all-powerful group, a hard-won plan or project can be destroyed as quickly as in a prairie fire, and the teacher then has to build up confidence from scratch, with every tedious detail repeated. The tendency of the adult is to get angry on discovering that these, bright curious human beings are so unstable.

When the subject matter is attractive to them, many preadolescents are able to motivate, discipline, and even judge themselves. They like to make their own plans and often reject the opinions of others. They no longer accept the adult's word as gospel. Their slogan is "Show me!" or "Prove it!"

They prefer details to whole units. They have a passion for collecting, which satisfies their newfound urge to sort, categorize, and classify. They get enormous pleasure out of these studious explorations and collections which gain the admiration of their peers and sometimes win new friends they could not have inspired to interest in other ways. A child who is considered puny or sissy, for instance, may share with a popular sports-minded child some mutual collecting enthusiasm. Children also can win praise from adults who are impressed by the extent and fastidiousness of preadolescent collections.

The world of reality dominates the thoughts of this age group. They are turning from the imaginative fancies of early childhood to seek facts about the physical world, about themselves, about their relationship to others. Although their imaginations go on developing, the highly inventive play disappears at about this age; unreal fears are replaced by an apprehension of real dangers. In their search for facts they are constantly asking, "How does this work? How was that made?" Reading choices confirm their overwhelming desire for objective information—science and mechanics, fiction with realistic themes. Their artwork shows the same bias in both subject matter and execution, as, for example, in the following paintings—"The Nervous System" and "The Horrors of the French Revolution."

Grade six—boy

Grade five—boy

The mind of the preadolescent, as compared with the minds of his younger brothers and sisters, understands cause and effect. Concepts also begin to bloom, and the ability to solve simple problems, especially ones in which the child himself is involved. Relationships between physical, mechanical, and natural phenomena are perceived. The preadolescent, fortified by his gang or clique, has begun to move away from solitary interests to group exploration, and he therefore becomes more and more aware of the variety of ideas and beliefs surrounding him. A concept of time begins to grow, very slowly. These children begin to contrast the present with the past and are curious about living conditions and people of long ago. They can be stimulated by studying history, though their chronological understanding is still dim. As they pass through the preadolescent period, they make real progress in recognizing time sequences in both their personal lives and the historical past.

On the whole, they remain interested mainly in the immediate present and in exploring, acquiring, and building skills. Their intellectual ability expands as fast as their reading skills permit. Certain children, usually those from a middle-class background who have been exposed to books and ideas at home, acquire the reading proficiency of adults at this stage, learning to use the library and source materials such as dictionaries, atlases, and encyclopedias. The amount of leisure-time reading they do now is greater than it will ever be again in their lives. Books satisfy their yen for adventure and increase their power to share vicariously the experiences of others. Their art is often inspired by their reading. However, the underprivileged, especially the city ghetto children, often have such serious reading blocks that they cannot share in this important preadolescent experience. Nonverbal activities such as art often release some of the tension involved in the reading failure and help these children gain some status in the group and begin to bloom intellectually.

One of the preadolescent's saving graces is his sense of humor, which takes the edge off his belligerency. Though, as Gesell describes it, the humor of the ten-year-old is "mostly obvious, often heavy and labored, and usually not funny to adults . . . corny and smutty" and usually concerned with elimination, the very fact that humor is operating at all is reassuring. It is a sign of objectivity and release from tension. By the time the child is twelve, he occasionally can even make fun of himself and be "funnier from an adult point of view" (7: pp. 343–44).

Preadolescents like riddles and formula jokes. The younger ones often invent their own stories, which tend to be rambling accounts of violence, expressed in symbols. A child, usually a boy, will act out the funny story with spontaneous fantasy gestures and horseplay. Below is a painting in the slapstick spirit of the age.

33

Grade five—boy

The older children like to show off a whole repertoire of jokes, with the verbal account not dependent on comic behavior. "Increasingly from about eleven or twelve on, children tell jokes in anecdotal form, in which the telling is not a verbatim repetition but leaves something to the ingenuity of the teller" (8: p. 233).

Joke-telling children are popular with their peers. Being able to laugh also "aids in self-acceptance; it increases . . . feelings of self-importance and superiority," as Elizabeth Hurlock suggests in *Child Development* (9: p. 525). Humor depends on seeing discrepancies, and this faculty grows in preadolescence, along with the development of such concepts as money, size, time, honesty, and responsibility. The more intelligent child will grasp the discrepancy earlier.

Grade six—boy *Robot*

The concept of death is more real to some than others, the middle-class children being, on the whole, more protected from its actualities. Ten-year-olds associate death with old age and are not much concerned about what happens in the afterlife (7: pp. 491–92). Eleven-year-olds may be curious about funerals and want to attend one. They may refer to reincarnation and to souls returning to earth. By the age of twelve, the child is more personally concerned, realizing the connection between death and the possible loss of his personality. He speculates with his friends on what it feels like to die, what is the most painless death, and whether immortality exists.

No matter what his age, however, the preadolescent worries about losing his parents. He feels it very deeply when a member of his family or a pet (especially a dog) dies. Preadolescents become passionately attached to animals, which can be loved without reserve and which cannot talk back or tell them what to do. A dog gives companionship without strain or competition and brings out early stirrings of parental affection and responsibility. For these reasons, the death of a pet is not taken lightly.

Grade six—girl *Funeral*

Shown on page 36 are two animal paintings. In one, the story of a bloody battle is told. Love of animals and mother love are important themes for girls of ages ten to twelve. The mood of comfort and security has been well realized here. Preadolescent girls like to paint horses. In this painting the rhythmic beauty of the body, the sweeping curve of the neck and the swish of the tail, has been caught. Again, the theme of mother love. Note the delicacy of the hoof action as the colt playfully nuzzles its mother.

Grade five—boy

Grade six—girl

According to sociologists, the ten-year-old does not do much thinking about God. God is an invisible man who can be talked to and is generally protective. Very young children associate God pretty much with their fathers, and ten-year-olds retain vestiges of this habit. At the age of eleven, God becomes an imaginary spirit who is vaguely related to one's behavior, rewarding or punishing. Twelve-year-olds may develop religious obsessions; God is by then connected closely to man and his concerns.

Grade six
The Creation

All this varies widely, of course, with the specific child's religion, observance, and family emphasis on religious education. In his art, the child may express some reaction of his own and other religions, as in the following painting. After reading about and discussing how God created the world in six days, one child responded in a statement so compelling that it makes us pause in wonder at the power of human beings. Notice the flowers with their roots, the grasses like hands reaching toward the power of the light and dark; these are personal symbols devoid of clichés. In another painting God is seen as a fabulous king. Where God is, the sun shines persistently; strange but benevolent creatures are lucky to be near him. He wears a crown, and His arms turn into wings if he cares to fly.

Grade five—
boy *God*

Moral concepts are only half understood by preadolescents. Honesty and loyalty, for instance, can be applied in specific situations but are not easily transferred from one type of incident to another. Value judgments such as right and wrong, good and bad, are simplistically clear to children in the fourth grade, but by the sixth grade, children are less sure and dogmatic, more doubting and tolerant. They are, after all, breaking away at this point from blindly accepted parental values and seeking their own.

It is in games especially that honesty, loyalty, and "fair play" are developed in children. By the age of ten, fair play has become the prime moral virtue, recognized by all. As Havighurst says, "The child's attitude toward rules of games is really his attitude toward moral rules in general, for rules of games are rules of conducting what the child regards as his most important business" (10: p. 54).

Children develop personal reputations through their behavior in organized games. Every boy and girl wants to be regarded as a good sport, a good loser, an honest player, a loyal member of the team, with respect for the rights of the other players. Not all preadolescents are able to live up to these standards, but they do their best, knowing that dishonesty and irresponsibility will mean rejection by their group. In their artwork they build many images around the important sports, such as baseball or football; they also paint the athletic stars who, to them, exemplify all the virtues aspired to by the preadolescent (and often the adult) society.

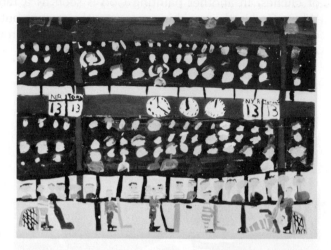

Grade five — boy

Altruism can emerge in preadolescence. A child may be capable of doing a service to others, though the gesture tends to be immature, unrealistic, and inconsistent. Boys and girls will stand up for members of racial, religious, or social groups different from their own. They may express sincere belief in democracy. They have an inherent interest in children in other parts of the world, and under any circumstances they will champion the underdog, feeling perhaps that they play that role themselves in relations to adult society. For example, in response to the topic "What civil rights means to me," a boy painted the march on Selma.

Grade six — girl

Preadolescents also understand some reciprocal responsibilities: parent to child, employer to employee and vice versa, doctor to patient, society to individual.

One might, in the light of these examples, call the preadolescent already socially conscious, however antisocial he may become under the stress of his maturation. The film of his mind has now been partially exposed to reality. He is becoming oriented to what and where things are, even if he cannot quite find his place among them.

Preadolescents need teachers who are sympathetic and objective, with a good working knowledge of their students' needs and anxieties, prepared for the ambiguities and hostilities, willing to move and shift and travel at the children's pace, enjoying their enthusiasm and drive. Though in our culture preadolescence seems to be a destructive, difficult period, regarded with understanding it can be viewed as a very touching phase in a child's life, both immensely sad and deeply exciting. It is at once a death and a birth. It is at this point that the individual boy or girl chooses, out of countless possibilities, a specific form of being and specific modes of behavior acceptable to our society. In the process, certain unique qualities of the individual must atrophy while others grow.

We teachers of art who assist in this transformation are by nature dedicated to preserving the mysterious potentialities hidden in each child. At the same time, we must give children tools of knowledge and the emotional strength they will need in the battle of growing up in our age. At best, we try to offer an education that will serve them in two ways; first, to secure their survival, status and personal adjustment within the culture; second, to protect the lifelines leading back into the inner resources of their unexplored selves. Thus fortified, some of them may be able to act with imagination, to question the established ideas of their times, possibly to make innovative contributions to American society.

REFERENCES

1. Mary Jane Loomis, *The Preadolescent,* Appleton-Century-Crofts, Inc., New York, 1959.

2. Margaret Mead, *Cultural Patterns and Technical Change,* A Manual Prepared by the World Federation for Mental Health, Mentor Books, New York, 1955.

3. Arthur Witt Blair and William H. Burton: *Growth and Development of the Preadolescent,* Appleton-Century-Crofts, Inc., New York, 1951.

4. Harold W. Bernard, *Human Development in Western Culture,* Allyn and Bacon, Inc., Boston, 1962.

5. Erik H. Erikson, *Childhood and Society,* W. W. Norton & Company, Inc., New York, 1963.

6. Betty Lark-Horowitz, Hilda Present Lewis, and Mark Luca: *Understanding Children's Art for Better Teaching,* Charles E. Merrill Books, Inc., Columbus, Ohio, 1967.

7. Arnold Gesell, Frances Ilge, and Louise Bates, *Youth, the Years from Ten to Sixteen,* Harper & Brothers, New York, 1956.

8. Martha Wolfenstein, "Riddles and the Legend of the Moron," *Causes of Behavior: Readings in Child Development and Educational Psychology,* Judy Rosenblith (ed.), Allyn and Bacon, Inc., Boston, 1964.

9. Elizabeth Hurlock, *Child Development,* McGraw-Hill Book Company, New York, 1950.

10. Robert J. Havighurst, *Human Development and Education,* Longmans, Green & Company, New York, 1953.

A Special View: The Disadvantaged Preadolescent

2

The underprivileged children of all ages who come into our middle-class public schools from a lower economy and a different, if not foreign, background have many epithets thrown at them not unlike those thrown at any American preadolescent, rich or poor, of any race or creed. These range from *sullen, slow, apathetic* and *unresponsive* to *disorganized, rude, impulsive,* and *violent.* Since all children from ages ten to thirteen are considered "unreachable, irresponsible and often obnoxious," does it follow that the underprivileged child, as he comes into preadolescence, does not stand out in the middle-class teacher's view as so very different from middle-class children? Or does he have a double dose of incorrigibility?

The latter is in some measure unfortunately true. Poverty, undernourishment, racial discrimination and alienation from the affluent society, plus the frequent language barrier, add immensely to the problems that make preadolescence for any human being anywhere a time of anxiety and ego crisis. Furthermore, while the deprived child is going through the same difficult transition as the privileged child, he seldom receives the same help or understanding. School administrators and teachers often have rigid, preconceived and unhopeful attitudes about his academic potential and his social behavior. He has usually done poorly in all his subjects. By the time he is in the sixth grade, he is probably "reading at a level approximately three and one-third years below grade level . . . considerably retarded in arithmetic and other school subjects" (1: p. 21) and is so dissatisfied with school that he has no hope of learning or of enjoying activities in the classroom. He has very possibly been classified by now as either retarded or deficient and is in a special class, having retreated into silent, defensive hostility broken only by outbursts of aggression.

The conventional rationalization of his deficiencies is that no, or very bad, English is spoken in the home; that he has had neither books nor adequate food, clothing nor living space; that he has never been motivated to pursue education. Sometimes racial traits have been unconsciously or deliberately blamed for backwardness in school—and they still are, though such an undemocratic sentiment is no longer freely expressed.

Current attitudes have more psychological depth and inherent optimism. The learning difficulties of these children, as Fred Powledge writes,

found on such a large scale cannot correctly be attributed to brain damage, birth defects, disease or myths of racial inferiority. They can be attributed only to the attempts that society has made . . . to withhold certain vital, fundamental experiences and concepts from the lower-class child . . . Dr. Deutsch[1] refers to this as "stimulus deprivation" and "environmental disadvantage." They are negative factors that easily can destroy a child's motivation to do something once he enters a public school, especially when the school is predicated, from kindergarten to diploma, on middle class American traditions, habits, and beliefs [2: pp. 18–19]

Sociologists and psychologists believe that conscious or unconscious discrimination against the poor and the racial minorities, not only in classrooms but also in PTA meetings, guidance offices and testing programs, serves to alienate both child and parents from the school. This increases the anti-intellectualism of the poverty-ridden family. They find no place in the school where elements of their own subculture can operate or even be acknowledged. Often, too, contributions such as original humor, sensitivity to art and music, physical skills, colorful myths, mores, food, and dances are either ignored or denigrated. Parents are apt to withdraw from contact with the school. As for the children, they must suddenly learn to sit still for hours on end; they must adjust without preparation to tests and memorizing; learn new words and suppress the old; ask questions (this is often not customary in the underprivileged home); and somehow make sense out of the strange, unfamiliar environment. Psychologically it has proved to be a more dubious practice than throwing a young child into the river and expecting him, instinctively, to swim. Only a few do.

After extensive research, efforts have been made to work out programs like Head Start to help the underprivileged enter the educational mainstream with enough know-how to keep their heads above water. The pioneer agency in the field of intensive supplementary education was the Institute for Developmental Studies, now affiliated with New York University. Head Start's orientation sessions are designed for the very young, of course, and it will be years before teachers in preadolescent grades

[1] Dr. Martin Deutsch, director of the Institute for Developmental Studies.

will feel the benefits. Also, these programs are still very few and far between. Prospective teachers of preadolescents have the benefit, nevertheless, of the research that has been done, which should help them understand not only the human potential that has been and is being wasted but also the special ambiguities the ghetto children bring with them to school.

Teachers of the underprivileged should also come prepared for the "disadvantaged child's tendency to shy away from verbal and other sorts of assistance when it is finally offered to him by a sympathetic adult" (2: p. 18). Teachers who are sincerely dedicated will acquire a body of knowledge about the various backgrounds of their students, but they will find it is useless without sufficient patience in the face of rebuff and the humor-plus-empathy needed to deal with the diverse traumas of poverty and the color line.

Though the civil rights movement has dramatized the situation of the black child in the inner cities and the Deep South, deprivation is not exclusively a racial problem in our country. Black parents with middle-class status and income have far better luck than poor whites with their children in the schools, and probably at least one-third (the number is increasing fast) of the black children in our large cities test as high as white children. (1: p. 5). The underprivileged come not only from our racial minorities but also from white urban and rural slums. They come not only from the foreign born but also from our truest "natives," the Indian population, living on reservations and in growing numbers in city ghettos. They come from isolated mountain towns, from the Canadian border, and from trucks of migrant workers, American or Mexican, in California and the Southwest. There are no states in the Union and almost no school systems that do not include them. Often industry brings them and in its cycles abandons them; many are victims of a changing agricultural economy; many more are victims of an educational system that rejected their parents and grandparents. They belong to varying cultures—some with little or no heritage, others with rich traditions, strong religion, warm family life. Essentially, they emerge, in all colors of skin, from poverty, handicap, and illiteracy.

NOT SCHOOL-WISE BUT LIFE-WISE

The disadvantaged are emotionally set for or against education, depending on early experiences and parental drives. But there are some generalizations that can be made. Recent studies and events (such as struggles to gain community control of schools) indicate that a good proportion of the parents of deprived children see education as of the utmost importance. Learning may not mean the same thing to them, however, that it does to middle-class parents. According to Frank Riessman, the latter are more inclined to see schooling as acquisition of knowledge for its own sake and "for the development of self-expression, growth, and the like" (3: pp. 12–13), while the former tend to take a more utilitarian approach. They want their children to be educated in order to improve their chances for employment and financial security. Science is held to be more useful than the humanities. "The deprived child feels powerless in most spheres of life, and he sees science as giving him control and strength, at least over the outer world . . . he sees a career in this area much more readily" (3: p. 13). It is a moot point, in our opinion, whether the middle-class parent's aims for his children are less materialistic, or whether he has merely learned to disguise his real fears and desires. But there can be no doubt that parents who have suffered all their lives from lack of education are apt to wish ardently that their children should have a different fate.

Yet even with this drive behind him and his own desire for education, the disadvantaged child is apt to turn against school. Resentment against discrimination and an ingrained anti-intellectualism can be reasons. The feeling that the practical things of life are much more important than what is contained in books may keep some children from opening their minds to abstract ideas. Since they have been physically rather than verbally oriented by early environment, they may find conceptualization difficult and need to go step by step through a problem. This is time-consuming, and in our mass-production, speed-adjusted schools, they are soon left behind. The slower style of learning is denigrated and stigmatized even when it is natural to more privileged children. Discouraged, the slow learner is all too often apt to drop out. Research now indicates that this type of student may indeed learn more thoroughly and permanently than the facile pupil. Unfortunately the custom of putting certain children together in one section with the pejorative label *slow* does not encourage them to stay in school.

The underprivileged are apt to take longer in solving a problem or taking a test because of unfamiliarity with subjects and formal language and social insecurity in the school setting, as well as because of their previous orientation to the concrete and physical. They function at a speedy pace when involved in activities that call for physical prowess and when verbalizing in their own idiom. They are able to make adjustments and decisions often by picking up cues from another person's facial expression or bodily gesture. They make judgments that can be based on concrete fact. They may not be book-wise but they are life-wise. They have what Riessman terms "hidden intelligence" (3: p. 68).

While the deprived child does not easily get into a problem, once he is thoroughly involved "he is often able to work tenaciously for long stretches at a time. This may be a characteristic of the physical learner, because in order for him to learn he needs to have more of his whole body responding, and this requires a longer 'warm-up' period" (3: p. 67).

Irving Taylor, project coordinator on the staff of the Institute for Developmental Studies, has, according to Riessman, some new ideas about the untapped creativity of disadvantaged children, whom he finds not nearly as nonverbal as has been thought. Taylor discovered that in word tests their responses were more original, unusual and independent, and that their language is both more visual and more flexible. Also, they permit language to interact more with other kinds of communication, such as gestures and pictures. This ability allows them to break through the strict meaning of words. He has found a similar approach to language in creative people whose nonaural senses are more acute and who respond to visual, tactile and kinesthetic stimuli (3: pp. 77–78).

For the art teacher there are valuable clues in this research. The underprivileged child, who because of formal language blocks has found neither success nor encouragement, may be drawn out by teaching methods that stress the visual, physical, active and *colloquial.* In the art studio the child can look and do —rather than sit and hear—moving around, using the body, using his own home and street language. If the supposedly inarticulate child can find expression in the studio, he may carry his new-found voice into other classrooms and other disciplines.

SUBCULTURES: BLACK, WHITE, RED AND BROWN

There can no longer be any doubt that the academic and creative potential of the deprived child is linked up with his freedom to express himself in his own cultural terms. It may be contended that no matter what the subculture, the underprivileged mimic and seek to take on the prevailing mores of the larger society in which they live. But there is another view—that the under-privileged represent a contraculture, rebellious, angry, and always in opposition to the attitudes and behavior of the dominant class. Certainly some of our current subcultural manifestations bear out the latter theory. The truth probably lies in between; both imitation and rebellion are operating, producing contradiction and often neurosis. This is reflected in the behavior of preadolescents, who are, to compound the conflict, at an ambiguous stage of personality development. The confusion and anxiety may thus be doubled for the eleven- or twelve-year-old from the poverty class who is at the threshold of society at large and cannot see clearly which way he is going to jump. Often, in the end, the decision is too hard to make, and he may spend his life drifting.

Some knowledge of that variegated terrain which some sociologists call contraculture and others the subculture of poverty is essential if a teacher is to promote a working relationship with the deprived child and provide methods and materials that will be meaningful and allow him to find some success.

A clear distinction should be made between the culture and the environment of the disadvantaged child. Often in the starkest environment, such as that of the American blacks in the South before and after emancipation, a surge of artistic creation will take place. The Negro genius brought music from Africa and the Caribbean and combined it to give America perhaps its only great native art: jazz, a strong, coherent, poignant blend of African and American strains. This is the proud heritage of every black child. Black culture has always been strong; the environment has always been difficult, both physically and psychologically. Black leaders are seeking now to alleviate the trauma felt by black children in a predominantly white world by substituting pride in their heritage (music being only one element of this) for the "blues" and resignation. They are seeking to build a new psychological environment for their children in spite of the fact that improvement of their physical scene is so slow in coming.

Rural isolation   Some of our white poor seem to be living almost in a nonculture. Children in the Deep South, Appalachia, northern New England and the northern Great Lakes region may present the most difficult challenge of all to the teacher. They are "the people left behind," as described in a 1967 report by the President's National Advisory Commission on Rural Poverty. Without the stimulation of the city and other cultures, without aspirations or hope for change, these children have very little between them and crime or the pathology of fascism. "Early American" values are diminishing and almost gone. Middle-class commercial values seeping in from the cities can only frustrate these children born into destitute tenant farms, abandoned agricultural districts, and dead coal mining and mill towns.

There are 14 million rural Americans who are poor, and a large proportion of these are destitute. Dr. Edward Moe, in a recent conference on educational problems in sparsely populated areas, emphasized: "With our overriding confrontation with the city and urban, we must not neglect the rural, the small community, and the sparsely settled areas. Had we been more aware of what was happening over the last century, we might

have reduced somewhat the burden now placed on the city"
(4: pp. 18–20).

The country child may differ from the city child in that while
he grows up equally fast sexually, he seems to be emotionally
dependent on his parents longer, and may not make the transition
to peer group life until he reaches high school—or drops out.
Geographical separation of families, of course, makes gang life
almost impossible in some localities. The lack of social stimulation may account for the predominance of intellectual apathy,
which is more of a challenge to the rural teacher than aggressive-
ness in the classroom. This apathy may also be a product of the
cultural lag in rural schools, which are more in key with nineteenth-century education than are city schools. The younger
children are suppressed and regimented by old-line teachers, and
the curriculum is more hidebound. By the time of adolescence,
academic failure, plus smoldering resentment against mal-
nutrition, lack of clothes, and the embarrassment of being on
relief, have turned a great many youngsters away from school.
Guidance counselors are scarce. Drugs have infiltrated many
rural regions, compounding the delinquency problem. Too many
administrators expel students summarily for offenses ranging
from drinking at dances to not having frequent or "suitable"
haircuts, instead of creating opportunities to discuss changing
values.

There are of course many exceptions, and general educational
changes are coming, with the help of federal grants and the
beginning of government research into the needs of the rural
deprived. These children may be the last in the country to
experience art education because of distance from cultural
centers and reluctance to stretch already tight budgets to include
anything as "impractical" as art, not to speak of the anti-intellectual conservatism of the majority of parents and local school
committees.

Appalachian children are a very special case, with a language
problem almost as severe as that of children who migrate here
from a foreign land. As Vincent Skinner reports, they suffer from
a "lack of familiarity with standard American English as an *oral*
language system, which is a prerequisite if they are to learn to
read printed material in the text books" (5: p. 131). Their geographical isolation in a mountainous region ruined by the Industrial Revolution and then abandoned to destitution trapped them
in an ancient English dialect, isolating them further from society.
Like many of the Indians, they cannot make a living in either
city or town, and are wards of the welfare state. The children
eventually leave, totally unequipped for modern life. It is to be
hoped that the slow tide of educational reform now creeping
into other rural areas will also reach them.

Inner-city children The disadvantaged child in the ghetto has one advantage over his middle-class contemporaries—self-reliance. Boys and girls are left alone sooner by their parents and must take care of younger children and fight and fend for themselves in the streets. It might be said, too, that they have a psychological advantage over the more protected children in that instead of being subject to anxiety and guilt (induced by parental training methods), they are on the whole motivated by an anger that they often have an opportunity to act out. This inevitable aggression, born of deprivation and resentment, can of course make them a disruptive force in city classrooms when it is released there instead of in the playgrounds or on the streets. Children from subcultures are more or less aggressive and hostile in the classroom, depending on their family's position in the civil rights struggle, home training, quality of personal experiences, and values of their ethnic group.

Some sociologists believe that ghetto family life, especially in the case of Puerto Ricans and Mexican-Americans, is on the average healthier than that of the affluent, because it produces cooperation, based as it is on "mutual aid between family members that extends beyond the nuclear family typical of the middle class. It embraces uncles, aunts, grandparents, cousins. . . . The

Grade eight—boy—John Henricks
The life of the inner-city child

child has a sense of being part of a large and extended family . . . and these people are available to him as a resource in times of crisis" (6: p. 80). Leon Eisenberg believes that this produces collective rather than individualistic values and that inner-city children are not so easily beguiled as middle-class children by concepts of status and prestige. "They have more genuinely equalitarian values" (6: p. 81). Riessman feels that in the crowded, busy, noisy home where no one child can be focused on or overprotected, there is little jealousy and competitiveness, and many of the classic family problems, such as the Oedipus complex, are avoided (3: pp. 36–37).

Considering the spread and variety of our deprived class, it may be impossible to generalize with any truth about family life, which can change drastically in national economic crises, such as depressions and overinflation. Nor can the neuroses created by racial inferiority feelings and constant hunger *all* be purged by anger and group solidarity. Nor is tribal security always enough to allay intense fear, jealousy, and suicidal impulses when one is exposed daily to the competitiveness, dangers and materialistic display of city life. Each ethnic group has its own neuroses and its own ways, for better or worse, of dealing with them.

49

Black children There are records of great male leaders in every generation of Afro-Americans since before the Civil War, usually ministers or educators. But on the whole, it was the women, with their maternal drive, who kept up the morale and social mobility of the race. The black males were feared as soon as they were freed; society accepted only their great musical contribution and no more. The women (always good at a defensive holding position) went on adjusting to a subservient position for the sake of survival. They had to become strong, almost Amazonian, a tremendous number of them without male support. For that reason, probably, the black schoolgirl does better in school than her brother; she starts with a confidence passed down to her through many generations.

Black boys have suffered from the ego denigration of their male forebears and the unhealthy situation of growing up in a female-dominated home. Until recently, especially in the South, they have been prone to give up school at an early age. In integrated Northern city schools, they have felt discriminated against by teachers and administrators. Now the civil rights movement has given fresh hope and specific educational aims to all Afro-Americans. Black power has come forth from black matriarchy to challenge its rule. Black males are leading the movement, and their sons and younger brothers will undoubtedly reap the benefit in the form of a new image of themselves, and, it is presumed, a stronger will to stay in school, although the fight for more equable education has only just begun.

These children are taught independence at a very early age; in fact, they are punished for dependence. They have always been weaned abruptly by their mothers, who were, and still are, often the sole breadwinners and forced to be out of the home. Children are toilet trained, assigned chores, and taught to take care of each other much earlier than white, Puerto Rican, or Mexican-American children (7: pp. 268–87). As a rule, the black boy's "early experience in fending for himself results in precocious social maturity, independence and emancipation from home" (1: p. 79).

There can be little doubt that art activity is useful for cognitive development in other school subjects, as well as for training in visual perception and in organizing the talent for expression. A new art curriculum in black ghetto schools, as suggested by a group of black and white teachers and educators (24), should be centered on the humanities and involve all the teaching personnel in a school in its conception and growth. The inclusion of film-making and photography would be both pragmatic and stimulating. Every opportunity should be given Afro-American children to utilize their tactile and kinetic senses. Projects that make use of their ready knowledge of television, cartoons, and movies could be devised. The humor of the black child is something to be encouraged, not stifled; it is a path toward objectivity to be prized and praised. Teachers can also utilize the dialect of the streets, which is colorful, direct, and descriptive. If black children are allowed to express themselves in their own natural idiom, a start can be made toward expression in more structured English.

African art, especially the unique and wonderful carving, should be featured. American Negro history is another subject which can strengthen self-image and pride. (Black college students have been agitating for this.) In this connection, it was suggested that teachers make a point of the differences between blacks and whites, dramatizing these as interesting, rather than ignoring them. This might enlarge general tolerance of human diversity as well as ease tensions.

Teachers of black preadolescents, especially white teachers, come into a loaded situation, one demanding the utmost sensitivity and self-confidence. A lot depends on how the "monolithic confrontation" that may result from "growing estrangement between European ethnic groups and Negroes," pointed up by Nathan Glazer, will work itself out (8: p. 143). Unfortunately, the eternal problem of skin color will probably continue to make the black child a more special case in our schools than the paler Puerto Ricans and Mexican-Americans.

Puerto Rican children   The Puerto Rican culture, centered predominantly in New York City, is the newest addition to the melting pot, now more politely dubbed by sociologists "cultural pluralism." There were only 11,000 new immigrants from the island settled here in 1944; by 1950, there were more than a quarter of a million. A small proportion have very dark skins; these, confronting racial prejudice for the first time, often merge with the blacks or return to Puerto Rico. The rest, of mixed origin, have a nondiscriminatory attitude toward color that may in the end be their great influence on North American society. In general, as Glazer and Moynihan put it: "The Puerto Ricans add to a rather tough and knowing cast of New York characters a new type, softer, milder, gayer and more light-spirited" (9: p. 131).

Their love of music and dancing will affect the city's folk culture; it survives in spite of the physical conditions they live in and the difficulties they have in adjusting their rural-feudal-Spanish mores to the pace and dangers of New York. They have something new on their side, however: the current trend against too rigid Americanization and a growing respect (learned the hard way) of other subcultures. The Spanish language, for instance, is not suppressed in the schools; there are Spanish signs on the New York streets, in libraries and in hospitals; priests give services in Spanish; teachers are encouraged to become proficient in the language. Mexican-Americans on the West Coast and in Denver, another Spanish-speaking subculture, are gradually feeling the benefit of the same liberal trend. They differ, of course, in that they are part Indian. They have had to fight harder for mitigation of the language barrier. Nor do they have, like the Puerto Ricans, the possibility of a quick and cheap flight home when the going gets rough.

Adolescence and preadolescence are, on the whole, new concepts for Spanish-speaking peoples. In their native lands, young people are either children or adults, ready to marry and reproduce in their teens, without the long wait in semidependence typical of our North American system. For this reason, any analysis of the psychology of Puerto Rican girls and boys as compared with that of other ethnic groups must take into account the development of sex roles and the anxieties and behavior patterns they create.

In Spanish cultures, the male has always been the cock of the roost and the wife subservient and faithful to the home, which it is her duty to hold together emotionally, though not without strain as her husband indulges in a certain amount of adventurism. As a father, however, he has always provided for his family with fidelity and pride. On the island, Puerto Ricans lived in great family conclaves (the extended family), and godparents took over as "a second set of parents . . . if the first were burdened with too many children, too many woes, or broken up by death or desertion. Children were overprotected . . . but they were not resented and neglected" (1: p. 90). Families were large; birth control was resented by the male as an affront to his dominating position.

The same families in New York, living in small ghetto apartments instead of in rural combines of cabins set on a fertile land, find their tribal security undermined. The families are as large as ever, producing an unhealthy situation for the father, who cannot support them all and must accept welfare. His skills are not industrial. He often refuses even to try to learn the new language, since it would humiliate him to speak broken English. He often retreats into hypochondria or real illness; there is a large incidence of mental breakdown.

This is a difficult ambience for the Puerto Rican boy, and his self-image and incipient sex role have suffered along with his father's. He is shorter and slighter than the Italian and black boys in East Harlem. He lives in constant, eroding fear of being bullied, knifed, or robbed. "The children complain about the older boys from higher grades . . . who hang around the school and bully them," writers Patricia Cayo Sexton in *Spanish Harlem*

(10: p. 117). Independence and self-reliance are not encouraged by their mothers. Traditionally, good children are defined as "obedient, respectful and docile." Many children are kept close to home or inside, even in the summer. Yet by the age of fourteen, the Puerto Rican boy is considered a man!

Both boys and girls are preoccupied with sex from the ages of eleven to thirteen. "No wonder they can't learn anything in school," remarked one youth worker in East Harlem. "They have sex on their minds twenty-four hours a day" (10: p. 11). The newer immigrants, of course, keep their girls under strict supervision; they cannot go out at night without an adult. These restrictions are beginning to break down in the third generation. But compared with the independence and self-confidence of the black schoolgirl, the Puerto Rican female is definitely at a disadvantage. Her fundamental role is not to get educated but to get married and bear children.

The art studio can be a joy and a boon to Puerto Rican children. Art teachers who work with them are struck by their natural and spontaneous response to color. Often, unlike the average middle-class children, they have strong sensuous response and no rigid preconceptions about what colors should "go together"; their combinations are unexpected, creative, and warm.

A long tradition of remarkable folk art is behind them, tied in with music, dancing, pageantry and drama stemming from medieval church ritual, processions, and celebrations of saints' days. Also, from the Indian branch of their culture, they have inherited a tradition of ceramics and weaving. (In Puerto Rico today one still finds the beautiful hammocks woven from reeds and fibers.) The Spaniards brought in majolica ware, and its warm colors were incorporated into the folk art already developed by the Taíno Indians. Puerto Rican polychrome sculpture, with the same Spanish medieval origins as the work of this kind found in Mexico, might provide teachers with valuable clues to motivating these children in what is still for them an alien, gray-colored environment.

Spanish-American and Mexican-American children   The Spanish-speaking people who settled in what was once northern Mexico and is now our Southwest have long enriched our society with folk art, music, dress, food, church art and domestic architecture. Too proud of their racial heritage to be "acculturated," they have remained virtually outside our public establishments. The children, while going to white middle-class Anglo schools, have always started off so far behind because of the language barrier that education has never gone very far. (This, of course, applies to the reservation Indians as well.) The new trend toward teaching English as a *second* language and admitting rather than brutally prohibiting the use of Spanish in the schools may change the lives of thousands of these deprived children.

It is a slow process, subject to bureaucratic delay, but it has been greatly accelerated by the migration of the Mexican immigrants, the "wetbacks" of this century, into Northern cities, where they have been stimulated by contact with militant blacks and the tensions of city life. Mexican-Americans, differentiated from (and snubbed by) the families dating back to the Spanish conquest, are a mixture of Indian and Spanish and seem to have a quality of endurance and enterprise which supersedes the tendency toward passivity and resignation found in the Southwestern Spanish-speaking small farmers or in many reservation Indians. Spurred on by the civil rights movement, their cultural pride has intensified, although their environment—ghetto rather than rural—can hardly be said to have changed for the better physically. Like the blacks, they are demanding a reasonable education for their children. There are 1.7 million Mexican-Americans in California alone, 80 percent of whom are at least second generation. A recent article in the New York *Times* by Homer Bigart reveals both their plight and their insurgency. Here, he describes the confrontation with the standardized middle-class school:

Besides being confronted with an alien language, the Chicano pupil finds that the attitudes, social relationships and objects depicted in his lessons are entirely outside his experience. Mexicans are expected not only to speak American but to think American as well. . . . Cultural rape is a term frequently used . . . [11: p. 54]

One of the severest difficulties facing both the Mexican-American child and the teacher who is trying to communicate with him is that he is criticized by his own community if he becomes Anglicized, yet even if he makes the effort, he is looked down upon by the Anglo children because of his accent and origins. Many children, torn between Spanish and English words, end up with no real language at all. There are still schools, though pressure is being brought to bear to change them, where Chicano children are spanked if they are overheard using their own language in the halls or even on the playground.

Family life, which bears a great resemblance to that of the Puerto Ricans, is changing for Mexican-Americans in Denver and in the cities of California. The lingering Spanish mores inevitably have become modified. Moreover, Head Start programs have already begun to attempt some orientation of children in the Western ghettos so that they may enter school with less sense of inferiority. At present, their dropout rate is the greatest of any minority group in the country. (This high rate is, of course, partly explained by the fact that so many Mexican-Americans are migrant workers whose children find it very difficult, for obvious reasons, to master the most elementary education and who are perhaps the most truly "deprived" of all.)

The need for art programs goes along with the need for bilingual schools. Here again, as in the case of Puerto Ricans, the traditional Mexican feeling for color and proficiency with clay may be keys to release creative expression and help the children find success in school. The pageantry and drama of the Catholic ceremonies were blended in Mexico with the already existing folk art; Mexicans have brought this infusion of color, life, music and dance into North America, and it would be a grave mistake to let it die out through hostility and lack of nurture.

For both Mexican-American and American Indian children, their heritage from the Indian past—Aztec, Inca, Maya—is enormous, and they should be made familiar with it. It is now accepted in many schools and colleges with Afro-American attendance that the genius of African carving should be emphasized and that all possible illustrative material should be available. By the same token, South America and Mexico could yield many inspiring objects preserved from the ancient Indian cultures. Knowledgeable travelers and archaeologists report that museums in Peru are crowded with art that is disintegrating on the shelves because of lack of air conditioning and preservative techniques. A minimum allocation of funds would allow us to borrow them and give our children—all our children, white, black, red or brown—an invaluable experience.

American Indian children   For many years, Indian children were taken away from their homes during preadolescence and put in Federal boarding schools to be taught English and presumably to forget their "pagan" ways and beliefs and become average Americans. This system did not work out very well. Nor did suppression of their religion. Both programs produced neuroses, alcoholism and despair. The situation was made worse by the fact that they were given the poorest land in the nation for their reservations and were thus deprived not only of their culture but also of a workable economy. Those who stayed on the reservations and the hundreds of thousands who moved to the cities, totally unprepared for urban industrial life, have lived for the most part in sordid poverty. Only a very small middle class has emerged.

There seems to be something deeply fixed in the Indian philosophy and temperament that will not be homogenized. It finally became obvious that these people were not going to become "acculturated" by forced feeding, and for the last 20 to 30 years an effort has been made to provide public schooling for Indian children without wresting them from their homes, to withdraw federal paternalism, and to establish a few civil rights. The ban on practicing their religion was lifted under the aegis of John Collier, the Commissioner of Indian Affairs from 1933 to 1945. This great Indian sympathizer has written movingly about the Indian way of life and the mysticism at its base. Their power to survive, he feels, comes from the "ancient lost reverence for the earth and its web of life" (12: p. 17). In 1966, members of a federal commission on Indian rights, liberties and responsibilities stated that the Indians had preserved against all odds "a religious appreciation of nature which imparts strength and teaches the worshipper how to overcome tensions so prevalent in our modern age; a deep respect for individual differences in contrast to our struggle for homogeneity; and an emphasis on conservation" (13: pp. 145–46).

When the Indians were allowed once more to practice their religion, "the response was a rush of human energy, a creativity industrial, civic, aesthetic" (13: p. 7). The population began to rise; roads and schools were built. At the same time, educational policy went into a confused transitional period that is still going on. Serious language barriers, isolation, and too-slow reform in teaching methods still preclude any satisfactory education for Indian children. Of the 56,000 schoolchildren in Arizona and New Mexico (there are 76,000 more scattered through the country), "not one in a hundred starts school with a knowledge of English or of the non-Indian world around them" (14: p. 11). It is therefore imperative for any teacher who wants to communicate with these children to become familiar with their world.

Apart from language, what are the main differences between Indian and Anglo children? First, it should be stressed that they differ drastically from tribe to tribe, coming as they do from different stocks that settled in different parts of America; second, that where interbreeding with whites and assimilation has taken place, it is difficult to distinguish between personality and culture traits.

A consensus seems to have been reached, however, that all Indians seem to possess a time orientation different from that of Anglo children, a reluctance to excel or stand out above peers, and a supernatural rather than a scientific approach to life. "Anglo-Americans are future oriented, Indians tend to live in the present in the 'exaltation of the now'," writes Miles V. Zintz in *Education Across Cultures* (15: p. 9). They do not believe, especially the men, in long drudgery toward a materialistic goal; like the Southwestern Spanish-Americans, they share with each other rather than hoard. Zintz asks the inevitable knotty question:

Should Indian boys and girls be turned into typical white Americans? "Are the educational goals of economic efficiency, civic responsibility, self-realization . . . equally as applicable to Spanish-speaking and Indian people as to Anglos?" (15: p. 12).

Again, like the Spanish-Americans, Indians belong to extended "kinship" families, as compared to the Anglo nuclear family. They give their children an enormous amount of love. In most tribes, parents seldom mete out punishment themselves. A member of the tribe is assigned the role. It is he who is used as a threat and called on when children misbehave. Or the matter is taken to the tribal council. As the children grow older, they are shamed and punished for clumsy, inept behavior, which may explain their shyness and fear of making a mistake in the classroom (14: p. 14). They are taught to learn by observing and never to bother busy older people.

Indian children are scorned by their peers if they stand out in individual success or get too far ahead of the others, for instance, in school. They seem never to have learned any of "the coercive and aggressive verbal techniques available to children in other cultures" (16: p. 305).

Premarital sex is common in the Indian villages of the Southwest. The Navahos, for example, have no word for illegitimacy since they believe that "reproduction is the ultimate human and supernatural purpose—a man cannot therefore be conceived in sin" (17: pp. 66–71). Among the Zunis, pornographic language is very common, even among third graders, according to Zintz, but the average Indian third grader in that region is eleven or twelve years old, and smutty humor does not mark him as very different from the average inner-city preadolescent.

New educational light and an Indian youth movement—the National Indian Youth Council—spurred by the example of black militants may bring changes. Members of the Youth Council are pushing for recognition of Indian culture and encouraging themselves and their peers to formulate and follow the Indian way of life in the midst of modern society. The aim is to preserve the best aspects of the tribal system. Stan Steiner quotes one of the leaders, a Sioux named Deloria, Jr.:

I suggest that tribes are not vestiges of the past but laboratories of the future. . . . The tribal groups are in transition but to a new form of social understanding. If understood by other people, their way might solve some of the pressing social problems of today. . . . [18: pp. 155–56]

This spokesman told the author that Indian boys in boarding schools are writing home for books on legends of their tribes and for Indian words they have forgotten. This movement will certainly spread eventually to younger brothers, and the teacher of the Indian preadolescent may soon face a different atmosphere, perhaps more difficult but also more rewarding.

Art teachers working with Indian children have a distinct advantage and opportunity. An Indian Bureau study of interracial differences throughout the country found that there is among Indian boys and girls "a higher incidence of individuals who can sketch or draw accurately from memory things they have seen than is true of the general population of school children" (19: p. 93). This has been reconfirmed by many teachers and observers. A tradition of centuries of hunting and of observing closely and concentratedly all aspects of nature has undoubtedly evolved this talent in a large number of the population. Relevant art programs not merely teaching the children to repeat ancient crafts already overexploited but geared to their present environment and interests might use this aesthetic strength and make a difference in the students' orientation to the rest of their schooling.

Eskimo children   Eskimos are today assuming a Western orientation, and difficult economic, social, educational, and psychological problems are besetting their once completely self-sufficient culture. Traditionally the Eskimo child has been reared in a manner which has given him much personal security. He is a member of a large family in which both sexes enjoy affectionate relationships and every member plays a vital role in family affairs. Early participation in daily activities has brought him not only a sense of well-being, usefulness, and importance, but has also trained him to assume the roles and responsibilities of adulthood. The changes brought on by increased exposure to Western culture no longer make it possible to identify clearly what his adult role should be. Preadolescents and especially adolescents feel confused and unprepared to face the future. School teaches them that they are a small minority in a world of larger, more complex cultures. They feel that they are not receiving the skills and exposure to qualify them for participation in the modern world. Norman A. Chance, anthropologist at Stanford University (to whom the reader is referred for further reading on this subject), recommends that the government and its professional representatives (including teachers) understand the culture with which they are dealing and allow the community to manage its own affairs: "if the Eskimo are to gain greater self-initiative, a greater sense of personal worth, and a greater measure of control over their own future, they must be included as active participants in the development program" (22: p. 99).

Teachers in Alaska are making efforts to include the Eskimo language, gift of storytelling and dramatic interests in the school programs for Eskimo children. They also recognize the superb skills these children possess and their keen sense of observation, displayed masterfully in the long tradition of visual arts. Works such as Saradell Ard Frederick's "Analysis of Two Dimensional Pictorial representation with Relevance for Art Teaching in Alaska" (23) will greatly assist teachers in this locality.

In all our inner cities from the Atlantic to the Pacific, the dis-advantaged grow up earlier, are exposed to more media, get together more in groups than the rural child, and quite naturally present a denser phalanx of smoldering resentment against their housing, the economic plight of their parents, the shabbiness of their circumstances, their records in school. They are hungry — not only for a full meal but for all the pretty, shiny, fascinating objects they see advertised and in the department stores, which they are sure the more well-dressed and secure children possess. They are hungry, too, for even a few crumbs of success, for respect, for even a modicum of sympathetic understanding. Where middle-class children may rebel against smothering parental love, extremely poor children often resent the lack of nurturing, the weary indifference of parents, the lack of com-munication in the home. They are hungry, angry, and very often afraid.

ANGERS, FEARS, GANGS

One of their primary fears is of not making the grade with peers. Schools that serve several economic classes and are inte-grated both racially and socially produce many tragedies. In *The Leftouts*, Sandra A. Warden points up many of the problems in heterogeneous schools:

Although the upwardly aspirant Leftout is eager for social acceptance, he may well be at a loss to know what norms to conform to. He may be subject to pressure toward some norms at home, others from his teachers, and still others from his peers. [20: p. 100]

Trapped in these cross pressures, he may be overtaken by

enough anxiety to incapacitate him for learning. If an already deprived child tries and fails to be accepted by the power group, his sense of deprivation and his resentment are reinforced.

It is obvious that the less one accepts oneself, the less one is apt to be accepted by peers. A vicious circle is set up. The preadolescent who most needs the support of a clique or gang because of a chaotic or nonexistent home life often lacks the social confidence that will make him acceptable. Children who have strong parental support are usually more self-confident, but in preadolescence "models outside the family may be important sources of self-ideals" (20: p. 127). It is the deprived boy and girl who need these models the most. The clique or the gang provides for many of these youngsters the security they seek. It can also be an adventurous and active experience. far from grown-up supervision and warnings. A boy may find an opportunity to be a leader. Boys and girls can get together in ways their parents would never approve. A gang can be both constructive and destructive; a school has a hard time competing for a child's allegiance or even for his attention when his gang is against learning.

Gang resistance to school can be a fairly standard phenomenon in many black communities. A boy will be "unwilling and often afraid to upset his status in the gang hierarchy . . . doesn't want to be considered 'seddity' or 'chicken' by going along with the teacher and showing an interest. . . . He cuts school because members of the gang do; he provokes teachers because this is part of the gang code" (21: p. 39).

With the occasional exception of sports, underprivileged boys seldom participate in the school's extracurricular activities because they never feel they belong in the environment in any meaningful way. Girls are allowed to participate in plays, music and art, but for boys they are "sissy." Usually no one in the school has introduced either the boys or the girls to humanistic values in language they can understand.

By the age of ten or eleven, most inner-city children have seen sights and heard sounds that would be unbearably shocking even to adults from the middle class. They have learned to hustle, peddle drugs, hate the police, and live from day to day on whatever turns up and on what food their mothers can provide. Family meals are the exception rather than the rule in the overcrowded ghetto home. The street is the real home, and the operating values are the gang values. In the gang, they feel, there is honesty and fair play.

In the light of these facts, it becomes all-important for teachers of these children to accept, condone, and in subtle ways *make use of* clique and gang.

How can we change our attitudes and methods to provide a more reasonable atmosphere and training for the vast population of the American poor? Educators have been meeting for several years in various parts of the country to share research on the learning hangups of deprived children. New York University's art education department organized a conference of black and white art teachers from schools in the metropolitan area in the spring of 1968 (24). They discussed ways of teaching art to the urban black child which would reduce his tensions, draw out his talents, and help him find success in other school work as well. Deficiencies of art training became all too evident during the discussions: total lack of interest in the subject in the rest of the school; inflexible scheduling; no relation between the art curriculum and deprived children's lives; and no correlation between the arts. Administrators have failed to recognize that the disadvantaged need special teaching techniques, subject matter with which they can identify, and an atmosphere to put them at ease and allow their intelligence and talents to emerge.

In 1966, the Brooklyn Museum (under an Office of Education grant) had sponsored a conference in Gaithersburg, Maryland, organized and directed by Hanna Toby Rose, educational curator. The conferees came from all over the country and included teachers, artists, actors, writers, administrators, and a few anthropologists and foundation members. Everyone agreed that the importance of art education for the disadvantaged is incontrovertible, though a great deal more testing and proving must be done to discover the right sort of art education needed. The value of art programs for the poor is multifold: they provide a continuing sense of accomplishment and accompanying joy; bolster self-esteem; develop taste and sensibility; and open up minds that have been starved for sensory and intellectual experiences. The discipline involved teaches the child how to work. If words are a stumbling block, he learns to communicate feelings and ideas in a new way. The right kind of program can increase a child's capacity for reading, writing, and mathematics (25).

It is by now a truism that self-expression improves one's emotional health. The art studio, moreover, provides an opportunity for concrete, personal action. A child constructs something of his own, or adds his own contribution to a group project. It also can open up for him new and stimulating social relationships.

One of the participants in the conference, Julian Euell, former director of the Haryou Act arts program, reported that there is a hunger in the ghetto for the arts as an antidote to the sordid ugliness of the scene and the lack of museums, art galleries, and little theaters. Community projects may be the most immediate answer—hundreds of them have sprung up all over the country in the last few years—but the schools, too, could do a tremendous service to slum children by making art an accepted and important part of the curriculum.

SOME SUGGESTIONS FOR ART TEACHERS

There are interesting hints for the art teacher among the research results presented at the conference. In assessing the development of drawing skills of approximately 1,100 elementary schoolchildren, Elliot Eisner at Stanford University exploded his own hypothesis that disadvantaged children should draw better because their environment is richer in sensations of all sorts than that of children from middle-class homes, where all mess is immediately cleaned up. He found, on the contrary, that deprived children on the whole had less drawing ability, even in the first grade. In the course of the experiment, he discovered another fact that surprised him: the gap in drawing facility between the two groups of children narrowed, "unlike the gap that widens between the advantaged and disadvantaged in academic subjects over time" (26: p. 21). By the seventh grade, the disadvantaged had caught up with the advantaged group.

For teachers of preadolescents this research may be significant. There is the possibility that the slum child, less achievement-geared because of academic failures and fatalistic hopelessness and less interested in middle-class orientation, is more capable of pouring his energy into art than the affluent child. He may not read fast enough to catch up, he may be too blocked in arithmetic to aim at a career in science, but he *can* learn to draw and paint as well as if not better than his middle-class peer. Physically less inhibited, and frequently more emotionally disturbed, the deprived child may be freer to release his imagination in more graphic ways than boys and girls who by the age of twelve are in high gear to push ahead, control themselves, pass tests, prepare for high school, accumulate practical know-how—in short, to conquer some corner of the world.

Ronald H. Silverman, from California State College in Los Angeles, reported conducting tests to determine whether the disadvantaged child is helped most by broad exposure to the visible arts, with brief periods of working in several media, or by working with a limited number of media over prolonged periods of time. He has since published his results, stating that "it would appear to be clear that only a depth art curriculum will begin to eventuate in bringing about important behavioral changes" (24: pp. 64–65). He found, moreover, that the depth approach to teaching art can do much to improve a child's spatial orientation and increase his ability to formulate more sophisticated concepts. He also believes that art teachers of the disadvantaged are more effective when they rely on media which they themselves have developed: "Teachers who are able to conceptualize clearly what they intend to teach are ... most capable of developing an understanding of art vocabulary and spatial orientation attitude" (26: p. 65). Silverman marks as his study's "most salient insight" that "it is the art teacher who is the key to bringing about behavioral changes in disadvantaged learners, and not art, per se" (26: p. 68).

The author's personal experiences and observations have lead her to a few conclusions. First, the inner-city teacher would be wise to bear always in mind that these children are independent, that they have "been around," and that all assignments should be related to the reality they know. "Baby stuff" turns them away. Second, most decisions on projects should be arrived at through discussion with the class, never dictated summarily. Third, these children require an enormous amount of freedom to move around and be physically active.

Teachers of preadolescents anywhere — city, town, or country — need a sense of humor in order to survive and succeed. A tough, "cool" approach that is at the same time empathetic is the ideal recipe. The ambiguity of children with regard to teachers is doubled in deprived preadolescents, since the teacher represents middle-class authority and can all too easily fall into the category of the hated policeman. Yet when the child discovers that the teacher is not just a disciplinarian but really on his side and willing to put up with many variations of bravado and disrespect, he may turn to that teacher for help and even for new values.

The teacher who will succeed with the rebellious, rude, or apathetic preadolescent of today must be neither a disciplinarian of the old school nor a sentimental patsy. A growing self-consciousness has turned the black pupil, for instance, into a person who is at once more promising and more difficult to control. He does not demand a black teacher rather than a white one; he demands someone who has some idea of what is in his mind.

In addition to understanding the plight of an individual student, a teacher must be willing to get involved. This is the meaning of the word *dedicated*. Ghetto dwellers and their children despise do-gooders who go through a stint of slumming and then escape into their more comfortable bourgeois environment. Yet everyone realizes that a truly dedicated helping hand from the outside world can provide the lift out of the ghetto (21). It takes stamina to keep extending that hand in spite of distrust, hostility, rude rebuffs, and icy withdrawal. To extend that hand to the clique that ignores it, and turns you off; to extend that hand to the strangely coiffured and dressed, to the dope-ridden youngsters who sleep in their seats, or to those who leave the room when they please, or use abusive ghetto language or a foreign one you have neglected to learn—this takes toughness and a heart. It also takes research, preparation, and intelligent use of intuition.

Even beyond these qualifications, a teacher who goes into a racially mixed school must believe deeply in the absolute equality of the races of man. Any person who shrinks from the brown or black face, from hair of a different texture, who has a latent horror of miscegenation or subscribes even unconsciously to the clichés of discrimination should be wary of teaching.

The children of the poor pretend to be indifferent to those whom they do not believe will give them respect in spite of their poverty. Many are also unwilling to respond to the same motivation that stimulates more affluent children to push ahead and plan for the future. Far too many of them do not believe that they *can* get ahead. Their pessimism is based on the lives of their parents, uncles, and aunts, who look back on their education as a nightmare or a short dream on another plane of existence.

Some minority-group children refuse to speak English as a symbol of resistance, the last refuge of self-respect. They set up blocks against learning because they are already so ignominiously far behind. If a teacher can relate the subject matter of the different disciplines to her pupils' rather than to the bourgeois world, their curiosity can be aroused and they will begin to listen. If the teacher can drop the defensive mask of authority and punishment, the exchange of ideas will begin to take place. The quality of the children's speech changes; a new vocabulary slowly supplants the profanity. Too many teachers—and the administrators who hire them—are afraid of the permissive, communicative atmosphere which would allow the hurt or maimed or buffeted child to feel free to participate. The children are afraid of failure and humiliation; the administrators are afraid of anarchy and chaos. The result is a standoff. It is up to those in power to make the next significant moves—extending the surprises of humor, comprehension of different languages, unshockable patience, and imagination.

REFERENCES

1. Benjamin Bloom, Allison Davis, Robert Hess, *Compensatory Education for Cultural Deprivation,* Holt, Rinehart and Winston, Inc., New York, 1965.

2. Fred Powledge, *To Change a Child,* A Report on the Institute for Developmental Studies, Quadrangle Books and the Anti-Defamation League of B'nai Brith, Chicago, 1967.

3. Frank Riessman, *The Culturally Deprived Child,* Harper & Row, Publishers, Incorporated, New York, 1962.

4. Edward O. Moe, *The Changing Rural Scene,* Conference on Solving Educational Problems in Sparsely Populated Areas, Denver, March, 1969.

5. Vincent Skinner, "Why Many Appalachian Children are Problem Readers— We Create the Problem," *Journal of Reading,* Newark, Del., November, 1967.

6. Leon Eisenberg, "Strengths of the Inner City Child," *Disadvantaged Minority Groups,* ed. by A. Harry Passow, Miriam Goldberg and Abraham Tannenbaum, Holt, Rinehart and Winston, Inc., New York, 1967.

7. Imogen D. Cahill, "Child Rearing Practices in Lower Socio-Economic Ethnic Groups," *The Urban R's: Race Relations as the Problem in Urban Education,* Frederick A. Praeger, Inc., New York, 1967.

8. Nathan Glazer, "The Peoples of America," *Minorities in a Changing World,* ed. by Milton T. Barron, Alfred A. Knopf, Inc., 1967. (Originally published in *The Nation,* Sept. 20, 1965.)

9. Nathan Glazer and Patrick Moynihan, *Beyond the Melting Pot,* Massachusetts Institute of Technology Press, Cambridge, Mass., 1963.

10. Patricia Cayo Sexton, *Spanish Harlem,* Harper & Row, Publishers, Incorporated, New York, 1965.

11. Homer Bigart, "A New Mexican-American Militancy," *The New York Times,* Apr. 20, 1968.

12. John Collier, *Indians of the Americas,* New American Library, New York, 1948. Reprinted in *The Indian in America's Past,* ed. by Jack D. Forbes, Prentice-Hall, Inc., Englewood Cliffs, N.J., 1964.

13. *The Indian, America's Unfinished Business,* Report of the Commission on the Rights, Liberties and Responsibilities of the American Indian, University of Oklahoma Press, Norman, Okla., 1966.

14. Norman and Gilda Greenberg, *Education of the American Indian in Today's World,* William C. Brown Book Company, Dubuque, Iowa, 1964.

15. Miles V. Zintz, *Education across Cultures,* William C. Brown Book Company, Dubuque, Iowa, 1963.

16. Rosalie H. Wax and Robert K. Thomas, "American Indians and White People," *Phylon,* vol. 22, no. 4, 1961.

17. Gladys Reichard, "The Navajo and Christianity," *American Anthropologist,* January–March, 1949.

18. Stan Steiner, *The New Indians,* Harper & Row, Publishers, Incorporated, New York, 1968.

19. *The Indian Child Goes to School,* A Study of Interracial Differences, Bureau of Indian Affairs, U.S. Department of the Interior, 1958. Distributed by Haskell Institute, Lawrence, Kansas.

20. Sandra A. Warden, *The Leftouts,* Holt, Rinehart and Winston, Inc., New York, 1968.

21. Helaine S. Dawson, *On the Outskirts of Hope,* McGraw-Hill Book Company, New York, 1968.

22. Norman A. Chance, *The Eskimo of North Alaska,* Holt, Rinehart and Winston, Inc., New York, 1966.

23. Saradell Ard Frederick, "An Analysis of Two Dimensional Pictorial Representation with Relevance for Art Teaching in Alaska," unpublished doctoral dissertation, Teachers College, Columbia University, New York, 1970.

24. *Art Education for the Urban Black Child,* Report of a Greater New York Metropolitan Area Conference, ed. by Dr. Angiola Churchill, sponsored by Office of Educational Research Services, New York University, New York, 1968.

25. Judith Murphy and Ronald Gross, *The Arts and the Poor,* U. S. Department of Health, Education and Welfare, U.S. Government Printing Office, Washington, D.C., 1968.

26. Ronald H. Silverman and Ralph Hoepfner, *Developing and Evaluating Art Curricula Specifically Designed for Disadvantaged Youth,* U.S. Department of Health, Education and Welfare, Los Angeles, Calif., 1969.

In the past several years a number of art educators have embarked on important research and projects in the area of art education for the disadvantaged child. For further reading the reader is referred to the works of:

Doris L. Barclay	Vincent Lanier
Pete J. Carr	June McFee
Robert D. Clements	Ronald Melvin
Harold L. Cohen	Robert J. Nearine
Florence Rand Diamond	Max Raymond Rennels
Elliot W. Eisner	Mary J. Rouse
Moana Hendricks	Ronald H. Silverman
Frances K. Heussenstamm	Dorothy Westby-Gibson
Ralph Hoepfner	

Their findings, reports and discussions will be found in the following two major art education journals of the last two years.

Studies in Art Education, a journal of issues and research in art education, published triennially (Fall, Winter, Spring) by the National Art Education Association, Washington, D.C.

Art Education, published nine times a year (October–June) by the National Art Education Association, a national affiliate of the National Education Association, Washington, D.C.

The Preadolescent as Artist

3

Between the ages of eight and twelve, most children go through an artistic crisis. During this period, most of them reach a stage of intelligence and perceptual power which causes a conflict between their current level of artistic expressive ability and what they come to know as reality. [1: p. 66]

NATURALISM

When asked to consider making a painting of the George Washington Bridge, a first-grade child made a memorable response. "At night the bridge is like a string of pearls swinging across the river." A group of sixth graders offered quite different comments: "It has two levels." "The speed limit is thirty-five. I remember my uncle said so when we went to Blauvelt." "It's held up with cables, and at night it lights up with light bulbs."

This does not mean that the sixth-grade child is incapable of poetic responses. But it illustrates the different kind of involvement he has with the outside world. Of course, he is more guarded in his speech than in his art, but there is much the same factual response in his painting, sculpting, movie making, and multimedia work. He is inevitably more down-to-earth and less spontaneously fanciful than his little brother or sister.

It follows that preadolescents are apt to strive toward realistic representation on the two-dimensional field, with infinite details to exhibit their growing knowledge of life. Compared to the looser paintings of the very young, the ten- to thirteen-year-old's work shows self-consciousness—in the general stiffness of the forms and the precise manner in which they are handled. For the changes in imaginative activity that will be completed in adolescence are beginning now. As Michael says,

For the child, imaginative activity is unconscious while for the adult it is conscious and controlled. This change . . . should be one of the most important concerns of the art teacher at this pre-adolescent period. [2: p. 16]

At a time just prior to the "advent of adolescence" the art teacher has an excellent opportunity to help the individual hold onto his creativeness through art experiences.

The young child mainly depicts body feelings, tactile sensations, and a subjective relationship to space. The older child
tries to show the outside environment; his figures relate to natural
and man-made objects. A generalized representation of the
human figure is no longer adequate. Clothing to indicate sex,
for instance, is very important to this age group, though visual
observation may not be operating very well, as indicated by the
hemlines of the skirts or the awkwardness of the arms. Details
are excessively applied, and they are apt to prevent any mobility
in drawing the human figure. When a seven-year-old draws the
body, it is not possible to remove one section, such as the arm,
and still preserve its identity as an arm. In preadolescent painting,
on the other hand, each item is separately treated and completely identifiable. In the paintings below, each girl wears
distinctly designed clothes, as does each boy. The color changes
from person to person. The giraffes carry their characteristic
patterns; the grass has its own texture; and the other vegetation
is highly articulated in its structural features.

Grade two—girl

Grade five—girl

If we compare the clay sculpture of older children with that
of younger, we find the same interest in details and realistic proportions appearing. Since they possess more factual knowledge,
older children also are more skillful in making a given material
perform a greater variety of functions.

In preadolescence, the fight against gravity is being won. The
children learn to distribute weight so that their animals and
people can stand up. Parts are differentiated more realistically,
and the tactile sense is developing to render real textures of hair,
skin, hide, bone, cloth, etc. For the younger child the tactile
pleasure of manipulating the clay is much more important, and
the proportions of the figures are based on emotional responses.
The preadolescent also likes to manipulate the clay, but he needs,

in addition, the sense that he is capturing visual events and often may not emphasize as much the emotional significance of what he is making. The older child is more aware, too, that free-standing sculpture will be seen from all sides, and he considers this in his rendering. The arms of the clay figure by a second-grade child were perhaps made long enough to help support the body. We cannot discern, from any distinguishing features of dress, the sex of the figure. It is a combination of four or five geometric forms. By contrast, in the figure by a sixth-grade girl we see a little vest with buttons on it. Underneath the blouse there are puffed sleeves. Her skirt is pleated. She has pompom buttons on her shoes and a ribbon in her hair. The older child can use the finer muscles in her hands to roll and attach bits of clay. She can also figure out how to reach with her fingers into difficult parts to attach and shape details; she knows how to use tools, too, as extensions of her fingers.

Grade two—girl   Grade six—girl

Younger children often render a single object on a sheet of paper, ignoring what is going on around it. Preadolescents produce more and more elaborate scenes as their knowledge of the world increases. They are paying more attention to their environment, and objectivity is controlling, often suppressing, the emotional response. They are curious about experimenting with color and may become intensely conscious of similarities and differences of shades and tones, and how the mood of a work can change by changing colors. Great care was taken in the portrait shown to select muted shades to render gradations of skin color; shading was used to delineate the hair and clothes. Even the shadowy background is a composite of tints and shades of the same color—an impressionistic technique to give the illusion of depth and atmosphere. The infinite patience it took to make this life-sized collage from small pieces of magazine cutouts shows how eager children of this age are to achieve realism (instructor: Tad Krumeich).

Grade seven—girl

SPATIAL CONCEPTS

All children in our culture develop along certain recognized lines in their representation of two-dimensional space, whether they are poster-making, printing, drawing, painting, making collages, using mixed media, illustrating, or sewing. They seem to travel a prescribed path—faster or slower depending on their interest and concentration. (The following analysis is based on the work of Victor Lowenfeld as he presented it in *Creative and Mental Growth* [1947]). Fundamentally, preadolescents discover more elaborate ways of indicating space in their work than the symbolic base line concept used by younger children, who put all their objects or people on a single line denoting the ground.

In the paintings below, both done by the same boy, we see dramatically illustrated the development of spatial concepts which can take place in two years. The title of both paintings is "War." In the painting done in the fourth grade he used a number of symbolic ground lines to accommodate men, horses and martial equipment. In the painting done two years later, we see a remarkable illustration of the kind of transformation possible during preadolescence. Here the human figures have been reduced to relate to the vastness of the terrain. The boy provided an expansive aerial view utilizing the plane to give a sense of depth.

Grade four—Allen

Grade six—Allen

Many children, by the time they reach preadolescence, make full use of the plane, but since each child develops at a different rate and perceives the world uniquely, spatial concepts differ widely. The following examples attest to the wide range of methods used by preadolescents to achieve the illusion of space on the two-dimensional surface. Some of these are used consistently by certain age groups.

Objects and figures are placed on the given surface without regard to their relation to each other in the whole format. (This is a spatial arrangement generally used by preschool children.)

Grade five—boy

The following painting still employs a ground line concept except that the sky is filled in (usually arrived at by the age of six).

Grade six—girl

Objects and figures are enclosed in a space designed within the given format. In addition, an aerial view is provided, as if we were birds looking down. (Use of space more typical of primary-grade students than of preadolescents.)

Grade five—boy

Space-time pictures are more typical of younger children than of preadolescents, but sometimes the latter make them in order to explore certain concepts, to demonstrate their knowledge, or to relate an experience. In the following painting, a fifth-grade boy gives us an x-ray view; we see the outside of the building as well as the people inside it. He also shows us the various positions of the bullets coming from the plane.

Grade five—boy

Fold-over pictures, diagrammatic views, and mixing of plane and elevation are used as early as the second grade. The fold-over concept is usually dropped, but the other two persist in the upper grades. In the painting below, entitled "Camp," a fold-over method is used for cottages, combined with a frontal view of trees.

Grade six—boy

In the painting entitled "City," a diagrammatic view of the roads is combined with a frontal view of the houses. They might be considered as being on different ground lines.

Grade six—girl

Up-and-down, or vertical, space is used often by children from ages nine to twelve. The child feels he is achieving distance as items are placed one above the other on the page, starting from the bottom. Some children make objects smaller as they go up on the page, adding to the sense of distance; others include the use of overlapping as well. There is enormous variation here, as there is in their other treatments of space.

Grade five—girl

Preadolescents are aware of and use some simple devices to achieve perspective. Through the use of diagonals at the angle of his paper, the creator of the painting at the top of page 75 has achieved a sense of movement into a room.

Grade six—boy

Converging parallels leading to a vanishing point on the horizon are often used by eleven- and twelve-year-olds to give a sense of spatial depth on the picture plane.

Grade six—boy

Just as often, reverse perspective is used by this same age group. The vanishing point then converges on the observer.

Grade five—girl

Some preadolescents want to learn more about conventional perspective. It is then important that they be helped to gain an understanding of the principles and guided in their practice to achieve the skills involved. It should be made very clear to all children, however, that this way of depicting depth is but *one* way, and that it is *not* the ultimate degree of perfection attainable. (The painting of the subway below demonstrates a good understanding of one-point perspective.)

Grade seven—boy

A preadolescent will feel most at home with one particular space concept. Since this natural bent arises from basic physical and psychological sets, it is harmful and confusing to try to change it. Instead, the child should be encouraged to accept it and build on it. There is a prejudice among children and Western society as a whole in favor of Renaissance perspective, but when a class is shown the many alternatives that artists have used over the years, this prejudice can be modified, and each child will either feel fortified in his own way of ordering or perhaps be stimulated to try a new one.

It must not be forgotten that some children tend to be more and others less visually minded. The latter will usually have little interest in discovering how perspective can make space perceivable on the two-dimensional surface because they are basically involved with their work in an emotional way. Their spatial feelings are inseparable from the feelings of self. Individual visually minded children, if interested, can benefit from the teaching of perspective and should be given instruction, but it is not wise to force it on the whole class (3: pp. 258–279).

Children of this age are not consistent in modes of expressing spatial qualities but may vary them somewhat from painting to painting, depending on what they are trying to depict. Two boys in the same group made the following paintings, illustrating the enormous differences in spatial concepts one finds between children of the same age. Joe showed an adept but more conventional use of space in his painting of the hockey game than his classmate Michael. Michael drew the figures to overlap the desks but was unhappy when he could not find an empty space for the teacher (figure standing). The art teacher suggested that he make a figure on a separate paper, cut it out, and try it around the room he had drawn until he found a satisfactory place. The mixture of spatial concepts in his painting is complex. We view the plants in the left-hand corner from above. The teacher, door, and two students are on the ground line; the rest of the group occupies the plan view. Because of the location of the door, the whole work might be considered a transparent box (x-ray view) into which we are permitted to look.

Grade six—boy

Grade six—boy

How is the preadolescent likely to order his representational work on the two-dimensional field? Occasionally he will sketch in briefly, using directional lines, the kind of spatial order he wants to create, before giving his full attention to the major figure in the painting, drawing, print or collage. Often, however, he uses an additive method, starting directly with the most important figure, completing it in full detail, and then adding other figures, objects, and details. Finally, he puts in the background.

COMPOSITION

This method of adding the decorative elements piecemeal leads to stiffness. The figures are apt to be confined to frontal representation, and there is little experimentation with space. Children will cling to this simple organization if left to their own devices and not encouraged to grasp the idea of an interwoven, unified expression of rhythms and balances.

The child who does not relate to the whole format of a given space finds he has tiny figures within a huge area that he then has to fill. His story does not come across because the size of the figures prevents him from articulating all the parts. Perhaps he makes them small because he is timid, feels he cannot draw and has an urge to hide his work. Or he may feel that since he is more grown-up now, he will not get emotionally involved in his figures but instead draw the environment accurately. After all, as he is learning, man is small when related to the physical world. Graphically the problem is always painful at this age level. A child may often have insufficient skill to fill in the background without obliterating the infinite details he has drawn with such care on his minuscule figures or objects. He is likely to become disappointed and discouraged. The teacher cajoles and then finally commands him to complete the picture. He then may add meaningless objects, such as cliché birds or clouds, or a sun or moon, to the background space. These fillers are usually distracting, sometimes completely out of context, given the meaning of the work. The result is that neither child nor teacher is satisfied, and aesthetically nothing has been accomplished.

Moreover, preadolescent children are dissatisfied with the sort of ordering that places objects and figures as on a stage, facing the viewer. They have done it since the age of five or six, and they want a more grown-up spatial look. Many are incapable of analyzing and adopting alternative methods without help. If the teacher can anticipate their restlessness and encourage them to examine a variety of ways of composition, they then have the pleasure of choosing for themselves, according to their subject matter. Preadolescents often abandon art activity altogether because they are not provided with the challenge, knowledge, and experience of techniques they need in order to lift their work out of the realm of what they feel is babyish expression.

ABSTRACTION

Some preadolescent artists choose, in different ways and varying degrees, to turn away from objective reality. Susanne Langer, writing about abstraction, says:

Anything about reality that is to be expressed or conveyed must be abstracted from reality. There is no sense in trying to convey reality pure and simple. Even experience itself cannot do that. What we understand we conceive, and conception always involves formulation, presentation, and therefore abstraction. [4: p. 93]

Symbolism means a selection from reality, reduction, or exaggeration. This sort of abstraction demands the real participation of the viewer. Picasso's bull, goat and electric light, and Miro's amoeba shapes are personalized symbols, with special significance for the artist. But the viewer can learn to respond to them not only in the way the artist meant them but also as they relate to his own experience.

In the right-hand painting below, Brian interpreted his milieu in terms of personal signs and symbols. He made small vignettes of recognizable objects or events, related or unrelated, but sensitively attuned to each other through color, value and rhythm of line. Whether his inspiration came from subjective or group motivation, his style persisted. His clay piece shows the same manifestations of private symbolism.

Grade six—Brian

Grade six—Brian

Below are shown two social commentaries. One is symbolic and emotional—the black man, congestion in the city, cramped conditions of city living. The other, representing the accident in the city, is literally interpreted.

Grade six—boy

Grade six—boy

The hand pierced by a nail below is consciously symbolic in intent. The group was motivated to do paintings suggesting stories but limited to the use of the hand and some props or objects. In this work the girl used symbolism, combined with a strictly representational style (lesson by Phyllis Stepper, student teacher; instructor: Tom Vega; director: Lois Lord).

Grade seven—girl

In the assemblage made by a boy, an entire circus is created symbolically by a ladder, a few wires, and a figurelike form in the ring.

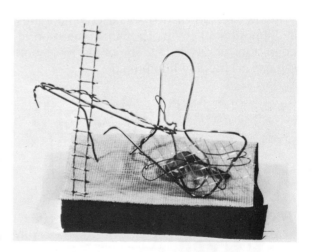

Grade six—boy

Symbolic statement in sculpture often occurs when a story or event is being depicted. In painting the environment can be easily and extensively represented, whereas in sculpture it must somehow be incorporated, compressed and thus symbolized — to show, perhaps, whether the sun is shining or the animal is drinking from the river, or if the figure is in a large field of flowers. In collage or assemblage, of course, the objects assembled very often have symbolic and associational connotations — individually, and in combination with each other.

NONOBJECTIVE EXPRESSION

Certain children are interested purely in the manipulation of nonobjective elements, with the representational connotations remaining obscure. Rhythm or color may be the motivating drive, as in the painting below, in which intricate linear imagery is organized into compact clusters of bright primary colors.

Grade six — boy

Joe, who made symmetrical paintings, moved from normal-sized paper to mural-sized. Sensing that his centrifugal and symmetrical arrangements had power, he added size and increased his effects. His entire sixth-grade year was spent in the production of oversized paintings. He worked independently, without asking for guidance, pausing between works only to accept with obvious pleasure the admiration of his teacher and his classmates.

In a free studio situation there will usually be a few children who are moved to concentrate on this sort of symmetrical work, which can be linked to the mandalas Jung has made famous and which Herbert Read (5: pp. 179–185) has analyzed so thoroughly as cropping up in children's art. Many children do both objective and nonobjective work. As Matisse said, art arises from two deep impulses: "the first is to share with others something of the quality of experience; the second is to make an icon, a holy thing" (6: p. 14).

Young children, of course, are moved more by the latter impulse than the former; they make more mandalas than preadolescents. But students in the fifth through eighth grades, when not overdirected by teachers, will also make their "holy things." Note the lush mandala by a fifth-grade girl, featuring a shell-like center.

Grade five — girl

Children who are involved in making mandalas seem to be completely immersed, quiet, and at peace with themselves, sure of and satisfied with their choice of lines and colors. They are not easily distracted and work steadily and privately. They go to great pains to mix their colors and achieve exactly what they want. On the whole, the colors are apt to be bright, clear and potent.

One does not try to influence a child to change a color or a shape when he is doing this kind of painting, for he emanates a strong feeling that he has the work in complete control. There is little repetition from one painting to another, yet the work will all have the same intent. Even among those children painting mandalas there seems to be no conscious attempt to imitate each other. One feels that there is almost something magical about the process and that to break the spell between the child and his work would be unfortunate. After a painting or collage, assemblage, or sculpture (for children make mandalas in all media) is completed, the child seems happy and relaxed and ready to be praised for what he feels is a worthy object.

On page 83 is a collage in mandala form, made of materials including cardboard, cloth, feathers, and felt; also a symmetrical "push-me-pull-you" in clay.

Grade five—boy

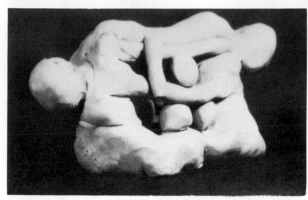

Grade six—girl

Read explains that the word "mandala" (Sanskrit for circle, or magic ring) refers to many varieties of concentrically arranged figures having a center.

It often takes the form of a flower, cross, or a wheel, with a distinct tendency to assume a four-fold structure. As a symbol, the mandala occurs not only throughout the East, but also in Europe during the Middle Ages. [5: p. 183]

Both Jung and Read believe that mandalas are an expression of the unconscious mind and that they have to do with identity and psychic integration. Read felt they should be encouraged in the art expression of children. Jung traced them through Chinese, early Christian, Byzantine, Celtic, Gothic, ancient Egyptian, Pueblo Indian and Rhodesian art (7). Read later divided them into four groups: 1) cellular or womblike forms, often with concentric rings and nuclei or loose-trailing tendrils; 2) more dynamic lines of force, with whirling lines, like flames or water or cones; 3) perfect circles and spheres floating in space; and 4) isolated spheres split into four regular parts (5: p. 184). On page 84, see a painting featuring the concentric circle, another using the cross, and a third in which an amoebalike form appears.

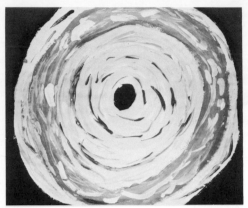

Grade six—boy

Grade six—girl

Grade five—girl

Rhoda Kellogg, who has collected many examples of the symbols used by very young children in their artwork, describes the mandala as having basic appeal, though she does not subscribe to the theory of the collective unconscious. After analyzing Read's interpretation of mandalas as images of wholeness and integration, she makes her own modification:

. . . mandalas are images of perfect balance and coherent structure; they can be enjoyed by all as esthetic experience, regardless of one's subjective state of emotion; great works of art tend to have a balanced structure that contains the four directional lines of movement found in the mandalas. . . . [8: p. 235]

My own observation has been borne out by that of other teachers that the production of symmetrical, mandala-like forms provides some children with an experience that is not only calming but fruitful. It is interesting that twentieth-century artists have been pioneers in the collection and appreciation of all forms of ancient magical art, primitive art, naïve votive art of peasant cultures, and the works of children. Kandinsky, Picasso, Kirchner, and Klee all have been enthusiastic students of these forms. For Haftmann,

the silent life of things possessed a special aura of strangeness, mystery, magic, which in the contemplating, reflective mind evoked . . . a sense of deep kinship. . . . The thing "of the hardest matter" became a component of human sensibility, and the unity of the outer and the inner was once again achieved. [9: p. 167]

In speculating about why preadolescents feel the necessity to create nonobjective art when they are at an age level of over-rationalism and surface conformity to the group, as well as of painful self-consciousness, one must give full thought to the theories of Jung and Read. There may be something in the concept of maintaining control of the environment, including one's own balance, through magical signs and symbols.

REFERENCES

1. Howard Conant, *Art Education,* The Center for Applied Research in Education, Inc., Washington, D.C., 1965.

2. John A. Michael (ed.), *Art Education in the Junior High School,* National Art Education Association, Washington, D.C., 1964.

3. Viktor Lowenfeld and W. Lambert Brittain, *Creative and Mental Growth,* The Macmillan Company, New York, 1964.

4. Susanne Langer, *Problems of Art,* Charles Scribner's Sons, New York, 1957.

5. Herbert Read, *Education through Art,* Pantheon Books, Inc., New York, 1943.

6. Roberta M. Capers and Jerrold Maddox, *Images and Imagination: An Introduction to Art,* The Ronald Press Company, New York, 1965.

7. Carl Jung, *Archtypes and the Collective Unconscious: Collected Works,* vol. 9 part 1, Bollingen series (edited by Phelix Adler), Princeton, N.J., 1968.

8. Rhoda Kellogg, *Analyzing Children's Art,* National Press Books, Palo Alto, Calif., 1969.

9. Werner Haftmann, *Painting in the Twentieth Century,* vol. I, Frederick A. Praeger, Inc., New York, 1960.

PART TWO

TEACHING THE PREADOLESCENT

Overcoming Blocks to Creative Expression

4

The willingness of an individual child to struggle with creative problems depends on how he values art, how others around him value art, and whether in his life and art experiences he has found some joy and confidence in discovering his own ways of seeing, feeling, and expressing. It depends on his need for security, his fear of mistakes. It also depends on whether teachers and other adults have tried to nurture his independence.

Some children, faced with the challenge of doing expressive personal work, become very insecure and look to formulas, stereotypes and copying in order to stay within the bounds of conformity. They also overemphasize the need for skill. They find safety in doing work that is noncommittal, deliberately pre-conceived, minutely planned.

These symptoms are not only the product of their characteristic preadolescent uneasiness. Their previous school life has often rendered them incapable of taking flights into fancy and finding challenge in self-directed experimentation. Factual, step-by-step progression has in all likelihood been their training.

Conditions in the art room can perpetuate this trend, if the teacher is incapable of creating an atmosphere of breakthrough. The blocks will remain, and the children will reiterate their fears of performing independently or doing free expressive work with complaints like "I can't draw," "It's no good," "It doesn't look like it," "I made a mistake."

Remove these conditions and perhaps there will be a different sort of response.

As teachers let us ask ourselves some questions:

Have we communicated incorrect ideas about techniques and skills?

Do we intimidate with our set of values involving great art, poor art, perfection, perseverance, and personal accomplishment?

Are the children victims of a tight educational complex forcing them into certain behavior patterns which destroy their confidence?

Is the new atmosphere of today—one of shared communal experiences and perishable, nonskilled, transitory art—more conducive to individual growth?

89

Has there been such a change that our attitudes toward art are passé and not workable for the child who was born only about ten years ago?

These are not questions which are easily answered, but they must be to some extent pondered when facing the blocks against creativity in our average school.

Another block to free expression is the attitude of parents and the neighborhood society. Whether the child lives in a ghetto or middle-class suburb or small town, the value placed on anything but the most undisturbing, representational art is apt to be minimal. There are of course exceptions, but our culture as a whole, while accepting certain works of art as objects of commercial value, still looks on the artist with suspicion until he or she has reached a large public with work that can be understood—which means work at least fifty years behind the modern trends. Modern art in its constant state of flux is obscure, bewildering, and upsetting. The preadolescent for whom deviation from the norm is difficult may suppress his instinctive creative reaction to innovating art and new sensations in favor of the conventional reactions of parents and neighbors.

PLACING VALUE ON INDIVIDUAL DIFFERENCES

Each child has his own distinct way of living in a visual experience of painting or three-dimensional construction. These differences are a source of anxiety to the conforming preadolescent and can discourage him from aesthetic effort. Various writers have categorized child art in different ways. Roberta Capers and Jerrold Maddox feel that differences may be caused by differing sense satisfactions in the work of artists:

To some the delights of the eye—color, light, and the patterns of shapes —will mean most. To others the pleasures of tactility, of varying textures and solidity, will count for more. Still others will find in movement, or in bodily action, the greatest satisfaction and interest. These preferences are usually a matter of degree rather than of exclusive preoccupation. . . . [1: p. 64]*

Lowenfeld (2: p. 64) makes a specific outline of these differences. He singles out two arbitrary personality types: children who are mainly interested in what they see and those who respond to the environment mostly in terms of feeling and meaning. He calls them *visual* and *haptic*. Below are two responses to a crab which fall easily into his two categories. Both boys observed and handled a live crab before painting it (children's Art Class, a diagnostic study sponsored by New York University under the directorship of Howard Conant, and taught by the author).

*Roberta M. Capers and Jerrold Maddox, *Images and Imagination: An Introduction to Art.* Copyright © 1965, The Ronald Press Company, New York.

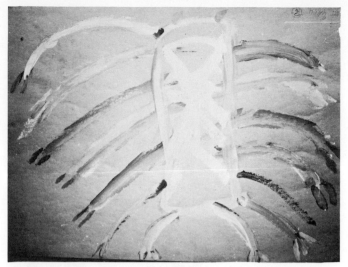

(Haptic)

One rendering of the crab is essentially subjective. The claws are the most important part—we can imagine being caught by them. The other comes closer to objective representation. The size of the eye is in exact proportion to the claws, and the coloring and texture are carefully recorded.

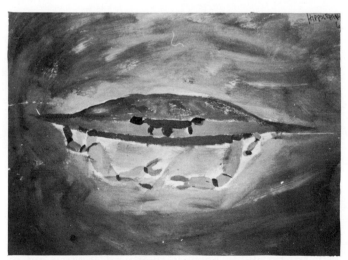

(Visual)

In the tunnel picture at the top of page 92, the child's response to a train gives a real feeling of being underground and pushing through the earth. The sides seem to close in; the light at the top of the engine seems to peer dimly through the darkness. It is a stirring experience for the viewer.

(Haptic)

One gets less emotionally involved in the second tunnel painting, though it shows logical observation of nature. The colors are graded reasonably in a sequence to the hole of light at the other end of the tunnel. The observer is made aware of visual details which have a certain independence from the whole, which lessens the impact on our feelings, appealing mainly to our logic.

(Visual)

Haptic children are often severely handicapped by the feeling that they lack artistic ability because their work is often out of proportion, full of exaggeration and distortion, and apt to be ridiculed by their peers. That is why many of them stop making any effort at all. The art teacher who is alerted to different qualities of expression can encourage the more subjective, less visual child to find pleasure in his approach and help him achieve more status in his own eyes and in the eyes of others. Situations can be created that give all children a chance to explore the art experience with other senses than the eyes. This concept is becoming more popular in the schools today and widening the views of both teachers and students. The youth culture has moved the whole country in this direction—there is an emphasis on the interaction of objects, people, environments. One teacher may provide an eating experience and suggest that the children depict an image of the path of the food as it progresses through the body. A project to paint what happens when one rides in an elevator (with the children actually taking an elevator before they start painting) has brought some impressive reactions. Touching, smelling, exploring an empty shell and then drawing the living animal who lived there can induce a creative tactile involvement. Through such experiences, those children prejudiced against more expressionistic work gained insight. Others (haptic) realized it was not necessary to strive to meet visually oriented standards when such standards are not natural to them. Every child should be supported in the means of expression most suitable to his temperament, since fine and sensitive work can be achieved in no other way. An important fact to remember is that most children use a combination of both approaches—with few working at either extreme.

One student teacher, faced with the apprehension of many in her class about skill in delineating space and making things look real, thought of a way to reassure them and reduce the frustration and disruption in her art room. She took the time to organize an extensive exhibit in which a typical embryonic scribble, or drawing, or painting by each child was pinned up next to the work of an artist with whom that child had some affinity. It might have been color relationships, quality of line, texture, shape, composition, bold inventiveness, a methodical quality, introversion, or romantic mood. The children were not only pleased but thoroughly engrossed as they contemplated their work in relation to that of notable artists, and read with interest the teacher's comments on similarities. They began to realize that every successful artist has his own special style and that being oneself is something worth working for (student teacher: Linda Sampson).

Stereotypes   One of the pitfalls for the preadolescent artist is that he may persist in automatically producing a certain formula over and over, and thus keep his feelings or any new idea out of his work. Stereotypes are often the answer to the problem of drawing "realistically" (3: p. 50). Disturbed children may do them

COUNTERACTING STEREOTYPES, COPYING, AND MISCONCEPTIONS ABOUT SKILLS

in order not to deal with any painful contact with self, and thus avoid both their own psyches and the environment (except when these crop out in disguised forms) (4: pp. 119–20). Their works are apt to be projections of daydreams, or symbols from comic books, movies, or TV shows, such as skulls and crossbones, giants, Indian headdresses, shields, swords, knives.

Stereotypes often come out of the group repertory. One finds the same symbols for tree, house, man, and woman in one child's painting after another, or one encounters the same way of rendering waves, texture of grass or hair, color of sky, or shape of clouds. These shortcuts occur in all media—painting, collage, construction, assemblage. One child will discover that bottle caps make good eyes on a puppet, and practically every child in the class will do the same thing. Wool may be used for hair, and no one will look for possibilities in any other material. In abstract work, certain kinds of shapes will be automatically combined in painting after painting.

Children fall back on repetition when they are "turned off," when they are not stimulated to see and feel things in new, personal ways. It can also be a sign of alienation and resistance.

Constant outlining is another kind of escape. Often children are taught this device, as in a project to produce stained-glass windows. Or a few will discover it on their own, and the rest will follow suit. They will realize that colors seem brighter when outlined by a dark color and that a painting looks neater and more "finished" when forms are contained within a unifying fretwork. A child may be so sensitive to the spatial power of color that he feels threatened by its control over his work. His recourse is to confine it with a strict, decorative format. He may not want to give up this device because he doesn't know how to produce contrasting colors of differing intensity. Such knowledge—provided by an alert teacher—can satisfy his need for vibrant colors and give him the confidence to let his colors breathe back and forth on the surface independent of a constricting framework. Many factors—habit, lack of skill, and possibly a compulsive neatness—can keep a child prisoner within this stereotype.

Directed observation of real life can lead also to the abandonment of such cliches as the "pretty girl" face to which preadolescent girls are so attached. One teacher gave a group of girls a full-length mirror and a private area for work, to minimize embarrassment, while they discussed their figures, measured their faces and bodies, and compared themselves with each other. When the excitement was over, each decided to paint a life story of her ideal girl. "A Day in Her Life," as shown in the following paintings of Susan, went well beyond the stereotype of the pretty face.

Dressing

Working as a photographer's model

In our recent past, glamorous magazine illustrations, beauty queen contests, and the whole sex-symbol movie-star tradition have created a stereotype of the ideal American beauty. We are only now in advertisements, TV shows, etc., giving attention and enthusiasm to other kinds of male and female attractiveness: Jewish, Black, Mexican, Puerto Rican, Indian, Greek, Italian, Middle Eastern, Oriental. Children deriving from these racial and cultural backgrounds have in the past tended to conform to the restricting clichés of facial beauty, probably with feelings of resentment, inferiority, helplessness or smoldering anger. Eldridge Cleaver, in *Soul on Ice*, describes the harm that the idealization of white beauty has done to black boys. The consequences are bitterly and brilliantly laid before us (5).

Important social changes are affecting every American's view of self and others. In many art studios there may still be jars of paint and packages of paper labeled "flesh," all of them pink in color. But many minority children are now creating images of their ideal face nearer to what they themselves look like. The child who not long ago might have hesitated to paint his self-portrait in dark tones now realizes, and acts upon the concept inherent in the "black is beautiful" message.

Adherence to a single concept of attractiveness is detrimental to individuals and to all of us as a culture. Teachers must resolutely help children resist and reject such stereotypes by encouraging them to see, understand and develop an openness to all images of man.

Sometimes children can be moved to more creative goals if they are motivated to use the stereotypes they seem to love in a broader, more original context. In a city school, children were stimulated to create a modern supercity complete with all the favorite elements—supermen, pretty go-go girls, and rocket ships. The boys and girls first copied the figures from comic books and other sources and then started to elaborate and enlarge upon them, creating all sorts of original heroic figures floating around in a community, doing superdeeds. Through the use of the overhead projector they enlarged their drawings and transferred them to mural-sized paper. By allowing use of an old, secure format, each child was finally able to allow his imagination to take hold (student teacher: Enid Glaser; instructor: Julie Kermish).

Grade six—boy *Frankenstein*

Grade six—boy *Batman*

Grade seven *Class mural*

Detail from mural

Copying   Preadolescence is a time when many children turn to copying, though there are always some in a class who feel so secure in the progress of their work that they have no need for it. Except in a residue of old-fashioned schools, copying has become a practice that fills teachers with dismay. They have battled for years to make sure that children are allowed to express themselves spontaneously instead of slavishly copying strokes rendered on the blackboard. Child art has been nurtured by teachers and parents and revered by artists for several decades. Young children have been freed to play, discover, draw, and paint their feelings and experiences exactly as they flow out naturally.

Why then should many nine- to ten-year-old boys and girls want to copy enough to do it surreptitiously when it is (as so often) forbidden? There are several possible reasons:

1. They have reached a point where they no longer value their earlier spontaneous way of doing things; they consider it childish; they want to draw immediately according to some preconceived adult standard. Furthermore, they are curious and want to find out how grown-ups perform. They are avid to know how things are put together. By copying they are perhaps vicariously entering the culture that is in store for them—a culture which, by the way, rejects almost all art except accurate (and prettified) representations of reality. These children therefore want to make their objects and people look "real."

2. The teacher may be failing to stimulate them with enough challenges, or to help them master specific skills they need to further their creative expression, or to spur them to observe from life. There may not be enough content provided in the studio relevant to the real concerns of preadolescents—their environment, contemporary life, contemporary ideas. Teachers are now fully able to bring in slides, tapes, movies, and other media devices made available for motivation.

3. Some children may be copying for the same reasons they use stereotypes: fear of self-revelation, of ridicule, of failure, or exposure of their lack of skill.

It is the author's belief that when copying becomes an irresistible need, it can be used as a stepping stone. First, the teacher should not turn it into a hidden sin, but help the children examine what they are copying, why they are copying a certain work, what its artistic value may be, what it means to them, and where it might lead them with respect to their own work. This sort of analysis must be done with each individual child. For instance, if a girl is copying from magazine illustrations and inferior prints in order to find out more about drawing horses, then the teacher's course might be to show her paintings by men who have handled the subject expertly and then reveal to her in some dramatic way that these horses were one and all drawn from life and not from pictures. An expedition to sketch from real horses would be an ideal next step. If this is not possible—though in all cases it should be—then the child might be led to choose some few details directly relevant to her need for certain information about the shape of a horse, rather than copying the whole horse. At all times, copying from photographs is better than from drawings or paintings, since the information to be gained is more accurate and less distorted by personal incapacity (skill) or plain insensitivity or banality. Giving credit to her sources helps children keep clearly in mind what is theirs—copying skill—and what belongs to the original artist or photographer, namely the whole idea and execution.

Comic strips command the greatest attention as copying material for the preadolescent. Inventive teachers have turned this interest in copying them into the study and practice of creating them. Comic strips are analyzed—the more significant artistic devices in them studied—and then the children are encouraged to try their own. These often are wonderful, a very natural and contemporary art expression for today's children, dealing with subjects of interest to them, and combining pictorial images with written material. For youngsters with reading and writing disabilities they are an excellent learning tool.

In order to move copying into more personal expression, provide mixed media of great variety so that each work will have to be different because the material demands it. Have the child add other objects and elements to the one he has copied—interesting environmental settings, etc.—so that the whole thing will be lifted into a new context. The original combination and the look of the whole result will build up the child's confidence. Collage and assemblage are means of broadening and expanding copying and freeing the child to start a composition that will be entirely his own.

One teacher had a remarkable collection of birds, undersea plants, and fabulous insects which the children used for reference. They used seeds, beans, etc., to reproduce the shapes of the plants and insects, instead of painting them on paper. These were then combined into a large complex mural. In the course of making this a good deal of creative adjustment had to be made on the designs which increased the originality of the work.

Another path is to show the child how to stretch the copied material into the area of surrealism: to fragment and abstract the elements and make new associations in the manner of modern art. This means that the child will be allowed to appropriate certain images and skills he so desperately wants and at the same time develop his own inventive ideas as he places them in an imaginative context.

Copying should never be suggested or encouraged, and it will not take place to any great extent if things are really alive and booming in an art room where the students are too busy building their own world and responding to exciting materials and experiences. It will crop up, however, and should be dealt with in a creative rather than authoritarian way.

An episode that took place in an inner-city school is enlightening. (It could have happened anywhere in America.) A gang of boys decided they would come to art class. It was their intention, the leader said, to learn to draw, then to make pictures and sell them. They produced several picture postcards, some cartoons, and some paintings bought in Woolworth's and proceeded to copy them. The subjects were hula-hula girls, swaying palms in Florida, and cute puppys sitting on pillows. During the first lesson, the teacher (Martha Zola) talked to them about mixing colors, textural qualities, ways of sketching preliminary lines. At the next lesson, she brought her own selection of Woolworth's best, saying, "Okay, let's talk business and not art for a few minutes. Guess how much each of these cost." Not one was over $2. The boys argued that theirs would be "hand painted" and worth a lot more. "All right," she said, "why don't you go out and do some tests—ask people what they will pay for hand-painted copies. If you are in business, you should know what your market is." She then showed them reproductions of fine works of art with similar subjects. She pointed to one, and using a newspaper article as proof, told them that the original had sold for $85,000 at Parke-Bernet Galleries last week. The boys were intrigued. What made these paintings so valuable? The following art periods were lively and engrossing with discussions about works of art and examination of them. As they talked, the boys began to discover the fact that paintings are records of human feelings, comments on social conditions, evidences of the human mind tackling ideas and techniques. The teacher brought in a sympathetic gallery owner who discussed paintings and how they were sold. The boys began to visit museums to see great paintings. They were in the end excited enough to start painting their own subjects and stories, based on personal experiences.

Skills   "Skill in any art should be regarded as a refinement of insight" (6: p. 189). Preadolescents find it difficult to understand this concept. They tend to think of skill as simply related to rendering in a realistic style as in the pictures they see in magazines or comic books and, in rarer cases, in museums. If one had the craft, they feel, one could make great paintings.

The adults around them at home and in the neighborhood tend to encourage this view. The craftsman is admired, and when children show evidence of this sort of aptitude, we are impressed. Parents and even teachers may praise a child more for his technical skill than for the "feeling" aspect of his expression.

A work of art of high caliber is of course skillfully rendered, but the message of the work must be of import. In great art, it is impossible to separate—be conscious of separately—the force of the skill and the force of the insight behind the work. In a low-caliber painting or sculpture, we may feel the presence of skill and the absence of insight. A banal idea rendered with perfect technique still produces a banal work. This must be made clear to preadolescents and illustrated with examples.

The student's desire for skill is commendable, since his skill will be an integral part of his expression, allowing him to make his idea visible. But he must be disabused of the notion that in painting and three-dimensional work skill means merely the ability to mirror reality.

The acquisition of skill is linked with experience. If a preadolescent has had extensive opportunities through his younger years to experiment with materials and many kinds of subjects, and thereby developed a correlation between his inner creative life and his hand skills, then he will come into the studio with some confidence and an experimental attitude. But if he is stuck with habits of stereotyping, or the conviction that some colors are "right" together, or fixed on certain ways of drawing or modeling the human figure, then he will be blocked and unable to express the increasingly complex concepts that occur to him in preadolescence, and incapable of satisfying the special craving for skill he feels at this age.

The preadolescent will find as he proceeds from problem to problem that no single inflexible skill, and not all but only some of the techniques that served him well in the past will be sufficient to deal with each new problem. New skills, new personal techniques and ways to use tools are always required to express the new ideas and feelings that crowd up within the changing boy or girl.

Techniques that are taught should be the kind that do not indoctrinate, but make for fluency and flexibility, and capitalize on those unpredictable discoveries cropping up in the course of a work. There are no easy answers as to what skills to concentrate on. A taught technique which will hamper one child may help another. It is essentially a matter of developing in children habits of exploration—and sensitivity to materials—which will give them courage to select, reject, use, or perhaps rediscover methods which will serve them best. The willingness to play hunches imaginatively is a function of the spirit and the will, and there is no formula for guiding this development. One can merely try constantly to understand a child's particular need at a certain time to express a particular thing, respect his individuality, and become sufficiently involved in the experience he is undergoing.

A great deal in the production of enjoyment of art is intuitive, but the use of the principles of design can be rational, and when the child reaches an impasse in his production, a rational approach can profitably augment intuition. [3: p. 64]

Preadolescents can increase the power of their expression by consciously working with some of the principles of design and giving a craftsman's attention to tools and materials. They can ask themselves: If I repeat these colors and shapes, will I unify my painting? Are these colors related to the mood I want to convey? Should I use a subdued color range as well as a bright one? Where shall I put the strong emphasis? Such analysis may lead them to think about how they are applying the paint or making the most of the crayon or oil pastel to achieve the wanted texture and intensity of color.

With the help of a teacher's steady guidance, a child will learn to look at his own methods objectively: Have I utilized the given space to its best possible advantage? What did that material do for my idea? Did I think enough of varying the uses of my line? Did I break up my space in the most exciting combination of shapes—did I create various heights, make use of odd balances? Did I make the most of my brushes? Were there other tools I might have used?

The child needs a great deal of support from the teacher in this struggle with technique. The teacher must study constantly what individual students or groups of them are embarking on, and give them the unstinted benefit of his or her own experience and knowledge as an artist. This means keeping a weather eye on their progress and their roadblocks, and being ready with discussion, advice, demonstration, and use of references and resources relevant to what they are trying to achieve. If a child is wrestling with perspective, he should be helped with it; if a student is having a frustrating time because he puts too much or too little paint on his brush, this should be pointed out. No one should be allowed to founder uninformed and undirected, for he will develop negative attitudes toward art.

It is important to remember that preadolescents love technical things of all kinds. This enthusiasm should be made to count. Exciting technical experimentation can become a fruitful part of the art program—activities that demand a process such as printing, for instance, will satisfy the desire to make things involving a craft, and for a taste of the machines that are a major part of the adult outside world. Success will bring satisfaction and a sustained interest in perfecting a technical skill. This, in turn, will surmount the need to reproduce clichés and stereotypes in lieu of original work.

There are today numerous slide strips, cartridge films, and movies demonstrating techniques in all art media. These can be used for specific problems; they are also enormous aids in developing curricula geared to special projects; they provide independent study material. Perhaps even more important than these films on techniques are the films showing how each artist struggles with various methods to perfect his skills—skills that will enable him to communicate with clarity an idea or feeling that is his alone. Children watching these films become aware that medium, idea, and skill are inextricably entwined, and that personal sensibility and quality of idea give direction and value to skill.

PROMOTING FIRSTHAND EXPERIENCES

Studio activities that involve observation from life, drawing and painting from live things, studying live things, touching them—that is what lifts children out of the mire of clichés and stereotypes. To be spontaneous with subject matter, a child—and an artist—needs to have great familiarity with it, to study its nature intently, and make it part of himself in as many ways as the senses and imagination allow.

Freeing the body to help the hand and arm work is one of the ways to help children improve their lines, their coordination and the general grace of their work. Let them move around, turn, crouch, swing their legs, stand up, stretch; encourage them to feel the directions of the lines of their drawing in their muscles, and the construction of forms in their own balance of weight and tensions. Once they get the idea, they let loose their extraordinary physical energy and endurance and direct it into their paint strokes or into the gestures of a three-dimensional structure. Weak, hesitant lines and tight, cramped forms can to some extent disappear, depending of course on the inhibition or lack of fear in a particular child. Curiously, this factor is often neglected in the teaching of art. Children are confined to cramped seats and must hunch over their work—often elbow to elbow in too small a space.

The body can be turned into a tool in the graphic arts as well as in dancing and music. The freeing of the body helps to free the imagination. Although there may be no audience, there is a moment of performance in visual art, a peak of expressive energy reached without self-consciousness if the atmosphere is conducive to it.

Nonobjective work has as one of its salient features that it releases the springs of the unconscious. Teachers often ask pre-adolescents to try it, convinced that such activity will counteract formulas and tightness and reduce the emphasis on acquiring skills for purely representational work. This is often true, and experimentation is successful with some children, who become interested enough to pursue this path of expression in serious fashion. Others will misinterpret the experiment, feeling that one only does this kind of thing when incapable of the skill and discipline required for realistic rendering.

Teachers often fail to pass on to their students the real meaning of nonobjective art. This may be because they themselves have no more than a superficial understanding of it. If one has not become immersed in the significance of this twentieth-century art form, how can one communicate to children anything except that it's fun, it loosens you up, it all depends on wonderful accidents, manipulating the flit gun, dripping, sponging and "we are having a fine time relaxing." The idea that the playful, the discovery, and the unpredicted can be turned by discipline into personal and significant paintings that communicate ideas and feelings will never get through to the children if the teacher does not believe it.

In this case, one fails the children. For preadolescents, though they want to have fun, are serious in their intentions to grow up and do work that is worthy and gain them praise.

A teacher has three important tasks here. The first is to gain knowledge (and firsthand experience) and think through his or her own attitude about modern art. The second is to develop in her students an understanding of why one feels moved to express oneself in nonobjective terms. Third, it is vital to point out in discussions with the children the artist's prophetic role in society and the honor he must be given in his own time for the innovations he stubbornly carries through, thereby furthering and heightening the consciousness of man. Nonobjective art has been produced for many, many years; the children have seen it (or should be shown it) in museums, in countless lobbies of office buildings, banks, movie theaters, possibly on the walls of their own or their friends' homes. They are ready to learn about the derivations of modern art and what it is all about.

Every teacher has her own approach to the question, "Why nonobjective art?" One teacher has developed this idea: Human beings can be compared to receiving and transmitting instruments. The senses are indiscriminate receptors of a multitude of auditory and visual messages (also messages received from gestures, glances, spatial relationships). Through instinct and inheritance we receive messages from the past. In sleep they come from our subconscious. We are so delicately tuned that

DEVELOPING
CONSTRUCTIVE
ATTITUDES
TOWARD
NONOBJECTIVE
EXPERIMENTATION

there is even some possibility of predicting future messages.

If we are artists or children working with materials, we have a strong urge to transmit our experiences to others; we try to find ways to tell what is happening to us. Since many of the messages that come to us are complex, superimposed, never seen or heard before, what form can they take? What should they look like?

The artist gives them whatever shape seems to come closest to what he feels it is important to express out of this inner multi-level world. The nonobjective painter uses shapes, colors, and movements to express symbolically what he has lived and felt. When we look at such painting, we reach out for the messages in it with our feelings. If we are truly receptive, the symbols will be transmitted to us easily because they come from a human being living in our time and we can to some extent understand them, translating them into feelings or thoughts we have had, or into words if we wish. A nonobjective painting is an image of our time, and the artist is telling us things about today and tomorrow.

Through discussion, children can be made aware of the social and prophetic power of the artist. The ideas expressed in the following quote from McLuhan can be transferred into language they understand:

To prevent undue wreckage in society, the artist tends now to move from the ivory tower to the control tower of society. Just as higher education is no longer a frill or luxury but a stark need of production and operational design in the electric age, so the artist is indispensable in the shaping and analysis and understanding of the life forms and structures created by electric technology. . . . in the past century it has come to be generally acknowledged, in the words of Wyndham Lewis, that "the artist is always engaged in writing a detailed history of the future because he is the only person aware of the nature of the present." Knowledge of this simple fact is now needed for human survival. [7: pp. 70–71]*

The role of the teacher is to support the emerging individual within each child and to provide the children not only with the tools but with the attitudes that will bolster their self-esteem and strengthen them to meet the onslaught of culture. They must be exposed to differing ways of thinking, perceiving and behaving in art so that they can choose for themselves their own paths of expression.

Torrance's studies (8: pp. 36–43) are very significant for teachers of art. They indicate that wherever independence and creativity occur and persist, there is always an individual—not a member of the peer group—who plays the role of sponsor. It is the spon-

*From *Understanding Media* by Marshall McLuhan. Copyright © 1964 by Marshall McLuhan. Used with permission of McGraw-Hill Book Company.

sor's part to encourage exploration, deviant behavior, experimenting, and questioning. The sponsor also protects each individual from his own peers, and rewards all inventive thinking. This, then, is the role the teacher is to play, and it is an exciting and creative one. It is up to the teacher to keep each child glowing with his own independence, and to keep the playfulness, nonsense, even contrariness bubbling along. For the very random joy of the art experience can counteract the forces of conformity and of the deadly practical seriousness which is apt to paralyze the human spirit.

REFERENCES

1. Roberta Capers and Jerrold Maddox, *Images and Imagination,* The Ronald Press Company, New York, 1965.

2. Viktor Lowenfeld, *Creative and Mental Growth,* The Macmillan Company, New York, 1947.

3. Helen Merritt, *Guiding Free Expression in Children's Art,* Holt, Rinehart and Winston, Inc., New York, 1964.

4. Edith Kramer, *Art Therapy: in a Children's Community,* Charles C Thomas, Publisher, Springfield, Ill., 1958.

5. Eldridge Cleaver, *Soul on Ice,* McGraw-Hill Book Company, New York, 1968.

6. J. L. Mursell, "How Children Learn Esthetic Responses," in the 49th yearbook, *National Society for the Study of Education,* Part I, Learning and Instruction, University of Chicago Press, Chicago, 1950.

7. Marshall McLuhan, *Understanding Media,* Signet Books, New American Library of World Literature, Inc., New York, 1964.

8. Paul E. Torrance and Paul R. Henrickson, "Some Implications for Art Education from the Minnesota Studies of Creative Thinking," *Studies in Art Education, a Journal of Issues and Research in Art Education,* National Art Education Association, spring, vol. 2, no. 2, 1961.

Working in and through the Group

5

School is the place where most children work out the task of learning to get along with age-mates. Whether the teacher pays any attention to it or not, the child's chief concern is with this task. Often the key to understanding a child's difficulties with his school subjects, or to understanding a discipline problem in class, is given by a knowledge of his difficulties in achieving this particular developmental task. The skillful teacher studies and understands the peer culture of her school and community. [1: p. 31]

This chapter describes several teaching experiences at the sixth-grade level in order to show ways a teacher can work within and through the peer-group structure.

The sophisticated student in the field of education will understand that it is never possible to repeat exactly the same teaching methods used in one school, in another. The conditions differ too much, and each institution has its own special ambience. In fact, even in the same school a given lesson will seldom be repeated. The following examples are important, therefore, only as they enlighten the student as to the milieu in which teacher and pupil operate and learn at the preadolescent group level.

Here is what happened. Two art teachers were given permission by the school administration to work as a team. First, one of the teachers would assume responsibility for a given number of classes, with the other acting as assistant, and then the roles would be reversed for another series of classes. Such an arrangement allowed the teachers to utilize the natural flux and variations that occurred as the pupils grouped, split, and reorganized themselves according to their needs and whims. In this way, the autonomy of a gang or clique could be preserved and developed at will, and without interference; instead of breaking up a group arbitrarily, the teacher could make use of it to increase these sixth graders' feeling for art.

At the same time, of course, periods of individual, independent work were allocated, to be interspersed with group projects. It is well to remember that not all children will participate in a group project. The teacher's discretion and knowledge of the individual

07

child are very important here. A child should be allowed to make a decision of this kind himself.

In studios where preadolescents are encouraged to select their own pursuits, they often separate naturally according to sex. Within these two large groups many arrangements are possible. Sometimes each child works independently, or there may be a small group working within the large division. At other times the sex segregation will not hold, and there may be a smaller mixed group. The teacher soon becomes familiar with the pattern of grouping and regrouping, which is based on the social needs and volatility of the age group.

The teacher who permits this mobility and fluctuation faces certain responsibilities. Studio logistics must be arranged and plans made for directions to be explored and for the supervision required to bring out the best development of individuals and of special cliques, in terms of what the subject matter has to offer in scope and depth. The fundamental discipline of learning to make and to look at art cannot be given short shrift even under these fluid and changing conditions.

The freedom to make their own groups and to choose their own projects seems to produce in children self-reliance and independence, which in turn make them more apt to shoulder tasks willingly and accept the teacher's assistance when it is extended to them. The educational experience unquestionably means more to preadolescents in the framework of a natural peer group.

The group is ready to restructure when its members have done all that their skill, maturity and interest span permit them to accomplish in a given project. Some children become restless, unable to keep up the pace set by some of their peers. Others are ready to move into a new group because the pace is too slow and unchallenging. While all the children may not be ready for a change, the teacher may decide to sanction regrouping and new activities in order that the majority can end on a note of high success. Or it may be best to siphon off a portion of the group, allowing the rest to continue until they are ready to stop. There are occasions when outside forces bring on a restructuring: a big social event, a disaster, or a public holiday that temporarily captures the interest of the group. School events as well as personal problems of individual children are always cropping up and need to be considered. The teacher is constantly choosing between alternatives, making the best of all possibilities. Some elements of the daily program, however, some motivating and evaluating, must be planned as solid, unshakable and inevitable, in order to make progress in the direction of curriculum aims for the whole class.

During transitions, teachers may encourage short-term activities of various kinds, to gain time for new groups to gather. In this period, one must watch out for the disruptive behavior that is apt to emerge when children are not engrossed in purposeful activity. Faulty timing at this stage may end up with students drifting too long without direction, or perhaps settling into something not appropriate for the group, and prone to failure, or even counter to the philosophical-artistic aim of the program. Teachers and children then reevaluate these plans and develop sounder ones. This sort of guidance precludes many time-consuming projects that have little or no educational worth.

The teacher at this juncture must play several roles. While the children search for a new project that is significant to them, the teacher stands by passively but ready to fan the flame of some idea that seems worthwhile, perhaps to point out its advantages and expand it to give it more meaning in relation to the general aims set up for the class. Various new ideas may be presented in connection with the children's original thought. This exploratory suggestion period is followed by a period of tryouts; some ideas are rejected, some developed. Finally one is agreed on. Groups may begin to coalesce at this point either because of the interest of certain children in the chosen project or because of friendships alone.

Once the selection is made, teacher energy and inventiveness go into planning the steps of the project so that the children will have the enthusiasm, skills, and endurance to deal with it and personalize it to the limits of their ability.

In the projects that follow, as they began to take on definition, each teacher gave her concentrated attention to a single group or to several smaller groups. The two teachers discussed what was occurring or should occur. They analyzed possible avenues for each group and divided the responsibilities. At various stages they checked with each other as to what was growing and crystallizing, estimating how long it would take for this or that to develop, what signs of regrouping were appearing, what material in relation to the curriculum was being covered, and what kind of regrouping they would encourage when the time was ripe, so that learning aims could be fulfilled (teachers: Lera Beth Lumbley and Angiola Churchill).

EXAMPLE 1— SMALL GROUP OF SIXTH-GRADE GIRLS

There were ten girls, aged eleven to twelve, who were supposedly painting in one room while the boys worked on constructions in the adjacent studio. The class met for a 90-minute period once a week. A single boy was working in the same room as the girls. For the past several weeks he had been experimenting with linear perspective. The girls were capable, most of them with drawing facility, but so absorbed in keeping in step with each other and following the leader that they were not doing work commensurate with what they had done at earlier grade levels. The group consisted of:

Nancy—a leader, feared by the other children because she had the power to turn the other girls against any individual by means of catty remarks. She had more knowledge about sex than the others; she had a history of rebellion and bravado in relation to the teachers in the school; she was known to make derogatory remarks about her parents. She was not particularly good academically. She was a good dancer and wore clothes that teachers considered inappropriate for her age, but the other girls thought them "groovy." Her artwork, which consisted only of pretty-girl clichés, was greatly admired by all the others, and she helped them copy her style.

Alice—Nancy's best friend, more introspective, but quite like her in all the other ways described. She was a capable girl both academically and artistically, and very well satisfied with her art expression. She was not open to suggestion and never explored her own potential as a painter.

Beth—good-looking, popular with all the others, an attractive black (light-skinned) girl and one of Nancy's friends, at least in school. She was a good athlete but had problems with academic work. She copied Nancy's style religiously.

Stacy—a high academic achiever, younger than the others, and generally ignored, because to be childlike is an unforgivable handicap at this age level. Her immature artistic expression was considered to be absolutely disgusting. She was unsure of herself and tried to imitate the others, but her attempts were laughed at.

Carol—a high academic achiever, black (dark-skinned), organized, who had been capable of exceptional creative work in her younger years. Now she was moody, uninspired, removed from the group. Though admired by the other girls and respected and accepted, she chose to be a loner. She made no particular effort with her artwork, completed nothing, received no joy from it, and seemed determined to isolate herself.

Mary and Jill—girls who formerly did excellent creative work. Now they had lost confidence; their values were confused; they did not know if Nancy's style was truly the standard or not. Socially they were followers in this particular class structure.

Grace—new girl in school, physically handicapped and anxious to be accepted. She was completely dominated by Nancy.

Susan—a nervous, disturbed child, incapable of maintaining friendships. She was often the butt of Nancy's sarcasm and always in the midst of some verbal battle with other children, ending up with tears on her part and screaming refusal to participate in projects, either her own or those instigated by the teacher. She

111
Working in and
through the Group

was ostracized by the children and had refused to paint or take part in any activity all year.

Jane—good academically, but a social loner. She was friendly with the more independent girls and disliked by Nancy. She sometimes challenged the latter but secretly tried to imitate her style. Nancy pointed out her failure in this regard.

The mood of the group was destructive. For several studio periods the girls had been bickering, gossiping, and viciously criticizing each other. Little factions of twos and threes were forming under temporary leaders, disputing points too numerous to mention since the topics changed so frequently. Emotional declarations of likes and dislikes ran rampant: clothes, films, girls in other classes, some teachers' behavior, a recent party some of them had attended. With all this going on, no one was paying the slightest bit of attention to what she was painting. The brush merely served as a weapon to slash on a color when an opinion was being given emphasis; the selection of a new color merely meant an opportunity to dramatize turning one's back on another person's comment and leaving the scene in a huff.

The art teacher was grasping at straws in an effort to stimulate these youngsters to pursue some constructive goals. She had tried to motivate them at the beginning of each period, sometimes during the period. She threatened, she bullied, she tried to get them sufficiently calmed down to listen to suggestions, but she did not succeed in capturing and holding their attention. She tried punishing them.

At one point she demanded silence under threat of not allowing them to come to the studio and tried to work with individual children. As quickly as she built up someone's confidence, someone else came along and pronounced judgments that tore that child down again. The teacher even tried to compete with Nancy and offered bigger and better ways to do the pretty-girl cliché. Even this did not take hold, because while they erased and fussed over an eyebrow or the turn of a curl, and ranted hysterically when it seemed imperfect to them, and called to Nancy to make it right, yet it was not really important to them at all. They were searching for something else, something they could be truly serious about. They were looking for ways to calm some of their fears about themselves, about who they were in the group and how they could achieve.

Preadolescents make it difficult for the teacher to give them the help they are crying for. They are often drowning and need the hand the teacher extends to them, but they resent that hand. It represents their dependency—in their eyes, their inadequacy. They turn to each other for help first, but desperation results when they realize they are all floundering. Then they are forced to accept a little help, occasionally, from the adult standing by, but they make it hard and accept it only on their own terms. They will not reward a teacher with kindness when one has been particularly understanding; they will be quick to point out, brutally, one's faults and inadequacies; they keep one guessing; they are full of surprises.

The teacher who knows and loves this age level plays the game with pleasure and deliberation; summons up the wisdom and patience to wait, go through the paces, pay the forfeit required by the children—in other words, to be a sport. Such a teacher still represents the straightjacket of society, yet allows the students their head, believing that they are born to be independent, that they will make their adjustments in their own styles, in their own time, on their own terms.

These children truly love the person who can survive their treatment and come back for more, who does not humiliate them but is capable of teaching them the techniques and giving them tools they can use to function in their culture. In fact, they respect the person who provides them with the power to restrain their emotional outbursts, who helps them reason out and perceive themselves in all their various commitments and activities.

In this particular group—and this is not uncommon—there was one special child who needed extra attention. She was incapable of relating to either peers or adults. She had no confidence in herself, and her reaction to any frustration was tears and screaming. Her peers had no use for her, and she became the scapegoat of the entire class. She was tiny for her age, which added to her problem. She could work at something for about 10 to 15 minutes and then had to create a disturbance violent enough to disrupt everyone. Many teachers thought she should be removed from the group, which they felt was being unduly penalized by her neurosis. Meanwhile, she made it much harder for the art teachers to help the group find its direction.

As the group of girls foundered, the boy, who was working in the same room, was reaching the end of his interest in the problems of perspective he had been tussling with. The teacher tried to arrange special time to furnish him with the additional techniques he needed to continue. But as so often happens to an art student, the realization finally came that perspective is a scientific device and limited as an artistic tool. The boy, who was scientifically minded, had become interested in its potentialities but began to realize that artistic emotion and judgment must enter in to change the purely mechanical elements, and that perspective has to be tempered and modified if the work is to express anything personally significant. When he found that this scientific tool was not capable of allowing him to create the effects he wanted, he began to lose interest, and like the girls, he was at loose ends, looking for something else to do.

113
Working in and
through the Group

The teacher, whenever she could leave the girls, tried to help him find new directions. Many avenues were explored, but nothing took hold. One day he worked on something and then threw it into the nearby wastebasket. Lifting it out, the teacher demonstrated the possibilities she saw in it, the various shapes and colors, hoping to give him some insight or stimulus by demonstrating that there are things in one's own work that one may be overlooking.

As a general rule, working on a child's painting is not recommended. It is better that children at this age do not see how a teacher works creatively, as many would be inclined to copy her, thinking this a way to gain her favor or considering it a requirement. But in this case, it proved to be constructive, because it was an unusual event and because the girls were trying to establish a relationship with the boy. He was, incidentally, a leader in the class and popular with both boys and girls. The girls gathered around to see what was happening, and utilizing this moment of group attention, the teacher emphasized that possibilities exist in any work but that for various reasons an individual often fails to develop them. She gave some of these reasons and illustrated, using the discarded painting, ways of surmounting them. She was hoping to "hit home" with some of the girls in the group.

Within minutes, many of the girls saw possibilities in the painting and asked if they could work on it. Gradually, under the leadership of the boy, they formed a group, lining up to take turns working on his discarded painting. Later, they all worked together on a fresh paper, and finally several works were enthusiastically completed in this fashion. The significance of this spontaneous occurrence was pondered by the teacher, and it influenced her future plans for the class.

Susan had participated in the event. Though at first hesitant, she had added two tiny dots with her first turn, and with each subsequent turn her boldness and freedom increased. The teacher concluded that the previous practice of working with this difficult child separately from the others had only served to isolate her more from the group to which she desperately wanted to belong. To find ways of working with her as part of the group might bring more substantial results.

Group and teacher rapport began to improve. Several points about individual styles and personalities seemed to make some impression on the children. The group was working together; they were also willing to think about some of the ideas put forth by the teacher.

The teacher thought about how she might broaden the project. Working on larger, mural-size paper would give each child more space to elaborate ideas and see them more clearly. It might be valuable to introduce group paintings done by others—frescoes of Altimara, Lascaux, Tassily, in which images were painted one upon the other without regard for composition—and then later to move to those murals conceived as a harmonious whole.

If, however, the class preferred to pursue the notion that had taken root in the previous session (beginning with the boy's discarded painting), the teacher would be ready with a group of slides showing how several artists chose a similar subject but arrived, each one of them, at a unique expression through feeling, technique, and personality.

When the group met again, the girls wished to continue the activities of the previous week. But when they discovered that the boy was no longer interested and had elected to work with the other boys in the other room, they now had a million reasons against continuing. The teacher presented the two alternatives she had prepared, and they unanimously chose to see and discuss the slides showing the same subject matter treated by different artists in individual ways.

During the viewing of the slides, the teacher said very little, while the girls talked, argued, and laughed among themselves. The leaders chose their favorites, and the dutiful followers backed up their choices; nasty digs were directed now at this one, now at the other. Stacy's remarks were pronounced to be baby stuff. Carol chose not to comment. Susan started several arguments. One of the children booed the whole business, but the group turned on her. Thus they survived a critical moment that might have broken them up.

Finally Nancy declared it would be a good idea if they decided on a subject and all tried to paint it. The others went along because they really did want to work with paints, and agreeing was a way to get something started. Nancy's purpose in suggesting this project may have been to continue her control of the group, feeling that they would all follow her lead and she would emerge, as usual, as the best.

The teacher counteracted this influence by stating that, like the artists depicted in the slides they had just seen, the girls would of course do very different things, since each one of them was an individual. This notion touched a deep chord, for within herself each girl knew she was indeed unique, and this had a reality and a significance for her. Therefore, while Nancy cried, "Follow me and you will belong and be liked!" there was another call from the self, "You are yourself strong, you are unique; your own way of doing things is valid; the others will like you because you are yourself."

Choosing a subject they could all agree on was the first hurdle. Nancy wanted to paint people because she felt confident about drawing them; those who had less confidence were hesitant. "A person in a room" was finally chosen as the title and subject matter, after the teacher had assured them that she would help those who could not draw well. Others were intrigued with the possibility, put forward by the teacher, of painting a room that gave the feeling a person was inside it without actually drawing the person.

115
Working in and
through the Group

Project 1—a person in a room[1]   Knowing the difficulties the girls would face in their first attempt to achieve a finished painting and a sense of wholeness after their long history of unfinished works and disconnected compositions, the teacher gave them colored construction paper (18 x 24 inches) to provide them with backgrounds that could unify their work, speed up its completion, and assure some measure of success.

Nancy

Jane

Susan

The girls were quite pleased with their work. They were happy to have been able to complete a painting within a short period of time. They discussed what they liked in each other's paintings.

[1]All the pictures shown in this chapter were made by the children of the Ethical Culture Schools, New York, under the direction of the author.

The teacher pointed out the various individual qualities in each: in Nancy's, the broken line and the movement she achieved; Jane's beautiful color (varieties of green) and pattern. Recalling the slide presentation, one child mentioned Bonnard in relation to Jane's work. Susan's precise techniques were greatly admired — the glass effect on the dressing table won the day. Her interesting use of the background color in the other objects was mentioned. (Matisse's red studio was reshown on the screen.) Susan's painting, as well as Beth's, was full of clichés — snake, eye, window, picture on the wall, and so forth — but these were not mentioned in the evaluation.

It was the first painting Susan had done in a year, and it was accompanied by emotional tantrums that exasperated both teacher and class. The strain of keeping up her confidence to continue her work was sometimes too much for all of us. Occasionally, the group asked her to leave before it was finished. But she came back to the studio to work with the teacher at several prearranged times. She wanted to keep up with the class and made supreme efforts to control her hysteria.

At the end of the first project, the girls felt it would be interesting to go to a museum and see some of the works they had been shown in slides, since the teacher had mentioned a loss of color in the reproductions. A visit was arranged for the next session.

Project 2 — wallpaper cutout The girls still wanted to work together. They discussed themes but were not really excited about them. The teacher, of course, tried to be prepared with several suggestions. She felt it was essential to keep them together, since it meant that each member was willing to make concessions and modify her behavior in order to belong, thus increasing both her effort and the quality of her work.

Many suggestions were rejected, some of them better than the project finally chosen. As it happened, the children had brought some terribly designed wallpapers to the studio which they greatly admired. They were not discarded because the teacher was interested in seeing what creative use they could be put to. She suggested that each child pick an element she liked and build a whole painting around it. As can be seen in the results on page 117, only Nancy used cliché mountain and water textures. Even Beth did not follow her lead; her interest in the theater began to supersede her desire to be approved by Nancy. She was complimented on her choice of colors and the courage in tackling the staircase. Being able to see through the glass was also considered an artistic feat.

Spatial effects were discussed, and making objects smaller to indicate distance. Since the inverse perspective bothered no one, it was not mentioned, but some noted the use of diagonals to get the sense of linear perspective. The girls did not like

Stacy's painting; they thought it was sloppy and the subject matter ridiculous. But they were as tactful as it was possible for them to be, considering their usual behavior toward her. The teacher managed to divert most of their comments while not actually defending her. To defend her would have only made it more difficult for her, as they would have teased her for being under the teacher's protection. Children in Stacy's position realize they have to make it on their own and reject the teacher's assistance, though they need the assurance that the teacher is aware of what is happening and will keep the situation in hand if the teasing is too rough.

Susan, who fussed and agitated over her painting to an extreme degree, finally cut out the figure from the first painting she had made and mounted it on the new paper. She was thus able to get a sense of two rooms, a spatial quality the girls greatly admired. She still required attention and support for every small decision. She cried when she was dissatisfied with an effect and came in before and after school to improve it. It was the means by which she was actually beginning to be accepted by the group, and she held on to it desperately.

117
Working in and
through the Group

Nancy

Beth

Susan

Stacy

Project 3 Given shapes   On a piece of paper 12 by 36 inches, which is a difficult size and shape for composition, the teacher painted three marks of yellow, orange and blue. The girls were asked to compose a painting incorporating them.

Project 4 Textured paper   The girls were asked to paint any suitable object inspired by an 18-by-24-inch piece of curiously textured paper that had been given to the school.

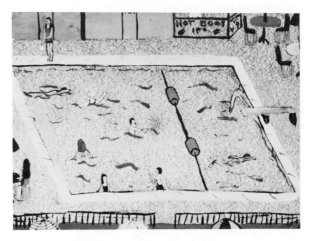

Mary

Evaluation proved interesting. They talked about applying paint with texture instead of the same old flat way. Several artists were referred to who were able to make interesting effects with their brush work or the way they applied color (Pissarro, Van Gogh).

Project 5 Collage   This was an experiment on a gray background, 24 by 36 inches, using every scrap of three sheets of colored paper, with paint added if desired. The fact that every

Jill

scrap had to be used led to very inventive and creative forms and textures. Also, it turned out to be a lot of fun to see that no one cheated. Laughter released many of the tensions that had existed within the group. Several youngsters enjoyed each other's company in new ways. Stacy was appreciated for her sense of humor instead of being scorned by the group. The new girl clowned in a way that gave definition to her personality. This sense of play and release also contributed to the aesthetic expression, which became more imaginative. Courageous approaches were tried out because it was a game and it was all right to be laughed at.

119
Working in and
through the Group

Discussions and evaluations of the projects often led to viewing the slides again for new sources of inspiration. What did artists paint about the city—crowds of people, emotional subjects, poverty, war, sad situations, the nude body, dancers, and so on? Abstract subject matter was often discussed by the teacher, but the group was not interested in it. The use of slides and reproductions was invaluable motivation. A projector was always available. In fact, work was done in a darkened room with electric lights, and slides could be shown whenever one child or the group needed them.

The students' ideas received the first consideration, although the teacher always came prepared in case they had none. After a few moments of observation and of questioning individual children, and sometimes a brief general discussion, the teacher presented some of her ideas or elaborated a student's idea by her own contribution. Sometimes an idea rejected in one period would be remembered and utilized in a later session.

The main objective of the group was to work together, and any device that accomplished this was considered. At times, materials held them together—a motif, a textured paper, a limiting condition. Most often it was a theme.

On one occasion, the teacher showed the group some examples of her own work that were abstract enough to keep the children from being overwhelmed by pictorial standards. There were about ten drawings of the same two figures. The children estimated that if they could make one trial painting each period, it would take them ten weeks of working on the same theme to achieve success with one painting, as it had taken the teacher. This example served to show them they should not be inclined to be too quickly and easily satisfied, as painters work for long periods on one idea before it becomes successful and reach a solution only through perseverance.

On the whole, though the teacher made suggestions, the girls always chose what they wanted to do. Everybody threw out ideas, but the leader, Nancy, usually made the final decision, or rather, she rallied more girls to her support than anyone else. The group was allowed to run the discussion in whatever manner they wished. The teacher waited and interjected ideas just like any member of the group, but did not insist on any one of them. Children talked freely, visited freely, worked where they pleased. Clean-up was not too good, but passable. Generally they gathered at one spot at the end of the period where the paintings were put up, to look and talk about them. At the beginning of a period, they gathered in one place to make decisions as to what to do that day. The teacher worked with them individually from time to time, helping each child not only to keep up but also to gain a bit of glory with the group in one way or another.

The teacher's role was on the sidelines, motivating, guiding, and helping individual children to articulate their ideas. She did not manage the group; its own leaders were in charge. She insisted only on retaining her single voice and vote, and with that wielded sufficient power to help the girls find worthwhile enterprises.

Music soothes the savage breast, and the girls often borrowed records from the music department to make their working atmosphere more pleasant. Dimming the lights was another means used by the teacher for controlling distractions, getting attention, or soothing some flaring temperament. Harmony was thus subtly preserved.

Project 6—a crowd There was a discussion about overlapping, which most of the children were using unconsciously, that served to bring new awareness of its possibilities. The project required them to include at least eight people on 24-by-36-inch paper. The object was to get quickly the feeling of a crowd without necessarily worrying about details.

Carol

Nancy

121
Working in and
through the Group

The illustrations on page 120 show the excellent progress being made by several of the students. By now the girls were working quickly and with a sense of wholeness. They were no longer dependent on the colored background for unity, having gained the confidence and ability to choose color relationships that would produce cohesion.

In Carol's painting an important thing is happening: each person in the crowd has a black face. This was the first time she had ever done this. The stark formalizing and the empty faces succeed in communicating a mesmeric effect. The color and the stillness are powerful.

In Nancy's work, we can see that a revolution and growth have taken place, more dramatic than in any of the other students. The "pretty girl" died a little in each of her paintings. And as she began to be divested of her position of complete power over the group, Nancy began to understand that to keep her status she needed more than her drawing ability; she had to adopt and explore a more creative approach. Of course, as former "art teacher" of her clique, Nancy was too proud to ask for help. This would have meant loss of face. When help was offered to her, even in disguised and unobtrusive forms, she rejected it, even though it might have gone unnoticed by the others; she was very perceptive and sensitive on this point. The teacher therefore began to assist her by making general remarks to the group as a whole that applied directly to Nancy's unique creative problem. The girl was clever enough to get the message and begin to experiment. Once she got started, the teacher directed more and more of the motivation to her. The other girls were unconcerned, for they were busy with their own problems, with which they were helped individually by the teacher.

When Nancy began to get recognition from the group for her new direction, she became more willing to ask for "advice," as she termed it. Her crowd painting shows her progress; it has poetry and sophisticated composition. There had been much discussion about achieving a feeling of a crowd without drawing in details of faces and clothing. Nancy continued to improve and showed some qualities of elegance in her work. Everyone appreciated it, but *no one tried to copy.*

Project 7 — animals For children this is a subject that is enjoyed but often avoided because of lack of firsthand knowledge. A trip to the zoo would mitigate this problem, but that is sometimes difficult to arrange. Our files of photographs were used as substitutes, along with visits to the animals in the school.

The aim of the project was to paint a real subject with imaginative color. As seen in the work of one of the girls, overlapping had become a persistent interest as a means of achieving a cohesive statement. After seeing the work of Franz Marc and others, color had also become important to her.

Alice

Project 8—poverty The children had seen other artists, like Daumier and Picasso, depict poverty.

Beth

Project 9—use of transparencies A given number of colors in cellophane were experimented with for overlapping color and form. Like the previous project, the main aim was *color.* When they chose a subject like poverty, the girls became conscious of color as a means of conveying feeling. In the exercise with transparencies, more emphasis was placed on luminosity, subtle color, mixed color, achievement of a sense of space and atmosphere through color. The teacher had felt they needed to give their color more attention and kept motivating the group in this direction.

Project 10—the nude The children had noticed, while viewing the slides, that nudes were often a favorite subject of artists. Concern over body changes and curiosity about the body are natural when one is a preadolescent and still finding out about oneself. The girls chose the project themselves, after discussion of some slides they had seen. They were nervous and embarrassed and giggled a good deal. The paintings were done from memory of other works they had seen, but they posed for each other for legs, arms and position.

123
Working in and
through the Group

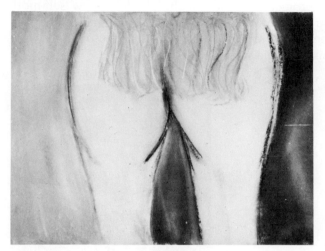

Jill

More than any other project, this one brought cohesion to the group. They helped each other with real diligence. Even Stacy, who made a major effort to participate in this project, was encouraged by the girls. Complimentary things were said about her painting. "There is a feeling of mistiness in her work, as if the figure is on the beach," said Alice.

Shading and modeling and giving the illusion of three-dimensional forms were discussed by the girls. The teacher's aim was to emphasize composition, putting the figure on paper so that it was interesting. This removed the need for accuracy of anatomical structure and detail. Texture of skin and hair was also a feature they could concentrate on. The unusual body color in Mary's painting was noted; she used a gray paper which came through all her figures. Jane's unusual view was the prize of the lot, and brought about much laughter and good will. The girls were very proud of their work; they wanted to show it to favorite teachers, friends, and some parents.

This led to the idea that they should have a group show, which eventually finalized the project. An afternoon and evening were reserved for an exhibition opening in the studios. Children, teachers, and families came. The girls even received compliments from the boys in the class on this formal occasion.

Project 11—dancers These paintings were done on 18-by-24 or 24-by-36-inch paper in mixed media. As can be seen, the class had by now gone far beyond the desire to represent prettiness. The abstract, the suggestive, the essence had become much more important. Occasionally one could even hear a criticism to the effect that "The face doesn't go with the body. Don't fuss over the face so much; think of all the parts," and so on.

Before this project was chosen, the children, now self-motivated, made a list of all the possible ideas suggested in the past. The group then made a quick selection and got right to work. The use of mixed media was their own idea.

Mary

CONCLUSIONS   Working in a separate group, away from the rest of the class, these ten girls had the privacy that created opportunity for discussion of the many special problems that disturb children of this age. Therefore a calmness and confidence began to prevail, and the children were free to enjoy the intrinsic qualities of the art experience. They were able, as time passed, to take on more challenging assignments.

Susan, who needed so much individual help, is an example of growth that a cohesive group makes possible. The intimacy meant chances to talk things over. Gradually, she improved in both mood and behavior and seemed happy to be accepted. She made

125
Working in and
through the Group

a real effort to control her upsets and to keep up. It was discovered that she was a perfectionist and could not accept any work that did not turn out exactly as she had envisioned it. Through discussion and example, the other girls helped her see that we must all accept some failures, that certain projects are bound to prove difficult for one person or another, and that we have to be good sports. Susan slowly realized that sometimes the desire to do a good job is more important than the end results.

Susan thus functioned with her peers for the first time. Others had a similar experience of adjusting and finding status in the group. Nancy no longer held complete power. Decision-making was shared. Leadership became a matter of who was most capable at the moment of doing the job that was necessary. Thus many had an opportunity to be leader. Nancy herself became too interested in what she was accomplishing in her own work to worry about whether the girls were following her lead.

Evaluation was perhaps the single most important aspect of the program. Constant reference was made to the qualities represented by the works of great artists. The urge to make good in a larger world became more important than power in their own limited preadolescent domain. The assurance that as far as painting was concerned, they could have success within their own group, made it possible for them to reach out to the "real" world of adults. In this connection, the teacher's selection of the works of great artists to show to the children is an important planning element. The students must have the opportunity to choose examples with which they can make immediate connection, and which they can assimilate at a very elemental level into their own attempts.

It was a workmanlike atmosphere, with each person developing independently yet capable of asking the group to consider her specific problems when necessary. There was no urge to imitate. If someone saw something in another's painting she thought she would like to incorporate into her own, she usually said so, and usually it was incorporated so well that it took on new character and meaning. Otherwise, it was soon abandoned as a poor decision.

In eleven weeks, the girls saw about 500 slides or reproductions, plus a group of originals at the museum. As a game at the close of the term, the girls wanted to see if they could name the artists they now knew, and jotted down names as a series of pictures was shown to them. They felt they came out quite well.

This particular group program ended because the girls were ready for new media, especially clay, and the boys were also ready for a change. As a single group they moved into an intensive clay experience, and then back to painting again. The confidence and personal sense of direction they had developed in small-group experiences served them well, and they now had the ability to concentrate and work independently within the larger class group. The mood of antagonism, bickering, competition and threat seemed to have been largely removed. The girls seemed happier, more affectionate, less tense. They were able to keep their feelings under control and manage themselves with more stability. As a result, they felt more secure, and more creative too.

**EXAMPLE 2—
LARGE GROUP
OF SIXTH-GRADE
BOYS AND GIRLS**

This class of twenty-four boys and girls met for a 90-minute period once a week and completed thirteen projects. It was a very different sort of group—a rather wild bunch of sixth graders, with little experience and no particular interest in the arts, unable to draw at all and very discouraged about not being able to make anything look "real." Many of them lacked the will to concentrate; their confidence had reached an all-time low, and experimentation was nonexistent. The boys spent their time talking sports; sporadic frictions and fights erupted among the girls' cliques, and there was continuous teasing play back and forth between the sexes.

Group cohesion began to come into being when the teacher posed the question: "Do any of you feel you are learning anything in this class?" As children of this age are quick to see faults in others sooner than in themselves, they replied candidly: "You don't teach us to really draw like they do in real art school" and "We're tired of kid stuff," and "You say our things are good when we think they are just junk."

An analysis of these typical answers is enlightening. First they say: "Teach us some skills with which we can meet adult standards." The second remark means: "Treat us differently now that we are grown-up." And finally, they are saying: "We are confused by your values and standards, which are different from those of other adults. Which are we to believe?"

The teacher's ultimate proposal to the children took account of each of these appeals.

She first took on the issue of the art teacher's values versus generally accepted adult standards of what is "good" art. Through discussion and slides, she showed in how many instances the creative artist and the public have been and are at odds (examples: Rembrandt in his day, the French Fauves of the early twentieth century, and today's pop art). It was also pointed out that society in the past has often rejected the innovations of scientists, inventors and statesmen.

Then she dealt with the issue of teaching methods. Some old

127
Working in and
through the Group

lessons that grandparents might have been given were investigated; their own parents' experiences were noted. The association of teaching methods with real people and an estimation of just how effective the old art education had been, made an impression on the children. They became more interested in their teacher's efforts to develop improved techniques of teaching from which they might benefit.

In answer to the appeal, "Treat us differently now that we are grown-up," the teacher suggested a plan whereby she would teach them some of the concepts evolved in a pace-setting high school for the specially gifted in art, which she had attended. She told them that their group was qualified to meet some of the artistic challenges posed to older children, *if* the class would make a real effort to control emotional reactions to failures and curb violent references to likes and dislikes; otherwise, she would not be able to help them. The students, somewhat motivated to show that they could indeed handle high school projects, and happy to be preparing for the future, were eager to start.

Finalizing the plan required the teacher to evolve methods suitable to the temperament and capacity of preadolescents. These children's tastes and aspirations tend to go far beyond their abilities. The teacher therefore worked out graduated steps toward each desired goal, so that the children could experience the measure of success needed to encourage them to proceed.

From past experience, she knew that children of this age have a tendency to work in an additive way, building a painting from detail to detail until the total is achieved. The serious limitation of this method is that it is time-consuming, and children in the group we are describing were rarely able to complete a painting and thus tired out before they had the pleasure and revelation of making a total statement. The teacher felt that their confidence could be bolstered and their interest increased if they were taught techniques and encouraged to choose subjects and themes that were conducive to a spontaneous total expression. The additive method of working might, of course, be well suited to certain temperaments. Therefore the teacher planned that, after the initial exposure to the general project, each child would be free to adopt his own working procedure.

As will be seen, the children were given opportunity to include all the details they wanted in their work after the first broad expression of the theme had been made. This satisfied the urgent need of preadolescents for factual details.

The projects were divided into three categories:

1. Those building toward achievement of a total composition.

2. Those emphasizing the rendering of the human figure.

3. Those aimed at expanding techniques and proficiency.

Certain developmental characteristics of preadolescents had to be kept fully in mind: their intense interest in social interaction; their tendency to be distracted, their nervousness, and short interest span; their need for adult recognition and acceptance; their drive to develop personal standards and to feel they are maturing; their need for fun and play; their enormous energy.

The timing and pacing of the projects were extremely important features of the program. A fast-moving schedule, greatly varied, full of surprises and dramatic events, with time out for laughs and social relaxation, seemed most suitable. The projects, though limited to painting, were structured to require a variety of responses from the students. One project, depending heavily on the quality of the material used for its effectiveness, would afford a child a quickly realized success. The next, however, would make demands on technical skill or imaginative capacity. The 90-minute period was paced to allow for a variety of moods and responses. Intensive demands and challenges were kept up for only brief periods. For example, silence might be demanded for 10 minutes, with complete concentration, followed by 3 minutes of releasing, unrestricted activity, followed in turn by 10 minutes of taxing, quiet, private work. After this came 10 minutes of activity that allowed uncensured social interchange—work requiring relaxed attention, culminating perhaps in a carefully guided, evaluative, sharing, group time.

The child who wished to concentrate during a social period was given a chance to do so. The one who found it difficult to accomplish anything because of his urge to socialize was provided with the means of doing work and still not missing out on anything. In fact, the structure of the program gave the unpopular child opportunities to become part of the group in ways he never could have managed on his own. In general, the pacing gave each of these children a form in which he could give vent to many changing and erratic moods without creating a problem for teacher or peers.

The entire venture had the aspects of a complicated game. It contained some features of a marathon race. It took physical endurance to participate—and at this level children have plenty of that—and to enjoy the new-found prowess of their developing bodies. The projects were devised to give them a feeling of adequacy of some kind, if not in art expression. Whether they could render the human figure convincingly or not was not the major issue. The important thing was whether they could keep up with the gang and the exhausting rigamaroles. The children found the game dramatic and stimulating. It was only later, when they began to understand that they were also doing exciting paintings, that they began to appreciate that aspect of the project.

A brief description of one of the lessons will show how time

129
Working in and
through the Group

and logistics were manipulated. Every step of the activities planned for this particular 90 minutes had a duration of not more than 10 minutes. Stopwatch and bell were essential. At the beginning of each phase, instructions were given clearly—only once, loud and brief. The children were asked to "freeze" when the bell indicated the end of one phase and the beginning of the next.

The task to be completed during each phase was considerable, placing the children under pressure. The resulting mad rush, accompanied by clowning and giggles, added to the tension and excitement of the game. The individual projects were calculated to allow the majority of the children to finish at about the same time. Those who were slower received maximum help; the faster ones were given small additional tasks to do. Projects involving intensive output were usually followed by more relaxed ones, so that slower children could catch up on the previous task without objections from either peers or teacher. On the whole, they usually managed to finish together. (In a few cases, children came in later, at some free time, to attend to minor details.) The real appeal of this game was that it gave a child a chance to qualify, to belong, and to identify with the group.

The physical arrangement of room and materials and the freedom the children had to move around had much to do with the success of the program. The teacher managed to invent new and dramatic ways to use the space. For instance, she might tell the children to duck under the table they were working on and spend a few minutes in free play. Huddled in close quarters with old or new friends, they would squeal with delight at this unexpected pleasure. Or the teacher might say, "Everybody on his back on the floor and relax!" or "Let's sit on the tables, pretending they are boats, and look down on a sea of paintings floating around us on the floor below."

The rules for procuring and returning materials were simple but well established in the school, and the children had been held to them strictly in their earlier years. During this program, however, the rules were often relaxed, as an extra bonus and a concession to their new status. The children recognized this and showed their appreciation by good sportsmanship, putting forth a real effort when it was demanded of them. From the teacher's point of view, relaxing a few rules resulted in much progress, cooperation, and rapport.

This group project, with its special dynamics, would be especially appealing to disadvantaged children. They like changing scenes and ideas superimposed upon each other as in movies and television; they take commands of a quick kind; they like competitive games involving physical endurance. Moreover, they are conservative in their inclinations and approve of learning skills rather than pondering concepts and feelings. The condition set up in the studio is not too different from their everyday environment, which is a shifting atmosphere in which ingenuity and ability to adjust count the most. With the removal of rigid standards, deprived children will lose their fear of failure or of making fools of themselves. Here their cleverness and cunning will work for them. The rapid change of pace and of rules precludes any disruptive behavior, and they can avoid the humiliation of punishment. In fact, they will have a hard time keeping up with the rules even if they want to disobey them.

Five projects—to gain a sense of wholeness in painting

Project 1 This took two art periods to complete. During the first session, the children were taken on a sketching trip around the neighborhood. Their equipment was 9-by-10-inch drawing paper clipped to carboard and graphite sticks. During the second period, a large gray bogus was pinned on the wall (18 by 24 inches) and trays of paint (six colors), sponges and water laid out. *No talking* was the rule—not strictly held to, but enough to reduce distractions.

The children were relaxed and lying around on the floor as they looked over their sketches and recalled the experiences of the previous art period. They were asked to decide which of their drawings recalled the mood and character of the neighborhood they had visited. After deciding, they were asked to go to the paper on the wall and sponge on their ideas as quickly as they could, then return to lie on the floor. There they looked over their sketches again carefully, to pick out detail that emphasized the theme or mood; the next step was to get up

Boy

again and this time with a brush put in the details. After this, there was a period of comment and discussion.

131
Working in and
through the Group

The children were eager to talk and to see what others had done with the same subject. They wandered around and exchanged opinions and ideas, since they had been told they would not have to do the cleaning up that day. They were gay, relaxed, and receptive to easy discussion about the work.

Project 2 Here, the children were asked to experiment with "visual research." It was pointed out that artists are constantly researching in his manner for their larger paintings. The children were asked to search out some soft and lyrical forms, as well as some hard, angular shapes. These were to be found not in the objects in the room but in the air spaces between the objects.

As expected, the research resulted in pages filled with unrelated bits and pieces, many hopefully pertaining to the two major categories. The teacher then asked the children to use their sense of selection and preference, their feelings and ideas, to choose and omit; to strengthen, through color, size, and contrast some aspect of their visual notes; and in the end to create a unified statement of interest to them.

The class enjoyed the challenge of this project. Several started to name their compositions, and all soon followed suit. Many children asked to come to the studio at a special time to try it again on their own. In the following example, the upper part represents the research and the lower part the finished painting.

Boy

Project 3 This was intended to provide experiences for developing a sense of the whole and a consistency of theme by the use of color as mood and line as action. The final works were to be done on bogus paper (18 by 24 inches), using chalks. The children were asked to chalk in shapes and colors on three papers, understanding that they were to be used later as backgrounds.

Slides were shown of modern paintings, grouped by themes: war, fighting, love, dream world (surrealism). Then the children were asked to choose one of these themes, select the original background paper that best fitted the subject, and then draw figures or objects on it.

The resulting work, showing effective mood, action and unity, was a sign that the class was gaining confidence.

Girl   *Dream world*

Project 4 This lasted for two periods, the first of which was taken up by a trip around Manhattan by boat. The children took sketch pads and graphite sticks. The objective purpose was a group composition made up of individual panels. The materials were construction paper and paste. The aesthetic aim was to achieve dynamic compositions from their own sketches within elongated formats.

The media used made effects possible which increased the children's confidence in their neatness and precision. (Most of the forms were cut on the paper cutter.) This was important only because at their age and in this particular art course, strict neatness had never been required of them. They took great pride in impressing their classroom teacher.

133
Working in and
through the Group

Boy

Project 5 This was divided into two 30-minute periods. The materials used were scissors, manila paper, bogus paper, felt pens, paste, and a still life set up by the teacher. The aesthetic purpose was to give the class experience in overlapping and in composition.

First 30 minutes: the students were asked to cut out from manila paper each item in the still life without drawing it first, and then to paste the items in a composition as seen in the still life on the table. They could draw in details if they wished.

Second 30 minutes: they were asked to cut out the entire still life at once from a single piece of paper. The previous experience

First Picture David

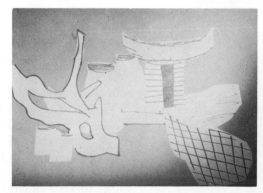

Second Picture David

had familarized them with the objects. Then they were asked to paste it to the bogus paper and use felt pens for detail. This part of the lesson proved too difficult for some of the class to complete, but before they began they had been told how hard it would be, and that even trained adults would find it difficult. They made an enormous effort, and many were successful.

By the time the children had completed these five projects, they began to be impressed by the speed and sure success of their output. Their interest in their own work began to mount, along with their curiosity. What was the teacher up to? What new adventure would they find when they came to the studio next time? Not only were they having fun, because the scene changed so often, but also they had no tiresome waiting between events, because the teacher had paid so much attention to organization. They found some of the projects easy, and yet others were hard and challenged their ingenuity. They had begun to work hard—not only to keep up, but to find out. The fast pace suited their temperament.

Five projects—working with the human figure

The aim of this series of lessons was to overcome the clichés and stiffness typical of preadolescents when they try to draw the human figure. The lessons were organized to encourage the class to:

1. Consider the human figure as a total shape.

2. Use line in fluid movement to express the figure.

3. Sense bulk and density in the figure.

4. Develop an awareness of the relation between background and form.

5. Encourage more experimentation with edges between forms.

Regular drawing tools were strictly avoided; it was felt that might be one way of dispensing with clichés. The materials used gave quick and to-the-point results. This taught the lesson more directly than words and was more effective than the standard way of teaching drawing, which involves attainment of many skills before students can see results.

Only occasionally was a single model posed. Usually the stand was jammed with as many youngsters as it would hold, all wriggling like eels. Posing was considered a part of the painting experience, and each child spent as much time posing as painting. This minimized the self-conscious drawing that results when a single figure is posed and the student tries to render it to perfection. Furthermore, it gave the children a certain empathy with the poses; they felt the stresses and strains of the positions in their own bodies.

135
Working in and
through the Group

Project 1—to become aware of the figure as a total compact shape Scissors and paper were used, and there was no pre-drawing. The children used scissors as a pencil, cutting as they looked at the model. Moderate talking to near neighbors was allowed. The poses were arranged for 5 minutes each, with 2 minutes more for details. There was one break for relaxation, socializing, and free movement around the room. The children were asked to arrange the figures they had cut onto vellum and paste them into a pleasing composition, adding details they wanted. Time was allocated to make several of these works. At the end of the period, the work was quickly displayed and the class encouraged to look and comment.

Girl

Project 2—to experience the feel and character of fluid line and thick line Colored paper, 24 by 18 inches, roving (string) chalks, and paste were used. Three children posed on a table. The roving was not to be cut until the figures were completed; color added if desired, and roving pasted down. The models posed from 15 to 20 minutes.

The rules required that a continuous string be the drawing tool. This proved to be an artistic challenge as well as a source of entertainment and fun. Prevented by the quality of the medium from rendering a realistic version of the live models, the children found pleasure in taking advantage of the fluid linear effects possible as well as of the comical effects. As seen in the drawing below, a continuity and compactness of grouping was achieved, and shapes (both positive and negative) were observed and articulated.

Boy

Project 3—to emphasize economy of means in expressing an idea
Colored paper, string, felt pens, and paste were used. The theme was "A Rain Storm," inspired by the torrent of rain that had hit the city that morning. The composition was to include no fewer than five persons and three umbrellas.

Girl

137
Working in and
through the Group

Although no mention was made of economy of means as an artistic concern, the children noticed, during an evaluation of their work, that it was not necessary to include every detail in order to get an artistic point across, and that sometimes details interfered with the total impact of the meaning.

Project 4—to achieve a sense of unity between the background and all the objects in the composition; to sense bulk in the figure; to eliminate hard outlines between forms Materials were colored construction paper, plus mounds of torn bits of paper for each child. The children took turns posing. There was discussion about the fact that all objects, inanimate or living, are made up of particles of matter, and that we tend to forget that other things beside ourselves are important in the natural world. We become stiff and self-conscious about the human figure because we are so concerned with our physical beings. When this happens in our paintings we all too often have a tight representation of the figure without any true relation to the rest of the space and the other objects in the composition.

The children were asked to create figures by pasting bits of colored paper on the construction paper so that they formed figures. If they wished, they could use felt pens to suggest the remainder of the composition. They found it tedious but enjoyed the intellectual idea and the novelty. Motivated by the teacher, they began to consider the artistic purpose of the project. The tactile sensation of placing the bits together gave them a feeling that they could actually manipulate the bulk and mass of the figure. They saw reasons for eliminating rigid outlines. The concept that they, like the rest of the universe, consisted of moving particles got through to them.

Boy

Project 5—to produce interaction of figures and background
The children used sponges, paint, and water. They posed in groups or singly. The class loved the slapdash quality of this painting experience as they sponged in the background first, and then the figures. They laughed as they compared each other's efforts. Occasionally they discussed the relationship between background and figure, and between the different figures.

Boy

Four projects—emphasizing media and use of the body

Project 1 The aim was to appreciate transparency and the accidental qualities of poster paints. Each child had a basin of water, sponge, and white vellum (18 x 24 inches).

Three musical selections were played, each creating a distinctly different mood. During each piece, the procedure was as follows:

1. The children listened quietly as a part was played through.

2. As they painted, it was played again.

3. When the music stopped, they were asked if they were willing to wipe out the entire painting.

4. While listening again to the same piece of music, they painted again on the same piece of paper.

Many children wiped out their work and expressed their idea over and over again, refining it each time. There was much dis-

139
Working in and
through the Group

Boy

cussion about how it felt to destroy one's work. Several of Picasso's remarks on this subject were read aloud, and a series of reproductions of paintings that he did on the same theme over a protracted period of time were shown to the children. They remarked that it was rather amazing to be able to retain an image of the essentials of a painting after destroying it, and to repeat these essentials, meanwhile improving the total statement by eliminating the nonessentials.

They seemed to have gained a sense of power over their work as a result of this project. They realized through discussion that the work of Pollock and others, which looked like "nothing," as they said, could be achieved only through exceptional control. They began to understand that they also could have control over their painting even when using this very fluid technique, and that the artist is master of his media. They learned not to be afraid of making mistakes; one learns through them.

Project 2 One of the motives behind it was to help the children accept modern art and thereby appreciate more their own experimental expression. Materials were paint, sponges, basins of water, paper napkins, and rolls of paper as large as desired. In a preliminary discussion, we recalled several lessons in which body movement had been important, such as water-color sessions and posing and drawing the human figure. We looked at some American and Oriental gesture paintings. The class became interested in the idea of the body as a tool in itself. Then the children were asked to remove their shoes and dip their toes and their whole feet in the paint and use them instead of brushes. (Paper towels and wet sponges were at hand for cleaning up.)

There was shouting and general elation. Little of aesthetic value resulted, but after washing up and calming down, with a piece of candy stuck in each mouth, we studied the effects we had achieved. There was a discussion about how free one could be in expressing oneself. Though this session was rather wild and mostly for loosening inhibitions, there was some constructive talk about reproducing the texture achieved by the foot painting with a brush, and perhaps using some of the other qualities in future work. We looked at some paintings by artists who were using rather unusual methods to achieve interesting effects.

The children were learning not to scoff at unfamiliar things and not to go along automatically with the conventional attitude found in our culture that art and artists are "crazy" and do useless things. They were also beginning to realize that we can be as free as we want in the painting process, and that the artist's body, through the empathy he feels when portraying action through the human figure and the gestures he uses in applying the paint, is physically involved in the resulting work.

Project 3   The aim here was to experiment with *visual texture* in order to gain a sense of the whole and become sensitive to the surfaces of paintings for their tactile qualitfes.

The materials were potatoes, paints, brushes, and 18-by-24-inch paper. The potatoes were first cut into very simple shapes. Then, using them as stamps, the children created textural patterns over the whole surface of the paper. The next step was to convert, either with a brush or a potato, the textual surface into any abstract shapes or realistic objects that the patterns suggested.

There were some very interesting results. Many children

Girl

envisioned figures running, fighting, or playing. Motion and action was the almost unanimous and quite unexpected reaction to the experiment. There was talk about using this technique, when the need arose, in their regular paintings.

141
Working in and
through the Group

Project 4   The aim was to create *actual texture,* to experiment with the use of aggregates. Materials were sawdust, sand, plaster, paste, and paints. The children were asked to paint on any subject, using these textured materials to create qualities of actual objects or the feel of them.

The class was shown the work of artists who had used aggregates to give special substance to objects, or for the purpose of an overall textural quality.

Boy

The program as a whole proved to have considerable merit as a unifier of the group and a means of changing the many negative attitudes toward art originally held by the children. Their three demands had been met, with more or less success. They had learned some skills; they had been presented with high school challenges and not treated like babies; they had been exposed consistently and pleasurably to artistic values and standards other than those of the conventional, nonart world and now had the potentiality of making up their own minds about them. They had worked hard in the studio, learned many new things, and had fun with their friends. A spirit of confidence and comradeship emerged in which the teacher and the shy or unpopular children were easily absorbed into the group's plans and activities.

When the children went back to free paintings, they seemed

very capable of facing and handling their own problems from one piece of work to the next. Their paintings had a quality of unity and were executed with assurance and speed. A general atmosphere of independence and interest prevailed for a good portion of the school year.

Girl

Boy

REFERENCE

1. Robert J. Havighurst, *Human Development and Education,* Longmans, Green & Co., New York, 1953.

Building Skill in Rendering the Human Figure

6

If the preadolescent cannot learn to render the human figure in some medium and with some degree of verisimilitude, he will feel unsatisfied and incapable of participating in many art activities, particularly where drawing and painting are involved. It is often at this barrier that the child stops for good. "I can't draw" or "I can't make the figure stand up" are soon followed by "I don't like art."

There are profoundly important reasons why human beings want to make images of themselves, reasons connected with man's concept of "self," of his relation to the universe. The self-concept, which begins to grow not too long after birth, as soon as the ego emerges, is distinguished from self-awareness and has been called by various terms throughout the ages. Self-pride, ego, or simply self-confidence—whatever it is named, this self-image is affected by interaction with other individuals and groups and is modified by success and failure in tasks and social relationships. The self-concept of minority-group children has become an object of much discussion and research; in general, consideration of the self-image, how it grows, how it is often twisted or deformed, is now a potent factor in the effort to improve the education of all disadvantaged children (1). Correlation has been found between what Elden Snyder defines as "the organization of qualities that the individual attributes to himself in varying situations" (2: pp. 242–46) and his academic success.

The child's self-image is constantly changing and directing his behavior and role playing; this image is greatly affected by the expectations and support or nonsupport of "significant others"—i.e., parents, siblings, peers, and, most important for our purposes here, teachers, (3 and 4). It is a cliché by now that teachers as well as mothers and fathers can undermine the confidence and self-esteem of the children in their care, through attitudes toward poverty, background culture, race, etc. The issue that concerns us is: How can the art teacher help children through their artwork to project, objectify, and in a sense reduce the distorted mirror images which are bound to assail them as they move into our complicated society?

Painters and sculptors—indeed, artists in all media—project images of themselves to some degree and, depending on their scope, an image of the *Zeitgeist* of their time. They release these to be recognized and contemplated. The creation of two- or three-dimensional figures, faces, and masks twisting, glorifying, and abstracting the human form seems to be a permanent artistic urge. Disturbing but healing, these images have served both magic and therapy. Their release is an especially relevant activity for the preadolescent, who is in the throes of developing his physical and mental identity, and is asking himself: Who am I? Who are the others?

In his search to place his emerging personality in today's social setting, the preadolescent cannot help but feel all around him the dehumanization of our culture; individual man has become less and less important in the complex world of technological marvels. As Paul Goodman writes: "Growing up is now interpreted as a process of socializing some rather indefinite kind of animal. . . ." (5: p. 8).

Early in our century, painting and sculpture began projecting a sense of psychic loss. Udo Kultermann provides an interesting quote from Giacometti, describing how and why that artist felt compelled to make his emaciated projections of humanity.

When I tried to create from memory what I had seen, to my horror the statues became thinner and thinner, only when they were very thin did they achieve likeness, yet their dimensions startled me; unflagging, I began over and over again, and in the end, after many months, I was back at the same point. . . . It may be that in all this I am no more than possessed, from causes unknown to me, or compensating for some sort of deficiency. [6: p. 13]

Giacometti, working from living models, produced unrealistic-looking sculpture. Kultermann refers to what has occurred as "a kind of obsession which, in the demand for greater accuracy transforms not only reality but also the image of man" (6: p. 13). After 1960 themes of devastation and disintegration no longer absorbed the artist's interest. He turned to "existing forms of contemporary people, as they appear in television, in films, advertisements and magazines, particularly in big-city life" (6: p. 14) for his representations of humanity. Contemporary man was imaged "as idealized, stereotyped, intact, authentic, rather than phenomenal, reality" (6: p. 14). Is this "pop art" figuration a satire on the materialism of our times? Preadolescents, once their conventional attitudes toward the rendering of the human figure become more flexible, will react with interest and empathy to images of this kind, although the full irony may be beyond their conscious understanding. For these are indeed figurations of the world which they are about to enter.

Pop artists have done much with the portraits of our film stars. Marilyn Monroe, for one, has been portrayed as epitomizing various symbols of our culture, such as sex, money, success, and the fragility of success. Andy Warhol, employing a contemporary advertising technique, has placed her image before us as reproduced *ad infinitum;* he is telling us what victims we have become of mass media. Another pop artist, James Rosenquist, presents us with fragmented images—odds and ends of her physiognomy commenting on the shattering effect of our culture upon the individual. (7)

By exposing the preadolescent to these modern images of man, we expose him to the idea that man's view of himself is constantly being altered by the impact of his culture and environment. Ours has been basically altered by science; medical research has revealed biological man as never before. During the Renaissance, people suddenly became aware, through the works of painters and sculptors, of the outer structure and anatomy of man; in our age, his inner anatomy has become painfully familiar. X-rays have penetrated the flesh, and we can see, on still shadowy topographic maps, the internal terrain. We measure blood pressure and blood content; whole organs can be reconstructed through operation and transplant. New blood can be pumped into a baby before it is even born. So much is known about bodily functions that astronauts can be put into isolated capsule suits and sent into the upper solar world, while their heartbeats and digestive processes are sent back by computer to the laboratory on earth, and the men themselves are brought back by devices that seem so miraculous that the world has not yet fully comprehended them.

The brain of man, the seat of consciousness, is being explored as intensively as space. Psychoanalysis, drug experimentation, and research into the nervous system provide yet more images of internal reality, though we are still on the threshold of this domain. All these new aspects of modern consciousness have become subjects for modern art. They symbolize knowledge, fear, excitement, triumph or disgust.

PREADOLESCENT REPRESENTATIONS

The preadolescent will, of course, be primarily interested in the more physical and concrete aspects of figuration—what he can touch, how the body is formed, and how it works, since his own growing body is going through exciting and disturbing changes. He will want to render the figure realistically, not symbolically or subjectively; he will be interested in mastering the external physical dimensions—the typical form and shape that a body should take. It reassures him to do this and is quite natural when one considers how frightening it can be at this age to consider all the mutations of growth that could crop up and turn one into a freak. Children should not be pushed, but merely nudged gently into awareness of all the extravagant potentialities of the artistic rendering of the human body.

In the preadolescent's drive to concretize his ephemeral identity as a body with flesh, bones, muscles, and nerves that mobilize them, the initial problem is that he wants to draw or sculpt immediately as the great artists of the past did, or else as modern illustrators do for commercial success. He may not have the skill to achieve either of these goals. He has to be weaned away from his frustrating desire and encouraged to face the artistic problems within his range of powers.

First of all, he can be led to understand that even if he had the skills, it would be inappropriate for him, in the second half of the twentieth century, to draw like Rembrandt or sculpt the human form as artists did in the Renaissance. With enough exposure to past and present art, he will recognize and be reassured by the fact that different societies have varying interpretations of the human body and face. His ideas about figuration in general can be expanded to help him traverse the formidable barrier of inhibition and fear—fear of ridicule, fear of failure, and in some cases, fear of facing his own self-image.

The teacher works to keep the children flexible and to show them that the true rendering of what they look like, or what a friend, or a motorman on the subway, a salesgirl, or a baseball player really looks like, is a changing, movable combination of various aspects of physiognomy, emotion, displacement of space, sociological conditions, etc. Are they convinced? Maybe not, because the human condition is too vast and complicated for them to comprehend. The teacher helps each child with his special interest, of course, but does not create for him a false security leading him to believe that what he is thinking about is all that exists. All too often, children have been overprotected in this way—undersold, even incapacitated in this teacher-built cocoon, only to have the traumatic moment of realization later on, a moment which may not be easily survived.

**DEVELOPING
FACILITY AND
SKILLS**

The aim to keep in mind at this level is to build knowledge, familiarity, facility, and the pride of each child in his own uniqueness. The teacher provides both objective and subjective experiences, trying to keep a good balance between them.

There are exercises giving a child the opportunity to dissect, scramble, and reassemble the human figure in collages and assemblages, to play with it as a monkey plays with a peanut. Other exercises encourage the student to use the figure in the context of composition, making it a part of the theme to be expressed, making it important to the total effect in terms of elements of design, such as space and movement. Still other exercises allow the child to empathize personally and emotionally with the shape and tensions of the human figure—posing as a model, taking part in dramatic tableaus, dancing, marching, or playing roles in order to identify with the figures they want to draw, paint, sculpt, or represent in other ways.

Many techniques and media can be presented. Sometimes a child will become so absorbed in one of them that he is distracted from all anxiety about proportions. Or a whole group will do a great deal of work, moving so fast and so intensely that they learn about proportions without struggling consciously. Such intensive directed moments involving the figure should ideally be interspersed with periods of undirected, free, personal projects through which the children, choosing their own themes, can apply some aspects of the techniques of figuration they have just learned, altering them to make them their own. Suddenly, to their great relief, they will find themselves dealing courageously with the human figure in ways they never expected, utilizing their learning and gaining praise from their peers.

Use of the posed model   The posed model serves this age group well. It can stimulate both the subjective and the objective approach to figuration, making available size proportions, positions of the body in motion, and all the emotional possibilities implicit in movement, facial expression, etc. A model can be posed in action, playing an instrument, for instance, while the children work, or moving from spot to spot in a rhythm to which a child can respond. The children can be encouraged to make mobiles or wire sculptures of the moving model. Or a pose can be dramatized with props familiar to the children: standing in the rain with an umbrella (some fake rain effects would be interesting with lights on paper and wind fans), or riding a bicycle (a real one brought in) or on a sled. The model can be posed in a costume or a sports uniform, with still-life props of all kinds. Have the children observe the model from different parts of the room, or from above or below the normal eye line. Use mirrors so that the child can see simultaneous images of the model, and ask him to render these in sculpture, wire, see-through materials like gauze, lace, or chiffon, or in a sew-on appliqué.

The posed model can be useful for expressive work in all

media: photography, sewing, collage. Children can do soft (stuffed) sculpture of the posed model, using plastics. Or they can do a poured plaster sand relief.

Children know that artists use living models, and this gives the activity importance. Whenever possible, use outside models, as this brings the community into the classroom and makes the event more exciting. (A group project, with the children taking turns posing, also has its function, as described in Chapter 5.) During a storefront arts project in White Plains, a policeman in the community came in to see what the children were doing and was asked to pose. Life-sized renderings were made of him.

Use of dance, drama, music Playing the roles themselves in a tableau involves children in a graphic, kinesthetic way that can enrich their painting and modeling skill. Perhaps an English teacher can be asked into the studio to read a piece of literature appropriate to the theme of the tableau, or a record by a famous poet or actor might be played to inspire the children to imagine the scene. They can sing the songs that belong to the period, march around—if they are, for instance, being Washington's army or marchers in the Poor People's March in Washington, D.C. The more they live with their bodies inside the drama, the better their aesthetic expression of it in clay or paint or other medium will be. It is important for them to sense the movement of their limbs, the space they occupy, the concave and convex pockets created by the relationship between bodies, and the pathos, tragedy or jubilation of the story. The sound experience is also significant. What does a war yell feel like? How is it when the lungs fill with air and collapse? What does a mouth feel and taste like when it is shouting? One child may become so involved in the breathing and nervous contractions of the body that he will make them into an abstract interpretation of the tableau. Or the music may inspire a child to create another kind of abstraction—perhaps a montage or assemblage of the fleeting impressions received, or a composition in some medium representing the tempo and rhythm of the song. Preadolescents will thus discover that they are creating a "happening," combining many disciplines and media into one event. Mixing media in this way can do much to increase children's flexibility, hold their interest in rendering the figure, and in general deepen their perceptions.

Painting techniques
1. Pose a model in a colorful costume. Have the children paint the figure on one-half of a folded piece of paper (blot painting), doing it directly without first sketching it in lightly, since this project is most useful when performed in a limited

amount of time. Before the paint dries, have the children fold their papers and rub. When they open them, they discover two figures instead of one and accidental qualities that may be of interest and that can be developed, when still wet or when dry, with small brush details. The point here is for them to do many such blot paintings, as some will be pleasing and others not.

This technique can be used to produce more than two figures at once. The double image concept is very stimulating to the child as well as giving him an opportunity to learn about the figure. Portraiture done in this manner provides an opportunity for psychological exploration.

2. Add some liquid starch to paint and pour it into throw-away plastic squeeze bottles. Pose the model and have the children draw-paint with the bottles. They can combine it with flat brush painting if they wish. Working on newspapers or textured papers also lends variety.

3. Pose the model. Have the children wet their papers with a sponge and then draw in crayon, paint, or inks.

Printing and resist techniques

1. Pose the model. Have the children draw the figure with charcoal on heavy paper and then cut out the drawing, creating a stencil. Using a dry brush, proceeding from the edges, they then transpose the contour of the shape to another piece of paper. By using this stencil over and over, the children can gain a sense for composition. Overlapping figures turned upside down and in every direction will give effects that carry an artistic meaning which teacher and child can explore in terms of modern art— x-ray, simultaneous edges, fragmentation of the image, and others. The stencil can also be used for spatter paintings, with spray guns, atomizers, and window-spray bottles. The containers should be filled with thin paint and the spraying done within protected areas. Figures can be combined with three-dimensional objects or collage.

The use of screens, all sizes of mesh, wires, and strings, plus a vast variety of porous materials through which paint can seep, can create exciting shapes and inspire children to ambitious projects, once they master the technique. In addition to large works of their own, they can work in teams to create sizable murals if they wish.

It can be pointed out to the children that this technique is used by commercial artists for lettering and representational work. It is also used extensively by wallpaper and fabric designers. A visit to one of their establishments might intensify a child's interest. For disadvantaged children this vocational possibility might make the project more important. Stenciling often produces work which is very neat and professional looking, and this satisfies the child's need to feel that he is developing mature skills.

2. Monoprints can be made with fingerpaint or tempera with some starch in it, and the printing can be done on newspapers, newsprint paper, or any other simple material. First, spread paint on a waterproof surface. Have the model take quick poses which the child draws, making grooves in the paint with his fingers. While it is still wet, cover it with a piece of newspaper, press and rub, then peel back to reveal the figure printed on newspaper. This is very effective since the writing comes through, providing additional meaning and texture. Sometimes the child is inspired to make correlations between the writing and the action of the figure. Children have also added cutout clippings from the newspaper to develop their themes.

Elmer's Glue prints are made by squeezing the glue out or dripping it to draw the figure. When dry, apply water-based or another kind of ink, and print.

Prints can also be made by stamping. Use a single stamp made from an eraser, potato, or other found object, and an inked block.

3. From the posed model, have the children paint with liquid wax (resists) on paper. Have the children brush watercolor washes over the entire paper. To remove wax, cover with a piece of newspaper and press with a warm iron. Or have the children draw the figure in the crayon and then paint over the whole paper with a thin paint mixed with water. Or, using waxed paper over a piece of white paper, have the children draw the figure on the waxed paper with a blunt instrument, then brush thin paint over the wax lines, making the figure appear. The element of surprise in this project enchants the children.

Sculptural techniques   There is, of course, an infinite number of experiments in building the human figure for children to do in the media of sculpture. These will be treated in detail in Chapter 9. Though landscape, interiors, and objects are important features of sculpture, the figure remains the most important theme.

Sometimes it is helpful for children to manipulate clay, wire, papier-mâché, and carving materials at the same time they are drawing and painting the human figure. It gives them a more concrete sense and understanding of the body. They can use the awareness of three-dimensional bulk to discover and discuss with each other and the teacher how to give the illusion of mass on a two-dimensional surface. Drawing from their own sculpture is a useful experience and one that reveals to them how bulk and volume are attained in differing media.

An interesting exercise is to paint the figure or portrait on corrugated paper or on a cardboard sheet on which boxes of various heights have been pasted. Have the children paint the figure at these varying levels. Or have them build a raised surface themselves with papier-mâché (using tissue paper) on which they finally paint the figure. Or they can fold or crush an ordinary sheet of paper, fasten it to another surface, and paint the figure on this combination of uneven surfaces. Such experiences give them a sense of volume and movement.

Composing the figure within a format

1. Using tempera paints in three values, draw-paint the posed model in a variety of poses on individual papers. Do this for several periods. In one period, discuss and study figure works of mature artists, pointing out how figures are related to each other, how objects and figures are related, and so forth. During the final period, cut out figures and arrange into compositions. Other objects and other figures can be added as desired. Below is a sample collage (chairman: Philip Helo; student teacher: Ada Landis).

Grade seven—boy

2. Pose the model. Fit the figure into an unusual format which may result in a dynamic composition. Have the child put the figure in a vertical pose but a horizontal format, and then vice versa. Or fit the figure into a circular space, or square, or some irregular shape. The exaggeration that results accustoms the child to a less realistic approach to figure drawing. He becomes so concerned with the problem of fitting the figure into the space that he forgets conventional proportions.

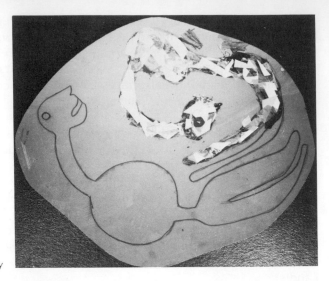

Grade six—boy

After each child has put his individual figure into a given space, ask him to combine his work with the work of friends in a larger format, after selecting a unifying theme or story. As auxiliary motivation, make a study, with the children, of artists who filled given formats, such as ceilings, niches and other architectural spaces. Possibly some children will develop three- or two-dimensional projects of their own along these lines.

3. Have the class construct out of huge cartons a large "environmental wall" within which they can place sculptures in a variety of materials occupying certain niches in humorous and inventive ways. They can then add painted figures in cramped quarter and odd positions, spilling out of a box, or spreading over a combination of boxes.

4. Have the children carve from a block. Zorach's sculpture might appeal to preadolescents, as well as the vivid analysis of it by Sam Hunter, who speaks of the "cramped compact form" which the sculptor "pressed into unity" by forcing it into the "narrow confines of his stone blocks" (8: p. 165). Another sculptor, John B. Flannagan, is described by the same critic as drawing his forms out of their stones "as a chick from her egg, or they were shown in cross-section, usually within a womb-like enclosure. The cyclical movement of emergence, and return to the source, made a modest but convincing allegory of birth and death" (8: p. 166).

5. A sophisticated project could follow, in which a survey is made of difficult formats. The Parthenon frieze can be shown at this point. Rising to this challenge, a group of children might be stimulated to tackle the same problems, using a circus, military parade, or protest march as a theme. They can select a

suitable location, such as a school library, a church, or another public place where a plaster relief can be accommodated. Each child in the group can make a portion of the relief, which is then assembled on the spot.

An introduction to the study of "street art" (presently an important expression for artists in the urban scene) can be developed at this time. Teachers can seek permission of property owners in the community to allow children to paint murals on such surfaces as building walls, excavation fences, and doorways. For children living in mixed ethnic areas, the adventure of using live models from the community in their work can help reveal to them the variety of interesting personalities in their neighborhood.

6. To increase the children's flexibility and awareness of format, suggest that they take a given shape (such as a rectangular piece of paper or cardboard) and work their way out of it, destroying one format by making a new one. After drawing individual figures from the posed model, have the children place them in such a way that they burst out of the format, as in the picture below.

Grade six—boy

7. In the painting by Jasper Johns entitled "Studio" (1964, Whitney Museum of American Art), wires, painted cans, and cardboard objects from the artist's studio dangle free of the canvas, imparting a greater sense of physical reality to a nonobjective painting. The preadolescent will find numerous objects in the environment which he will enjoy adding to his flat works (possibly to the figure) inspiring up-to-date associations and liberating him from traditional ideas of format.

8. To help the student relate the figure *to* other objects in the composition, give him several shapes in highly textured

materials and have him make a composition combining them with figures he has painted. Relate this to the work of Matisse, Bonnard, and Vuillard.

Learning to render the figure in action

1. One way to help children express action in their figures is to use inexpensive Halloween skeletons with movable joints. On large mural paper, they can pose and trace the figures as they wish, according to their chosen themes, dressing the figures in any way that carries out the idea. Emphasize movement and intricate poses. In the finishing stages, have them discuss and dramatize the unique personalities they have created. In the work below, the student traced his mannikin in many poses, then decided to make a mural with almost life-sized figures representing drunken men.

Grade six—boy *Mural*
6 x 6 feet

2. Show the class how to construct a figure of any size out of oak tag. Joints should move by means of brads, and the children can dress the figures by painting them or by using collage or three-dimensional materials. Some children might enjoy doing this as a group, with a theme in mind. The figures can then be arranged in action poses on a large format. One group made enough life-sized figures to dance and prance throughout the halls of an entire school.

3. Use a strip of movie film. Show how the action can be broken down into a series of still frames. Ask the students to go through simple movements in slow motion—yawning, for instance, in which the back is arched, the head is turned, chest thrust out, elbows possibly raised above the head, eyes shut, and

mouth opened and closed. In this way, the child comes to realize the complicated series of movements that can make up a single action.

4. Ask the children to paint or draw a figure performing a single action, using either different colors for each drawing in the series or a layer of transparent paper for each section. Generally the pictures should be separated by spaces, but in some places superimposed on each other. Five stages might be preferable. The child should practice the movements himself and identify with the poses. As he is drawing, he should occasionally go through the action again to get the feel of it.

5. This lesson can be expanded or motivated differently by showing how an illustrated "flip book" gives the illusion of figures moving when the pages are flipped over. Or show a slow-motion movie of football or baseball and have the children paint as they watch the players. The model moves very slowly from one position to the next. Explain to the children that the goal is not to draw a recognizable figure but to express movement itself. Relate this to the work of the futurists.

6. Show the children pictures of sculptures and paintings, such as those of Michelangelo, Rodin, Daumier, and Goya, to explore the concept of how themes, ideas, emotions and moods have been expressed through the human figure alone, without the aid of props or an indication of locale. The imaginative teacher will find other sources and resources. Sculpture has always expressed ideas through the human body: the worker tired from his labor, loneliness, distress, despair, generosity, justice, tragedy, illness, equality, and freedom. (The theme expressed here is loneliness.)

Grade six—girl
Loneliness

Persuade the children to get into the pose themselves before drawing it or expressing it with clay or wire. Ask them to make the appropriate sounds that go with the gestures. Ask them to close their eyes and listen to the sounds produced by the other voices in the room; also the stamping, shuffling, rising and falling of limbs that express the shapes and gestures other bodies are taking to express themes. Preadolescents have much to say about the human condition. Many young people are experiencing or witnessing situations in which emotional stress is poignant.

Whatever they depict and however they render, for preadolescents a variety of media and methods is the best grist for the mill. These children belong to the approaching age, and it is they who will make and live the future that modern artists are now projecting intuitively and extraperceptively. As the children grow to be sixteen and twenty, they will be more capable of communicating with modern art than we, their teachers are—that is, if we keep them flexible and receptive to the image of man as it appears in all media, based on hope or despair, rendered seriously, comically, satirically, or romantically.

The portrait   It goes without saying that of all forms of art the portrait has the most direct relationship to the self-image. The depicted face has more magic, more power over the mind than the rest of the body. The presence is in the face; it is more nearly alive. No matter who is being portrayed, the portrait partakes of the artist's self-concept and his intuitions about mankind in general. As Frank Seiberling says, "In a deep sense, all portraits are self-portraits of the artist" (9: p. 188). He also sees in portraiture the "loneliness and pathos of man's individualism" (9: p. 198). Another reaction might be that the portrait is the triumph of man's individualism over death and a hint of the strength of the spirit.

In Egypt it was customary to bury the portrait of a dead man along with his mummified body, in the belief that the soul would pass into the portrait if the mummy failed to survive. While these images were likenesses of the dead persons, the countenances were, universally, masks of calm self-assurance. The statues, intended to become the living body in the world of death, were regarded by living men as already creatures of another realm, and their unruffled features reassured the living that there was nothing to fear in dying.

The Greeks saw themselves in the images they made of the gods. The bodies and faces of their gods were glorified concepts of the human form. According to their myths, men and gods were at times equally unreliable, but beauty and grace of form and gesture were eternal attributes of the deities. The Greeks created in sculpture a noble world of supermen in which reality and make-believe merged, a world maintained by clear intelligence. Greek art is assembled from attributes of the Mediterranean face and figure and from an intellectual image of what mankind *should* look like. This formalized, refined image has remained in the Western world ever since, perhaps becoming a subconscious archetype, influencing our taste, and prejudicing us against any other kind of facial beauty. Even the practical Romans in their declining centuries renounced their original concepts and adopted in their sculpture what became a devitalized "look" based on the Greek concept of beauty.

Earlier Romans, superrealists, practiced making masks of their dead that left nothing to the imagination. Death meant immobility—muscles without tension, jaws that dropped. The dead man was imaged as exactly what he had been in life, with all the scars of his valor, labor, avarice, or decadence on his face. His character was the heritage he left, and his family carried his mask in processions on special days. Later, during their heyday, the Romans made realistic portraits of the living. These also were frank representations of severe and intense men who built and maintained an empire.

After the Roman Empire fell, the facial image of man seems to have been submerged in darkness. We have few artifacts portraying the faces of the barbarians. Their lack of skill at first prevented them from leaving evidence, and perhaps their sense of inferiority too, and the frightening chaos of the times. Then with the emergence of Christianity, images of God and Jesus, saints and disciples became plentiful, slowly evolving from bad Roman-Greek versions to the emaciated, noncorporeal, ascetic images of the early Christian age. The portraits of the martyrs became the ideal—sick, mutilated bodies, mortified and denied all sensuous pleasures so that the soul would reach heaven and its reward.

With more economic stability, less carnage and improved law and order, confidence returned. The towns, the bourgeoisie, and the monasteries supported a new image of humanity. We see it in portraits and in the art inside romanesque cathedrals. The common people begin to emerge: the characters with the crooked noses, the squinting eyes, the robust, round faces of the artisans and serfs, the characteristically national features of the Virgin of Autun. The Bretons and the smaller nobility of the French and German countryside appear in the images of the Virgin Mary, and the common babies of the poor are immortalized as the Holy Child. Later in Flanders, Holland, and Germany, influenced by the Renaissance, portraits were made of the prosperous burghers and their wives, marriage contract portraits in materialistic settings representing what they owned and what they ate. These portraits are symbols of the power the bourgeoisie wheedled and wrenched away from a weakening landed aristocracy—portly men, overly somber, thick, with their florid, overfed women, feathered and tastelessly attired. Further along in this period, portraits show us the peasants at their feasts—the coarsened faces, heavy hands and feet— indulging in their joys and vices.

Meanwhile the High Renaissance had come across Europe like a glorious ship bearing a new image of man, one that had risen from the ashes of the ancient classical world. But it had been altered to fit a new, virile conception of mankind and of individual man. Capers and Maddox sum it up in *Images and Imagination:*

Portraiture is an area of subject matter which, as one might suppose, waxes and wanes in popularity in accordance with the role the patron plays in the instigation of art. In the Renaissance, the interest in human personality and the importance of the individual in the social scene led to a development of portraiture unparalleled since Roman times. Antonio Pollaiuolo's *Man in Red* . . . is presented as the embodiment of human power. His is an arrogant self-confidence; he has an air of rejecting intimacy. The clarity with which his figure is silhouetted against the void of negative space about him tends to present him as a type, as a mental image of "the man of the Renaissance." While the portrait is unmistakably a likeness, the theme is a very general one: the self assurance of a man who believes that he has a god-given right to use and enjoy the world in which he finds himself [10: pp. 52–3].

Here was a peak of confidence in man's powers. In the eighteenth and nineteenth centuries the image became a more mannered, paler, diluted version of Renaissance man, less arrogant, less sure. For generations the desire has persisted to emulate that peak which in art was a mixture of the idealized "beauty" of the Greeks and the duskier Italianate version—luminosity of colors and sensuality of lip and heavy eye. Every country's artists tried their hand at it. The English painted their country gentility looking like Velazquez figures in pastel. Charles V sacked Rome and wounded the pride of the Italians, but the paintings of courtiers and royalty of the time are warmed-over versions of Venetian portraits. When Napoleon built his empire, his artists dragged out the classical faces and forms and surrounded him with a world of pseudo refinement, excluding the faces of the rabble (the ugly ones) who had fought for him. Colonial America brought over the same aesthetic dream from Europe, even while rejecting the politics and religions of the Old World. It is still living.

To be sure, along with this persisting archetypal image we have had almost seven centuries of realistic, probing portraiture, such as Rembrandt's. Picasso and Matisse have hankered after the classical ambience, but on the whole the self-conscious twentieth century has produced psychological rather than idealized images of man. The artist has been compelled by the agony as well as the social science of his time to summon the unconscious life of the sitter into the painting, at the same time pondering aspects of relativity and measuring the validity of his own perceptions.

Self-portraits have been done by artists since the beginning of time. It is all-important to encourage the preadolescent to take advantage of this experience. His self-image, or concept of his own attractiveness, is a pivotal point in his progress toward personal assurance. The attempt to project even a farfetched image of oneself is a step toward objectivity, an exorcism of the curse of inferiority feelings. Elizabeth Adams Hurwitz in *Design, A Search for Essentials* writes movingly about the therapy of projecting emotional images into art:

In art, when you put into tangible form the well-loved images and sensations you feel are good, you find you understand them better. This can happen also if you give some visible form to things you hate, fear or dislike. . . . Once we have made these things real, we are no longer at the mercy of the destructive, disintegrating effect they have on us. The very fact that we have the power to shape the material in their likeness helps. We may find that they are not real, but unfortunate combinations of experience in our minds, freak associations [11: p. 64].

A good teacher, by using reproductions, slides, physical descriptions in literature, and documentary movie shorts from all the world's cultures can help to destroy the obsession with one single brand of facial beauty. There are many exercises aimed at increasing the child's perception of the human face. When preadolescents feel they are being taught techniques that will help them make their faces more realistic, they are much more willing to do portraits of themselves and others.

Grade seven—boy

Grade seven—girl

It is a good idea to encourage the children to use a variety of media. As suggested in the section on figuration, this gives the child the best opportunity to discover some combination of technique and material that will bring him enough success to satisfy him. Various suggestions follow:

1. Have the children build their portraits in layers of transparent tissues of different shades, pasted with liquid starch. This produces wonderful translucent effects which preadolescents appreciate since they make the skin look lifelike. It is also a valuable color experience.

2. Have the children work directly with their hands or with tools that permit wiping, scratching, scraping, or brushing (mono prints). They can draw portraits emphasizing depressions and raised surfaces or other aspects that the teacher thinks important. This monoprint technique builds knowledge of the anatomical structure of the face, while not permitting excessive preoccupation with representational details. The medium also encourages expressive responses to the differing shapes of the head.

3. Have the children use a simple printing device or stamp to build the density that produces a modeled effect, in one color or many, to get the sensation of broken color. The emphasis should be on the use of values and on experiencing the dynamics of broken color. A form of pointillism can also be used, with paint or with ink.

4. Ask children to reduce the face to basic geometric forms. Suggest some means of using gradation that will give these shapes depth. (Compare Rembrandt and Durer.) Have the children try one with a plain background and one that has a feeling of atmosphere, as well as developing their own individual ways of achieving a three-dimensional effect.

5. Have the children take turns modeling for each other for given periods. Have the one who is posing make two facial expressions, a sad face and then a happy one. Ask the children who are drawing to notice what happens to the various features: the sad face sends the corners of the mouth down; the eyes may droop or close; the head may hang down slightly or turn to one side; the tongue may protrude slightly. As they paint or print, ask the children to imagine a color or colors which would give the face an even sadder expression. As they sculpt, print, or make a collage, ask them to try to show the facial expression changing visibly from one mood to another.

6. Suggest a game to the children in which they pretend they are police artists aiding in the location of a missing person or criminal. They should work in threes: one draws, while a second describes a third pupil hiding behind a screen. The description should include: eyes, their shape and size in relation to the

face, and where placed in relation to nose and temples; the whole face, its shape and size; cheekbones, where placed; chin, distance from mouth, and whether pointed, square, or receding; nose length, width, shape; hair color, texture, shiny or mat; mouth size, shape, relation to chin, nose, and whole face. The teacher can invite a police artist to come to the class and demonstrate, possibly giving some of the children vocational motivation as well as knowledge.

7. Pose a student behind a sheet, with a light, and have the other children cut out or paint a side view of the face (silhouettes). This is a good way to encourage the children who hesitate to attempt a profile. It also promotes facility with the proportions and positions of features. Emphasize the overall shape and contour by having them ignore details. Then have them cut profiles out of transparent papers and from a separate piece of transparent paper cut out the full face. Finally, have the children paste the transparent views over each other on a format, so as to see all the positions of the face simultaneously.

8. Pose the children against highly figured backgrounds and have them paint each other. The works of Bonnard, Vuillard, or Van Gogh would be highly stimulating here. The vitality of color and design of the background will emphasize qualities in the sitter and/or give new insight into the use of color and energy of stroke as they affect the quality of the rendering.

Grade six—girl

9. Placing a strong light on the face will produce shadows and make the underlying structure more pronounced. Some children might be motivated to draw and sculpt with this aid.

10. Suggest drawing the face from many vantage points—from above, below, and as seen between objects. Encourage the combination of as many views as possible in a single work.

11. Using hand mirrors, get the children to make self-portraits, some to include the reflection of another student as it comes into the mirror. This is a very popular exercise. One boy drew himself looking into a mirror in which an ape was reflected.

12. Suggest that the children experiment with pieces of mirror, incorporated into either a sculpture or a collage, that give the viewer a view of himself as he is studying the portrait of another. The experience of merging with another personality in this mirror-image way has connotations the teacher might develop vis-á-vis social studies, literature, music, etc.

13. The full-length mirror is always an important tool. The children can pose themselves with animals or working on some favorite hobby. Many portrait painters in the past have used animals as props to reveal the personality. Since live animals are often not allowed in schools, have the children bring in sketches or make use of visual aids.

14. The relation of the parts to the whole can be emphasized by asking the children to outline and cut out two identical shapes representing the face and torso. Have them paint in features in natural but slightly different positions on the face, ending up with completely different personalities in spite of the similarity of the shapes. This can also be done in three-dimensional media.

15. Reducing the face (and torso) to provocative shapes can be a very useful exercise. Show the children various slides or reproductions of works by artists interested in this simplification (Modigliani, for instance). Posing a model, have the children reduce their portraits to some pleasing basic design. Unusual patterns and psychedelic color intrigue preadolescents.

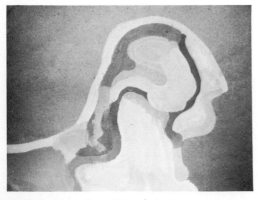

Grade six—boy   *Portrait into design*

Grade six—girl   *Hide-and-seek drawing*

16. Hide-and-seek pictures and collages interest children of this age. Have them surround and obscure their portraits with patterns and designs created to express the elusiveness of the personality, or perhaps to evoke some other meaning. (Relate this to Pavel Tchelitchew's "Hide and Seek," 1940–1942.)

17. The varied and subtle colors, often patterned and textured, to be found in magazines, provide an excellent source of collage scraps that can be used to create portraits. Used in careful tonal sequences, they can make for rich modeling effects.

Another project might be started by first constructing a papier-mâché life-sized or over-life-sized bust or full figure on which the magazine scraps are pasted. Using the pictorial or representational pictures in the magazines, children can assemble original conglomerations of objects, figures, or portraits which have amusing, outlandish meanings as well as inventive imagery (teacher: Martha Vega).

Grade seven—boy

18. Preadolescents can be encouraged to portray neighborhood personalities. The class can be taken through the neighborhood to do sketches of people and then use them in the studio as the basis of finished work. For instance, the mayor, the editor of a newspaper, a star reporter, or the police chief and some detectives might be persuaded to spare fifteen minutes and let the schoolchildren make sketches of them. Or a fireman, postal director, postman, hospital director, or a chief nurse might allow themselves the experience of having a serious group of preadolescents make drawings of them and of their professional territory.

Cray-pas oil colors in stick form, felt-tip pens, or other easy-to-handle tools with color would be suitable for the children to use on these excursions. Such contacts with the people who run and service the community are beneficial, and it is an important enough enterprise to please the preadolescent. The same types of expeditions could be made in small groups to sketch business and professional men, sales people, bus drivers, taxi drivers, restaurant owners, hair dressers, and so on. Certain people could be invited to the studio to sit for portraits in all media—fathers, grandparents, religious leaders, school principals, and special teachers whom the children want to portray. Well-known sports and entertainment figures might come, also, as well as visitors from other countries.

Grade six—boy *Soda fountain man*

19. Group portraits have an enormous appeal for this age level. Show children the double or group portraits which are our inheritance. Boys like to do pictures of their gang or members of their club; girls like family group pictures (see page 165). Get them started on research about an ancestor or an ancestor they would like to have had. This can lead to many humorous inventions and is, moreover, relevant to their self-image and its objectification. On page 165 see two paintings. One is by a boy who said he had an ancestor who came from overseas and was tough, with a tattoo on his chest. An uncle who was remembered for his hairy chest is portrayed eating a banana.

THE GROTESQUE

The grotesque in art may be expressed in various ways. In general, it is exaggeration or deformation of the human face and figure, though in many instances animals and other forms from nature are subjected by the artist to expressions of strangeness and deformity. The aim of these radical distortions of familiar shapes seems to be to evoke fear, repulsion, even horror in the viewer, with the deeper aim of objectification and purge of fear, repulsion and horror.

The earliest artists of the grotesque made the masks and distorted figures we see in our museums and which to our Western

eyes appear as sacrilegious destruction of the "normal" human
form. They seem less strange, however, when we learn that they
are based on animism and sympathetic magic and had a communal
function. We begin to understand the emphasis on the human
reproductive organs and the recurrent theme of metamorphosis
from animal to human. These artifacts played an essential part
in the ceremonies which evoked forces to protect society from
destruction by enemies, by famine and sickness, and to keep
it increasing. The figures were often designed to frighten off the
spirits of disease; the artifacts were themselves considered to
be spirits. Robert Goldwater speaks of the energy supposedly
invoked by the masks, figures, and other sculpture created by
aboriginal nontechnical cultures (African, Oceanic, American Indian, Eskimo): "These forces belong to another world, therefore
the inventiveness of the masks, their stylization and impressive
exaggeration" (12: Intro.).

The mask is an important aspect of portraiture, especially
for the preadolescent. When presented by the teacher as a
universal object made by practically all cultures of the world
in order to allow a man to alter himself and become a god, a
dead ancestor, a malevolent or helpful spirit, an animal, or a
different human being, the child may be moved to make use
of it himself. He may be able to transform some of his fears and
compulsions as well as the creatures of his imagination into
three-dimensional substance by creating and wearing his own
grotesques.

Greek masks are interesting objects for the children to study.
They represent aspects of the personality, such as rage, grief,
craftiness, happiness, and elation. And in our own culture, the
Halloween masks and the Mardi Gras creations are relics, much
diluted, of practices that go far back into history. It is worth
noting that only when the masks are worn do they have any
real significance or effect. On All Souls' Day, the men who wore
them were theoretically transformed into departed spirits, con-
gregating for their *danse macabre.* In this way humanity paid
attention to the existence of the dead and expressed its consciousness of mysteries that remain forever unsolved.

The therapeutic value of ceremonies and the artifacts created
for them cannot be overestimated. Capers and Maddox refer to
an interesting observation made by J. A. Hatfield in *Dreams and
Nightmares* on the subject of the dramas children instinctively
use to counteract trauma and fear:

It is recorded that during the Battle of Britain, bombed-out children
first suffered a period of shock, and then they began playing at bombing.
By this means they apparently subdued the terrifying phantoms of their
nightmares and found their way back to psychic health. The artist "play"

also deals on occasion with the painful reality under the comforting coat of make-believe. [10: p. 166]*

The authors elaborate on this theme, suggesting that "most of the monsters and grotesque creatures of art owe their ultimate origin, and certainly their vitality, to the same mysterious source from which our nightmares come" and that the artist makes them to "objectify the dread creatures: to have them out where we can take a good look at them in broad daylight" (10: p. 166).

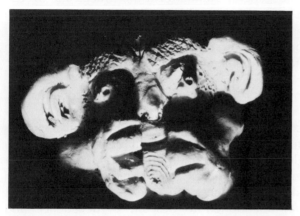

Grade six—boy

Grade six—boy

Our fears about death, our dependence on the terrible power of the elements, and our belief in benevolent or malevolent gods who interfere in man's affairs have undergone drastic transformations. Yet still we feel the fury of nature's self-destruction, and of human self-destruction, which has taken on through science a terrifyingly vast scope. The meaning of death still cannot be fathomed; mysteries are as rife as scientific breakthroughs. Longer life, relief from pain, and reduction of hard physical labor seem to be matched by increased tension and greater fears for the survival of the race. Our contemporary artists create out of this situation a new kind of grotesque. They no longer create subjects, such as substitute bodies and masks, for us to use as intermediaries with divine powers, but instead they show us what is wrought on the human body by the shocks of our times, by the machine and fear of war, by strange diseases, by cosmic loneliness, by our dislocation from this earth—in short, the fears and horrors of our century. And we are drawn to these artifacts, transfixed as any primitive man before his images.

Roberta M. Capers and Jerrold Maddox, *Images and Imagination: An Introduction to Art.* Copyright © 1965, The Ronald Press Company, New York.

Many talented painters, from the Second World War to the present, have alternated between nonobjective art and figuration, proceeding from the world of cubism and expressionism to abstraction and the genre of disfiguration. De Kooning has attacked the figure, overpowering and deforming it. His violent brush strokes symbolize the impact of society on the individual. Pellegrini writes that "in new figuration, subjectivity acts on the world of things, reconstructing it, deforming it," and that today the artist, resisting the dehumanization of the machine, the computer, and the general standardization, "faces the world, reproducing it in its grotesque and absurd aspects, and often the images take on an aggressive, caustic, burlesque appearance. This humor is not comical; it is wounding and brutal, often morose; it is what has come to be called 'black humor'" (13: p. 198).

Francis Bacon paints the tragedy of contemporary man, projecting psychological trauma on biological replicas. Pellegrini calls Bacon's work more serious, more "ethical" in its significance than most of tne modern figurative work. Bacon is "a voice for order and against indifference" (13: p. 200). He forces us to admit the reality of our day: the face of naked cruelty, the cold, satirical face, the face empty of humanity, or incomplete, or abandoned to despair, to decadence and confusion. Such art as Bacon's will initially repel the preadolescent; it is created to produce fear, repulsion, horror. But twelve-year-old boys and girls who spend most of their waking hours on the city streets will recognize its reality and respect such a strong statement.

The grotesque in art has an enormous appeal for the preadolescent. For him it is an adventure into the unknown, where his imagination runs free and where he can rebel from the demanding pressure on him to conform to society. In this form of art, he can express his fears and hostilities without suffering either ridicule or recrimination. This form of release should be made available to him. It might perhaps be a safety valve against delinquency and the random violence that is apt to originate during this period. When he paints or assembles his grotesques, he can play all the gory and unconventional roles he wishes and can vicariously experience deviations from the norm. The teacher should not hold back timidly and worriedly on the sidelines, afraid that the child is being morbid and unnatural but, instead, bring into view all the wealth of artistic exploration of the grotesque from the dawn of recorded time to the present. Many children will gain an understanding of the real meaning of art through this sort of expression as perhaps through no other, for it reaches into the depths of man's unchanging nightmare—his fear of universal powers that are beyond his control.

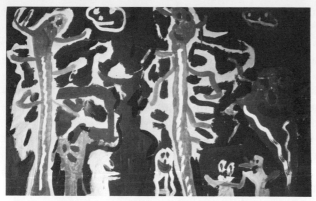

Grade six—girl *Trees become malevolent spirits*

Grade six—boy

Some teachers think it is safer to avoid the whole thing, as they do the subject of sex. But that is the way to lose contact with the children. As an example of good teaching, there is the story of the boy who went to a museum to see the Egyptian mummies. Back in school, instead of doing the usual tight little drawing of a mummy, he asked to be allowed to make a "real one." He made one that was all of nine feet long, using wadded newspapers for the understructure and then wrapping it in medical gauze treated with plaster. He put a set of false teeth in the mummy's mouth (a plaster replica supplied by his father, a dentist). It was a superb mummy, such as had never been seen, bigger than any in the museum. Everyone in the school came to admire it, not only the younger but also the older children. One can imagine the glory that fell to the child who made this mummy. It was a rewarding experience such as he would probably never forget—a remembered vision of himself as a person who could accomplish, *do.* The boy's teachers made it possible for him to carry through his idea, macabre though it was, by encouraging him and helping him to find the proper tools and materials. They sponsored and believed in him (Little Red Schoolhouse, New York University; teacher: Walter Kendra; student teacher: Marissa).

This is only one example, among many, of how an interest in the grotesque can spark accomplishment. There are many projects along these lines:

1. Construction of a new face out of parts of many faces can be an amusing exercise. Direct the children to paint or make in some three-dimensional medium an eye of one member of the class, lips of another, right eyebrow, left eyebrow, and so on.

It does not matter if boys' and girls' features are both used; a mixture is best. Materials used may be of different colors, textures, etc.. It is best when the lesson moves fast and all the children participate in the game. As a final step, ask them to combine the parts into a strange, often absurd, whole.

2. Using an actual skull or full skeleton, have the children create symbols of death, death-in-life, or a creature from the world beyond our life.

3. Pose a figure or several figures. Project slides of fruit or vegetables onto them. Strange forms will appear on their faces and limbs. Children can produce fantastic and imaginative works in all media in this way.

4. Ask the class to do x-ray pictures or sculptures of the inside of a head or body. Some do it imaginatively and some scientifically. They may use transparent plastics three-dimensionally or show a figure lit from within by electric lights.

5. Have them create sinister figures wandering through the city, or men and animals from Mars, Venus, or some other galaxies.

Grade six—boy

6. Using cutouts of faces from magazines and newspapers, have the children put all manner of paint, collage, or decollage on them in fanciful detail.

7. Make full use of any available masks and ancestor figures of primitive peoples. Have the children create masks symbolizing special qualities, such as a god in control of rain, storm, sea, clouds, sun, moon, lightning, volcanoes; or a god with power over vegetation, or over life and death; or deities of laughter, pranks, sex, or murder.

8. Have the children put together a portrait from highly figured materials (stripes or flowers) and create op qualities—with stripes going in different directions, for instance.

9. Have the children take a portrait they have already painted and using a paper cutter, cut it in a given pattern and then reassemble it so that it gives the effect of movement. This can be done in clay as well. Or have them make a head, cut it up, and reassemble it in a fantastic arrangement.

10. Have the children create slightly human combinations from pictures cut from magazines—a walking advertisement of some of our contemporary manias.

Here is a collage in which the child artist built associations derived from foods we eat. He is fascinated by a man made of ice cream with an orange for a head. Many artists in the past have been preoccupied by this concept. (Student teachers, Special Project District 10: Marjorie Doe, art supervisor.)

Grade six—boy

Children can find human associations in vegetables, flowers, and animals of all kinds. Papier-mâché can be used effectively. All manner of found objects can be used to create people. (Picasso has playfully populated the world with such strange human replicas, as has Marisol.) It might be possible to motivate the children to use the human figure and portrait in combination and to present them as outgrowths or adjuncts of furniture or other objects.

Once the imagination is let loose and the child has been exposed to the many notions that once involved so-called primitive man and today concern our painters and sculptors, the image of the body and face of man can be found everywhere and formed in all media.

CARICATURE AND SATIRE

Unlike the grotesque, the exaggeration in a caricature is not employed to transform the object into another being. The person depicted—successfully characterized by exaggeration of a notable gesture, disproportionate feature, or unusual characteristic—is rendered distinctive by the very exaggeration. Charles de Gaulle's protruding nose and receding chin have often been emphasized, and the general's not unreasonable height of 6 feet 1 inch was extended so that he appeared to be about 7 feet tall. The result was a lampoon, and viewers were deeply amused by the ridicule, no matter how fond they were of their leader. Even the general himself may have been amused, accepting it in good humor, liking to think of himself as a unique individual whose fame and distinction had made his physical attributes worthy of comment.

Toulouse Lautrec, an artist with a technique and intention far beyond that of the newspaper caricaturist, used a more subtle type of exaggeration, making his music hall and saloon figures slightly distorted and blown-up for more sophisticated expressive reasons. Lautrec did not lampoon, yet we are struck by his characterizations. The lighthearted, capricious caricature is considered journalism by devotees of the "fine" arts, yet many superb fifteenth-century Dutch and Flemish woodcuts similarly caricatured the life of the times. We are perhaps in another era in which the artist is moved to caricature (and thus satirize) aspects of the society which he seriously distrusts and wants to destroy by means of his art. Marshall McLuhan writes: "Humor as a system of communications and as a probe of our environment—of what's really going on—affords us our most appeasing anti-environment tool. It does not deal in theory, but in immediate experience, and is often the best guide to our changing perceptions" (14: p. 92).

Grade six—boy

Grade six—boy *A sheriff becomes a horse*

The preadolescent enjoys the humor of caricatures. He should study many profound works of satiric art (Daumier and others), as well as political cartoons. He could try some himself and be motivated to look deeply into the character of the person he is satirizing, so as to avoid the obvious clichés that can so easily cheapen this type of expression. Ask the children to study favorite personalities on TV programs and do numerous quick sketches of them, or, using found objects, to do assemblages. Have them pick from their sketches the characteristic facial expression and the gesture that is repeated over and over. With the use of transparent papers, the child can eliminate confusing details and choose the significant lines and shapes which express his subject. Encourage the children to make serious studies of these personalities. As a follow-up exericse, sending the results to the subjects might bring interesting reactions.

They should be shown the negative aspects of satire and caricature, how it can be a derisive and cruel humor that tears down other people in order to build up one's own sense of superiority. The positive uses can also be demonstrated:

The social purpose of satire is to ridicule people and institutions so that they will change . . . although laughter is involved, satire is a *serious* art form, serving to puncture pretension, to cut the mighty down to size, to dramatize the gap between official purpose or promise and actual performance [15: p. 55].

The clown represents a caricature combining, in a profound and touching mode, the tragicomic aspects of the human personality and existence. This is never sufficiently explained to American children. Italians have Arlecchino and Pagliacci and the French their Pierrot and Columbine tradition. Our children are asked to paint the clown, and so they usually do—a cliché of one type of clown patterned on Emmet Kelly. They should perhaps be asked to make a study of clowns. What do their faces say? What sort of pathos is expressed in the specially designed eye? What is the meaning of the traditional mouth design? Of the attire? Of the gestures?

Since preadolescents are just beginning to see relationships and discrepancies, they are usually not capable of sophisticated humor or satire. They are much more likely to indulge in the grotesque. The teacher need not be too much concerned with developing the art of satire, except in those children who are particularly interested. It is perhaps a form reserved for the gifted few. Some children will possess a natural talent for it, and the teacher should be prepared to help them understand the true purposes of satire, one of which, according to Christensen, who writes about Eskimo masks, is to serve society "by acting as a check on the excesses and misapplication of power" (16: p. 67).

In our affluent time, the special situation of disadvantaged minorities who do not share in the American prosperity may generate more interest in caricature and satire among preadolescents than ever before. If they themselves are disadvantaged, they are completely conscious of exactly how and why, thanks to the enlargement of communications and the emergence of minority leaders. Perhaps black children, for instance, could be channeled away from their exclusive preoccupation in art class with lettering signs that say "Kill Whitey" over and over again by encouraging them to try political satire. Skill with lampoons and caricatures might give the youngsters a chance to analyze, objectify, and aggressively assert their grievances, as well as to promote humor, pride in their skill, and a healthy exchange between black child and teacher and black child and his white classmates. The ideas of some of the outstanding black writers can be springboards for these children's self-expression, and they will learn, incidentally, some of the more sophisticated ways of effecting social change.

The power of an Al Capp or David Low or the great Georg Grosz in the Germany of the twenties can be demonstrated to preadolescents. "To be laughed at by a community or by substantial groups in the community . . . is an exceedingly severe kind of humiliation. . . ." (15: p. 56).

SUMMARY

It is advisable, when working with the children in practice sessions devoted to the human figure, to develop a series of exercises that culminate in some unified statement. This gives the class security, a beginning and an end to things. They can then adjust to the intervals in between, when they may feel lost and wonder where they are going. If a child does not receive any immediate satisfaction from a single exercise, he may have the patience to wait, without discouragement, for success in the next exercise, which may suit his talents better. Giving children a choice of many experiences, during which they can find their special abilities and work from many points of view, helps sustain their interest. A child will succeed here and (in his own eyes) fail there, and this is much better than getting him to put forth a vast effort in a single direction with the possibility of failure.

The teacher should try to keep the children working with the figure for a number of consecutive periods. Such in-depth exposure increases their chances for success and allows them to see their progress. A suggested sequence, culled from the procedures described in this chapter, is as follows: 1) experiments without the brush (to help overcome clichés); 2) experiments with collage and paint, 3) stamping experiences followed by use of the brush; 4) some three-dimensional work; 5) drawing the gesture; and 6) using previous work to build a total composition.

There can be no doubt that skill with the human figure gives the preadolescent personality a satisfaction that goes beyond that of conforming and producing recognizable rather than abstract, fantasy forms. It is a subtle fortification of one's identity as a standing, moving, feeling human being. It can be a purge of repulsive self-images. It can also be a straight kinesthetic release of life force, fear, sex and general tension into an artifact that seems almost as alive as oneself.

REFERENCES

1. Tena Roseman, "Relationship of Northern Born and Reared Negro Children and Southern Born and Reared Negro Children in Terms of Self-Concept," unpublished doctoral dissertation, New York University, New York, 1962.

2. Elden E. Snyder, "Self-Concept Theory," *Clearing House,* vol. 40, December, 1965.

3. Gerald Knowles, "Teacher-Pupil Relationships as Related to Self-Concept Needs," unpublished doctoral dissertation, University of Illinois, Urbana, Ill., 1966.

4. Dorothy Skeel, "Determining the Compatibility of Student Teachers of Culturally Deprived Schools by Means of a Cultural Attitude Inventory," unpublished doctoral dissertation, Pennsylvania State University, University Park, Pa., 1966.

5. Paul Goodman, *Growing Up Absurd,* Vintage Books, Inc., New York, 1956.

6. Udo Kultermann, *The New Sculpture, Environment and Assemblages,* Frederick A. Praeger, Inc., New York, 1968.

7. Ray Faulkner and Edwin Ziegfield, *Art Today,* Holt, Rinehart and Winston, Inc., New York, 1969.

8. Sam Hunter, *Modern American Painting and Sculpture,* Dell Publishing Co., Inc., New York, 1959.

9. Frank Seiberling, *Looking Into Art,* Holt, Rinehart and Winston, Inc., New York, 1959.

10. Roberta M. Capers and Jerrold Maddox, *Images and Imagination,* The Ronald Press Company, New York, 1965.

11. Elizabeth Adams Hurwitz, *Design: A Search for Essentials,* International Textbook Company, Scranton, Pa., 1964.

12. Robert Goldwater, *Sculpture from Africa in the Museum of Primitive Art,* Museum of Primitive Art, New York, 1963.

13. Aldo Pellegrini, *New Tendencies in Art,* Crown Publishers, Inc., New York, 1966.

14. Marshall McLuhan, *The Medium Is the Message,* New American Library, Inc., New York, 1967.

15. Edmund Burke Feldman, *Art as Image and Idea,* Prentice-Hall, Inc., Englewood Cliffs, N.J., 1967.

16. Edwin O. Christensen, *Primitive Art,* Thomas Y. Crowell Company., New York, 1955.

The Creative Process of Self-appraisal

7

The result of creative self-appraisal is continuing refinement of the expressive powers of an individual through sharpening of the senses and expansion of the intelligence. There is no limit to this development, and the artist, like the scientist, seems to have an insatiable desire to move to new problems and new forms of expression. Without self-assessment, he would stay on the same level; it is the spur that keeps him growing. (Matisse once said that when he did not know what else to do to a painting, he went on to the next one. He felt that a single painting was not a complete entity but merely one unit in an endless chain, and that they were all necessary to the true, complete projection of his idea.)

How does one learn to assess one's work? How is it taught? Guggenheimer defines evaluation as "gaining greater control over the brain's practical role of censor" (1: p. 50). It involves a disciplined effort to evaluate the whole of a work through steady appraisal of each of its parts and learning to choose between alternatives. It may mean total censoring of a project in favor of another overall approach.

Is it possible to teach children to see the different interpretations and solutions of a single problem? There is no easy answer to this question, just as there is no easy rule or standard by which to determine a particular child's degree of intelligence or intuition.

In the arts, especially the visual arts, creative judging of one's own and others' work is even more mysterious than in other disciplines. Moreover, intelligent self-appraisal is even more of a personal challenge nowadays than it was in the past. Our present culture is characterized by highly individualistic styles and modes of expression. Although there are groups and movements to which certain artists belong and which provide standards and critiques, the general tendency is to go it alone. This means that each artist must find his own method of self-appraisal.

Critics of modern art face a complex problem, though perhaps it has always been true, as Leo Steinberg says, that modern art "projects itself into a twilight zone where no values are fixed"

(2: pp. 45–46). He gives an interesting exposition of how he felt when contemplating Jasper Johns' work:

What I have said—was it *found* in the pictures or read into them? Does it accord with the painter's intention? Does it tally with other people's experience, to reassure me that my feelings are sound? I don't know. I can see that these pictures don't necessarily look like art—which has been known to solve far more difficult problems. I don't know whether they are art at all, whether they are great, or good, or likely to go up in price. And whatever experience in painting I've had in the past seems as likely to hinder me as to help. I am challenged to estimate the esthetic value of, say, a drawer stuck into a canvas. But nothing I have ever seen can teach me how this is to be done. I am alone with this thing, and it is up to me to evaluate it in the absence of available standards. The value which I shall put on this painting tests my personal courage. Here I can discover whether I am prepared to sustain the collision of novel experience. Am I escaping it by being overly analytical? Have I been eavesdropping on conversations? Trying to formulate certain meanings seen in this art—are they designed to demonstrate something about myself or are they authentic experiences?
    . . . It is a kind of self-analysis that a new image can throw you into and for which I am grateful. I am left in a state of anxious uncertainty by the painting, about myself. And I suspect that all of this is right.

It is in this spirit that art teachers should look at the work children place before them.

There are no systems of aesthetics for the appraisal of today's art. The artist himself can evaluate his work only on the basis of his intention and the successive levels of his results. Inevitably his yardstick must be: Have I grown in the direction of my goals? What new insights has this piece of work revealed to me?

For the child involved in art activity, the same thing is true. Neither pupil nor teacher can assess work against the standards of the Renaissance or, say, abstract expressionism. Hopefully, children will find their own manipulations of space, line, and color. Assessment of performance and growth must come as much from them as from the teacher, whose role is to clarify individual pupils' ideas, ambitions, and goals, along with helping them develop the skill to proceed.

If one took too seriously the idea that children do not bother about the future and center all their concern on the immediate present, one might decide that they were incapable of self-appraisal. But self-criticism is a process linked up as much with day-to-day performance as with future goals. Constant evaluation is an integral part of the artistic act. As a child works and reworks his art object, the concept of "future goals" or "growth" will probably never enter his mind, but he is appraising every minute, censoring, discarding, obliterating, beginning again—a creative routine that grows in depth and sensitivity the more it is carried through, and one that affects his development in the years to come.

For some children—especially preadolescents, with their short attention span—there is the danger of being satisfied with the excitement of a momentary experience and then abandoning the work before it is fully realized. Sustained and disciplined effort may require the passage of time, and they may have to return several times, after giving in to distractions, to bring to their work any genuine critical insight. The teacher plays an important part here, becoming, one might say, a superego for the child, helping him to sustain and judge his own work. It is the teacher who can make the child feel that his experience is meaningful and that he is creating something real, creating "a new being that nobody would ever see, either in nature or otherwise" unless the artist "caused it to exist" (3: p. 123).

It is only when mutual trust and consideration and sharing of sensibilities are built up that an exchange of any validity can take place between teacher and child. It must be understood that a child's creative life is involved here, and what he believes he can do and what he is able to become. The teacher's role is to become a friend and live with the child through his experiences, so that the child can discuss what he is doing and finding out. The teacher has opinions and artistic techniques to put at his disposal, as well as greater experience of viewing and enjoying art. She presents these so that the child may choose, consider, try out, adopt, or reject. In the end, the child has the ultimate decision; it is his work, not the teacher's. All too often the teacher lives and works vicariously through the work of the child; she makes the choices and he carries them out. He may derive some pleasure from manipulating the material, but he cannot grow and change if he is deprived of the power to decide for himself.

The preadolescent, with his great desire to learn and to grow up, is ripe for the revelation and discipline of creative self-assessment and will achieve it if the atmosphere is conducive. Following are examples of interchange between teacher and pupil that resulted in considerable success along lines of self-appraisal and actual art produced:

1. Robin's paintings were consistently nonobjective. Every time he came to the studio he selected his materials, made one of his designs, and completed it, usually in one session. If not, he came back at a free moment to complete it. He always made it clear that he did not want to be interrupted, but when finished,

**TEACHER-PUPIL
INTERCHANGE**

he sometimes wanted to discuss the painting with the teacher. Sometimes they discussed only the current work; at other times, they dealt with it along with several previous designs. Certain questions dominated the discussion: What is happening in this new one? What is its relation to previous designs? The teacher found that it helped her to see what was happening if she made a simple sketch of the major shapes and movements of the painting. Robin seemed to find this device helpful and took to doing it himself after finishing a work. Robin liked the mixed colors he had used in this one, and he felt that the repetition of triangular shapes was interesting. There was some motion in the wavy lines, fast in the diagonals and slow in the large circular form. But what he found new and exciting was the figure outlined in white, and next to that the purple outlining the yellow, because they emerged and gave a sense of space.

First painting

Both he and the teacher hit upon the idea that in his next painting he should perhaps try to create parts or sections with more contrasting values, and, since he liked the wavy sensation, to emphasize it.

An examination of the second painting showed Robin that certain shapes—those heavily defined—came forward, while others sank into the background. But although he liked this second work better than the first, he was dissatisfied because the background was static compared to the rest of the painting. He noticed that although he had divided it into two or three sections in an effort to give it life and involve it with the foreground, he had not succeeded in building a dynamic relation with the rest of the forms. He was determined to do this in his next painting. Also, though he had managed to put rhythm and movement into his line, it became choppy at the top of the painting.

Second painting

Robin considered the third painting his masterpiece. He repainted the yellow shape at the right. Result: a sensation of spatial movement. He had simplified his color. His line moved with rhythm across the surface and became simultaneously the silhouette and the edge of the shapes. Robin now felt he had eliminated the static background. He became interested in the power of the shapes themselves to create movement and the sensation of space. He also perceived how color functions to create movement.

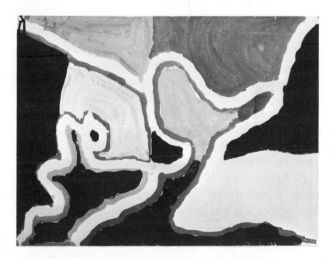

Third painting

In his next painting, Robin emphasized shape, though he did not entirely eliminate line. He consciously limited his color, trying to repeat colors so that they occupied differing spatial positions. He was working very consciously here; thus his line was weak and his composition cramped. He noted these qualities and was not altogether satisfied with this painting. He felt he was struggling for new understanding, for some idea that had not as yet become quite clear.

Fourth painting

The teacher listened attentively to Robin while he analyzed his work and made decisions about what he wanted to emphasize and what to discard. This boy was very definite about the kinds of shapes and movements he wanted, and he had the discipline to eliminate the ones he did not feel were right. The teacher helped by analyzing with him the routes he might take to achieve his predetermined goals.

Robin worked on his abstractions in this way for the entire sixth-grade year, even when others worked on class or small-group projects. Still, he joined in the group discussions and analyses of projects with enthusiasm and interest. He was given opportunities to explain his own project and goals to the group. Robin was given a one-man show to which he invited family and friends, and with the guidance of the teacher he wrote an introductory statement for the exhibit, describing his artistic purposes.

2. Jane, like many preadolescent girls, was interested in painting horses. Although she herself rode and knew a good deal about horses, she had difficulty drawing them. The teacher found time to give her special attention during the art period, or early in the morning, or at various free moments during the day. Jane brought in sketches of horses she had drawn in the park, and the teacher looked at horse photographs with her to try to clarify certain details that gave the student trouble. Then Jane decided to pretend she had been given a colt and told the

story of its life in pictures. The story included twenty paintings which took her half a school year to complete. Some of the scenes depicted here show the colt being born, broken to saddle and groomed for a show.

The colt is born

He is broken to the saddle

He is groomed for a show

During the months that it took to complete the series, the teacher not only tried to help Jane with the anatomy of the horse, which constantly plagued her, but also encouraged her to show different views of the animal. Jane's greatest success was with the frontal view (6). The teacher had suggested alternatives, but to Jane this was a very difficult view, and she was satisfied with the depth she was able to achieve.

Jane's color was very literal. The same brown and green are used throughout, with the same blue sky. The teacher constantly suggested that there was a range of possibilities within the three colors and brought out papers of various shades. She even premixed shades of paint to be ready for use, but Jane was not interested in experimenting with them.

Along with the rest of the class, Jane participated in an experiment introducing the children to the effect of light on color: light outdoors at different times of day and in different kinds of weather, and how it changed the colors of buildings, and trees. This exercise did not change Jane's brown, green and blue. She did respond, however, to texture motivation, and in each of her paintings after the first, she discussed textural qualities and made small side experiments with the grass, bushes, straw, sawdust, and blossoms. She wanted to change these from painting to painting and consciously worked at it. She also discussed with the teacher the strong contrasts she employed so successfully.

Jane loved her paintings and went directly to work after the formal greeting from the teacher. During the lesson she always asked for a conference. Her questions went along these lines: "Can you think of anything that will improve this part of the painting?" or "I wanted to give the mane a silky finish but not too much because it really feels coarse when you touch it. Does it look right—like I want it?"

The teacher supported many of Jane's reasons for doing things but also guided her toward future explorations. Often, when they were ready to plan the next episode, the teacher suggested that they take a fresh look at all the paintings in the series so far. After painting 2, the teacher tried to make Jane aware that her trees were stereotypes. That is why the texture of the hedge in number 5 was greatly improved. Jane looked at many photographs of hedges, and in preparation for number 6, she did sketches of trees from the studio window and worked in the same way to achieve the wall in the park, number 7.

3. Pearl and Barbara were good friends. They had the idea of working on a project together, apart from the others. Barbara's skills were advanced; she could render objects in deep space and proportion the figure realistically. Pearl's paintings showed a mixture of spatial concepts, combining the use of the ground line with minimal movement up and back on the picture plane. Figures were represented, in most instances, as a combination of geometric shapes (see example). Because of this discrepancy between the two girls, the teacher suggested that they work separately on different parts of a whole, to produce perhaps a book of paintings on a given theme or a hand movie. The girls chose the movie.

A hand movie is a group of paintings taped together and placed on a simple device consisting of two rollers, one at each end. The paintings can then be unrolled in the desired sequence. Pearl and Barbara chose the subject of rich girl-poor girl—how they lived, how they became friends and remained friends even after both had married.

One sample of the series painted by Pearl is shown. It

illustrates the part of the story telling how the poor girl had to go to bed early because she has no clothes and no friends with whom to go out.

Grade six—Pearl

In planning the scenario, the girls decided they would first show each girl getting up, then the poor girl going to work, the rich girl going to lunch, and a fashion show, and so on, alternating between them in sequence until they meet and become friends.

When they began to work, both girls chose white paper (a favorite with preadolescents). In contrast to Barbara's work, Pearl's looked unfinished, scattered, patchy, and lacking in impact. Noting this, and Pearl's growing anxiety, the teacher called the girl to an informal discussion. Pearl was an introspective child whose work was not naturalistically skillful. Her concepts of figure and space were drawn from her feelings (haptic), and she was neither aware of visual detail nor as interested in it as her partner and friend, Barbara. Some of the characteristics of Pearl's work resulted from the fact that she was at least two years younger than the others in the group. Enormously gifted academically, she had been advanced twice to a higher grade, and like many children who are pushed ahead, she was apt to be nervous and full of anxieties.

It was the teacher's intention to help her analyze some of her most immediate problems with technique and find solutions which would give her work greater force, unity and clarity. "How do you feel about the movie so far?" the teacher asked. Pearl thought Barbara and she had worked out the story sequence beautifully. But she was having some difficulty with her painting; the people did not stand on the floor, and the colors were not right somehow. The teacher said then, "I notice that Barbara has started to paint her girl's room a light pink on the wall, and the floor will have a pink rug. Do you plan to color the poor girl's room—the walls and the floor?" (At this point, Pearl's painting consisted of a few sketchy objects and people in the middle of the paper, which was still its original white. There was no impact of color. Consequently, mood was lacking, and the whole composition compared unfavorably with the richly colored, carefully painted scenes done by Barbara.) Pearl said she planned to paint everything in drab colors suitable to the poor girl's environment, but she had two problems. First, she could never remix the colors once she got a shade she liked and never had enough paint to do all the walls. Second, she had trouble painting around objects. Her hand often slipped, and she would lose part of the figure she had already painted.

The teacher said, "Let's take each problem separately. How do we get around the first?" Pearl herself arrived at the idea that by mixing in a cup, she would not run out of paint. The second problem required some experimenting. The teacher showed her how to dip the brush so as to avoid drips, and how to place the edge of the brush against the object she was surrounding with paint so as to control the brush more firmly and avoid obliterating important details. Then the teacher demonstrated (on a separate sheet of paper) how a dry brush technique or sponge might give color as well as texture and make it unnecessary to paint around the figures. They also experimented with putting paint over paint, in case Pearl wished to add objects and figures after she had made the background. Wash effects were also suggested and tried.

In the course of this exchange, the teacher was obliged to leave Pearl to attend to another pupil's urgent problem. When she returned, she found that Pearl had discovered a solution to her difficulties on her own: she had made a selection from a number of colored papers in the subdued green and tan range. She was excited about her find and was beginning to plan in advance the rest of her part in the movie. The colors, she felt, set the mood she wanted, and she called Barbara over and told her about it. "You see, my scenes will be dark and dreary, and yours will be all ice cream and cake—beautiful pinks and yellows and pastel colors. My girl couldn't afford pastel colors. The walls get too dirty where she lives, and she has to be practical."

Thus the girls moved into the second phase of their analysis and evaluation. It was the discovery of the colored paper that brought Pearl's work into relation with Barbara's, and it was this device, too, that made the girls discover that their hand film had to have visual continuity. They discussed how else they might bring harmony to the whole, and came up with these ideas:

They could use similar hues, in different values, from frame to frame, to give repetition without monotony.

Some frames could be complicated and full, while others could be quiet, calm, and subdued.

Certain exciting frames could build to a climax and others lead to or away from them.

Directional lines or rhythms were needed to connect the frames.

Textural passages would add interest.

In order to achieve the desired effects, the girls took to tacking the different frames on the wall, shifting them around and altering them until they achieved better cohesion. Gradually, as they saw more in their work, they came to realize that in the initial stages of their movie they had been concerned mostly with the written or spoken story and that only later did they begin to make the visual components operate. They admitted that another time they would have begun with sketching, laying out colors and relationships, shapes and directional lines, in order to get a sense of the visual aspects of the movie in general, before addressing themselves to the details.

This was not an easy learning experience for either girl. They often pointed out how their styles were so different from each other—yet they also noticed, and the teacher pointed it up, that this difference might be the very challenge of the film and the element which gave it an interesting quality: Pearl's rough, moody characteristics juxtaposed to Barbara's lighthearted qualities. Poverty and affluence were sharply brought into focus by this contrast.

Everyone agreed that it had been very fortunate that each girl had kept her style intact, since this had helped the film significantly. Although it was not discussed, the teacher felt that both girls had gained by working together: Barbara, by appreciating that Pearl's subjective, emotional approach had as much value as her own accepted representational style, and Pearl, reassured that her method had enough force and value to give her the confidence to proceed and grow within it.

A PRODUCTIVE CLIMATE FOR EVALUATION

Both teacher and child want and need to know if each finished work represents growth and progress, however slow. Certain conditions foster this search. First and foremost, a child must not be so overwhelmed with adult criteria and routine evaluations, such as marks, that he cannot build confidence in himself and empathy with the teacher. The best results come when pupils feel that their teacher is truly more interested in their development as a whole than in their performance on a certain day and in fulfillment of a certain part of the curriculum. The majority of marks given in schools are based on criteria that are never clearly understood by the children. Faced with too stiff criticism and too rigid a system of marks, children lose all joy they might feel from the slow accretion of insights, skills, and personal styles.

There are many ways beside a rigid system of marks by which the teacher can keep track of the progress of each student in the class. The alert teacher will be familiar with each student's individual approach, or potential approach, and thus be able to see whether he is developing or standing still. Is the child attacking new ideas, exploring new techniques and media? Is he evaluating his own work with care, or is he indifferent and apathetic? Is he putting his own self and environment into his work? Is he making something constructive out of his failures, or is he giving up?

At the preadolescent level, evaluation is both more important and more difficult than at any other stage of child development. The teacher needs enough flexibility to deal with two distinct attitudes taken by the child: 1) the negative mood that rejects adult assistance and tends to refuse defensively the communication with more skilled and knowledgeable human beings that is necessary for any real self-appraisal; and 2) the positive, curious, seeking attitude that comes through at times, willy-nilly, and saves the situation.

Rejection of the teacher is fortified by gang or clique formations. A child eager to conform to the peer group is afraid of getting too enthusiastic about any adult or school goals. Therefore, he constructs numerous barriers between himself and the teacher and between himself and his own potential enthusiasm. Disadvantaged children, with their inevitable resentment of society, make communication difficult for teachers in these days of racial tension. They do not "trust whitey" and do not want his advice any more than they want to take directions from him.

The positive attitude, however, can be called forth by sincere and at the same time sophisticated teachers who accept the shifting groups and cliques, move with the current, do not easily take affront, and do not offend the children's newfound sense of independence and group solidarity. As soon as children trust a teacher, they will be eager for new experiences and increasing numbers of problems. If the group in general has confidence that the teacher is not seeking to undermine it or break it up, individual members are then free to do self-chosen tasks with enthusiasm. They begin to respect discipline and standards. They begin to judge themselves, since deeply and instinctively they want to be brought up to scratch, as this means growing up to join the world of reality and to master ways of survival.

The paradox of this preadolescent negative-positive attitude can be both stimulating and exasperating. Quick shifts in group or individual moods make evaluation a very tricky exercise of wisdom. Objectivity, and a certain amount of card indexing, are important if the teacher is to find out in all this flux what is really going on inside each child.

At this age, children are outspoken and emotional in praising and condemning their own and others' works. Children often evaluate in terms of what they think adults like, and their verbal judgments may be very unreliable. Sometimes they are looking for praise when they condemn their own work. The teacher's role is to divert them from blanket judgments and to teach them to limit their criticism to specific details, such as, "The legs of this clay animal melt into the base, but you certainly get a sense of speed and force in the body movements." It is wise for a teacher to find out how a child really feels about his work before making comments, so that student and teacher together can judge how close the child came to his goal for a specific work. Often, when a child is satisfied, he wants and needs praise.

In such a volatile emotional atmosphere, teachers are needed who can keep their heads in court, so to speak, and file away perceptions and judgments in their minds in the midst of action. In general, teacher evaluation is a process of aiding the child to become aware of his own growth and of considering with the child his strengths and weaknesses in an atmosphere of encouragement and support. Sensitivity to preadolescent inhibitions and fears and the pain of growing up can make a great difference. A combination of sympathy and firmness allows the child to face without ego loss the hard facts of any arrested growth and thereby to intensify his efforts in a positive direction. And it cannot be stressed too often that since self-appraisal is a vital part of the creation of any work of art, it is an important factor in the teacher's final estimate of a child's progress during a school term.

Children should be motivated to keep private diaries or journals about their artwork, to be shared by others or by the teacher if they feel like it. Looking back at these with the teacher after, say, half a year of work can be a valuable experience. Any student who is interested enough to keep such a log will inevitably see signs of progress, and the teacher may gain insight into problems that the child has been unable to talk about. The journals can be kept in a special place in the studio.

Every art room should have storage space to house the work that is done, since it goes without saying that actual samples

**ACTIVITIES
STIMULATING
SELF-APPRAISAL**

provide the best means of noting changes, problems, movements from one stage of maturity to another. Both finished work and work in progress should be kept in folders and carefully marked by name, age, sex, grade, and date. (Some teachers keep date stamps ready for use.) It is important to develop a system whereby children automatically put their names, grades, and the date on their works. Two folders, in the case of painting, collage and other two-dimensional work, are needed for each child, one for current unfinished work and the other for finished paintings. The current work folder should be easily available to teacher and child. It can be used in various ways. The child can enter the room, go to his current folder, and pick out what he wants to complete or just look at again. Before class, the teacher may want to refresh her memory about what this class is doing; she therefore examines the current folders. During class, a child will have some problem. Perhaps neither he nor the teacher remembers how it was handled last time, so they use the material in the folder for discussion and evaluation. Or the teacher may want to select from the folders of finished work several typical problems to which a whole group might give attention. Current work folders are also used by the teacher at the end of the period for the planning of future sessions. And, of course, the folders are important in the formal written evaluation of individual children if required.

Photographing or making slides of children's work is an excellent way to record growth and development and to stimulate the student not only to evaluate his growth from year to year but also to share ideas and ways of approach with others. Photos and slides are a great help to teachers. They can use them during talks with parents and in conferences, or to help other teachers in the school gain a better understanding of a child and become more aware of maturity levels. Teachers also find slides valuable for checking their own class procedures.

Preadolescents will enjoy making their own photographs, if properly taught and guided. Stills in black and white and even Polaroid films are not too difficult to manage. If a work is photographed in progress, a child can see a detailed evolution of his approach to a certain problem. By making a number of such sequences, children may recognize and learn to avoid some automatic responses and habits which have blocked them and have become personal stereotypes.

A more subtle stimulation of self-appraisal can be created by bridging the age levels and bringing preadolescents into contact with older and younger art classes in the school. Anything that gives them an opportunity to discover their role and status in society is important to this age group, for they are vitally interested in placing themselves and in belonging. When they meet older children, see their artwork, and talk about it, they often recognize some of the artistic problems that they have struggled with, more nearly solved. They find out in this way just where they are and where they can expect to arrive in a few years.

This technique is well utilized in many schools and has also been used to advantage in the art centers being developed in urban ghetto areas. Teen-agers are being paid to assist in these places, since it is a means of reaching this alienated group. In the White Plains Storefront art center, during the first part of the summer, one teen-ager merely instructed the young where to keep their clay, how to clean up, and other housekeeping details. Her general attitude was disdainful; this was "kid's stuff." The breakthrough in her attitude came after she created a wonderful clay rabbit. After this, she was more personally involved and could be more truly helpful as a teacher's aid, since she had experienced some of the joys and perils of the creative act (4: p. 1).

Occasions should be provided in every school for preadolescents to communicate with older children and make their voices heard. Neither adults nor older children should be allowed to dominate these sessions. Both will need briefing by the art teacher as to the goals of the session, which are to listen to the preadolescent and give him the respect he deserves. Exhibitionism on the part of any participant is not to be tolerated, and all exchanges should attempt to be honest, direct, and dedicated to the artistic purpose underlying the meeting.

Preadolescents will react to respect, reasonableness and honesty and give them back in kind. They will have a chance on these occasions to find out what some adults are really like, and as a result may become less defensive and more objective not only about grown-ups but about themselves, too.

The next step is to give preadolescents a chance to teach other youngsters some of the things they have learned to do well. At the Ethical Culture schools, for instance, the older children kept a weaving program going in most of the classes throughout the school. The shop teacher taught them to make hand looms, and the preadolescents, working in teams, visited other rooms to teach other children how to warp them. They also discussed the designs which could be enriched by using a variety of textures. They encouraged the younger children to bring string and wool from home; they taught tapestry weaving to the slightly older ones. They had regular periods in which to visit the classrooms and supervise. During the Christmas season, when everyone was involved in festive decorating, preadolescents were organized into teams to teach paper sculpture techniques. They also taught sewing, knitting, art history, collage, and construction, and were particularly useful when a class was putting on a play.

The art teacher's role was to train the teams and help them organize their materials, and to work out with other teachers schedules for the lessons. The children themselves did all the teaching and loved it.

Preadolescents can also plan for younger children interesting lessons they have gone through in their own studio, along with showings of slides and reproductions to inspire creativity. They enjoy taking on such teaching ventures in twos or threes. Small groups require minimum adult supervision, and this, of course, appeals to them. Large groups can be organized to do a series of lessons, but this requires elaborate preparation and closer supervision by the teacher. The small team is advised; it makes the whole thing more spontaneous. Two or three close friends can take on a teaching project to show what they can do on their own. A teacher gains their affection and trust when she is willing to send them out, without separating the clique, on such an important mission. To safeguard the younger children, she also makes sure that they will gear their lesson so that they themselves gain information about the needs, abilities and problems of the younger children. As a result, they see their own characteristics and abilities as distinct and different. Objectivity and self-appraisal are stimulated. Preplanning, paperwork, and discussion between art teacher and the team are essential. At this point, any misconception of the technique they are going to teach can be cleared up. During this analysis, the preadolescent learns to structure his own knowledge in very realistic terms and may even solve some personal problems in the process.

IMPORTANCE OF DISPLAYS AND EXHIBITS

One must see art to learn about art; there is no substitute for this experience. Displays of all kinds are of inestimable value for creative self-assessment. When they are soundly planned, they show the children what kinds of growth, changing, maturing, progress in skills, and progress in individual expression are taking place. Displays make students take a harder look, and visual sophistication is gained both through the eyes and through conversational exchanges.

An infinite variety of displays is possible. One can set up objects to show, for instance, how similar subject matter or similar feelings are expressed by 1) the same age level; 2) the same age level but different economic and cultural backgrounds;

3) various age levels; and 4) children and mature artists. One-man shows or two- to three-man shows can highlight some aesthetic idea, give needed recognition and encouragement, or illustrate some technical skill.

Keeping work in progress on casual display in the studio is a sound way of developing self-appraisal. Children coming in and out or visiting in the studio have a chance to assess their work in different moods and at varying distances. If they know it is on display or easily available, they may pause on their way to lunch, gym, or before school. Most artists contemplate their work in this manner. It is also necessary for the child.

All studios should be equipped with areas for displays. The teacher can use this space to show the work of an entire class and discuss goals, directions, and results or to make a special point by showing the work of one or several students. Discussions, exchanges, group involvement—all these are important learning tools. The method and the physical space are indispensable.

Furthermore, every school should have a hall with walls made for the exhibition of paintings and niches and cases for three-dimensional work. The exhibit should be changed by the art teacher at least every two weeks in order to keep up the interest of the children and of other teachers.

Formal exhibitions in which children have an opportunity to cooperate in a large social undertaking is a particularly suitable activity for early adolescence. Churchill and Lumbley, in an article describing the value of graduation-time exhibits, see this as an activity which makes the most of personal uniqueness but which also allows the peer group or gang to work and have fun together. For the eleven- or twelve-year-old, anything that makes him feel appreciated, accepted, and important has enormous appeal.

The selection of paintings for the show is in itself an exercise in evaluation:

All the work done up to this time by each child is looked over by child and teacher with a view to selection. . . . Whether choices coincide or not, it is a good opportunity to discuss progress and directions. Usually the favorites of both the child and the teacher are included. Some children find that they want to do more concentrated work in one or more areas in order to have more to choose from [5: p. 16].

The authors also point out that at a particular time, when academic pressures are strong, the exhibit marks points of achievement in the creative as well as the scholastic areas. Support and status are thereby given to the arts, in turn motivating the student to put forth a good effort toward the achievement of high standards.

An inventive teacher will also initiate, at various times during the school year, panel discussions, art conferences, and open house days. These bring in parents and the immediate community. Pertinent figures from the world of art can also be invited to participate with the children in discussing viewing, and evaluating the work on display.

RECORDS, TAPES, EVALUATING SYSTEMS

Taping a lesson is a very useful device. The children gain objectivity when it is played back; the teacher develops insights into individual problems and ideas for future planning. When students hear their own discussions, they often realize how much time is wasted repeating the same ideas, interrupting, creating distractions. They also understand the point of criticizing each other with kindness instead of cruelty.

One teacher had each child speak about his work in private, and she taped his words. With his permission, she played the tape to the class, showing each painting as it came up. The group response was enthusiastic. The tape was useful not only for self-appraisal; it also gave the children a chance to know each other better and to compare their feelings about their work.

In another session, the teacher carried this experiment one step further. She taped a panel of artists discussing their paintings and on the same tape spliced in some similar thoughts expressed by the children in her class. This gave them respect for their own ideas and opinions, a sense of their own importance and of the importance of art.

Another teacher had a tape recorder in the room at all times, and the students could say anything they wanted at the end of the period or between activities. To break the ice, they were told they might voice a complaint or frustration, or something lovely, or an art problem, discovery, or new insight.

Some teachers devote too little time to listening to the children, becoming too preoccupied with the mechanics of the lesson or the curriculum goals. The experienced teacher learns to keep one eye and both ears tuned to the total atmosphere, even when absorbed in setting up equipment or in other duties. At the same time, she must respond to individual children when they speak to her. This ability to pay general and special attention is a talent not easy to develop, but it comes in time. The student learns a great deal about what he is doing when he can talk about it. Very often he will be able to explain to the teacher in a lucid way something that was, up to then, obscure to himself and meaningless to adults, something he was able to draw or sculpt only after the teacher allowed him to articulate it in words. The creative process in art is largely covert, and is revealed mostly in actions, values, attitudes, self-concepts, and role expectations held while engaged in the activity" (6: p. 44). Creating a work of art can be seen as a progression of stages in which the artist makes a series of simple and seemingly spontaneous choices. Yet they all proceed from a complex of conscious and subconscious impulses and preferences, expressive of both individual personality and cultural influence (7: pp. 169–75). It is important for the teacher to try to understand how the child thinks and feels as he is working, because his emotions and thoughts are related to the object he is trying to create. They also reflect the effect that the art experience is having on his total personality development. The teacher should make as many notes as possible on each child, since it is hard to remember later everything that has happened during the turmoil and swift encounters of each session. Slides, photographs, the work itself, and tapes give a good kaleidoscopic view. But written data on each child's growth of skills, knowledge, and emotional attitudes is an enormous evaluating aid. There are devices to expedite records of this sort.

Inventing forms for recording student action and reaction is a matter of personal preference and ingenuity. File cards are very convenient. It is amazing to discover the kind and volume of information a teacher may gather by jotting down comments during the daily class. The cards can be prepared in advance and organized into class groups. Along with name, date and type of lesson, the teacher can add comments such as: "Has technical problem" or "Seems very dependent on Joe's opinion of his work" or "Negative response to suggestion regarding color experimentation" or "Involved, and has definite ideas" or "Likes privacy and no interference," "Seems nervous, unhappy, tense when working, looks around a good deal, behaves as if he wants to hide his work," or "Is struggling with the figure, particularly leg movements; will need attention."

It may not be possible to have a card for each child, to be used during every lesson. The teacher might systematically select a few children for this type of observation during one lesson, other children for the next lesson, and so on.

Referring to these comments after a period of time may be a very revealing experience. In addition, various types of checklists for the purpose of recording feelings, emotions, values, attitudes and preferences can be devised, to be used by either teacher or child. Some are forms to be filled out as part of a regular routine record; others are devised for use at prescribed intervals; and some are developed for specific situations when the teacher feels it is necessary. All these forms should, of course, be based on a soundly planned educational aim. They should be constantly examined with a view toward improvement, clarity, and utility—even for the sake of novelty. Children are apt to treat forms as unimportant when they can no longer recall their original purpose.

Two sample forms are included in Appendix B (pp. 417–419). The first, entitled *How I Felt While Working Today,* might be used either on a regular routine basis or only occasionally, depending on the quality of the group and on individual responses. The second, *I Am Finished with This Work,* can be used only by certain children when they decide to put a work aside.

Written anecdotal accounts of varying lengths are another form of useful record. They may be small stories about individuals or about a group. Here is a sample:

Name
Date
Grade

Joe is becoming discouraged. According to him, he constantly "spoils" his drawings by spilling over the edges when he uses the regular bristle brushes to fill in his drawings.

He needs to be helped technically, perhaps given a selection of small camel hair brushes which will let him draw directly. Also show him Japanese or other paintings in which drawing is done spontaneously and directly with the brush.

Arrange and prepare for a conference with him.

The data collected by all these methods through the school year should not be thought of as information merely to be used in summary evaluations or required by the administration from time to time. Nor should it be collected in ways that suggest a secret dossier on each child. This information, these hints, are merely notes on growing, acting, changing personalities. They are part of a continuous research into each child's development and into the value of aesthetics as an integral part of any curriculum. Checklists are not exclusively for the teacher, either; they should be made available to the students, as well, when needed for their own evaluation of themselves as artists.

To hand out monthly or term grades in art courses is neither logical nor practical. Growth of the imagination cannot be measured numerically, nor can creative expression be graded in conventional terms. According to many art educators, the most satisfactory type of report is one "that indicates as specifically as possible the status of the student in behavior and accomplishment and makes recommendations for further directions" (8: p. 120). In the more forward-looking schools, these statements take the place of grades.

The following is an outline which may be helpful to teachers in structuring term reports:

Growth of self-confidence

Individual qualities of expression

Areas requiring special attention

Areas in which there has been marked growth

Social behavior and its effect on the art experience

Behavior while working

Attitudinal changes (Both Conrad [9: p. 274] and McVitty [10: pp. 77–78] have devised criteria for evaluation useful in practical teaching.)

Annual reports evaluating the total art program may also be required by the administration. Such summaries of purposes, projects, results (learning, skill, growth, artifacts) are excellent tools for taking stock. Their value is exactly commensurate with the time the teacher devotes to them. (For further information, the reader is referred to Henry's comprehensive discussion on growth and evaluation [11].)

It is obvious that the student's self-appraisal is linked with the appraisal of the teacher. It could not be otherwise. The child in question is somewhere between ten and thirteen years old and still semidependent; he has not got his wings, though they are beginning to grow. The teacher is still very important to him in the learning process. He needs her cooperation as much as she needs his. In evaluating, and even in writing the final report for the authorities and for parents, a cooperative venture is sometimes in order. Pupil and teacher, in their own words, make statements about the year's work, to go out under the same cover. Writing their own reports to their parents about their progress is a revealing experience in self-appraisal for children.

Through such a process of participation, two-way communication can be built between teacher and child. The teacher proposes general goals and specific techniques. The student communicates through his artwork his still immature tones, modifying the general program according to his own creative urges and ambitions. If the teacher hears him, with the inner as well as outer ear, she can help him decide at the end of a period of time whether he has expressed a small part of his unique message.

REFERENCES

1. Richard Guggenheimer, *Creative Vision for Art and for Life,* Harper & Brothers, New York, 1960.

2. Leo Steinberg, "Contemporary Art and the Plight of Its Public," *The New Art,* E. P. Dutton & Co., New York, 1966.

3. Etienne Gilson, *Painting and Reality,* Meridian Books, Inc., New York, 1959.

4. Robert Burkhart, *Spontaneous and Deliberate Ways of Learning,* International Textbook Company, Scranton, Pa., 1962.

5. Angiola Churchill and Lora Beth Lumbley, "Exhibits Children Do Themselves," *Art Education Magazine,* vol. 57, no. 6, 1958.

6. Edward B. Feldman, "Process," *Art Education Bulletin,* Eastern Arts Association, April, 1961.

7. Lincoln Rothchild, *Style in Art: The Dynamics of Art as Cultural Expression,* A. S. Barnes and Co., Inc., 1962.

8. *The Visual Arts in General Education,* A Report of the Committee on the Foundation of Art in General Education for the Commission on Secondary School Curriculum, Progressive Education Association, Appleton-Century-Crofts, Inc., New York, 1940.

9. George Conrad, *The Process of Art Education in the Elementary School,* Prentice-Hall, Inc., Englewood Cliffs, N.J., 1961.

10. Laurence F. McVitty, "An Experimental Study on Various Methods in Art Motivation at the Fifth Grade Level," *Research in Art Education,* National Art Education Association, 7th yearbook, Washington, D.C. 1956.

11. Edith M. Henry, *Evaluation of Children's Growth Through Art Experiences,* The National Art Education Association, Washington, D.C., 1959.

Two-dimensional Expression

8

Rendering an image on a two-dimensional plane holds a double magic. With a few tubes of paint, pencil, ink, or scraps of paper and a clean flat surface, an illusion can be created of three-dimensional space, light and dark, volume, motion, and objects and bodies that appear to have solidity and texture and to possess animation. Even more magically, painting can make images of the inner experiences of the human consciousness: perceptions, thoughts, passions, sensuous reactions, and concepts of living. These pass from the mind of the artist to the canvas to the mind of the beholder. From a modicum of earth's vegetable and mineral stores, almost from "airy nothing," comes substance for the eye and the soul.

Drawing, painting, and printing have been used since the beginning of recorded time—perhaps from the earliest stages of cognition—to express a wide range of ideas both mundane and exalted, and have been adapted to the most simplistic and erudite revelations. Painting and drawing are pliable, highly flexible modes of expression, capable of recording quick changes of feelings, concepts and moods. The marks a painter makes on a blank surface are as uniquely his own as his fingerprints. Through these marks he perceives a dimension of himself that is new and different from, let us say, the sounds he makes or the way he looks and moves. (In many caves where primitive men lived, we have found the imprints of their hands on the walls, sometimes their footprints.) This objective representation of one's identity can be a spur to look for additional evidence of one's existence—or rather, of the special quality born into an individual—and for the significant differences and similarities between oneself and other beings. A person's perception of nature, his subjective, sensuous response to materials, and his choice of subject matter—all these are singular to him and possessed by no one else. They can provide him with a map or chart to follow in the long search for identity.

For preadolescents this is a definite boon. They are still insecure in their skins, not sure of what either body or mind

SELF-DISCOVERY

will do. They are prone to be fearful of what René Huyghe calls "the mystery which is to be found in man himself, his own body" that with "acts of insight, passion, sudden and unforeseeable impulses, disturbances of all kinds . . . stealthily introduces the threatening unfamiliarity of the physical world to the very soul" (1: p. 464).

STRUCTURING THE OUTSIDE WORLD

The preadolescent is especially bent on understanding and adjusting to his environment, the world not of his making. He is learning to adjust to the laws of nature, institutions, family life, machines, and ways of survival. The average child of ten to thirteen wants to increase his conscious scope, to make sense out of things, to reduce his personal chaos. This urge is both scientific and aesthetic. Like mathematics, like physics, art was born out of a desire to give structure to unstructured experience. Joseph Wood Krutch wrote:

Genuine art is neither a mere naturalistic report of events nor an escape into a dream. It is an ordering of the world of experience in such a way as to attribute logic and meaning to the world [2: p. 8].

The process of artistic creation has played an important role in extending the human consciousness. It has fortified our humanness, sharpened our senses of perception, our skills and intuitions, and probably increased our chances of survival. And as it did in the childhood of the human race, graphic expression today develops a child's intelligence and his grasp of the realities outside himself. Michael Kirby (Essays on the Avant-Garde) believes that

though consciousness precedes perception, certain perceptions are able to change the limits or basic character of consciousness itself. It is upon these changes that the significance of art depends [3: pp. 60–61].

Looking, making an image, recognizing, not only educates but gives intense pleasure to a child. Boys and girls on the verge of maturing find comfort in objective expression of the outside world which is or is about to be so important to them. A painting or drawing, while illusionary, is also a visual truth in itself. It can bring aspects of existence into focus. This creation of three dimensions on a flat surface excites children with its mystery; it also brings them in touch with objects, beings, and events they want desperately to absorb.

The objects children make are creations that have never existed in the world before and are as rare and precious as the individuals who brought them into being. Painting and other graphic media give a child the opportunity of being a creator now, instead of having to wait until he can build skills, or until he has lost his inspiration during laborious hours of preparing his material, as with stone, metal, or wood, wrestling with stubborn substances to make them take on the personal intentions of the maker. A painting instantly jumps from tabula rasa to an image of at least some part of the personality involved in its conception. A child of ten or eleven, with a short attention span and shorter patience, can spontaneously pour out patterns and color sequences having personal significance.

Aesthetic creativity is natural to all human beings, whether they are aware of it or not. We live in two realms, that of nature and that of art. Although of different substances, they share some elements; innumerable reflections pass back and forth between the two spheres. We are inextricably involved in both, though sometimes participation in the world of art remains below the surface of consciousness. The realm of art is man's own creation, therefore comprehensible and controllable. In spite of science, the natural universe in its totality is still unfathomed and unpredictable. Natural law does not seem to establish man as more significant than other forms of life. General purposes in this sphere are mysterious, seem unconcerned with human fears, joys, hopes, or survival. It is in defiance of this indifference that man has always sought to make himself the center of the universe, creating an ordered habitat in which he can think, feel, understand, and take emotional nourishment. Gilson states:

. . . painters confront onlookers with concrete objects, real things, or beings, which they themselves have made before which we all find ourselves in the same situation as before the things of nature. For, indeed, nature does not explain . . . nature is simply there for us to see. In like manner, instead of giving us words to understand, painting places under our eyes realities on which to meditate [4: pp. 132–33].

A communications network of high frequency runs between all the arts and within each separate one. Making a painting is an act not only of self-identification but of projection and transference as well. A complex message can be transmitted without words through the subject matter, the sensuous patterns, tactile qualities, and dynamics of line and color. The eye is the receiver and transmitter too, as the message passes from one consciousness to another. In his painting or drawing, a child can silently speak out his feelings in the images that emerge from all levels of his mind.

When painting, either by themselves or as a group, or reacting to paintings by mature artists, children live in a communion of feeling and creativity that helps mitigate their loneliness and insecurity. Edith Kramer, art therapist and long time observer of youngsters writes:

Children who paint together soon develop a remarkable degree of understanding and appreciation for each other's work, so that often their judgement will be more penetrating than the observations of adults. And this is not surprising if one considers how much the understanding of art depends on a common cultural and emotional situation [5: p. 19].*

A child's painting, drawing or collage may also serve as a socially viable outlet for frustrations and anxieties, or as an object to test attitudes on others and observe their reactions, to see what will or will not be accepted by the society. Preadolescents may also use this newly discovered circuit of communication to ask for help in moments of trouble. The art therapist working with the very disturbed uses this knowledge.

SECURITY AND SENSIBILITY

Like all other media, painting and drawing can be introduced to these tenuously balanced preadolescents in ways that will make them feel secure.

The first step is to encourage them to accept and give value to their own work and that of others without fear of ridicule and without ridiculing. This is accomplished through the creation of an ambience in the studio which puts a premium on individuality and tolerates all degrees of realism, fantasy, and abstraction and all levels of skill. Teachers build this free, welcoming atmosphere by the respect they pay to each child and by what they point out to praise in every work. Careful attention to exchanges between students is also important. Emphasis is laid on the value that each person's unique qualities hold for our all too standardized society.

Second, children need help in gaining skill. Unless technical skill is nurtured in relationship to the personal message of each child, many will be unable to find their way into the

*Originally published by the University of California Press; reprinted by permission of The Regents of the University of California.

creative current. The required help should be immediate, offering a choice of specific solutions to the problem at hand. By special attention to the individual, by introducing a wide variety of technical aids, by shifts in the tempo of art experiences, and by providing opportunities for both variety and mixing of media, the teacher gives the child a better chance to discover a way of rendering which satisfies him. Repetition of a single approach may stifle expression; one child's release is another child's frustration.

Finally, if there is to be any permanent value to the experience, preadolescents must be exposed to the sights (and discussion of these sights) that will develop their sensibilities. At this age, they have the potential to develop a selective appetite and taste that is beyond the ordinary and which will help them enjoy, and survive in, both the creative and mundane spheres of life, possibly contributing some discovery of their own. Children can be sensitized to the different ways that significant works of art speak of the human condition. As their perceptions sharpen, they will learn to respond with an energy that goes beyond the pleasure of mere recognition and comfort in a naturalistic scene. The less literal messages of abstract painting will also begin to come through.

THE CREATIVE PROCESS: MIND, HAND, MEDIA

How is the artist led to fashion and refashion until his form expresses an emotion or a revelation pressing inside of him? Intuition may serve as a springboard. It can set the tone, the colors, the scope of the painting, and it may articulate the organization. After this, the painter brings to bear his artistic knowledge, his power of assessment, consciously subjecting his intuition to evaluation. This experience may inspire in him more experimentation and further intuitive flights. In significant works both intuition and assessment will be operating in unison.

Pierre Soulages said, "I work guided by an inner impulse, a longing for certain forms, color, materials, and it is not until they are on the canvas that they can tell me what I want" (6: p. 198). Yet Soulage has a keen sense of order, of formal structure, and his works reveal his aesthetic intelligence in their bold interrelated forms, moving dynamically in great thrusts to create unity and harmony.

Picasso said that "a picture is not thought out and settled beforehand. While it is being done, it changes as one's thoughts change" (6: p. 179). He also called painting a series of subtractions. We may infer that a painter must make constant choices, to determine what is appropriate in a certain work. William

Baziotes used to say: "I put it on, I take it off. I put it on, I take it off." His painting appears at first to have sprung full-grown from a conscious and well-realized plan. But closer examination reveals the search he was constantly engaged in. Moreover, his process of applying-removing-applying often accounts for the rich luminosity which appears in so many of his paintings. His method made possible his mystical, fantasy-laden forms. The process itself took over.

Another type of discovery may come from the "doodle." Unlike the found form, which is already a plastic element, the doodle comes from within, an expression of the subconscious. The doodler may produce something that is entirely formless which may be transcribable into a form. It may even provide a theme or subject. It may offer no possibilities at all. It is interesting to note that the artist who doodles, even completely automatically and thoughtlessly, follows a mode in keeping with his current style of painting. If he wishes to use the doodle for true discovery, he must consciously direct his efforts away from repeating and imitating himself.

There is doodling, there is sketching for a projected work, and there is drawing. In recent times drawing has been neglected as an intrinsic part of the painting process. In fact it has come to be regarded as a separate discipline; in many art schools, drawing and painting are taught in separate courses. This may be partly because drawing, in relation to painting, has been historically considered as a kind of shorthand and merely a technique for making studies, for experimentation, practice work, "loosening up." Quick results with a fine pencil, pen or brush seem to be all one expects of drawing in a painting class. Though many drawings, past and present, have been executed with chiaroscuro, tone and form, the notion that a drawing is merely an outline still persists.

While such a use of line is valid, a deeper view reveals that it can be considered a formal element in itself. Use of line for form is clearly evident in the works of Miro, Tobey and Klee. These artists use drawing as an autonomous factor, not for sketch or contour or shorthand to be later translated. Their drawing is a statement in its own right.

Oriental calligraphers made little or no distinction between drawing and painting. Their gestures made when producing calligraphic symbols were as meaningful as the shapes themselves, both physically and spiritually. Perhaps it was the combination of mental and manual ritual that made their work so powerful.

The action painters and the abstract expressionists have renewed the importance of line associated with gesture. It is clearly part of the new emphasis on the importance of the artist himself as a performer in his work, which becomes an expression of his whole body, not merely his perceiving and sensing mind.

For artists, for scientists, and especially for children, playfulness, "playing around" with an idea or a shape or a mathematical problem, can often lead to creative discovery. Teachers are all too prone to equate the necessary relaxation of rigidity, which relieves fear of failure and nervous tension, with triviality and lack of concentration or purpose. Playing spontaneously with paint often improves personal expression, bringing forth greater freedom and force. Meyer Shapiro wrote of abstract painting:

The object of art is . . . more passionately than before, the occasion of spontaneity or intense feeling. . . . All these elements of impulse which seem at first so aimless on the canvas are built up into a whole characterized by firmness, often by elegance and beauty of shape and colors [7: pp. 38–39].

The child, when he is "just playing," may feel, because society has influenced him in that direction, that he is functioning in a void, without direction or aim. He may then be at a loss, confused and frustrated. The teacher's role is to reassure him, keep alive his response to all the manifestations that emerge from his unconscious as he plays, and encourage him to evaluate them. During one period of accomplishment, the child may be pleasantly surprised to find how interwoven work and play are.

Collage is a medium that stimulates playfulness and awakens unconscious emotions and images, often incongruous images, like bits of a dream. Scraps of material, newspapers or magazines will accidentally touch off nostalgic associations. For children they often release powers of spontaneous improvisation, a long chain of aesthetic responses. The process of choice is strengthened as the child orders and unifies these fragments of reality and dream into a unity that expresses his message. Richer compositional arrangement, color power, and spatial effects through texture and shape can often be more easily discovered by a child when manipulating collage materials than when painting. He is able to move quickly or replace each item on the surface, in order to discover how it behaves, before securing it permanently with glue. Technical proficiency is less important than it is for drawing and painting. There are no preconceived notions about what is right. There is no great historical tradition to intimidate the beginner. After all, collage materials are scraps. Mistakes do not matter. The material is plentiful and never expensive. There is less nervous tension when a child uses collage, and the creative mood is less vulnerable to feelings of inadequacy and to criticism.

Children will work nonobjectively in collage, advancing from one project to the next, sharpening their sensibilities and discrimination by experimenting with all kinds of surfaces, colors, textures, and ways of ordering. Often they like to work with found content, applying realistic textures to various portions. They can be stimulated, at the start, by the idea of exploring materials for contrast: Shiny-dull, rough-smooth, hard-soft, opaque-transparent, light-dark, pattern on pattern. For nonobjective compositions, they can play with big and small, squares turning into circles, lines turning into curves, repetition, balancing. Themes may be suggested to arouse creative associations: dawn becoming day, dusk becoming night, "myself in time," places seen in dreams, real landscapes, seascapes, or terror in city streets.

SUGGESTED EXPERIENCES FOR PREADOLESCENTS

It is a fearful exercise to reduce the complex practices and principles of the mature painter to experiences for children. Yet all indications point to preadolescence as the period in which a transition can be made from a predominantly intuitive to a more conscious grasp of art.

Like techniques, principles of painting are understood through seeing and doing, rather than talking. Discussion means little to a child. It is too abstract and is apt to build clichés. What an element is called—line, texture, or visual order—is not as important as its function for the child in his own expression, and perhaps in that of others. Children find their own words if they want to, and learn ours only when they feel it is important to do so.

The following suggested experiences may be useful as resources for motivation when working with individual children or with small or large groups. The majority have been tested by actual use. Many have been designed to provide the child with means to satisfy his desire for representational rendering through unlimited experimentation with media in unconventional ways. A combination of what children recognize as a serious intention to observe nature, plus an unusual means of rendering perceptions and ideas, keeps a child flexible and encourages fluency. At the same time, his desire for realism is respected.

All or most of the projects have the potential to stimulate nonobjective responses as well. It is recommended that the teacher give encouragement and equal status to nonobjective works. Too many teachers have been all too willing to let children fend for themselves in this manner of expression, failing to provide guidance. Insistence upon the representational stifles the child who can respond to color, action, suggestive shapes, accident with the medium, and the myriad qualities which receive attention from all abstract painters. Children tend to be in tune with their time, the work of contemporary artists making the natural connections with the present society. The following experiences are accompanied in most cases by references to specific painters, both representational and nonobjective. It is important for these children to see realistic and abstract work simultaneously. This teaches him to accept the entire field of painting with all its rich and varying possibilities.

VISUAL ORDER

Any art expression, if it is to communicate its meaning, has organization, whether planned consciously or intuitively by the artist. As Myers said, "The artist thinks in design terms as the musician thinks in terms of harmony and counterpoint" (8: p. 250). The painter uses a specific range of design elements and principles. They are the components which he puts in relation to each other in order to make his statement. He does not, in fact he cannot, use one in isolation from the other, although he gives emphasis according to his purposes and his personality.

The graphic artist, in order to achieve significance, arranges the elements of color, light and dark, value, line, shape and form, and texture. In addition, he will be concerned with the design principles, which include space, movement, rhythm, balance, emphasis (dominance and subordination), and proportion. Ultimately, and also constantly as his work develops, he will be involved in achieving unity while maintaining variety within the unity. Even in the most recent art, which seems to be unrelated to or in defiance of the principles of design, these components are present.

Compare the visual ordering of Matisse and Braque, both of the twentieth-century French school and both often painters of interior scenes. Matisse conceived of a room as a joyous, carefree environment. A delightful casualness prevails, expressed by highly decorated curtains, flowers, etc. Colors are high-keyed; drawing is spirited, fluent and sensuous. The structural order of Matisse is determined by his vision of existence. His interiors could hardly exist in physical reality, but they have another reality as structure, as idea, as the self of the artist. Their existence has been made possible by Matisse's unique organization of plastic elements.

Braque, with another concept of life, offers us an architectonic interior. By relating lights and darks and compressing planes which seem to interpenetrate, he builds a sense of three-dimensionality. The ambience is one of constructed security and the mood often one of brooding and contemplation. Thus did two painters unify the same painting elements and the same subject matter into entirely different coherent frameworks.

Time, as it exists in a painting, is closely linked with movement through an illusionary space, just as time, space and motion are linked in the universe. All art exists in a time-space frame. The composer and the dramatist manipulate time in obvious ways. "The symphony, the film and the ballet are spread out, laid down on a bed of time; the time spent by the auditor or spectator is practically predetermined" (9: p. 140). The painter, architect, and sculptor use time on a more suggestive level, involving the acrobatics of the eyes and the more physical participation of the viewer.

Stress, pause, interval, and the repetition of pulsations across the surface produce the sensation of time-space in a painting. At first sight, the meaning of the painting as a whole is communicated to the viewer: the impact is received and assimilated as a unit of feeling and sense impressions. After this the painting can be gradually savored, enjoyed, and comprehended. For complete experiencing, there must be a period of contemplation allowing for successive reactions as the viewer moves from one passage to the next, grasping relationships and making associations.

Balance is as important to the visual order of a work as rhythm. It is essential to the psychic as well as to the optic security of the viewer. Without balance, he becomes disoriented and unwilling to participate in the movements of the painting. This equilibrium may be achieved in many ways. It should not be considered merely as a strictly formal or mechanical balance of objects or elements; it is, instead, an interaction of elements to create a visual harmony. Oppositional forces producing asymmetry can often be more compelling than symmetrical arrangements.

Experiments, techniques, and materials Children benefit from experimenting with many and various ways to plan a painting. These develop flexibility, spontaneity and the painterly approach. Exercises in the following projects fall into two categories: those aimed at expanding spatial conceptions and those which encourage children to plan paintings as whole rather than as parts. Colored papers, manufactured textured papers, papers pretextured by crushing, crinkling, perforating, or stapling in overall patterns can do wonders to unify a work.

Painting directly, without preliminary sketching, should be encouraged at all times, yet many children of this age hesitate to plunge in without some preliminary planning. They feel more secure if they make a light chalk or charcoal sketch or use a thin water stain to draw, applying the more opaque paint to finish. Their whole bent is to become more precise than in their younger days, and they like to be able to try again after making what they consider "bad starts," "mistakes," or "poor drawings." Using tracing paper in series allows for elimination or addition as the child sees fit.

Broadening avenues to composition

1. Frequent changes of format help children become aware of the importance and possibilities of compositional arrangements. A thin vertical composition may expedite a sense of unity; a round format or a long horizontal one made from shelving paper may encourage children to make scrolls. (See Kenneth Noland, "And Again," 1964; Mark Tobey, "World," 1959; Frank Stella, "ifafa II," 1964; Robert Indiana's X-shaped paintings, quatrefoils, and oval shapes; Braque and Picasso's analytical Cubist paintings.)

Grade five—boy

2. Alternate the background to gain a more active composition. First, a child draws on a colored paper his main characters or objects, according to his theme or idea. These figures or shapes are then cut out. Successive layers of colored papers are pasted behind and around these cutouts in order to change and build

up the background. Painting may be combined with this project. The cutouts can be used to trace the original forms onto new forms. Thus the child works from the background out toward the surface, which gives him an exciting new vantage point.

3. Children can paint animals which they know or would like to know more about and cut them out individually. They then paint the animal's habitat, using the reference file for pictures and descriptive details (see page 410). The last step is to paste the cutouts onto the separately painted background.

4. Children can look through an empty picture frame made of simple cardboard at a selected subject and paint exactly what they see within its limits.

5. Ask children to consider entering their paintings with cut-out shapes from different edges of the paper. Shapes floating off the paper are captured in action, coming in from all directions, pushing down, floating up, entering through the sides and corners. Avoid placing shapes in the center of the paper, as this will result in a more static statement. To illustrate the carry-over from abstract to representational subject matter, it might be important to encourage children to do a representational work immediately after the exercise.

6. Using Matisse's "Red Room" as a starting point, have the children think about a painting in which the color of the background is repeated in at least three or four items. This will illustrate to them still another way of achieving unity.

7. Study and analyze the compositional arrangements of mature artists by using overlays of transparent paper over their works. Each child should pick his favorite and then set about to discover the dark and light patterns of the work; the linear qualities and the major rhythmic forces; directions, tensions, pressures; and the color qualities related to repetition and dominance. Then each child can paint (or dance or sing or write a poem), responding to the work he has just analyzed — the overall *feel of* it.

8. Use a still life for exercises in composition.
   a. Have each child choose an item in the still life, handle it, smell it, hear it, study it, return it to the table and then paint it. After they have done this several times with several items, ask them to deal with the entire composition. The familiarity gained with each item and the response evoked in handling it will bring forth a bold and assured distribution and articulation of parts, which at the same time gives vitality to the whole. Following are two paintings from a series of seven.

They show how Hank, who chose an eggplant and various other vegetables, was able to compose with ever-increasing control and finesse as he progressed.

Grade six—boy

Grade six—boy

b. Using the same still life, ask the children to stress different elements as they paint it. In one color's function in the total composition is stressed; in another, shapes; in a third, linear rhythmic qualities.

c. Children will enjoy interpreting the still life with collage materials. In three versions of the same still life, one stressed the quality of the bouquet of silver dollars using skrim, labels, felt and string; in the second, shown here, the artist is more interested in the total view and has organized it to make it appear more realistic, involving some interesting spatial qualities; the third showed a particular sensitivity to design qualities and the color action of the carefully chosen objects.

Grade six—boy

9. Using strips of colored tape, have children divide any given surface into rectangles and squares. After the tapes are down, have the children fill the squares and rectangles with colors, using small sponges for quick coverage. They should be able to do at least six in a 50-minute period. For some, combining the painting with collage might be interesting. Show the class Mondrian's or Ad Reinhardt's work. Also show some representational work with underlying organization based on geometric forms. Persian miniatures and early Italian Renaissance paintings are rife with interesting divisions by this device. Children can also be encouraged to do a series of spatial divisions, without the tapes, on large paper. (See Afro and Rothko.) Then, utilizing the drawings previously made when sketching outdoor landscapes, encourage the children to organize their subjects into more formal structures, stressing geometric shapes.

Along with this project, of course, there should be some discussion of what the early-twentieth-century artists were trying to do. Why did they feel the need to analyze objects and figures in terms of basic geometric forms?

10. Use oversized formats to develop compositional power. The huge picture, a particularly important phenomenon of our time, is highly appropriate for preadolescents. It can be a challenge to their energies and ambitions. Give them a format that stretches in footage in all directions, requiring an image larger than life-size and demanding an extremely physical act of painting—arm movements rather than merely wrist exercise. Working in this size is a kinesthetic liberation of body energy and is apt to lead the children out of previous preconceptions and clichés about form and shape and composition.

Large brushes should be used, plus some inventive tools like spray guns and others borrowed from other arts. Children will do remarkable things when they are allowed to choose their own size of format. The material should be rolled out by the yard to match the image or dream they want to project and to satisfy their own ideas about what they can accomplish. The preadolescent is looking for just such an adventure to expand his scope, fortify his ego, and gain notice from his peers. He will need the teacher's help and encouragement, either alone or as part of a group project. He will blossom as he undertakes a huge work; he will feel that he is coming to grips with the "real thing." (Show Michelangelo's "Sistine Chapel," Matisse's "The Dance," and Monet's "Nymphes.")

Large nonobjective paintings, unhampered by self-conscious attention to the human scale, often increase the emotional power of the painting experience and expand the aesthetic intuition. Pollock's work is a good example. Involving the whole body in its execution, it seems to have gained the force that is released by one repetitive ongoing movement, appearing to be one long breath. One also feels this in Newman's simple expanses of one color, traversed by strips of other colors to establish the scale.

By abandoning subject matter, in particular the human figure, the large painting becomes more of an entity, a "thing," an icon, a holy symbol. "Almost as much as the pyramids, it speaks of itself alone. It is no longer a window to a world, but *the* world, imminent and autonomous. It has size, and thus dignity, a dignity no longer intruded upon by fictitious agents in human attire" (10: p. 56).

SPACE

Preadolescents who are eager to represent reality and to employ the techniques which give the illusion of objects in deep space should be given the help they require. But as has been explained at length elsewhere, it is important for the teacher to proceed with caution, since each child perceives spatial qualities in a personal way. Lessons which involve spatial perception in ways radically different from the child's own conception may disturb his confidence and confuse him. It is salutary for the teacher to recollect and at times point out to the students the various and even contradictory space concepts used by artists in other eras and cultures.

Religion, for instance, often influenced treatment of space during the Renaissance. A Florentine nobleman who commissioned and donated an altar piece depicting the Crucifixion often asked to be included in the scene. Although he was placed in the immediate foreground, he was always much smaller than the central figures so that he would never appear to be considered as equal to the Christ figure.

Sensation of volume Giotto's greatness lay in his placement of man in space. He conceived of human beings in all their physical as well as spiritual reality; he gave men and women a solid existence on the canvas, in contrast to the symbolic antirealism imposed by medieval religiosity. Giotto's understanding of modeling—his use of lights and darks—resulted in forms that give the sensation of organic substance and strength. His landscapes are solid and earthy; his objects and figures exist as volumes displacing space and enveloped by it.

Recognizable and imagined space Michelangelo's "Last Judgment" offers the observer celestial, terrestrial and subterrestrial visions in a single work. Here is a combination of worlds known and unknown. The viewer makes the journey back and forth between material and spiritual spheres and feels no strain, because of the artist's consummate sense of harmonious space relationships. What might have been a confused composition was unified by certain passages and complex movements containing pervasive light and dark patterns. These patterns control and hold together the disparate parts. Each separate figure is treated autonomously; it has volume, weight and substance, yet is so integrated into the whole scheme that it never undermines the unity of the composition. This is done by congruity of color, shape, value, and movement. The figures are modeled sculpturally, but an arbitrary chiaroscuro produces a dramatically emotional and awe-inspiring effect.

Atmospheric space One might say that Leonardo da Vinci emphasized the spatial sensation in his works. His method was chiefly one of chiaroscuro, in which light and shade were used as an illusionary device to create the naturalistic (though idealized) forms of the Renaissance. Da Vinci placed less stress on sumptuous color than the Venetians and relied largely on merging his shapes by softening their edges, blending them so that they seemed to flow into each other. The result was a unity of interacting volumes, along with a pervasive atmospheric effect. While his colors were at times rich and full, his paintings could generally be called monochromatic. He was most involved with the movement through time, tension and balance of an atmosphere.

Cubistic space Cézanne subjected the objects he painted to a carefully systematized analysis which ultimately gave them more concreteness. He reduced them to cylinders, cones, and spheres, at the same time merging these basic solids without significantly altering their natural appearance. An apple still looked like an apple. Surface and depth became more closely tied together in his work than in the work of his predecessors, through the interlocking modulations of color tones as well as through the interpenetrating planes.

His preoccupation with solidity and space led others who immediately followed him into even more intensive involvement with volume and nonperspective spatial illusion. Cubism emerged from the work of Cézanne as much as from African sculpture, which both Braque and Picasso studied. They spoke of "cubic power" and conceived of atmosphere as well as objects made up of solid building blocks which could be structured to give a sense of three-dimensionality. They reduced their colors to a monochromatic range which allowed them to concentrate on expressing a three-dimensional physical reality. By means of "interlocking faceting," that is, locking together the "geometric faceting" derived from analysis of an object (11: pp. 98–99) and the atmosphere around the object, a powerful architectonic spatial order was created. The atmosphere around an object was conceived of as having a solidity of its own.

Later, these artists attempted to juxtapose as many views of the object as possible and to combine them into a single work. These paintings take on the appearance of compressed volumes existing within a space-time complex, which to the artists was undoubtedly a truer reality of space and substance than any heretofore achieved.

Surface flatness   Artists of the twentieth century have claimed that the illusionistic (perspective) space of the Renaissance was antithetical to the basic nature of the picture plane. The natural flatness should not be violated, they declared. They rejected chiaroscuro and endeavored to hold all their forms on the immediate surface, allowing them to move vertically or laterally but infrequently into the canvas. They did not want to create "deep space."

Flat, or lateral, space has been used by Oriental painters and, during some phases and periods, by Western artists. It has now been brought to a highly esoteric level by the current hard-edged painter, whose contours are clean and sharp and whose controlled space is the ultimate in flatness.

Illusionary color optics   Today's op art produces in the viewer the sensation that geometric forms or symbols are moving into alternating spatial positions. The artist is working directly on our optical senses, creating provocative, even disturbing or irritating spatial effects, at times shaking the viewer out of the complacency of his normal vision of space.

An unlimited field   Any, all, or some of the approaches to space in which artists have eternally been involved will provide provocative projects to pursue with youngsters. The important learning experience here is that *no one way is the right way.* Any system that a child may choose is as legitimate as another.

Means of achieving spatial illusion

Size contrast.   Although two men may be roughly the same size, the one who is farther away will appear smaller to the naked eye. This observable difference registered on the two-dimensionable surface convinces the viewer that there is distance (space) between two persons or usually equal objects when one is smaller than the other.

Very young children as well as adults in some cultures do not employ this illusionary technique and are more interested in assigning size according to emotional importance, or power (magic), of the object or person. But the preadolescent in our culture is generally anxious to make things look "real." In the painting below, the artist has placed an enlarged figure in the foreground, creating a sense of space.

Grade seven — girl

Identical shapes of different sizes cut out and organized into groups or graded into a regular progression can create a sense of distance or movement into the depth of the picture plane. Ask children to take a simple shape through such a gradation, as in the painting shown.

Grade five — boy

Use of sharp and diminishing detail (*atmospheric space*). It is a fact that the human eye does not see near and distant objects with the same clarity. Those far away seem blurred and comparatively lacking in definition. (Refer the child to knowledge he possesses of the focussing operations of his camera. Use this to motivate painting experiences.

Textural surfaces for spatial effects. Sharp, clean, bold textures tend to advance. More subtle, subdued textures tend to recede. When texture is distributed over the entire picture area, the flatness of the picture plane is preserved. These qualities can be noted by the students when they make collages and mixed media paintings or drawings.

Not showing depth on a surface has presented as much of a challenge to the modern artist as showing it. Using current works as a stimulation, the teacher can devise many exercises to give children an opportunity to experience this genre.

1. Have shapes touch each other to produce a sensation of very shallow space. (Marca-Relli)

2. Cover the picture completely with some uniformly sized single element, by stamping a pattern over the surface either before or after the major shapes are rendered. This tends to limit depth. (Klee)

3. Show that interwoven planes cut off perception of depth. (Cubists)

4. Show that overlapping transparent forms have a similar effect.

5. Spray mists of color over surfaces. (Rothko or Olitski)

6. Fill interwoven patterns with poured paint to create a richness which suggests depth but maintains the feeling of a flat surface. (Pollock)

7. Ask children to do a series of experiments by dabbing colors upon colors in thick dabs to produce a crusted rich surface interesting enough to engage the observer. (Pousette-Dart)

Directional lines. Line, when it implies continuous direction, creates a strong illusion of depth, especially when the emphasized direction is diagonal. Suggest subject matter to children or motivate them with visual aids to utilize these factors. Topics might be: serpentine paths in the park; twisting roads down a mountain; the zigzagging beach line; going up stairs to the attic; the curved slope of a hill; a circular driveway; a meandering brook.

Spatial qualities of color Modern artists since Cézanne have made us aware of the spatial characteristics of color, advancing their color up to and beyond the picture surface as well as into it. In this painting by a sixth-grade boy, color is used in such proportion and with such intensity as to cause the brilliant

Yellow Cab to appear to recede. Note that the bright red traffic light on the pole also stays back from the surface.

Grade six—boy

Ask the children to draw a simple objective shape like the taxicab above. Boats, oversized vegetables or fruits, and space ships are also good subjects. Using the object as a pattern, encourage them to compose several paintings of the same thing in different colors.

Realistic empty space   Large empty sections in a painting give a sense of spaciousness. Children can quickly become aware of this.

Children can create paintings in which objects or persons appear against an unmodulated stretch of background color. If the figures or objects have bulk and volume, the contrast between them and the flatness of the background will be exciting.

Overlapping   When one object partially covers another, the one in front appears to be nearer, regardless of size. In the painting of the crowd entitled "Demonstration" we see a very elaborate use of overlapping. However, most preadolescents often have difficulty with this concept. Note the ambiguous situation with regard to the girl behind the horse. The project pictured below was devised by the teacher to help the children with these problems if they seem worried about it. They were asked to use rectangular pieces of paper to represent people in a crowd. Some children, like this sixth-grade girl, will find it easier to overlap pieces of paper than to figure out how to discontinue a part and pick it up again where overlapping occurs. Many students can do it best by starting with collage and later translating the experience to drawing and painting. Painting a crowd as represented only by heads or legs will stimulate size gradation as well as overlapping.

Grade six—boy

Grade five—girl

Grade six—girl

Function of values   When a light source is assumed to be in front of the work, objects will appear to be in the foreground. The items in back will appear progressively darker as they move deep into the painting. When the light source is located at the back of the painting, the order will be reversed. Shadows sometimes aid in creating the illusion of distance. Advancing and receding values produce the impression that the various parts are ahead of or behind each other. A sense of space and volume is the result. Solids, volumes and masses rendered with gradations of values will automatically suggest three dimensions. Diminishing their sizes in contrast with one another will suggest distance. The teacher can create exercises along these lines for children who will benefit from them.

Position of the picture plane   Spatial effects can be achieved by going up on the picture plane. If the teacher suggests a subject such as the city, she may stimulate the desire to move up on the paper. Such a painting can be motivated by asking the question "Can you do a painting showing both sides of the street?" and suggesting that construction paper be used.

Use of transparencies Use tissue paper, gelatin, and cellophane (or acrylics which can produce glazes). Have the children draw, cut out, and then paste and/or paint objects which have appeal for them—a football, toy compass, diving goggles, baseball, flowers, or perfume bottle. They can then compose a picture in which the inner or the outer design is created by the overlapping parts. Children who can tolerate more complexity might be encouraged to draw the objects from many angles as well as overlapping them.

Expanding personal spatial concepts The teacher can help children expand their methods of showing space when they become dissatisfied with their present techniques. For example, a child had difficulty rendering a convincing crowd, and after some suggestions which brought no response, the teacher asked the child to cut out paper figures which could be placed around the right wing (see below). The child created with paper dolls which he pasted on. Another child complimented him and said he should make them of different sizes so that some would seem nearer.

Probably the new way of rendering space did not have real meaning for him as yet. Only perceptions which occurred through his own body would be the assimilated ones that he could render visually. Still, it is possible that through numerous visual experiments, he would come upon methods which would give him some satisfaction in this transitional period when moving from one concept to another.

Grade five—boy

Ask children to think what the world would look like from a swing, seesaw, or roller coaster, and render the experience. In a painting of the tennis net, the boy pretended he was a small insect, which enabled him to paint a common scene from an odd position. Or, as in the painting shown, ask the children to paint the world as viewed through a pair of binoculars.

Grade six—boy

Several sixth-grade girls were provided with textured paper and asked to use spatial concepts different from their usual practice. In their paintings the sense of plane was utilized. One used the textured paper as grass, another as water; a third made a rug out of it.

Children can experience different spatial possibilities by painting two aspects of their chosen subject, as in the faraway "general view" and close-up "specific view" of the orchestra below.

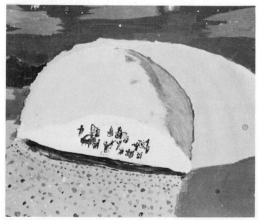

Grade six—boy

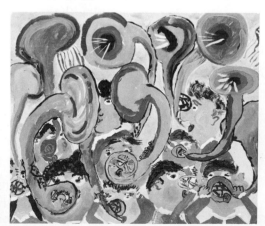

Grade six—girl

COLOR

It is quite widely believed that of all the elements of painting, color is the most dynamic, its impact the most compelling. The response to color is immediate and involuntary; emotion is stirred by the tonal sequences, by the intensity, and above all by the effect of juxtapositions. Though color is often used to describe objects realistically, it is capable of becoming a completely abstract element. Because of its relation to heat, light, and the survival of living things—it may be structured as harmonics, as power, as deep feeling, or as mood ranging from lyric to deathly.

For some painters, color can become the *raison d'etre*, superseding entirely the rest of the elements. For Josef Albers, for instance, color is stimulus, idea, experience. He has abstracted objective reality into his private world of interacting, moving, ordered color. Out of his esoteric experimentation in one painting comes the idea for the next.

The harmonies of Albers are entirely different from the bold drama of Hoffman; the spirituality of Rothko's color is a far cry from the somber moods of Reinhardt. The expressionists sought to reveal psychological realities through color, while the impressionists used it to put man into an atmosphere of lyric air and space. Persian painters created an opulent, sensuous environment; the Chinese chose a restrained palette to embody their view of life. Matisse wanted his paintings to express with their color a feeling of freedom, joyousness and love, and to appear casual and unlabored. Yet, he warned the aspiring painter, this could not be achieved through a casual knowledge of color. Its properties and structures must be studied before it could be used intelligently.

Mid-twentieth-century America saw a full release of color in abstract expressionism. Not all of the painters in this movement were accomplished colorists, but Guston, Pollock and Rothko are outstanding. Currently the optical school of painters, with their stress on pure color relationships, may come closer to capturing the essence of color. The forms are usually geometric or semigeometric, freed of associative overtones which distract the viewer from the primary aesthetic intent: pure color sensation and its spatial (optical) implications. What is color for the painter? According to Hans Hofmann, it is

the perception of plastic and psychological differences in the quality of light . . . color is an effect of light in relation to form and its inherent texture. In nature, light creates color; in painting, color creates light [12: p. 71].

Functions and qualities Fundamentally children should be brought to an awareness that simultaneous contrasts and interaction between colors are of utmost importance in creating with color. The eye must be trained to perceive the dynamic reciprocal energy of adjacent colors. This involves perception of vibrations, immediate transitions, the effect of light on color, color temperature, and weight—for some colors appear to be warm or cool, heavy or light.

On the technical side, it is essential to become aware of the active properties or characteristics of each color. Individually each has hue (red, green, blue, etc.), tone (dark to light), and chroma, which is the saturation, or amount of hue, in a color. With practice these learnings increase the child's power to use color dynamically.

Associative meanings   Local, or descriptive, color in the outside world gives us the red of an apple, the green of leaves, the blue of sky. It has an important function in representational painting.

Symbolic color has to do with the hues that have from time to time taken on different meanings in various societies. In Catholic countries, the fuchsia worn by the cardinals became a symbol of rank. Red and green in the world of technology and communication have come to mean danger and safety. Purple has connoted royalty in the Western world; in the Oriental world white is often the color for mourning instead of our black. The olive drab for the soldier, white collar for the middle-class worker, green or orange for the Irish spirit, red for revolutionaries demonstrate that color, through constant use, take on broad unofficial meanings. There are times when artists use these symbols for communication.

Expressionistic color has grown out of the belief that red, blue, yellow, and other hues have different effects on us psychologically and emotionally. The artist may understand the impact of emerald green and use it for this reason alone. Kokoschka's red nude is neither descriptive nor symbolic; it is a startling psychological punch, the degree of the blow depending on the disposition of the viewer and his reactions to red. We respond to symbolic color with recognition but to expressionistic color with a gut reaction. The latter establishes immediately an overall sensation, emotion, mood.

Whether employed for realism, expressionism, impressionism, or any other aesthetic purpose, color is always structural. It is composed, or ordered; it is related to the other elements; juxtaposition, hue, tone, intensity, and contrast are chosen to obtain a fully intended artistic result.

Techniques, tools, and methods of expanding color experiences   Experience in color can start the moment children see an attractive array of paints. To motivate and entice, colors should if possible be on display and in clear containers. When the child sees the colors next to each other, he automatically feels the effect of the colors on each other; no words are necessary.

When the children themselves are responsible for the arrangement of the paint table where selections are made, they often vie with each other for the pleasure of handling and sorting the colors. They can be encouraged to arrange them in families, as they are classified in the color systems, according to a graded scale. The teacher should have on hand large-sized visual aids as well as color demonstration charts of all kinds. A portfolio of visual materials from which such effects as simultaneous contrasts can be quickly produced, is very useful. They are often important in helping an individual child or a group with a problem and should be available when they count.

Mixing trays and sponges for rinsing the water from a brush before loading it with a new color are essential. A good-sized water container with a large bottom and a wide mouth is advisable. The children can become intrigued with equipping their trays. In one school they called the painting materials center the "painting cafeteria"; brushes were knives and forks, sponges were napkins, water the beverage, and the different paints the food. The paints should include tempera, poster, and powdered tempera, gouache, transparent watercolors, and synthetic water-based paints. In addition, the children should have colored chalks and pastels of all kinds, aniline dyes and inks, felt-nibbed pens, and crayons of all kinds.

Techniques of applying color which preadolescents can explore include wet and dry brush painting, spatter, sponging and squeegee application, resists, roller painting, marbling, stick and finger painting, encaustic, blockout (stencilling), Q-tip painting (pointillism), and airbrush painting (fixative).

Any surface is suitable for painting; vellum, bogus, manila, newsprint, and construction papers, and cardboards are usually available in school. These come in a range of sizes. Rolls of paper for murals come from 4 to 6 feet wide and many yards long. The teacher can provide more variety, depending on the budget. Canvas paper, masonite boards and stretched canvases would add dimension to the painting experiences. The view of many artists and teachers is that inferior materials hamper, and in fact render impossible, the development of aesthetic sensibility in depth.

Color mixing experiments. Teachers need to be inventive, playful, and (hopefully) well supplied with visual aids to assist them in making some color theory available and useful to their students. Color games of all kinds can be devised during which children pick up information about color mixing. For instance, one day have a "color-in" or "color happening." Using primaries, secondaries and tertiaries already prepared before the session, ask the children how they can express the knowledge they have gained in mixing colors in some sort of dramatic event.

Devise a human color wheel dance, in which children wearing or carrying their chosen color will combine with partners to create the proper secondary or tertiary. A caller, plus square dance music, would expedite the event with directions, atmosphere and rhythm. Or the children could paint large screens or cardboards to create environments within a given range of color.

Another type of review or test is to place a huge sheet of color at the studio door one day. As a child steps on the threshold, a James Bond type of voice says on a tape: "If you want to enter the art room, you have to give the secret color" (complementary color). Outside the door is a stack of various colors for the children to choose from and a box with a slot in it to receive the cards they pick. The child who does not remember can imitate the other students. (Not too much stress should be put on these games. It is far better for children to experiment freely with no possibility of failure involved.)

Using collage for color experiments. Color mixing should be encouraged at all times, but for children of this age collage is an excellent medium for exploring the dynamics of color relationships. It permits them to arrange and rearrange colors and to observe their powers. Collage eliminates the tedious mixing that may cause them to lose interest. Also, a child's choices are not so much conditioned by his previous, often limited, ideas about color. Collage avoids the danger of premixing a color which a child may find repulsive and which will discourage him from exploring beyond the primaries. Both ways of experiencing color are valid, but one may be more useful for a certain child than the other.

The range of color provided by dyed, patterned, and transparent or semitransparent materials far exceeds the range normally available to children using the tempera and watercolors provided in most schools. Other dimensions of color are realized through the texture and finish of materials—rough, mat, shiny. Color saturation experiences are apt to occur more often by manipulating dyed materials. In preparation for making a collage, it is useful for the children to pin a series of colors in a special place to see how they behave and then select the most satisfactory combination. A more formal lesson involves both paint and collage. One or two items are left unpainted in a picture. The child then tries numerous pieces of collage in the blank spots before making a decision. Making and then painting from a collage gives the class the opportunity of turning touched textures into visual ones, providing further insight into color qualities.

Nature's nuances   Leaves, vegetables, fruits, nuts, and other available natural forms can increase the sensitivity to subtle color. Asked to look at them simply as color and nothing else, the child can try to reproduce the mixture of hues and chromatic qualities these objects hold. If a child extends the color all over the page, he will eliminate all distractions of shape and line from the experience as he permeates the surface of his paper with color—the essence of orange, lemon, or spinach leaf.

Color moods: expressive potentialities   A color scheme in a representational work can be felt to be somber, gay, bold, brutal, bleak, etc. Empathy is at work here; color mood is derived from the natural tendency to identify with certain colors and read associations into them. Thus the quality of light in the sky, the gloom of a dingy street, or the joy of summer warmth will summon forth the projection of our emotions. Value dominance and contrast are involved in the creation of mood. Subdued contrasts in all elements are necessary for delicate moods, and forceful oppositions for moods of excitement, violent emotion, and the like.

Color for color's sake: chromatic abstractions   There are exercises and lessons that if properly related to the work of modern painters will liberate some children from their feeling that to succeed they must represent depth, perspective, and recognizable objects. If shown how color itself will provide meaning and subject matter, they will discover how to use color in this way themselves.

1. A first experience might be a series of paintings in which colors (thick tempera) are daubed evenly and consistently over the surface. All subject matter is eliminated, and the children become absorbed in the action of the colors. Ask them to do many paintings, one on top of the other. As they progress, suggest that they concentrate on the color effects in certain areas of the paper that interest them. They can be shown works of painters like Mark Tobey, Milton Resnick and Philip Gustin and encouraged to keep their shapes on the surface, or even in front of the surface of the paper.

2. It is possible to create an environment with color alone, using few or no shapes. If the children use pastels or some crayon medium mixed with turpentine, the translucent effects

will enthrall them. With gelatin, tissue, and cellophane papers, they can also experiment to create new colors.

3. Using a limited number of shapes, create a nonobjective painting, dividing the space simply into four or five divisions. Then repeat the design but change the colors, making the same painting in black, white and gray with matching intensities. Then use the same design, the same hues, but different tonal values.

4. Another project might involve a series of compositions entitled "Expanding Colors," "Contracting Colors," "Cold Colors," "Hot Colors," "Aggressive Colors," "Submissive Colors," "Inflammatory Colors," "Harmonious Colors," and so on.

5. Motivate the children (see Pousette-Dart, "Radiance") to make a nonobjective painting in which the center color seems to come forward toward one; to be followed by the opposite with the center colors receding.

6. Using slides of landscapes or seascapes, showing sunset, fall, winter, or summer forest, blur the screen so that only the solid planes of color can be seen. Explain the purpose of the blurring: to isolate color as an aesthetic reality with an existence of its own. The idea is to convey to the students the power of color masses and to eliminate as much as possible their dependence on detail.

7. Relating to Franz Kline, suggest that the children paint a path of energy against a given space, limiting themselves to one color. The point of this is to bring about some realization of the reaction of the negative space as it is invaded by an energy or force.

8. A trip to the United Nations on a clear, crisp day or to an industrial area on a wet, cold day can inspire subjective color in children's work. Or ask them to cut out a newspaper article that has made a great impression on them, involving some dramatic event, tragedy, war scene, etc., and in a painting to express their feelings about it entirely through color.

9. Reactions to language can stimulate subjective color experiences. There are words that evoke color, often mixed and subtle colors. To enlarge imagination and provide experience in color mixing, suggest that children create colors expressive of the following words:

dark	sun	sociability	floating
anxiety	despair	silence	sinking
laughter	sparkling	falling	sleeping
fear	boredom	flying	waking up
flying	unhappiness	crying	scolding

Children will enjoy comparing how differently each chooses to express a given word.

10. Tastes can also be linked to colors. Have the children paint, without reference to the realistic color of the food, the aromas of turkey, steak, candied sweet potatoes, french fries, chocolate sauce, banana split, onions. Or set up a still life and have the children paint a feast in colors that will either revolt or delight the viewer. Discuss advertising colors and the colors given objects, like toothbrushes, to make them palatable to the general public.

11. Encouraged to explore, children can find magical qualities when representing a wide variety of subjects. Ask them to paint the world around them when seen through colored glasses. A magical experience will occur when children wear paper glasses which have as lenses colored gelatins. A red gelatin will make everything appear red, to be sure, but the variations on the reds are tremendous. (Refer to Ad Reinhardt, "Red Painting," 1952.) A change to blue gelatin will provide other sensations and perhaps some new knowledge of color mixing, saturation, value, etc.

12. The more contemporary solution to representation of movement on the two-dimensional surface has been explored by painters who employ vibration of colors to cause optical illusion of movement. Using the works of Victor Vasarely, Richard Anuszkiewicz and Toni Costa as stimulation for experimentations along these lines will prove very fruitful with preadolescents. The use of cut paper is the simplest means to produce such work, but children can become so intrigued that they will find the patience required to work with paint.

13. Another valuable experience will be to scatter (using printing, painting or collage) dots, ellipses or any small shape across a brilliant field of contrasting color. Afterimages and vibrations occur. (See the work of Larry Poons.)

LIGHT AND DARK Man has always regulated his activities by the rising and setting of the sun and by the changing qualities of light and dark occurring in different seasons. Objects on the surface of paper or canvas would not be visible without the value contrast of dark and light in the whole painting, or without the relationships created by the values of individual objects and figures. It is understandable that the painter has made a cult of light. He thinks about it, watches it as it changes and plays on objects in the environment, and utilizes both its physical and psychological qualities.

Light and dark values interlock and help order the structure of a painting as, in combination with the other elements, they set the pace for the eye to move on a subtle journey of intermediate steps between contrasts and finally to the climax the artist desires. In addition, values may arouse the sensations of touch or weight, which in turn relate to balance and roundness and contribute to depth.

Symbolically and psychologically, light and dark have stood for good and evil. In medieval paintings, the saints were illuminated by halos and the background was gold, to indicate the divine light shining out of their bodies. In the Renaissance, light was used to model volume and convey objects realistically in three-dimensional space. Later Rembrandt, with his emphasis on human personality, used light both symbolically and realistically. While rays seemed to be coming from heaven as a special dispensation to penetrate the darkness in which man lives on earth, pinpointing humanity and providing warmth, these same rays might also be considered as Rembrandt's unconscious, intuitive preview of scientific facts later revealed by physicists.

To the painter of the nineteenth century, light became a symbol of infrequent clarity in a murky world. Beams of spotlights made objects emerge from the dense atmosphere, only to disappear again into the darkness. The message is one of man's mysterious, impermanent survival in an inscrutable universe. It is interesting to compare this with the general brightness of the Egyptian painted scene or the all-sky world of children (13: pp. 293–319).

The impressionists painted bright, luminous environments with the pattering of single brush strokes or dots (pointillism) distributed harmoniously and evenly over the entire canvas. A variety of light and dark (values) operates in each clump, or passage, to form shapes with no definite contours but with different hues. Pronounced local color ceases to exist, nor are there any real darks. Each brush stroke or dot seems to radiate its individual light (13: p. 320).

Cézanne and the cubists perceived light and shade purely as functions on the two-dimensional surface: dark shading toward the contour of a shape causes that shape to recede, and highlights make it come forward. A three-dimensional space resulted, an action back and forth in depth, toward the surface—all without illusionistic light or perspective. In this way the quality of light was achieved without treating it as connected to a natural phenomenon. Artists today use an abstract and inconsistent lighting in order to express their personal, subjective reality (11: p. 100).

Motivating children for light experiences Drill in the use of shading, modeling and chiaroscuro would be stifling and unnecessary for the majority of preadolescents. Many mature artists of the past and present have not been too concerned with accurate rendering of light sources and have been satisfied to use light as it suited their emotional or poetic moods. Chiaroscuro, or the method of conveying roundness through shading, perfected in the Renaissance, may interest some children, but the majority are not overly concerned with this technique, nor should they be, since it is but one of the many ways of responding to and expressing the phenomenon of light and dark.

Far more important than learning techniques, a consideration of light and dark gives the child an insight into the part that values play in the structuring and ordering of a painting. There is also the pleasure of learning through experimenting with values to communicate some of the intensely personal experiences of light that we all have, from the time we are born until we die.

Artificial light a source of inspiration: In the painting shown, we experience the quality of light in an empty office building; its lonely floors are being scrubbed by a hard-working cleaning woman. The drama of the light is the catalyst in this poignantly expressed scene.

Grade six—girl

After the children have chosen subjects based on their own experiences and have faced the many technical problems involved, it may be useful to engage those who are still interested in some basic exploration of light and dark, such as using dark paper to set the condition of night and then suggesting that the students record carefully the changes of color in the illuminated parts of a scene or a still life. (See Luigi Russolo, "Houses and Light," 1912, and Van Gogh, "Night Café," 1888.)

A film and lesson entitled "New York by Night" was created by Elizabeth Wiener while student teaching under Walter Kendra at the Little Red Schoolhouse in New York City. Their aim was to stimulate sixth graders to perceive various effects of soft and glaring lights—the patterns, shadows and spatial effects they make. The children responded to the film on black construction paper 24 by 36 inches in size.

The idea of painting scenes as if looking into lighted windows appealed to many children. One girl indicated the drama of black night and the quiet of the life within. A boy rendered the headlights of a car; one has the feeling that these are one's own eyes peering into the darkness. Another boy remembered important abstract shapes and expressed his feelings of the experience.

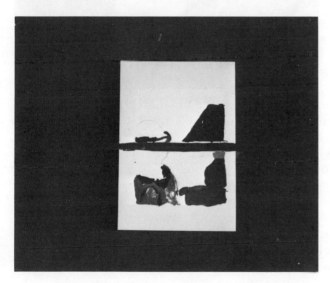

Grade six—girl

Natural light as a resource. Response to natural light in imaginative ways can be motivated by showing slides, films, or photographs of the effect of sunlight or moonlight on objects and landscapes. The children can then create their own lighted scenes in terms of their personal experience, their paintings featuring natural light of sun and stars and moon as poetic expressions of something remembered and now lived all over again in the realm of art: the moon shining through a mist-filled atmosphere as a plane flies by; a herd of horses in the moonlight, the shadows prominent in the meadow. The moon, made of metallic silver, is reflected in a stream. In the figure on page 234, a prehistoric animal bays at the moon.

Sharing these moments of past pleasure often brings children closer to each other. (To supplement visual aids, refer to Henri Rousseau, "The Sleeping Gypsy," 1897; Arthur Dove, "Rise of the Moon," 1937; Miro, "La Lune," 1948; Ryder, "Moonlight," 1880.

Grade six—boy

Firelight is another natural illumination that people of all ages find evocative. Visiting a nearby church or setting up candles in a darkened room can motivate exciting work. Use topics such as "The Campfires," "The Birthday," "The Menorah Candles," "Votive Candles," or "Firelight in a Room." (Refer to Loren McIver's "Red Votive Lights," 1943, or similar paintings.)

Prepainted papers are useful: the children paint a subject suggested by the value and color. Paper can be colored to suggest desert light, early dawn, icy dawn, twilight, fog, high noon on a clear day, light before a storm, or the light on another planet.

Cast shadows. It is not necessary to involve all the students in experiments having to do with cast shadows, but it is possible to give those who are interested some helpful pointers. To discover more about how a light source from a certain direction affects the shape of the shadow, take the children out to the playground on a bright sunny day so that they can trace each other's shadows with a stick on sand or on bare ground. They will play around, combine their shadows, etc., and in the process they will observe, discuss, and acquire some first-hand knowledge. Indoors, the same activity can be accomplished in the gym or any large open area, with the help of strong lights. Time should be devoted to discussion of artists who have utilized shadow not merely to reproduce reality with accuracy but also to communicate subjective meanings and to evoke imaginative connotations.

Below is a painting which includes shadows; the painter was quite aware that the images added drama to the mood and meaning of the painting and in fact were an integral part of the idea.

Grade six—girl

Shading and modeling. For those interested in realistic light and dark technique, the following simple experience may suffice. Choosing either to render an object or do a portrait, the children then use collage materials (limiting colors to black, white and grays to simplify the problem) to model a face or the form of an object by means of close values. Collage is usually a better medium for this than painting because preadolescents are too often impatient to mix the colors in all the values required to give roundness to a form. Scraps from magazine clippings provide a wide range of values and can be moved around until it is discovered where they function best, the children, of course, being still unaware of the anatomy on which structurally sound modeling is based. Most children of this age are quite content to use a nontechnical rendering of light and shadow, as is seen in a work by a sixth-grade boy (see page 236). His soldier's existence is tied to dull browns, yet he glows with a light placed where the young artist feels it should be—in the eyes, on the face, and a little sprinkled on details of the clothing and in the atmosphere.

Grade six—boy

Organizing values to achieve unity. Using a group of bottles stacked in a row, suggest that the children paint, on black paper, first the spots that gleam with the most light, then the less light spots, then those even duller, and so on. Since children are often poor judges of how much paint they should prepare, it is a good idea for the teacher, or students with her guidance, to premix, in large enough quantity for the whole project, a wide range of grays.

The next step is to repeat the exercise on white paper, letting the children choose as they wish from the grays, starting with either the darkest or lightest. Those who wish can turn their exercise into representational paintings by adding color and linear details. Topics might result such as "Horses Waiting Before a Race," "A Crowd," "Dancers Practicing," "The Team," "Homeless Refugees," "Immigrants," "The Poor," or "The Strike." The bottle still lifes can and often will be turned into nonobjective paintings instead. Some children will be satisfied with them as they are.

The final step is to make fresh paintings based on the students' personally chosen subjects, utilizing the range of premixed grays. It is important that the exercises be tied to color; the children shoud be asked to try to match a color to the value range and to do a subsequent painting with it.

Another exercise which expands awareness of the functions of light and dark was conceived by Elizabeth Barbrove, student teacher under the direction of Lois Lord in the New Lincoln School, New York City. Seventh-grade students were asked to make paper collages using grays, blacks and whites. In the collage on page 237, texture and value combine to unify the work.

Grade seven—girl

What is shape? . . . It concerns, first of all, the boundaries of masses. Three-dimensional bodies are bound by two-dimensional surfaces. Surfaces are bound by one-dimensional borders—for example, by lines. The outer boundaries of objects can be explored by the senses without impediment. But the shape of a room, a cave, or a mouth is given by the inner boundaries of solid objects; and in cups, hats, or gloves, outside and inside make up shape together or vie with each other for the title [14: p. 37].

SHAPE

We respond to the squareness, roundness or angularity of a concrete object as well as to its bulk and mass. In fact, these linear qualities define its mass or bulk in a painting as well as in reality. Shape in a painting can be modeled to show its volume or can exist flatly in two dimensions. In either case it has a basic force that operates on us both optically and ideographically. For as Arnheim says, "In the perception of shape lies the beginning of concept formation" (15: p. 27).

Building a vocabulary of shapes Selecting simple forms—stones, pebbles, driftwood, vegetables, pine cones, plants—for the children to handle and to look at is the first necessity, followed by rendering on the two-dimensional surface in a variety of media. Emphasis is placed on likenesses, differences, progressive sizes, angles, and curves as the children handle the shapes and draw them.

1. Variations within the same class of objects can be an eye-opening experience. Arrange still lifes to be called "Potatoes," "Onions," "Carrots," or "Apples" and have the children paint

or draw them, observing that each is shaped differently, though it falls within a general category. Varieties of man-made objects differ in design. Make paintings showing such design variations in sunglasses, diving goggles, or ordinary tools such as pliers, forks, knives, and spoons.

2. Display a group of objects with similar geometric structure: eggs, oranges, balls, crystals, beehives, building blocks, jewels, boxes, and shapes around the room that are combinations of these geometric forms. Ask students to make designs grouping similar or dissimilar shapes, or a combination of two.

3. For fact-loving boys especially, there are good experiments with the geometric shapes which they enjoy identifying and arranging into nonobjective paintings or drawings. Among these are the

trapezium	octagon
parallelogram	pentagon
rhombus	square
obtuse triangle	polygon
hexagon	rectangle
trapezoid	isosceles triangle
scalene triangle	ellipse

4. Albers, Hofmann and Mondrian are all devotees of the square and rectangle. Using these artists for motivation, ask children to make paintings featuring these shapes. (It is possible to repeat this project for every geometric shape.) For another lesson, show them the underlying geometry of the paintings of Cézanne and the cubists.

5. To capture students' interest, play a game in which each child has a piece of paper with various lists of different items; one list might include such a combination as a frog's tooth, an umbrella, five toadstools, and a hand. Another list might combine a lion's tail, an angel's wing, a rocking chair, and an electric stove. Each child then makes a painting using the shapes of the four items, incorporating them into a unified composition. Out of the aggregate of these items come brand new, fresh shapes. Such a game can be played with collage, drawing, and printing as well.

Use of the silhouette Exercises focusing on the silhouette appeal to preadolescents and are an excellent aid to perception of shape. It is not hard to make a portable silhouette screen. Buy an aluminum coat rack on wheels and hang an old sheet from the hat rack section. A simple spotlight can be used behind it. (Such a screen can be rolled away when not in use, or even disassembled and stored.) Place all sorts of items between the sheet and the light. Intricate shapes will do very well, for all shapes are simplified, making it easier to see their edges, size, and quality. Some exercises follow in which attention is focused on shape through use of the silhouette.

1. A good memory game can be played with the silhouette. First, display the item behind the sheet and have the children paint, draw, or cut it out directly from a piece of paper. Remove the object and ask them to cover up their drawing and do it again from memory. Another exercise is to have them paint the object as seen in silhouette, then bring it out in front of the sheet and have them paint it again in all its details and color. Many variations on this game will occur to the imaginative teacher.

2. The study of the silhouette as used in past art would be most rewarding. Extensive users of the technique have been the Africans, American Indians, and Australian aborigines. Their subject matter alone would interest the preadolescent: hunting wild animals with simple weapons; wars and daring raids with man-to-man combat; and feats of physical prowess, such as throwing spears, jumping, running, shooting with bow and arrow, and dancing in tribal ceremonies.

After study in depth of silhouette art as developed by early man, the children may want to do their own silhouette paintings on subjects like "Riding the Range," "The Stampede," "Indian Dances," "The Barn Dance," "Hunting with a Pack of Dogs," "Running after Game," "Street Fight," and "Block Dance."

Storehouse of shapes in city and country

1. A country landscape provides a rich array of shapes. If it is at all possible, children should have the opportunity of sketching them. Before going out, show a large reproduction of a landscape painting and ask the class to discuss, analyze, and sketch the four or five shapes into which the painting will inevitably be organized. After the children have brought back their drawings made in the midst of the country scene, ask them to do a scene in which all objects included fall into a few major categories of shape.

2. Show children paintings of landscapes by painters who distort the real shape of objects as a means of communicating some personal impression or emotion. Use El Greco's "View of Toledo," pointing out the flamelike shapes that appear throughout. Show them the billowing softness of the shapes in Renoir's "In the Meadow." Have them draw or paint a scene emphasizing some

special quality through shapes—angularity, roundness, elongation—as a means of adding emotion and meaning to the work.

3. Introduce children to the works of Ellsworth Kelly, tracing the derivation of his forms from plants. Ask them to see if they can isolate, enlarge and give unrealistic color to forms in nature which intrigue them.

4. If confined to the city, take children on trips to photograph objects of the urban environment. Focus attention on theme or one type of object. Later the slides or photos will be pooled and children moved to do a cityscape. Concentration by the group on one theme will allow for an in-depth exploration of it, a view enriched by the sensibility of many. Use of the camera promotes objectivity of vision, training the child to isolate and concentrate. Since the camera takes in more detail than the human eye, the child has more material to think about. Also the camera makes permanent, significant movements and transformations in shapes easily missed in the fast-moving events of life; on these the child can meditate.

Printing as a means of focusing on shape   Printing, like collage, offers versatility in teaching about individual shapes and in composing shapes into an interacting whole. In either, each shape can be held apart as a separate unit, manipulated, tested in various positions, and repeated to discover where it functions best. In painting, unless one has quick-drying paint, this testing can be a difficult process. It may be impossible to paint a light shape over a dark one. Printing is magical and quick; accidents can be turned into assets, an important feature for this age level. Furthermore, it is a technique that is logical and appropriate in our mass media culture. Warhol, Lichtenstein and other pop artists have structured their work on processes derived from the printing press and the panoply of advertising reproductive techniques.

1. Stenciling is a simple way to create a shape. Place found, cut or torn shapes on a piece of paper and pass an inked roller over them. They will mask out the ink and leave their outlines printed on the surface. In his book *Introducing Surface Printing* Peter Green suggests another method of roller printing which can lead to many new discoveries. Before printing, place forms on the inked roller itself, using silver paper, leaves, or anything which will stick to the surface of the roller.

2. Cardboard relief printing is another easy technique for exploring shape. The cutting, handling, pasting, and printing involved increases awareness of the quality of shapes.

Negative and positive shapes The background, or negative shape in a composition, is the part not occupied by the major figures, objects, or symbols, which are referred to as positive shapes. If there is a tension built up between these two elements, both of them may be more vitally realized as figure or ground, and every part of the composition becomes activated and interesting. Attention has to be turned on the negative shapes, which are usually neglected because the artist becomes so involved with the positive figure that he is fashioning. How his figure affects the dynamics of the whole often goes unperceived. Several suggestions have been devised to focus on this problem.

1. Using two pieces of equal-sized paper of contrasting hues or black and white, lay them over each other and cut a piece out of the top one. This gives the experience of taking away from the whole.

2. Ask the children to paint shapes on a paper. Then cut forms from the same paper (preserving the edge), perhaps cutting into the painted forms. New shapes appear when the original paper is placed on a fresh paper of another color. (See Hans Arp, "Mountain, Table, Arrows, Navel," 1925.)

3. Another project involves three pieces of paper and three steps. Cut several simple shapes from one paper. Arrange these on a second paper. Arrange on the third piece of paper the "negative" shapes left over when the positive shapes were cut from the first one. This exercise dramatizes the idea that both positive and negative shapes have force and importance.

4. Using folded sheets of many layers of thin paper, ask the children to cut out a number of identical shapes and arrange them in different series and relations on various papers. The equivalent power of the positive shape and the shape formed by the background will become obvious as it is seen how the negative shape changes and is activated in different ways as the cut-out shapes are put in different juxtapositions. Using one constant positive shape makes the background activity more discernible. (The works of Jack Youngerman, Al Held, and Ellsworth Kelly provide excellent resources.)

Shape related to mass, volume, and line How does the inside of a shape affect the contour or edge of it? What effect does a bulky shape—a mass—have on the space which surrounds it? These questions have perpetually stimulated artists in every age who have devoted experimentation and the passion of pursuit to their solution.

1. Take children to a natural history museum or a zoo. There have them draw animals in pastel or cray-pas, rendering as much as possible the sense of bulk and mass they observe. On their return, introduce them to the work of prehistoric cave painters, who rendered their animals on the irregular surface of the cave walls, utilizing the variations of the surface to give bulk and reality to their animals. Out of plaster or papier-maché a format resembling a wall with the same uneven surface as found in caves can be created. Using their drawings from the museum, changing them to utilize the bumps, swellings and concavities, children will be able to give three-dimensionality to their works and thereby understand more fully the close relation between linear contour and mass.

2. Contemporary uses of pictorial space deploy force, tension and stress of shapes. Shape, or form, and space are closely related; space is compressed by forms as they crowd in upon each other. This tension is felt by the viewer. An imaginative teacher can set up projects to illustrate this concept, allowing children to participate to some extent in the experience.

Have the children make a landscape in which the weight of the sky is pressured against the bulk of jagged rocks. Or show the force of the sea as it pushes against the resisting sky; the mountains thrusting into the atmosphere; underground gas pressuring the earth; the pull of gravity on the growing forms of nature; torrents of rushing water and the withstanding wall of the dike. If the children choose only the essential colors for these paintings and simplify details, the forces at work will be more obvious. Then have them paint the same pressures non-objectively. (See works of Nicolaes de Staël.)

3. Bring rocks to school which the children can then sketch or paint for mass and volume, trying to describe visually the activating forces inside and around them.

4. Put various objects in brown paper bags—solid objects, or at least those having mass—such as vegetables, fruits, bones, bowls, and boxes, along with skeletal objects which combine line with volume—seaweed, plants, sea forms, coral, clusters of leaves, twigs, etc. Have children feel them without looking into the bag. The sense of touch will bring new realizations about shape and the structure of objects.

5. Objects can be conceived of as having inside firmness which supports them and gives them shape. Children can be sensitized to these underlying structures. Have them dissect fruits, plants, vegetables, and animal parts to see and draw how they are structured from within, and/or have them study books on botany, medicine or biology. Such experiences reveal the relationship between line, volume and mass, provide factual

knowledge, and bring to the child a vast new world of shapes to add to his consciousness. For further reading see *Form, Space, Vision,* by Graham Collier (16).

Interpenetrating shapes Exciting paintings and collages can result from the use of interpenetrating forms. (Show children appropriate works by Picasso, Gris and Braque, indicating the reasons for their experimentations.)

1. Have children overlap and paste a number of transparent and translucent materials (tissues, cellophanes, gelatins) against a background of opaque or transparent paper. Where the papers overlap, they will find new shapes in subtle varied colors.

2. For this project, children are asked to draw or paint on individual pieces of paper various still life objects conveniently placed around the room and then to cut them out. They are then to overlap, cut, and combine these original drawings into compositions, emphasizing how the objects (shapes) seem to penetrate each other.

3. As a first step, have children paste a given shape or two on a format. Then, as they draw from a still life, they are to interweave these shapes as part of several objects. The result is a stunning interpenetrating pattern of shapes.

4. Impress children with the idea that they can paint what they *know* as well as what they can see of an object. Using a fruit or vegetable, motivate them to paint it from above, in front, from the side, and from below. They can render it flatly or with volume, in light and shadow, with texture, or in a combination of all these methods. Encourage them to cut, peel, and slice it in every possible way and draw all the parts. Study seeds, stem, and leaves, and draw them. Then have them reassemble the object by cutting and pasting together their own sketches.

In the final discussion of this project, point out to the children that they have gone beyond the mere external appearances and have penetrated to the essence of the object. They now comprehend it in its totality. There will be some who are scientifically curious and will be interested in such an idea. Some will gain a better understanding of the many aspects of reality which are of concern to modern painters.

MOTION

The twentieth-century artist has developed, according to Gyorgy Kepes, "Instead of the old fixed point of perspective . . . the perspective of growth; instead of static order, the dynamic of rhythm" (17: p. 196).

We have come a long way from the concept of a static universe with the sun moving around it. We know we are whirling on our own axis even as we move with the other planets around the sun. In fact, all matter is now considered by physicists as agglomerations of energy. Nothing is truly solid or fixed in nature; everything is merely moving at higher or lower frequencies. Discoveries involving internal combustion and electricity have fabulously increased the pace of twentieth-century living. We have achieved and passed the speed of sound. Computers do mathematics faster than by human computation. Concepts of mobility and change stir society everywhere.

Preadolescents, who are just coming into consciousness of the forces in the environment all around them, are very mobile creatures themselves. At a peak of physical energy, they are growing and changing and pushing rapidly from phase to phase, full of psychic forces often out of balance within themselves. They are in a hurry, and they are quite naturally interested in speed. At this age, therefore, children respond with enthusiasm to any lesson or discussions about movement in drawing or painting and have an instinct to express the dynamics they feel throbbing not only in the machine landscape around them but kinesthetically in their own bodies and minds.

In a painting, it is the interaction of all the elements—line, color, value, shape, texture—that causes rhythmic movement. The artist creates a time-related structure: up-down, left-right, light-dark, large-small, curved-straight, short-long. Movement is a linear path created for the eye. It provides both action and intervals of repose as it travels through the picture plane in a time sequence, progressing toward a culmination or emphasis which clarifies the ultimate meaning or intent of the work.

There are certain subjects that have always been associated with motion in painting—skaters, runners, dancers, horse races, and auto races. Such themes are natural for children, since their lives are so often involved with sports. They can easily understand and adopt the visual symbolism of relating, for instance, certain body gestures to running or skiing, indicating wind by flowing scarves or hair or swaying branches. They quickly notice the effect that undulating lines and strong diagonals have on the movement in a drawing or painting.

Many ways to stimulate works with motion involve using objects which themselves are capable of mobility. Motor cars, planes, boats, missiles, trains, and all kinds of machines can be shown on films to help recall experiences. Ask them to note how the natural elements, such as water, wind, rain, and sleet, can increase the sense of motion when represented by use of strong directional lines or patterns in association with them. The splashing mud as well as the shape of the vehicle gives a sense of action in the work of this sixth-grade boy.

Grade six—boy

Creating the illusion of motion   Blurring objects in painting will give the illusion that they are moving; a speeding vehicle appears blurred to the naked eye, and the viewer will automatically make the association. Suggest to the children that they experiment with this technique. Have children pretend they are inside the speeding vehicle looking out at the passing scene. Then paint their observations and sensations. A sixth-grade boy made this painting, entitled "Train." He used a blurring technique to indicate where the train had been.

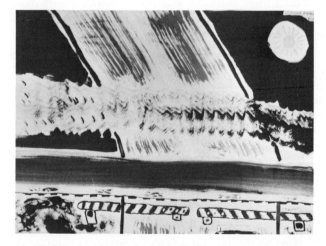

Grade six—boy

Repetition is an important technique in creating an illusion of movement. Encourage children to make paintings whose subject matter involves repetition naturally, as in the painting on page 246 by a sixth-grade girl. Note the directional surge; on the skating rink the children seem to be going in a circle. Details such as the clump of snow emphasize the direction. The texture of the small linear patterns which indicate that the wind is blowing enhance the sense of movement.

Grade six—girl

Continuous lines moving in the same direction create movement. An auto race or paintings involving streams or other waterways are subjects the children enjoy both for their associations and for the rhythmic experience they provide. If the children cannot achieve this repetitive effect, help them by suggesting that they draw one element of their painting, cut it out, and trace it over and over again. For nonobjective expression where repetition and rhythm are desirable, ask the children to cut out a number of identical shapes (folding the paper into many thicknesses reduces the tedium of making each shape). Then demonstrate to them how a steady progression along a given line will create a sense of movement. It is the intervals between the shapes that produce the effect. A rhythm or beat or faster tempo can be achieved by varying the spaces, color accents, values, or the size of the shapes. Compounded accents or intervals can create complex rhythms. The ingenious teacher can build an infinite number of experiences on these principles. (For instance, play a simple, favorite piece of music and have the children translate it into a rhythmic pattern on paper.)

1. Diagonals, for example, invariably convey a sense of motion. Line can instigate movement and beat within a two-dimensional work. Show children paintings illustrating the power of the diagonal line and motivate them with appropriate subject matter.

2. Shape affects the rhythm of a painting. The wedge, for instance, expresses more mobility than the square or rectangle.

Preadolescents know a good deal about velocity and streamlining and will enjoy using this knowledge in their work.

Shapes become active depending on the degree to which they slant or seem to be pulled toward the earth by gravity. Ask the children to modify the lines and shapes in one of their completed paintings. They will be able to discern that angular lines and shapes seem more active. (Show them Maurice Vlaminck's "Vase of Flowers," Juan Gris' "The Chessboard," or others.)

3. Abbreviation (recording only essentials) provides another means of registering movement. Have the children sketch a game taking place in the gymnasium, emphasizing the action in a linear way, using as few lines as possible. (Movies are also useful as motivation.) Show the class the works of artists who have used curtailed figures, stylizations, and broad directional movements to suggest action. (Drawings of Rembrandt, Rodin, Matisse, Picasso are illustrative.)

Symbols are abbreviated devices suggesting motion and action. Have the children cut out directional patterns, such as the arrow, from posters from magazines or from their own sketches on colored, patterned, or textured paper. Suggest they make a group mural combining their own work with found pictures. This gives them a chance to do intricate work at different rates of speed. Other symbols to use as themes are the glider plane, the bird, lightning, or a hand with a pointed finger. (See "The Early Bird," by E. McKnight Kauffer.)

In his wall paintings, primitive man used the dotted line or dashes as a way to express motion, to indicate the direction of an arrow, or the tracks of an animal, or a man running. Today this same device is used in comic strips. Children are familiar with these action symbols. In a fifth-grade boy's painting of a hockey game the path of the puck is painted.

Grade five—boy

Dynamism of modern life Crowds, the subway rush, airplane flights, police chases, war scenes, interplanetary combat with x-ray guns, the electric eye, and all kinds of motors and machines can be stimulating, action-packed subjects for expression in painting. The complex communication systems and networks of today also make fascinating material for youngsters.

Have children picture how vision and sound travel all over the world by wireless, radio, TV, cablegrams, walkie-talkies, interplanetary messages, from space ships, etc. (Use Herbert Bayer's "Messages through the Atmosphere.")

Suggest that they draw the paths of travelers—map pictures—motivating with such topics as "The Stanley-Livingston Story," "The Expedition of Lewis and Clark," or "My Trip to Camp Minipeg," "The Subway System," or "Path of the Number 2 Bus." A project can be devised picturing the dynamics of human activity—the throw of a lasso, wielding of a sledge hammer, casting of a fishing line. The idea can be taken further by suggested topics such as "If Looks Could Kill," "Taking in the Scene," "Exchanging Glances," "The First Time I Saw You," "Transfixed by a Glance," "Looking Around," "Seeing Places," and "The Hypnotic Glance." Or ask the children to show, nonobjectively, the path of a corkscrew form, a whirling disk, an electric saw, pistons, the jerk of the printing press, or the blast of the blow torch.

Responding to motion in natural phenomena Movements, pressures, eruptions, currents, floods, and raging atmospheres of nature can provide endless inspiration. Fish and bird migrations, windblown water, and shifting sand are conducive to nonobjective paintings emphasizing the undulation, speed, and changeability of the natural environment. Movies, photographs and

Grade five—girl
Waterfall

field trips for observation furnish themes and ideas. On occasion the children will discuss current natural disasters: a volcano eruption or other natural explosions, mountain landslides, a forest fire, a tornado, a wild coastal storm, or a blizzard. Through discussion and visual aids, the teacher can provide details children lack which will give their work the realism they want and a variety of new forms. Waterfall, river, sea—all moving water is an expression of mobility. (Movie closeups of the ocean dashing against the rocks are useful.)

The movement of birds, clouds, and colors in the sky can inspire children. The inventive teacher will find the phenomena of nature full of fertile opportunities. Movement in the sky is felt and seen in the whiplash of the wind or as the snow falls quietly in a simple vertical pattern.

Representing objects in motion   Analytical cubists broke the object down into its geometric components. This opened the way for the Futurists (Balla, Severeni, Carra, Russolo, Boccioni), who attempted to render the self-propelled object in motion and to imbue it with its inherent dynamism. A horse running is something entirely different from a horse standing still. "For instance, it must be given twenty legs!" as Haftmann writes. He continues:

At that time photographers, in order to illustrate motion, had superimposed pictures of individual phases of motion, obtaining a synthetic picture showing the individual phases in juxtaposition [11: p. 108].

The futurists were obsessed with "simultaneity." Their objects appeared as if multiplied in space, cut into sections by their own vibrations. The various images in motion penetrated each other in a geometric multiplicity. In an exaltation of speed they transmitted the pure optical sensation of motion, the compression of space-time into simultaneity. They were the first artists to take the machine for their subject matter and glorify the new development of transportation and communications. The frenzied appetite for speed that has characterized the twentieth century was prophesied in their works. "Here for the first time in modern art, the idea of movement takes precedence over the perception of movement or the emotions associated with it" (18: p. 43).

Rendering objects in motion   Each child can take one of his own paintings, not a favorite, and cut it on the paper cutter into patterns which are either vertical, horizontal or square, then rearrange them into their original format, but leaving spaces between the cut parts. A feeling of movement will result. A more dramatic movement can be achieved by stepping up or down each individual piece in a coherent pattern. The use of wavy cuts may be particularly suitable for certain subjects. Children may become confused if they cut too many at once. It is best for them to cut a few, paste them, then cut some more, and so on. (Show them certain kinds of advertisements using this technique.)

There are many ways to motivate children to paint the motion of objects. One project involves a fish tank minus fish, but full of water, mildly agitating. Dangle in the water some objects or shapes. Have the children paint the shifting sequence of images, either one over the other or separately, as they wish. Ask them also to change the spaces between the objects. If the teacher wishes to emphasize floating slow motion and the quality of suspension, the fish tank experience can be followed by a study of Miro's mysterious and vague sense of balancing in space ("Composition," 1933). As a follow-up, the children could be asked to paint objects suspended in the atmosphere, under such topics as "Dream Sequence," "Outer Space," or "Weightlessness." Another experiment can be done with an ordinary electric fan and materials that will flutter in the wind, such as strips of cloth or paper and/or objects that make noise when they move. As the children paint the changing forms as they are blown by the fan, emphasis will be on fast, fluttering motion. Relate the lesson to painters and sculptors who have reveled in this quality, such as the Greeks and Botticelli. Bicycle wheels or spinning tops can be useful in stimulating children to notice and render objects in motion. If they are interested, they can perhaps take off from such topics as "Buggy Ride," "Stage Coach," "The Bike Ride," "Hot Rod Race," "Speedliner Train," or "The Takeoff" (propellers). To show changing shapes on a two-dimensional surface, objects that the children have drawn can be cut out—fish, car, dog, starfish, star—in duplicate, using thin tissue paper in several colors. Arranging these to stimulate motion, they can be used for themes such as "Fish in Water," "Fish on the Line," "Dog Race," and so on.

The multiple image Twentieth-century interest in the multiple image grew out of the aesthetic concepts of cubists and futurists, who attempted to respresent a fusion of objective and subjective reality. They depicted different aspects of reality interpenetrating each other, paralleling Freudian psychological concerns. "Objects in motion and environment were fused, the inner and the outer were represented as one, simultaneously, without regard for natural appearance" (11: p. 109).

Using the preadolescents' desire for self-discovery and understanding of others, ask the class to make a painting called

"Memories," "The Passage of Time," or "My Childhood," utilizing, if they wish, mixed media to aid them in expressing the various reminiscences that occur to them, such as seasons and memorable or dramatic events. (Show them Marc Chagall's "I and My Village," 1911.)

A portrait of a person getting old before one's eyes is a stimulating theme for a multiple-image painting. Or the class might do a painting called "Evolution," showing the development of man from the past to the present or from the present into an imagined future. They will respond to this topic since it gives them an opportunity to show off some of the scientific facts they already know. Other topics could be "The Time Machine," "The Fourth Dimension," "Intervals of Silence," and "Space Travel." Science films showing the embryo or plants and flowers growing are very useful. The challenge is to capture the significant steps of structural change as these living things grow. Many time-space paintings will result from this experiment. Multiple-image pictures can also be inspired by such topics as "Watching a Tennis Match," "Talking to Two People at Once," "Reflections in the Water," or "Shadows on the Wall."

LINE

In painting, drawing, collage, and print making, line is an element which defines the limits and edges of shapes, masses, colors, values, or textures. Line exists as a threadlike substance which by itself can evoke emotional responses. Closely linked with motion, line may be a propelling force carrying the other elements into action. Depending on the format of the drawing or painting medium and the tool used, a line can appear as wide, narrow, prominent, or almost invisible. Each person has a characteristic quality in his expression modified by the medium used.

Children should be motivated to observe the works of many contemporary artists who have used the line almost exclusively and with great invention. Barnett Newman, William Turnbull, Morris Louis are painters working in this manner.

Tools and media   To give children a full experience with line, it is important to provide a variety of tools and media. Ink, glue, paint, chalks and charcoal and crayons of all kinds, felt-nibbed pens, brushes of different size, as well as objects found by the children which make a mark — all these contribute to the development of line sensitivity and the acquisition of skill.

Line and subject matter   At times, to broaden children's conception of line, teachers can suggest themes possessing opportunities to develop linear qualities. Windows in cityscapes invariably form linear patterns. Other man-made structures, such as bridges, bicycle wheels, and roller coasters, fall into the same category. Trees stripped of their leaves reveal their basic linear structure. Tennis net, made of twine can be represented only in line; the court, too, must be marked out in lines. When children are spontaneously painting or drawing from their immediate environment, they will naturally develop a sensitivity to the linear structure in both its two- and three-dimensional aspects.

Grade five—boy

Line and movement   To stimulate the sense of line as movement, use appropriate short sequences from certain films ("Indian Attack," "The Infantry," "Chasing the Robber," "Charge," "Retreat," "Racing," "Dancing," "Stampeding," "Horses," "Cattle," "Sheep," "Hens," "Movements of Flocks of Chickens," "Ducks," or "Gulls.")

After showing a sequence from a film on wildlife in Africa and a film on some domestic animals, play a game in which the children create line with the movement and gait of an elephant or giraffe, snake, hippopotamus, gazelle, monkey, chicken, beaver, rabbit, or pigeon.

Using the Charles Eames movie *Blacktop,* in which sudsy water runs in patterns over the asphalt paving of a school yard (or another film, perhaps one made by the teacher), have the children contemplate and express in any medium the lines created by moving water.

Suggest a subject like "An Abrupt Change of Direction," to be rendered with angular, curved or straight lines.

People and animals in action can be cut out, and with tracing paper the children can indicate major directions of their movements. Then from memory, not looking at either tracing or cutouts, they might compose the figures into a painting.

By pasting gummed dots at random, spaced at varying distances from each other, in a pleasing design on a surface, children can create abstract patterns or recognizable images by connecting the lines between the points. They may use one or several colors and thicknesses of line: wavy, dashed, or straight lines to make the connections.

Fluid, continuous line   It is a useful exercise to experiment with the unbroken line, overlapping itself and creating a flowing arabesque of motion. Water displays at a fair, fountains in the park, sprays from the garden hose, birds in flight, a plane lifting off, landing, soaring, or sky writing, billows of smoke from a chimney, a tea kettle steaming, or steam from a train engine all are excellent subjects for motivating nonobjective paintings. Some children might be interested in making the lines of a group of trapeze artists as they swing, flip over, and catch each other, or the lines a diver makes as he flies from the diving board into the water. They might combine on the same paper a swan dive, a jackknife, and a double flip. Or suggest the twirl of the drum majorette's stick in continuous linear movement.

By making a continuous line with paint that shines in the dark, neon signs can be created for nightclubs, restaurants, movie houses, etc. This would make an interesting exhibit ("The City") to be shown in a darkened place.

A line on a dark surface points up qualities of line not usually noticed. An object, group of objects, or a portrait can be painted using continuous light lines on black or dark surfaces. (See Paul Klee's "The Mocker Mocked," 1930, Museum of Modern Art.)

Morris Louis pours paints over the surfaces of his canvases to produce elegant fluid linear images. Preadolescents can explore and experiment in this vein.

Value and volume with line

1. Closely placed parallel lines or highly contrasting thick and thin lines create values. By cutting on the paper cutter various strips in different widths of one or many colors, the children can construct a painting, using the strips to pattern the clothes on their figures or describe their objects. Some may prefer to create abstract shapes with their lines. Ask them to make a portrait, piece of fruit, or a building out of strips. This is a good technique for achieving a sense of volume. They may need to outline the objects or faces in a light medium before they begin to paste on the strips.

2. Using some of their previously done paintings, they may enjoy creating linear patterns over all the surfaces in varying directions and thicknesses. Show them how painting parallel

lines across the breadth of represented objects will produce changes in value. Shading is not recommended as a technique to teach all children, but it might be of interest to a few. A child might do shading on various objects or geometric shapes, cut them out, and then combine them into a composition.

3. Volume can also be created by simple outlines or contours. Pose a model with a thick rope tied around the body and have the children draw only the rope. This will give them a sense of the volume (displaced space) inside the lines thay have drawn. Objects or persons in a landscape or still life, if drawn in outline, will also indicate volume.

Effect of line as texture Children will understand the relation between line and texture by using every possible linear effect to make patterns on small pieces of paper and then incorporating these in collages. (See Picasso's "Seated Woman," 1926–1927, Museum of Modern Art.) For homework, ask them to find, cut out, and bring to class pictures from magazines or newspapers in which linear qualities predominate. The resulting collection will provide a very useful class resource.

Line as structure Skeletal structure is delineated by line. The children can collect a large group of objects from nature to study and analyze for basic structures. Use rocks, stones, skeletons of ocean life left on the shore, toadstools, mushrooms, leaves, branches, driftwood, vegetables, pods, pine cones, plants, flowers, crystals, and jewels. The children should note these special features: changes in direction, spaces in and around forms, groupings and clusters, and variations in angles, sizes, and distances between things (16: pp. 7–16).

This project can heighten children's perception of nature; it gives them an understanding of how things grow and support themselves. The subject matter available in a museum of natural history is limitless. This is an excellent area for collaboration between art and science (biology) teachers. Show Leonardo da Vinci's drawings, for an example of how scientific perception of reality triggered the imagination of an artist, and how an artist researches a subject he wants to paint.

Lines seen and unseen Using a plumb line transformed into a pendulum, demonstrate its limitations. What distance does this pendulum cover? Left to swing, how long will it take to stop? Visualize the successive arcs it describes. Lengthen or shorten the cord on which the pendulum swings and note how the arcs are affected. If it had the force or energy to swing beyond these limitations, what shape would be described?

Following the demonstration, have the children draw various objects and/or models, encouraging them to visualize and render the lines which would exist if they extended freely beyond the confines of the subjects. The array and complexity of overlapping patterns will emerge to enrich the work. Or let children try to make visible in a painting or collage the sounds projecting into infinity, as well as sound waves coming into contact with each other. Motivate with such topics as "The Scream," "The Splash," "The Blast," "Thunder," "Drums," "The Chant," "Bellowing," "Howling," or "Arguing."

Space through interlapping lines

1. Precut strips of paper of all widths are used for this project. Starting with appropriate aids, such as films, actual objects, or sketching trips motivate the children to sketch bridges, outer-space equipment, radar screens, or nonobjective structures with strong linear qualities. Or suggest paintings entitled "Fishing Nets," "A Railroad Yard," "Ski Tracks in the Snow," or "Through the Screen Door." Or ask them to do nonobjective work using stripes in many colors. (The works of Piero Dorazio—a complex overlap of colored stripes—will provide an excellent example.)

2. Superimposed independent lines often make explicit the solid mass of an object. Prepare a background of colors and shapes, either abstract or representational, on which the children will superimpose linear forms. Transferring drawings already done from observation works best and avoids clichés.

3. Try experiments with simultaneous contours. Equivocal space is created when objects seem to occupy the same place. After a sound preparation and exposure to artists who employ this device, ask the children to draw objects that interest them, cut out the drawings, and reassemble them into a composition in which each object will share one or two contours with another object. Use aqueous media of various kinds to create a sense of line where the colors touch or blur.

An appreciation of individual linear sensibility   In viewing each other's work and in group discussions, children will notice the different ways each one works with line. It is of great importance to show and appreciate as well as to do in painting. Children can learn to take notice of instances of unique sensibilities, as in the work "Sledding in the Park" (p. 256), which shows a superb use of linear qualities. The treatment of edges is varied; note the decorative band of windows and the swinging movement of the ski tracks.

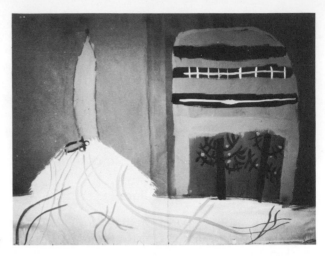

Grade five—boy

TEXTURE

Today there are few conventional restrictions against the use of any material for artistic expression. The last sixty years have seen a host of new substances and objects brought into the realm of art. Plastics, invented for industrial purposes, have been adopted by artists. Scraps, rubbish, and used material thrown off by our ever-increasing whirl of machine-made objects have brought forth new images. Inspired experiments of painters and sculptors have expanded the scope of their audiences. Haftmann has said of this twentieth-century phenomenon: "The more remote these scraps of reality seemed . . . the more useless, rejected, forlorn they were, the more evocative they became when held up as objects of contemplation" (11: p. 359).

Modern artists have searched with alert eyes the surfaces of things, the abrasions on metal, the scratches on sidewalks, the corrosions of rock, for the unlimited textural qualities presented by our culture, which would heretofore have been considered incompatible with any aesthetic purpose.

Seeing and touching Tactile response to the texture of a painting or collage intensifies the visual experience. Preadolescents react enthusiastically to the idea of a search for textural materials for a given project or to make a collection for future projects. They enjoy experiments that expand their sense of touch. Their yearning for "reality" makes it satisfying for them to find for collage or reproduce in paint some of the multitudinous textures that abound in the world of things and to use them to express their ideas, stories, and feelings. There is only one damper on the child's enjoyment of this process: the cultural prejudice that may try to convince him that these explorations have no serious purpose, that unorthodox media and preoccupation with texture are the pursuits of sensation and novelty seekers, and, though fun, should not be taken seriously. Preadolescents should be shown quite explicitly the valid reasons for experimenting with media and why the modern artist is particularly interested in fragments and relics from the natural and industrial world. The children can be shown that the artist always has to break away from the tight matrix of traditional techniques and media which develop into clichés and view himself and his environment with a fresh eye.

Finding materials   The students can easily get into the habit of looking for various textures. They can be given homework in the form of a treasure hunt; they enjoy planning these hunts themselves. One example of instructions for this game: "Walk into your house ten paces, turn right for three paces, turn left for five, and bring to school anything, found within a radius of two feet, of an interesting texture that could be useful in a collage or painting." Or: "Bring into class any object which gives a feeling of grass without being a picture of grass." The collecting instinct is very strong at this age. Suggest a textured paper collection: rubbings, stampings, oiled papers, resist papers, punctured, opaque, translucent, dyed, patterned papers, monoprints.

Small collections of objects with contrasting texture will give the children ideas for their paintings: mirror and velvet; fur and feather; leaf and fur; soap and towel; glass and cloth; fruit and basket; fish and cheesecloth. The contrasts of transparency and opacity, water and mist, solid and liquid, rough and smooth, shiny and dull, hard and soft can be realized somewhat through slides, films and paintings, if not through actual objects brought into class. Use master painters who have achieved and perfected these contrasts, such as Van Eyck, Chardin, and Corot. Surrealist painters will help to make this point also.

Take the children to the zoo or the natural history museum or, if possible, borrow stuffed or live animals. Ask the children to render in large drawings or paintings only the qualities of their coats, skins, and feathers, some of which the children will find interesting enough to consider nonobjective works they wish to preserve; some will be used in their representational work. Showing the works of Dadaists and surrealists may stimulate children to use some as incongruous textural effects in combination with objects.

Storage of materials   The hunt, storage, and display of materials are all teaching and learning functions. When materials come into the art studio from home or other sources, they can be classified and stored in plastic see-through boxes. Teams of children will volunteer to separate and store items; sometimes such an activity can become the day's lesson. Preadolescents love to sort and classify. It develops their perception of surfaces, sizes, shapes, and numerous other qualities. Boxes can be labeled: furry, shiny, transparent, linear, squares, circles, cubes, plastics, wires, textured papers (visual), textured papers (actual), patterned papers, patterned cloth, woven materials.

Invention of new media A time for media exploration in the studio can be exhilarating as both teacher and children become involved in the process of combining media in original ways. If you ask children to think up something they feel will be spectacular in a painting, you have started the ball rolling. Surfaces can be waxed and layered with thin papers which wrinkle in strange ways. Layered surfaces can be torn off in ways which reveal the different colored layers beneath. Images can be transferred from magazines, newspapers, or other printed matter (using turpentine and rubbing). Materials can be sprinkled to create a surface and then scratched or imprinted. These are only a few of the techniques for producing new-textured media. A representational painting using techniques that produce strong textural qualities is shown below.

Grade five—girl   (tempera resist)

Children should be encouraged to use mixed media. The use of sand, sawdust, plaster dust, and other materials makes an impasto which helps some children find a new dimension of expression.

Grades five and six. *Mural (sand added to paint)*

Finding texture in a subject   Sometimes the content or objects in the painting dictate the quality of the textural pattern which will be used: a brick wall, a stone path, or the patterns of branches in a tree. In the painting shown, the pattern and texture of the wall become central to the meaning of the work.

Grade six—boy

Using texture symbolically   Motivated by Dadaist and surrealist concepts, have children use unlikely textures to depict familiar forms: a furry banana, a terrycloth automobile, a sandpaper mirror. Use textures symbolically, as is sometimes done in advertising. An example is a Westinghouse advertisement which contains a statement about research projects on electric power and drinking water from sea water. A texture representing water is shown passing through both a drinking glass and an electric bulb.

Repeating a module to produce texture The mosaicists and the impressionists of the past used a unit or module which itself brought about an emphasis on texture. The Byzantine muralists knew the power of broken color and the effect of textures on spatial relationships. Seurat, through systematic use of the dot, created a physical and atmospheric depth that changed our vision of painting.

Control is achieved by clusters, density, flow, grain, and nets, that is to say, factors which affect equally the whole painting as a single system, rather than by balances of separate forms. In fact, the crucial element is, perhaps, not the grid but the point, the dot, the regular and repetitive unit [19: p. 90].

Children can be motivated to paint any subject that interests them employing this technique, using a brush or Q-tips, creating a uniform dotting or daubing effect. In the painting shown, the child was asked to experiment with short linear strokes to emphasize textural qualities. (Relate to the painter Bradley Walter Tomlin).

Grade seven—girl

An appreciation of the unique in feel and touch Discussion, looking at each other's work, and seeing the paintings of mature artists all develop awareness of the unique sensibility of each individual. Persistent, playful experimentation with textural qualities of different media will help the child find his own techniques. Three things will come clear to him as he works:

1. Textural qualities on the total surface are unifying.

2. Certain textures can sharpen the associative reaction of the viewer.

3. Texture can set a special tempo as it moves through a work.

Below is a painting in which preadolescents incorporated a tactile sensation into representational work. The girl who made this painting is particularly sensitive to textural variations. She has elected to work with a wide-bristled brush and a fine camel's hair brush. With the thick brush she represents the foliage and with the thin brush the branches, trunks, and carefully patterned windows. Note that while the buildings have a strong horizontal pull, the sky emphasizes a vertical pattern. it is also exciting to see how she has contrasted the wild abandonment of the vegetation in the park with the static and geometric composition of buildings and sky.

Grade six—girl

What preadolescents have to "learn" about art in general and their own art in particular is both simple and profound. By making art and by looking at art, one naturally begins to understand what art is. The teacher, who will have thought a great deal about art and should have had much experience in making art herself, will be ready to interact with youngsters of this age and build upon their spontaneous inclinations and pursuits to expand their art experiences. She will know that not every child needs the same thing at the same time. She will know that there are many routes to knowledge about art, only some of which are to be found in exercises aimed at refining techniques. The major reason for art experiences is to help the child to comprehend man as creator and himself as possessor of these same potentialities.

REFERENCES

1. René Huyghe, *Art and the Spirit of Man,* Harry N. Abrams, Inc., New York, 1962.

2. Joseph Wood Krutch, *Experience and Art,* Collier Books, The Macmillan Company, New York, 1962.

3. Michael Kirby, *The Art of Time: Essays on the Avant-Garde,* E. P. Dutton & Co., Inc., New York, 1969.

4. Étienne Gilson, *Painting and Reality,* Meridian Books, Inc., New York, 1959.

5. Edith Kramer, *Art Therapy in a Children's Community,* Charles C Thomas, Publisher, Springfield, Ill., 1958.

6. Allen Leepa, *The Challenge of Modern Art,* A. S. Barnes and Co., Inc., New York, 1961.

7. Meyer Shapiro, "The Liberating Quality of Avant-Garde Art," *Art News,* Vol. 56, No. 4, Summer, 1956, New York.

8. Bernard S. Myers, *Understanding the Arts,* Holt, Rinehart and Winston, Inc., New York, 1958.

9. Etienne Sourian, "Time in the Plastic Arts," *Reflections on Art,* ed. Suzanne K. Langer, Oxford University Press, New York, 1961.

10. E. C. Goosen, "The Big Canvas," *The New Art,* E. P. Dutton & Co., Inc., New York, 1966.

11. Werner Haftmann, *Painting of the Twentieth Century,* Frederick A. Praeger, Inc., New York, 1960.

12. Hans Hofmann, *Search for the Real,* M.I.T. Press, Cambridge, Mass., 1967.

13. Bates Lowry, *The Visual Experience: An Introduction to Art,* Prentice-Hall, Inc., Englewood Cliffs, N.J., and Harry N. Abrams Inc., New York, 1960.

14. Rudolf Arnheim, *Art and Visual Perception,* University of California Press, Berkeley and Los Angeles, 1966.

15. Rudolf Arnheim, *Visual Thinking,* University of California Press, Berkeley and Los Angeles, 1969.

16. Graham Collier, *Form, Space, Vision,* Prentice-Hall, Inc., Englewood Cliffs, N. J., 1963.

17. Gyorgy Kepes, *The Language of Vision,* Paul Theobald, Chicago, 1951.

18. Frank Popper, *Origins and Development of Kinetic Art,* New York Graphic Society, Greenwich, Conn., 1968.

19. Lawrence Alloway, "Notes on Op Art," *The New Art,* ed. Gregory Battcock, E. P. Dutton & Co., Inc., New York, 1966.

Three-dimensional Construction

9

Twentieth-century sculpture, future retrospection will show, was a highly transitional process, a brief labyrinth of changes. Already as a means of description, the term "sculpture" has lost its identity; it has become a misnomer for an art once concerned with carving and modeling for the purpose of simulating biological appearances, but which now designates all three-dimensional construction [1: p. 5].

Walking around a sculpture is an adventure of exploration. One may be flying with open-air shapes, tunneling through massive forms or peering into dark crevices, riding the swell and curve of voluptuous form or feeling the sharpness of an edge. Even more than viewing, the actual making of sculpture is a dynamic experience, one of the most important art activities that we can provide for preadolescents.

From first step to completion, a three-dimensional art construction exists as a concrete object, in contrast to a painting, which begins to exist only when all its various components are combined on a blank expanse of paper or canvas. In sculpture, the artist begins with a definite substance, shaped or shapeless, which he alters according to the skill of his hands and the quality of his tools. Sculpture has tangible three-dimensionality, measurable bulk. Its mass displaces real space, and its weight is subject to the laws of gravity.

It is only natural that the preadolescent should take to the direct physical experience evoked by three-dimensional construction. It is an art that is corporeal and sensual—qualities which give it a strong fascination for these restless, energetic children.

Moreover, three-dimensional constructions, especially in our day, are closely related to science, and many of the principles learned in science classes can be applied in the studio. Assemblages, moving sculpture, electrical kinetic forms, illuminated glass structures, environments and mock-ups will appeal to preadolescents in our electronically geared society. For better or worse, the throb of the machine is something that most of our children are almost as well adjusted to as their own heartbeats.

ADVANTAGES OF THE MEDIUM FOR PREADOLESCENTS

The link between science and art is as old as mankind. Jack Burnham suggests that there is "an abiding similarity between the artistic and scientific mind; it is as if both were motivated by the same pangs of discovery and a desire for the consummation of ideas into beautiful totalities." According to him, art, magic, religion and science have "joint origins," and each was "part of a common goal which could be ascertained as one of the four disciplines to achieve some degree of irremeable control over environment" (1: p. 5). Art has indeed implemented magic, served religion, and been served by science. In our present heyday of science, adult and preadolescent may find magic and technology synonymous. Voodoo figurines and masks have been replaced by talking boxes and computers as terrifying as angels and devils, wood figures and masks. Mushroom clouds are real-life monsters. These materializations summoned from nature by the power of the human mind inevitably capture our imaginations even when we revolt against them. Contemporary sculpture devastatingly expresses our hate-love for these manifestations.

Yet in spite of the high stimulation of all our electronic exotica and the magic of the lasar and quasar, the human image continues to be important subject matter for the preadolescent as well as the adult artist. Preadolescents in particular feel the need to make the biological replica; they still have the "artistic obsession for the free-standing human form and its life-emanating properties" (1: p. 1). They want to be able to draw the human body, but many of them will find it even more rewarding to model, carve, or reproduce it in three-dimensional media.

Figuration absorbs many modern sculptors. The association between the sculpted human image and the hypothetical existence of the spirit, or soul, seems to survive. The artist, as David Mandel prophesies, will be the counterbalance of the "surge of science";

. . . if we want to know what is happening to the human spirit, we must go to the artist. He is the soundest interpreter, if only because this is his essential task. . . .

Science, he says, is capable of a "closer analysis of our biological make-up and the energy that makes it live," but art "is the cutting edge of our biological awareness."

Its interpretation should be taken seriously, especially at a time when, as a biologist tells us, we will soon have to answer a new question. No longer, what creature is man? but, what creature should he become?" [2: pp. 124–25]

As philosopher, psychologist or simply as artisan, the sculptor has always had a deeply rooted desire to create objects which, because they exist in space and are carefully made, seem to be alive. Spirits were thought to inhabit the figures carved by primitive artists. The wearing of certain masks transformed individuals into gods or demons. Michelangelo felt strongly that he was releasing from the stone spirits who were waiting for him to do so. In many cultures, such as the Egyptian, sculptures were created as substitute bodies for the dead. Other cultures put terra cotta statuettes in place of real human beings in ritual blood sacrifices (3: p. 136). Sumerian figurines served as votive figures placed in the temple to pray in place of the actual person. Gods, animals, and even inanimate objects were often carved with human attributes. Here is a "devil dancer" by a modern twelve-year-old boy.

Boy, age twelve   *Dancer*

The study of anatomy was an early science and, like geometry, it inspired the graphic arts and served in the creation of the classic Greek figure, an objectification of man-in-God and God-in-man wrought in the purest, most durable materials, such as bronze and marble. The gods provided inspiration and purpose, but mathematical passion was the main drive in this pursuit of perfection.

During the early Middle Ages, when learning and science were submerged in the tidal wave of barbarism, religion, with the help of art, again had to make survival palatable. Gothic cathedrals were raised in thin spires to heaven, and anonymous sculptors depicted man as thin, emaciated, agonized, intricately distorted into the complexity of the architectural scheme.

With Christianity and the rise of the bourgeoisie, the wavering image of man appears to have become more stabilized. When the Renaissance began, learning and science emerged from monastic seclusion to join archaeological remains as sources of inspiration for new discoveries. Once more man believed he was mastering the earth. Sculpture again represented him as an individual of power and grace. Anatomy became as important as the soul; the sculptured nude emerged again, full of the life force and materialism of the times. As Elsen writes: "The classical nude reflects a man-centered world, one where man is the middle and measure of all things and is in felicitous equilibrium with nature" (4: p. 229).

Baroque and rococo sculpture were preoccupied with technical virtuosity. In effect, they were mass-produced to propagandize the divine right of kings and the glamour of the aristocracy. Public structures, palaces and grandiose gardens were decorated with effete, self-conscious, pseudorefined images of man in marble or other stone. No individual pieces were as important as the palaces, such as Versailles, or the monumental fountains, bridges, and squares that were created to adorn them. Artists, servants of the rising nationalism, sculpted figures that were still corporeal, but mannered and almost effeminate in their posturing. All transcendental presence had fled. Religious art, too, suffered from lack of dignity (4: pp. 229–248).

At the end of the eighteenth century, about the time of the French Revolution and the first bloody beginnings of the struggle for the rights of man, which is still raging intermittently in our own century, sculpture entered a period of revival of the most florid Greco-Roman styles. It took its insipid mannerisms from Hellenistic rather than classical sculpture and made use of historical and archaeological motifs. (Archaeology as a discipline was just being born.) The purified nude figure of earlier times, which had universal, nonpersonal qualities, became unnaturally "naked," almost lewd, in the prudish nineteenth century.

Sculptors no longer enjoyed hewing the stone with their own hands. They considered this labor too heavy and therefore made models in clay from which "artisans" made the finished piece in stone or cast in metal. It is no wonder that the work, while technically skilled, lacked originality and nuance and has little claim on our emotions. Nearly all the sculpture from the 1830s to the time of Rodin falls into the category of the *academic style*, a combination of Hellenistic, romantic and realistic forms (5: pp. 39–53).

A complete eclipse of corporeality in sculpture and painting took place during the "failure of nerve" period between the two world wars and the dark age of Hitler. By that time, scientific magic had so far replaced the religious that hardly a vestige of holy—even revived holy—content remained in art. The sculpted or painted human figure represented no longer the aristocracy but the ordinary man, real or surreal, as affected by existence in a war-torn, mechanized society. The anatomy of the unconcious mind superseded the anatomy of bones, muscles, and flesh, just as higher physics superseded geometry as inspiration for new forms.

Yet just as it survived through other cycles of history, the sculptured nude weathered the twentieth-century negative, invisible image of humanity, even outlived emaciation, repellent distortions, and cybernetics. In the human consciousness there is probably an ineradicable desire for this subject matter in art. The preadolescent, intent on mastering a true human likeness because of a profound psychic need, proceeds quite naturally toward carving or modeling the naked or near-naked form. In the process of constructing a figure, he can become so interested in the action of the pose, the mood, or the story he is telling that he may reduce the clothing to a minimum, just as artists of the past discovered that the body can best reveal its universal message when not encumbered by the garments of the day.

Unfortunately, the atmosphere of most schools is such that the preadolescent does not feel free to create his figures without clothes. The cultural mores—conventions of modesty and propriety—are strictly upheld, and the child who is at the age of self-consciousness and worry about what is right and acceptable in society dutifully clothes his figures. Furthermore, he is apt to want to show off his knowledge of worldly details and makes much of identifying his figures with male and female articles of clothing.

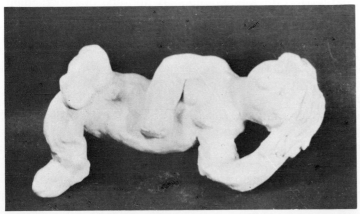

Grade five—boy

The recurrent activities and groupings of human beings appeal to preadolescents as subject matter: the family gathering, mother and child, man and animal, men at war, hunting, fishing, planting and gathering, sports competitions, and all manifestations of physical prowess. These various roles and occupations all have their built-in incentives to observe, to learn, and to belong. The preadolescent depicting them has an opportunity to display his newly acquired understanding of the world around him.

Grade five—girl

Grade six—boy

Preadolescents are also especially eager to fashion animal figures, an instinct they share with mature artists and which goes back to the roots of art and man's evolution from dependence on animals for transportation and companionship as well as food. Sculptors of the prehistoric past made effigies of animals in the hope of making them multiply; they knew them intimately —their habits and migrations—and, as hunters, observed them for hours on end.

Animal sculpture plays a diminished role in our culture, but it still survives, perhaps because we are becoming intensely conscious of the multitude of living beings that we have brushed off the earth with our machines, or perhaps because, as Udo Kultermann says, "the animal stirs the imagination . . . in terms of a subconscious memory" (6: p. 60). Preadolescents carry fresh from childhood their empathy with animals. Sometimes they love them more than they love human beings. For them this is a natural and rich sculptural field.

In social studies and in the rudimentary archaeology taught in schools, preadolescents will have already begun to learn the

relationship between basic sculptural shapes and universal human
needs, interests, and activities. The artifacts that have come down
to us were vitally associated with survival and with control over
nature. A good teacher will never let the student lose sight of
these connections. Even though it is obvious to all that our
modern household implements come off the production line in
enormous quantities, in materials not meant to endure, yet
the same relationship persists between man's needs, materials
and activities, and the objects he makes. The deep urge to make
useful things seems to exist in all children. The young child
working in clay will inevitably want to create a little bowl in
which he places things. The preadolescent will want to design a
modern utilitarian object which will have for him—no matter
how mechanically its basic material was produced—a satisfying
sculpted form.

Children are instinctive architects just as they are bowl and
pot makers and slingshot designers. They like constructing,
cutting out flats and hollows, making places in which to nest.
The author and a group of children used a large gym for a highly
successful project correlating art and social studies.

First, the children were shown slides describing the basic
building principles man has discovered and used in various
civilizations and the ways in which materials and science have
influenced form. Then the children were separated into groups,
with wood blocks, orange crates, planks and rigid cardboards,
to build in the various historical modes. They experienced directly
and physically the differences between styles of architecture and
came to some understanding of what inspired each one and
what technological limitations or breakthroughs were involved.

As the children piled, hammered, glued, taped and tied,
what had begun as natural, instinctive play became an aesthetic and scholarly experience as well. Using their own bodies,
they noted the various responses they made to certain enclosures, to the effects of light and darkness, to the mood created
by light. They heard the sounds the materials made when they
were combined in certain forms. They began to talk about how
buildings influence our bodies and what we do with them, how
they speak to us, put us in certain moods, recall memories.

As a culmination of our project, we went the next day into
a meeting place adjacent to the school, with the permission
of the minister, in order to experience a building—in this case,
a religious auditorium. The children were of many faiths; we
tried to put this aside and feel the essential purpose and quality
of the enclosure. We heard the faint sounds of the materials;
we walked on the rugs; we heard the rustle of our clothes. We
sang in the room; we divided the group so that half were
audience, half performers; we wailed and cried as in grief; we

played records of the special music that usually sounded through the building at funerals, at weddings and celebrations; we smelled the flowers. We also played with the dimmers on the lights and created moods with them. We turned out all lights and listened to our own breathing.

CHANGING SCULPTURAL VALUES

Since sculpture began, it has been controlled equally by materials readily available and the life and death styles of the culture producing it—that is, stable or nomadic, peaceful or warlike, ritualistic, materialistic, secure or in transition. The essential concerns of a people can be discerned in their sculpture.

The materials most often used in the far past were marble slabs, stone blocks, and tree trunks. Totemic, Egyptian, African, and Mediterranean ancient cultures have left us monumental works in these media. The static, monolithic forms that emerged inevitably from stone and marble suited the settled agrarian societies and also expressed important religious and psychological values. Restless sculpture with a quality of movement would have broken into the mood of timelessness and eternity that agrarian man sought in both ritual and environmental forms. Monolithic shapes also might be considered as reflecting the comparatively rigid patterns of his consciousness (7: p. 358).

Metal-working peoples wandered from the Asian steppes to occupy northern Europe. Small metal objects were infinitely easier to transport than those in any other durable material. Because heated metal lends itself to bending and to spiral and serpentine shapes, nomadic artifacts are characterized by linear and tensile rather than massive form. Complex, abstract, full of activity, their sculpture was the inevitable result of the life style which, even after the migrations were accomplished, meant war, conquest, and eternal forays as they wandered, destroying, learning, assimilating, reforming, and gradually coming to dominate northern and middle Europe. They were the "barbarians," deadly foes, but a dynamic, creative element in Western civilization. Feldman elaborates on the conflict between what he considers two major aesthetic drives:

On the one hand, sculptors from Michelangelo to Maillol have endeavored to preserve classical sculptural order; on the other hand, Romanesque and Gothic sculpture reveal the barbarian obsession with infinite movement, convulsive forms, and abstract ornament as opposed to naturalistic rendering of the human figure. . . . Indeed the revival of classical order during the Renaissance never succeeded in displacing entirely the taste for complex motion which had been whetted by barbarian art. . . . [17: p. 359].

The cloak of classicism imposed on gothic art wore thin, and the eighteenth and nineteenth centuries have left us sculpture that is in general considered imitative. It took a revolution in the life style of Western man, brought on by science, to free us from meaningless rewarming of leftover semimonolithic sculptural forms.

The Industrial Revolution and the psychoanalytic revolution have crucially changed man's concept of living and his way of looking at himself. New art—nonart to many traditionalists— was inevitable. In sculpture, the transition has been more violent and perhaps more difficult to understand or adjust to than the revolution in painting, because three-dimensional work makes a more intimate physical claim on us. Jack Burnham writes, in the Introduction to his exposition of modern sculpture:

For nearly twenty-five centuries the beauty and potency of sculpture was connected with an obsession for the free-standing human form and its life-emitting properties. Today sculpture has just barely preserved the prime attribute of palpable form; it remains a class of visible objects mirroring the process of psychic disbelief in its own being. With unmatched pathos it suggests still visible roots in the magic totemic objects of earlier ages while seeking sustenance in the austere soil of the scientific model and technical invention [1: p. 1].

In the early part of the twentieth century, the Constructivists threw aside the monolith in sculpture. New materials such as Plexiglas, new metals and wires, were at hand, ready for the shift from static to linear, open, psychologically disturbing forms expressive of the age of speed and urban living on a grand scale. At the same time, the break from the figurative tradition was made. Geometric, free-form and mechanical shapes gained supremacy. Leading artists in this movement of change, such as Tatlin, Gabo and Pevsner, found their creative impulses in physics, mathematics, and engineering. Naum Gabo, one of the 1913 Constructivists, introduced the concept of "space without weight"; his aim was to create a sense of solidity without using mass in the traditional way. He defined space as much through suggestion as through enclosure (7: pp. 362–363).

The explorations of Dadaism established additional new materials for sculpture. An anti-intellectual movement, its art was deliberately divorced from reason. Scrap materials began to take on inspirational values. Kurt Schwitters (1887–1948) combined valuable materials with garden-variety remnants of wood, twine, and paper into sensitive works of art. Hans Arp believed that reason (and tradition) had separated man from nature. He put objects together casually for contemplation, seeking pure discovery and a direct approach to organization.

He was inspired by the natural, such as eggs, leaves, clouds, and "biomorphic" forms of all kinds.

The urge to link art with the new scientific explosion of ideas and materials led to the creation of the Bauhaus in Germany in 1919. Later its founders came to the United States—Gropius to Harvard and Moholy-Nagy to the University of Chicago—to establish innovative institutes of architectural and other three-dimensional design. It might be said that architecture at this time gave sculpture room and board, almost absorbing it completely. Corbusier implemented a new concept of movement in space with materials and engineering feats that revolutionized both public and domestic building. The work of Frank Lloyd Wright affects us almost as sculpture.

From its position of "poor cousin," sculpture moved farther and farther away from mass, solidity and all association with stable structure. We now look upon Maillol, Brancusi, and Lachaise as the "old masters of modernism" (7: p. 361). New concepts of time and space, of the microuniverse whirling inside all matter, seized the artistic imagination. The two new magics —electronics and fission—began to work their way into art, especially into sculpture.

After the attempts of the cubists to create a new space in two dimensions had waned, after dalliance with the alluring fourth dimension and the satiric interludes deflating material-istic pretensions and vulgarity (pop), many sculptors have become involved again with creating objects which seem to emanate life.

SCULPTURAL FORMATS

Traditionally there have been two kinds of sculpture: in the round and in relief. The former stands free in space, an entity in itself. It can be moved and displayed anywhere. It is usually but not always created to be seen from all sides. Nowadays the elements of mass, weight and volume, which before the twentieth century characterized sculpture in the round, have been replaced by hollowness, directional linear movement, transparency, open interior spaces and actual movement. A mobile is a kinetic sculpture in the round.

Sculpture in relief is attached to a background and there-fore not seen from behind. This gives it a two-dimensional aspect, even when it is part of a three-dimensional form such as a free-standing column or block. Reliefs range from shallow incisions to forms so deeply carved out of the original surface that they appear to be rising in various degrees from the background.

Illusion is an important element of relief sculpture, as it is in painting. The traditional intention of relief was to produce within a limited area the illusion of a complete and fully rounded shape. Proper use of light and dark is essential. The artist makes sharp or subtle modulations depending on the amount of shadow he employs. The angles catch the light, and it is the relationship between the angles and the planes that makes a relief an aesthetically satisfying work. Much of the new box sculpture and many kinetic pieces in which form is created by moving electric light could be classified as reliefs.

It is a helpful simplification to reduce all sculptural work to two processes: the subtractive and the additive. Faulkner and Ziegfield (8: p. 465) add a third, which is actually a combination of the two: the replacement process, which is used for casting in molds when a more permanent material is to replace the original material used by the artist.

Today both the subtractive and additive processes are usually employed in the production of any one piece. Only in the traditionally carved single wood block, limb, or slab of stone or marble do we find the purely subtractive method. The modern artist may carve parts of his sculpture in the traditional way, but the accumulation of the separate parts into a single statement brings his work into the category of additive sculpture.

In carving, material is removed to reveal the form. It can be a tedious process when the wood or stone is hard. The original natural shape of a given block of material becomes the framework, or starting point, and its inherent density or softness in great part determines the resulting imagery. Carving materials are hard to come by in school because they are often expensive and require special storage space. Whittling wood or soft materials such as soap, Styrofoam, plaster mixed with vermiculite, clay blocks, fire brick, and certain cement blocks available in great variety are used by resourceful teachers. Carving is a fundamental sculptural experience, and some means should be devised to give it to children.

The additive method basically is one in which parts are accumulated until the sculpture becomes a unified statement. A tremendous array of sculptures come under this category. The artist nails, glues, welds, solders, or ties or binds together the various components. When working in clay or other soft materials, he simply presses and pushes the medium until it holds together. Most often in these flexible media the process of molding the material together is called modeling. Clay is, of course, the most flexible medium in which form may grow from the minimal to the whole, with the mass building up in stages. Other materials that are suitable for modeling are sculpt metal, clay substitutes, and plastics, which can be worked when in a puttylike state.

The word "construction" is used increasingly in sculpture. It originates from engineering and architecture and involves many of the same principles and concepts germane to those fields. Such terms as "fabrication," "cantilever," "solid foundation," "space utilization," and "flowing line" are used in both architecture and constructions. Indeed, another process by which sculpture can be formed, in addition to the additive and subtractive methods, is fabrication. Forms are folded upward from a flat material, such as cardboard, paper, metal and metal screens, and reeds or threads stiffened into woven cloth. The casting or replacement process, in which liquefied plaster, metal, plastics, clay, cement, or some other material is poured into a mold, can be done in many simple and interesting ways. Familiarity with these terms and processes helps the preadolescent link the things he makes with those produced by industry.

**MODULAR
SCULPTURE**

The module is used in sculpture as well as in architecture and is found in many natural structures, such as honeycombs, crystals, flowers, and microscopic life. Scientists assure us that the whole universe is built on combinations of basic modular units. All modular structures are formed of units that are constant in size and shape, or they may be combinations of these constants. Artists find this limitation of alternatives a challenge. Industrial standard units, such as bars, slats, and boxes in metal, plastic, or plywood are being used by some contemporary sculptors (Minimalists and Serialists) to create rigorous sculptural forms.

In their science classes, preadolescents will find or be encouraged to seek out basic biological forms and relate them to work in the art studio. Another motivation might come from a study of Buckminster Fuller's dome, which is based on combinations of tetrahedrons. Most architecture utilizes modular elements in great numbers (lath, studs, floor boards, shingles, bricks, etc.). Children will realize this as they look about them, and by making modular-based sculpture (an extension, actually, of the block building they did when they were younger) they will perhaps become excited by the aesthetic and technical challenge involved (9).

There are simple, uncomplicated ways of introducing children to the sculptural experience. An outing for the whole class at the beach may teach them more than days of structured lessons in the studio, no matter how well equipped it may be. By the sea, broken up into random bits and pieces, is the stuff from which some sculpture is made. Here are the fragments of granite, marble, mother-of-pearl, volcanic rock, shell, and smooth black alabaster out of which man has built things for thousands of years. When children gather them according to their impulses and tastes, an imaginative teacher can make clear many of the methods, values and elements of sculpture. How has the sea carved them? With their fingers the children can feel the swelling masses, the unfilled spaces, the weight, the texture (what a pleasure to handle them!), the coolness or hotness, the infinite and subtle variety of color and the change in color when they dry. There are linear contours flowing into each other. There are pockets of shadow as the stones are turned in the bright light, and new relationships of size and shape appear.

Gluing, with epoxy, stones of varying weights and shapes helps children comprehend gravity and the limitations it imposes. Balancing and counterbalancing, they begin to notice the practical and aesthetic meanings of weight, volume, and mass. Do they want to put nubbled with smooth? What is boring? When does contrast become meaningless? Repetition without monotony is a prime aesthetic quality which this experience with stones can teach. The sea casts up an infinity of almost similar shapes, colors and textures, along with startling variations.

An equally edifying experience is a day in a tool room, foundry, or production shop. Here, observing how men work with metals (and/or plastics), children become familiar with the complicated tools that have been devised to fabricate the objects of our culture. They learn about welding, metal casting, fabricating, cutting, piercing, forming, spinning, grinding, and polishing.

Visiting the studios of sculptors and watching them as they work in metal, wood, plastics, luminaries, marble, and clay can inspire children and whet their interest. This visit can make it much easier for them to understand that what they are doing in the school studio has some connection with adult purposes and activities. Movies of artists at work or films showing processes are also useful, as are visits to museums, where it is now the mode to provide dramatic explanations of artistic processes.

Combining visits to factories with visits to studios brings home the point that man-made objects have now become the "material" of sculpture, just as stones and trees are the raw materials for nature's art. Waste objects and scraps of our society are now used for art; visits to galleries and museums will provide graphic evidence of this. Perhaps the organization of a class scavenger hunt in a given urban or suburban neighborhood, or for rural children, through those back lot or car dump wastelands which abound, would help them see the possibilities in salvaging and giving a new role to industrial leftovers and discarded material lying around us. Scavenger lists require imagination to compose, and children require courage to ferret out the various items requested. The experience can be widening; it takes the scavenger into unfamiliar and slightly terrifying worlds. But are not such forays necessary for the preadolescent if he is to be at home in the environment science has brought into being?

Exhibits of found objects can heighten awareness and appreciation of their various qualities. Such exhibits can be the culminating activity of a scavenger hunt, or these objects can be further utilized to create art objects.

Weight, stress and tension Making sculpture underwater or on the moon would be a very different problem from creating it as we do here on earth. We have seen the legs of the astronauts seem to lift almost by themselves; gravity begins to look like a precious security. A child has to learn to adjust to the pull of gravity as soon as he begins to move and most dramatically when he stops crawling and tries to walk. By the time preadolescents seek to make an animal or a man in clay, wood or wire that will stand up, his knowledge of gravity has advanced from unconscious adjustments of his own body to include what he has learned in biology of the human backbone, the system of joints, and the tensile strength of muscles. He realizes more fully the problem of distributing weights in order for the structure to support itself, that "support must be physically equal to the load it bears" (10: pp. 146–147).

Films, slides and museum visits help children discover some of the many logical combinations which have been devised to adjust the weight and strength of materials to gravity. On such expeditions and during visits to artists' studios, they will also learn that many of today's sculptors are interested in pretending to negate the laws of nature by creating structures giving the impression of imbalance. This revolt against gravitational forces may be part of the sculptor's midcentury effort to dissociate himself from architecture and the new and dynamically engineered forms in building that have been edging into sculpture's domain. Yet basically it is an illusionary, esoteric movement; these sculptors are playing with an idea that is of special interest in our times as we prepare to explore worlds where little gravity exists. There can be no true countervailing of gravity on this planet, however, and the factors of weight and strength of materials remain basic to sculptural design.

Edges and lines It may be easier for children to appreciate linear quality in sculpture when dealing with wire, reeds, rods or similar materials which in themselves already possess a linear form. Yet there exist in sculpture many linear aspects which may not be at once obvious. Reactions to edges of massive forms or to the meeting of planes may require a subtle attention carefully nurtured by the teacher. Even in monolithic sculpture, the basic directions which bulks assume have a strong linear impact. The fluting of columns, for instance, can be pointed to as an example of how the strength of a material is increased through the use of a repeated pattern of lines.

Line in freestanding sculpture functions to lead the eye through and around. It also provides the psychological energy to arouse certain emotions by its rate of speed, by its width or narrowness, by the way it switches direction, or by the rise and drop or swing and jump of it.

Texture, patina and color Obviously the tactile impact as well as the emotional and physical influences of color are prime elements of a three-dimensional construction. A texture can be distributed over the whole piece to convey a representational idea (such as a hairy ape, scales of a fish, smooth baby skin, etc.). Or it can be produced on a portion of the piece to give emphasis or a special reality (a figured blouse, a person's hair, etc.). Or it can be made uniform to give an abstract, overall quality which takes on an identity of its own, apart from an associational meaning.

Texture used in patterns leads the eye from portion to portion of the sculpture. The teacher can encourage children to explore new tactile sensations, borrowing and adapting many ideas from the world of art, nature, and industry. They should be given special looking and seeking times, to enlarge their textural scope. If large scrap bins are kept full of interesting materials for stamping and adding to a surface and epoxy and white vinyl glues are kept on hand, the children will enjoy the discovery of new visual and tactile experiences. Sand sprinkled over an adhesive before it sets, scratching, or drawing graffiti may give the child the effect he wants.

Children can rub, polish, stipple, burn into, spray, or beat a piece of work until the finish satisfies them. Painting (aerosol-powdered paint, wrought iron paint, metallic sprays, casein), of course, provides another kind of patina, especially adapted to metal and wire sculpture.

Color, as it is used today by sculptors, can produce many illusionistic effects. The mellowness of wood is disguised to look like metal; metal is burnished so that it picks up reflections and creates the illusion of depth in mirror-glass transparency.

Lucy R. Lippard, writing about the modern relationship between sculpture and painting, says that "most abstract and some figurative sculptors are trying to avoid the connotations of the materials . . . and give the illusion of something autonomous and new in itself without reference to its antecedents—physical or historical" (11: p. 32).

Much sculptural work is being painted as one might paint a canvas; images of all kinds appear, and sometimes even brush work is frankly exhibited. Since sculpture is viewed from many angles, the color action must be carefully controlled.

It is used illusionistically to disperse and minimize volume, to separate shapes in space, making heavy shapes seem weightless, light ones heavy, near forms far away and far ones closer. And it is used to unify, to make a form more "real," isolating it from the environment and asserting the piece as a self-contained whole [11: p. 33].

According to Irving Sandler (12: p. 41), sculptors are greatly aware of "the possible incompatibility between the bulk of a shape and its thin skin of pigment. But the difficulties only make the attempt more challenging."

Light and shadow The shadows that appear when light hits an object are part of the working materials of the sculptor. All our creations are in fact at the mercy of light. Even as the artist is molding, adding, and subtracting, the sun and the darkness are mixing into the affair, changing things in provocative ways. Awareness of this process will make it very exciting for the preadolescent to create conditions in which light is, so to speak, caught in the act.

Electricity has changed our potential control over the aesthetic as well as over every other aspect of the modern environment. Perhaps even more than the painter, the sculptor has to watch the play of light on his work. He has to or must take advantage, perhaps electrically, of a happy coincidence of radiance and/or shadow so he can make the unforeseen—the accident—a permanent feature of the finished work. "Uncontrolled lighting is indeed the enemy of sculpture. It flattens form. It eats away at contours. It digs holes where highlights fall and tears masses to pieces" (3: p. 125).

It is very interesting to see the same piece of sculpture photographed by different people. Often the results look like entirely dissimilar works of art. Even if the photographs have been made at exactly the same angle, a change in light will make a great difference in the articulation of the forms. Such photographs are very convincing to children.

Shadow—lighter or darker as one moves around the sculpture or as natural light changes—also gives tonality and color, producing many pleasurable surprises. In works of natural wood, stone, or metal, the shadow adds elements of contrast and subtle variations as the color of the shadowed area blends with the color of the lighted portion. The Italian painters of the Renaissance noted this atmospheric blending of colors in the shadows on three-dimensional objects and perfected chiaroscuro to a degree unknown in painting before that time.

It is one of the great rewards of sculpture that because it is three-dimensional it creates its own echoes and reflections.

. . . the movement toward optical sculpture, as opposed to one defined mainly by volume, has been in progress for the better part of a century and in practically all styles: Cubist, Dada, organic, geometric, surrealist-organic, Expressionist, etc. Its impetus has been a slowly growing realization that light, controlled by color, transparency, or reflection— or a combination of the three—is one of the sculptor's most evocative stimuli [1: p. 160].

Size and shape   The size of a work of art orients the viewer in his own human scale. We feel small in relation to the central nave of a gothic cathedral, and we measure our bodies instinctively against the life-sized or outsized sculptured figure even when it is elevated on a stand. The element of size can be less easily experienced in painting, where objects and figures are generally reduced to miniatures (with the exception of some portraits), and the viewer must, with an optical-mental adjustment, reduce his own size in order to partake of the painter's intended shape relationships.

When they do large sculpture, preadolescents can use their own bodies for reference. In three-dimensional work, the transition in scale from actual size to miniature often requires a more concentrated stretch of the imagination than some can manage at this age. In fact, over the centuries, outsized sculpture, whether human, geometric or abstract, has been prevalent. It seems to carry a certain supernatural aura, imparting a sense of power to both maker and viewer.

Size, of course, does not exist without its carrier: shape or a series of shapes. Aided by light, shadow and color, shapes of differing sizes produce the illusion of movement in sculpture through a sequential progression of variations in scale. In a closed, monolithic work, the outer shape predominates; one sees first a total, unified configuration. The impression of the mass is easily encompassed. Then the eye looks beyond to the more subtle shapes stirring within it, perhaps created by shadows or by the artist's linear articulation. If the sculpture is an open form, we may grasp a totality of mass, but it is a more complex process because the shapes of the air within the body of the work can also be experienced as volumes or mass air spaces having bulk and dimension.

Where does inspiration for shapes come from? From primordial images perhaps as old as the first creatures with a central nerve cord, crawling around on a young earth; from direct observation and memories of hills, waves, lakes, clouds, leaves, branches, shells, cones, flowers, vegetables, stones, niches, holes, mounds, towers, wheels, hips, breasts, heads; from the squares, triangles, cubes, polyhedrons, spheres, all the mathematical verities, and from the machines and instruments born out of science; from jagged shapes of the electrical storm, from the rainbow, the aurora borealis, and the mandala that rises from our deepest identity to be a concrete symbol of unity and self-possession.

Shapes emerge not only through human association but also from the qualities inherent in the material used. A bird in wire and a bird in stone are hardly related, other than as birds. Cardboard pyramids can be obscenities. Pop sculptors like Oldenburg make fun of our materialistic culture, which they consider degraded, by reproducing functional shapes in inappropriate materials, distorting our sense of weight and texture, and deflating or inflating through exaggeration, as with all satiric humor. The Minimal Sculpture school, on the other hand, turns away from the multiplicity of the objects manufactured by our technology and relies on the shapes of solid geometry to the exclusion of any other distracting elements.

Most preadolescents are too innocent and inquiring to feel the bitter satirical urge and too interested in nature, human or otherwise, to confine themselves to mathematical shapes. When sufficiently motivated by the teacher, the media, or examples of contemporary or past art, they are fully able to summon up original shapes out of their subconscious resources, as well as to make sensitive selections from their environment. Below, we see how a child, in his construction of a crane in metal and wood, probably inspired by the giant derricks used in the building industry, has discovered a repertoire of shapes representing the function of the machine he is seeking to express.

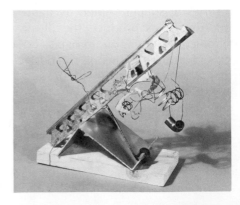

Boy, age eleven and a half

Clay is perhaps the most pliable of all sculptural media. No complicated techniques or tools are needed. It is readily available and fairly inexpensive. It can be handled directly, providing great tactile satisfactions. It can be fashioned into almost anything one could imagine. When fired successfully, it has durability.

Fifteen years of working with children in this medium, with most of the students using the clay two or three times a week, has convinced me that this material is, along with paint, one of the best that can be provided in our schools. Children of all ages find pleasure and success in manipulating clay, no matter what level of skill and invention they may have achieved. When one holds in one's hand the clay earth—soft, flexible, with its residue of ancient forms once living in nature—one experiences a true sense of identification with the human past. Children seem to feel this even when it is not pointed out to them.

Many educators have found it rewarding to provide for preadolescents as well as children of other ages a primary experience in the medium: digging the clay, refining it, wedging, forming an object or figure, then firing it in the ground as the American Indians and other early cultures did. Summer camps often offer this activity. It is appalling, on the other hand, to go into innumerable schools and see the students, who are supposedly studying the Indians, merely copying some designs on cheap manila paper with crayons—designs which the teacher believes are Indian motifs on the basis of one (possibly unreliable) book on the subject. On a recent trip to Puerto Rico, the author learned from art educators that although there are excellent clay deposits on the island once used by the original Indian inhabitants, they could not interest teachers in using this natural resource in their schools—schools which suffer badly from lack of material to work with in any area. Such a mine should be worked, both for education and for creative pleasure. Chandler Montgomery in *Art for Teachers of Children* gives us a fine passage on the qualities of clay (13: p. 84).

There is a warm quality to the material. Natural, fired, or glazed, it is not unlike the human skin, perhaps one of the reasons it was so widely used for statues, votive offerings, and funerary figures. Children work best in clay when modeling with their hands the human figure in the various, endless positions and scenes that occur to them. Other favorite subject matter includes monsters, imaginative creatures, and every variety of animal.

Temperamentally the child from age nine to thirteen wants quick success with a minimum of effort; he craves a feeling of mastery or confidence. Flexible, moist clay permits easy and rapid modeling, provides smooth finishes, and allows for the addition of the details preadolescents love to use as an expression of their developing realism. After the material becomes leather-

Grade six—girl

hard, it is suitable for carving and inscribing of linear effects. Sharp cuts and deep penetrations result in bold shadows which enhance the illusion of reality.

Moreover, clay objects can be finished in an enormous number of ways, depending on the time allotted to the program and the size of the budget. Color can play an important role here; with paint the preadolescent can satisfy his desire for a finished look and realistic detail.

Each child will respond differently to clay. Each will find his own way. Even beginners can achieve some success. The speed with which a piece can be finished is perfectly adapted to the preadolescent volatility. These children are always hungry to pass to new experiences. In transition emotionally and intellectually, they are often too distracted to sustain interest in a medium requiring tedious effort and perfection of technique, such as the resistive woods, stone, or metal. Quick results are desirable because only by making many objects and observing how they dry and survive or break in the fire can the child learn how to construct his piece solidly enough to endure.

The lack of in-between steps or extensive waiting also makes for spontaneity, a quality which is in harmony with the nature of clay. Details may or may not be added, casually or meticulously, according to the children's temperament and visual interest. At this age they may enjoy the idea of making pottery but seldom have the patience to accumulate the necessary skills, especially since they cannot help feeling that the machine can do it better. They like to use the wheel, one of the few pieces of mechanical equipment they are allowed to manipulate. But wheels are difficult to obtain in the schools, and this makes it unrealistic to develop in any one individual a serious degree of proficiency. Therefore, the following suggested experiences will concentrate on the sculptured figure or scenes including several figures with props, which children of this age create so freely and imaginatively and which provide a natural way for them to expand, with practice, the range and quality of their expression.

Depending on individual temperament, children create their figures and small dramas by either the additive or pull-out method, though the former is generally more common at this age. A few see the work as a whole from the start and are able to create it by gouging out parts from a lump of clay, making limbs that gesture and seem to move without attaching more material. The majority add coils for legs and arms and attach their figures to rolled-out slabs. Lowenfeld and Brittain, who have analyzed extensively these two methods practiced by eleven- to thirteen-year-olds, rightly insist that working methods should not be interfered with during the preadolescent period. They call the additive method (the putting together of parts) "synthetic" and practiced naturally by "non visually minded" children whose thinking "relates to details that are of emotional significance." On the other hand, "visually minded" children "use the analytic method of pulling out details from the whole" (14: p. 299). The differences between these two inclinations should be carefully noted by the teacher and taken into account in her motivation and evaluation of each child. The visually minded should be encouraged to pay attention to "the visual changes of form" and the non visually minded stimulated to express their subjective experiences (14: p. 229).

Teaching suggestions, setups, and procedures   As an early project, it might be suggested that children team up by twos or in groups to create a skit using clay figures. This will give them a sense of the power they have over this pliable material. Objects, people, and animals are made and then manipulated as puppets before an audience of other pupils. Arms are taken off and put back in other positions; heads are twisted about; figures are walked off and on the scene and are quickly propped into positions. Younger children like to participate in this kind of play. From it they learn about the material—what it will and will not do—and the methods each finds most natural to employ.

Enough clay should be provided for each child so that he can work with both hands and feel there is enough in reserve if he wants it. If the clay is skimped, the experience is hardly worth embarking on. Working on too small a scale prevents the child from actually feeling the medium with his hands and becoming so physically involved that the clay becomes an extension of himself. Most preadolescents work well, as a normal practice, with two balls or lumps of clay 5 to 6 inches in diameter. They should have a third piece in reserve. With this amount of clay they can make pieces that stand 5 or 7 inches high, adding a pedestal, and props if they wish.

Tools should be considered as secondary to the hands and fingers, and not introduced until the children have found out how much they can do without them. Then those tools which are extensions of the fingers can be provided. A kitchen paring knife with a short blade, blunted at the tip if desired, is good for cutting slabs of clay. A cutting wire is a necessary item. One of these for general use in the studio is attached to the wedging table. Others can be fastened to wooden dowels for individual use, such as dividing lumps of clay or lifting a piece off the table or the plaster bat. Loop tools are used to hollow out or carve. A wooden orange stick or tongue depressor, sponge, two tin cups and a plaster bat complete the list of simple tools, though in some cases the children may be provided with their own rolling pins so that they need not wander around the studio to find the one in general use when they want to roll out a slab of clay.

A child works well in clay without too much instruction, but usually there are two important techniques over which he must gain some control. Otherwise he will soon lose all desire to make any serious or creative effort in clay. First, he must be able to make his figures and animals *stand up.* Second, he must be taught to construct them so that they will *survive in the kiln.*

To stand up firmly and to withstand the fire, the clay must be of the right consistency. This involves proper wedging. All the children should understand how important and basic this first step is and should participate in it as much as possible. All art rooms can have a simple wedging table.

Children want to make figures that will stand up. The steps leading up to this accomplishment can be as formal as desired by the teacher or called for by the temperament of the children. Some teachers make an elaborate production of it because they feel that youngsters will derive both knowledge and enjoyment from the construction of solids such as spheres, cylinders, pyramids, and cubes. But in its simplest terms, to construct a figure one needs a sphere for the head, a bar rectangle for the body, and some cylinders for legs and arms. To make the figure stand, the most important factor is the quality of the cylinders—

or possibly rectangles—to be used for legs. If they are not solid all the way through, they will not support the weight of the body. If they are not skillfully attached to the body, they will not stick to it in the firing. The use of slip is well adapted to children's skills. They consider it a kind of paste and learn to roughen the surface where the joints will be attached add the slip, and then smoothing first in one direction and then in another.

Hollowing out the figure is done to avoid failures in the firing resulting from too much mass. Some instruction on hollowing out the bulk of the body is necessary, though this process may be omitted until the children have gained more knowledge and control.

At the important moment of standing up the figure, which has usually been made lying down, feet may be added to balance it more firmly. Now is the time for the child to decide on the gesture and movement he wants for his small created person and to move the arms, legs and head to create them. Now props and textural details can be added (clothes, eyes, shoelaces, etc.).

At the start of the year, under the influence of so much direct instruction, the results often come out looking like robots, not very different from each other. But this can be mitigated when details are added and command over the material has been achieved. Children learn as time goes on to remove some of the chunky quality after the piece has become leather-dry and will stand the greater pressure of tools.

Now that the figure stands securely upright and has been decorated, textured, and finished, depending on the ambition of its maker, his level of sophistication and skill, and the resources of the studio, the next step is the drying. After several weeks of this comes the firing. At the beginning of the year, the children have little or no idea why their pieces have survived or broken in the fire. As time goes on, they become more experienced and utilize more fully the various drying stages. As they work, they learn how dangerous it is to handle their drying pieces, which are most fragile at this time. Also, evidence of poor construction is made clear to them when their works dry too fast and fall apart before they are at the firing stage. For many of them, this reinforces their determination to pay more attention to the wedging, the solidity of their coils and attachments, and the initial drying process.

The lack of organization which sometimes occurs in studio management may contribute to the ruin of an individual's work and ultimately discourage him from trying again. The odds have to be pretty good that pieces created with love and enthusiasm will survive at least until they are completed—and, hopefully, for a while after that. The art teacher who cannot give some minimal guarantee of this will see her preadolescents hurrying to finish their work too fast, working with clay that is too wet or too hard, and discouraged because their pieces crack in the kiln or never even survive the drying period.

Use of coil The coil is a basic element in clay forming. The making of coils should be mastered early in the semester. Very thin coils are used for linear elements, such as hair and fingers. The coil is elemental, moreover, in the making of hollow vessels to be turned into pottery or utilized as hollow animals, masks, or figures. The South American Indians specialized in such anthropomorphic forms. Ernest Rottger's *Creative Clay Design* (15: pp. 9–51) includes many interesting projects of this sort, and there is, of course, a vast heritage of objects in our museums to use as inspiration.

The slab: Platforms, environments, pedestals, reliefs, mosaics Preadolescents must master the rolling out of a proper slab if they are to create with any success the elaborate compositions they like so much. The slab is made by pressing and rolling clay with a rolling pin between two identically thick pieces of wood. The slab must be even if it is to survive the fire and constructed solidly enough all the way through to support figures and objects. Children find it important to set their scenes on slabs, which can represent ground, floor, or any special place or material a child has in mind, as in the following creation. In this scene, a man is sitting on a rock with his can of bait beside him.

Grade six—boy

The slab itself, worked into figurative or abstract relief, can provide many exciting sculptural possibilities. A nonobjective project that might be suggested to a child inclined in that direction is to cut a slab into strips of clay and attach these in overlapping patterns to another slab. Some strips might be painted different colors or contain grog, while others could be left unfinished. The subtle variety of texture and color and interweaving lines can result in very interesting bas-reliefs. Of course, children will invent their own designs in many original ways without too much prompting. After seeing cuneiform writing and Egyptian hieroglyphics, they may want to devise a new language on clay tablets, perhaps writing coded messages to each other. Letters, numbers, geometric shapes, figures, and natural objects can be cut out like cookies and applied to a slab for interesting effects.

Long, complicated stories can be told through a series of coordinated reliefs, made either by one child or a group or by the whole class working together. Examples of these story-telling reliefs appear on architectural structures throughout history—for instance, on the Parthenon and in all Christian churches as the stations of the Cross.

Clay slabs cut into small pieces are useful in making mosaics. More readily available and cheaper than glass, clay mosaics can be produced on a large scale. The clay slab can be cut, bent, joined, or textured, to create three-dimensional forms. Boxes or other more amorphous forms can be designed as niches in which to place all sorts of fascinating objects. Representational and abstract forms, three-dimensional or flat, can be cut from slabs and ultimately hung as mobile structures. Wind chimes, bells, and puppets have been successfully created by preadolescents from the slab.

Surface finishes When children arrive at the point where they are eager to apply details of face, hair, fur, eyebrows, clothing, grass textures, sandy or rocky terrains, water and the like, they are ready for a large variety of experiments. They soon discover that there are two major processes which alter the quality of a clay surface: displacing material or adding it. In the first category, an impression is made on the surface with the fingers or simple tools to create pressed relief designs, or the child may scratch or gouge out the surface. The second method is additive; clay shapes, bits of clay, or clay designs can be applied to the original surface. Also, the surface can be covered with a glaze. Mixing the two methods can have exciting results.

1. *Incising, stamping, pressing.* Textures can be created in these three ways when the clay is in various stages of wetness. There are many tools to try out, all of them inexpensive and

consisting of ordinary objects and common kitchen tools—not to mention what can be done with finger impressions alone. As an eye-opening experience in perception, this activity is among the best and easiest to provide.

A texture box, containing interesting imprinting objects, is a must for every clay room. Children often become enthusiastic about finding new items that will make their clay works more effective. A good homework assignment is to have them bring in such things as buttons, paste jewelry, nuts and bolts, saw blades, shells, various-sized pebbles, sticks, spools, nails and brads, bottle tops, hairpins, hair rollers, screens or any kind of perforated material, corrugated paper, carved corks, and combs.

It is better for children to look around a bit before deciding what to apply to a piece of work. Help them develop the habit of not taking out of the texture box the first thing they see, or using the same old cliché over and over again. If they are considering hair texture, they might try a variety of textures on flat pieces of clay perhaps 3 by 3 inches in size. Then place each, in turn, on their work to see which one enhances it. Have them repeat the process for clothes texture, considering at the same time whether the object takes away from or enhances the design chosen for the hair. These small experiments do not mar the work, since they are tried on lightly and can be removed.

When a child comes upon a superior textural effect, it is a good idea to drill a hole in the piece, fire it, and add it to a permanent collection accumulated in some part of the room. Children ready to apply texture can go to this three-dimensional chart to find ideas.

Every once in a while, a class or a small group within it may enjoy making texture stamps. This involves making a tool out of clay which will imprint, once it is fired. These stamping tools must have holding devices; in the end, they sometimes become carefully made sculptures in themselves. Some children who have finished ahead of the others with their part of a class project may be encouraged to make them, for personal use or to be donated to the general collection.

2. *Adding to the surface.* One can stamp, cut out, or make by hand a series of shapes to be attached to the original clay surface in order to create a pattern. This pattern is sometimes stamped into for additional richness. Formal, random, nonobjective or representational designs can result.

3. *Glazes, engobes, slip painting.* Applying glazes or engobes to the surface is another way of finishing or decorating a work. Glazes have always been avoided by the author when working with preadolescents, because they are expensive and require much special equipment and a disciplined technique that is

difficult for children of this age unless much personal attention is provided. Moreover, the complications encountered in the firing are almost insurmountable when working with a large class. After observing many clay programs, I have noted one great weakness: teachers allow children to mar their pieces with cheap, streaked glazes merely to give the children the dubious pleasure of comparing them with the shiny objects they can buy in stores. Somehow the ultimate in both the teacher's and the child's mind seems to be the finish of the Walt Disney animal sculpture, or flower pot sculpture (Mexican donkey with cactus in his back or a white swan carrying a plant), or the many other eyesores prevalent in our discount stores—all with the Midas touch of sprinkled gold on them.

This is exactly the taste we as art teachers should try to counteract. The answer, in the author's opinion, is to encourage children to cherish the quality of the clay itself—the light and dark created by the forms and the textural qualities that can be imprinted or appliquéd to the surface. When enough attention is given to these qualities and children see the artist's use of them in many historical pieces, the children forget the shiny glazed surface and are perfectly satisfied without it. As ten- or eleven-year-olds, they find it hard to realize that a white powder will turn into a bright color and why it is so important to keep a separate brush for each glaze and to accept the accidents that will occur in the firing. It is far better to work with engobe at this age.

Engobes are colored slips—in other words, a liquid clay mixture plus pigment. Before firing, engobes appear to be light pastel colors; after firing, the color emerges as much stronger. Even the pastel version helps the child feel he has some control over the finish. Children interested in producing realistic scenes or expecting certain specific effects avoid the disappointments which usually occur when glazes run, crawl or stick. Teachers are pleased to minimize the time consumed in the repeated handling, delicate stacking and the double firing glazes require. Children can use the time saved to gain proficiency; twice as many pieces can be completed. (For additional reading on glazes and other useful teaching techniques, see Henry Petterson [16].)

On the general subject of finishes, it must be emphasized that children should be discouraged from thinking of surface qualities and details merely as decorative additions or illustrative information. Wonderful decorative pieces do exist in ceramic sculpture, and some artists have the personality and the need to do them. But too often the teacher's emphasis on decorative surfaces is out of proportion. The real significance of a work is what is communicated in feeling as a whole, and too much concentration on decoration of isolated parts and finish clutters the expression of subjective feeling. It is apt to distract the viewer from analytic appreciation of mass, monumentality, and other structural qualities.

Mixed media projects   It is usually the younger children in a preadolescent group who enjoy making panoramas, using not only clay figures but also many interesting materials that lend themselves to the scenes or events they are trying to depict. Older preadolescents are more interested in developing one idea or one sculptured figure in depth. The younger ones like to produce people and objects simultaneously, to manipulate them in play and pretend games.

In one school, art teachers appropriated narrow tables which were about to be discarded. Children signed up for these tables singly or in groups for 2 or 3 weeks at a time. They tabled their displays in the halls and had recorded music going for a few days, after lunch, when most of their classmates were passing through. The tables were in constant use for displaying clay scenes. Some depicted circuses, skating rinks, Martians, wax museums, houses of terror, and anything else that interested the children.

One solution to the discipline problem   A group of boys were making life pretty miserable for several of us who taught the regular art class. Nothing seemed important to them except their continuous sex jokes and showing off to any interested girl by some act of bravado, such as baiting the teacher or destroying a piece of equipment.

It was finally possible to get them located as an isolated group in the clay room, with the door closed between them and the girls. Then the real confrontation began between them and the teacher, who "played it cool" by busying herself with chores around the room. She was actually determined to find a clue that would indicate how to lead these youngsters into something with meaning for them.

At first they pummeled the clay, made snakes and balls and threw them at each other. Then they made male sexual organs which they hid under their hands while they nudged each other and laughed. The teacher, with her head in a cupboard or apparently absorbed in scrubbing a wedging board, was the butt of many a whispered gibe. Finally she decided the moment was opportune to call their bluff and, turning toward them, said something to the effect that if they wanted to make the naked body in clay, why didn't they do it? Nude human beings have always been the favorite subject of sculptors, she told them. There was nothing unusual about that.

The boys were startled and amused. "Only make things large so that we can see them!" she finished. They started fashioning some female bodies. Boys from ten on will occasionally do the female form but very seldom the male nude. On this occasion they made many female nudes, played with them as if they were dolls, then destroyed, then re-created them—all this very quickly, with absorption and pleasure in the clay and the idea. By the end of the period they were relaxed and nonaggressive; the experience seemed to have relieved their tension and self-consciousness. They leaned and lolled on the tables, and when the teacher asked for a hand in the clean-up, they buzzed around equably, squeezing water out of sponges with vigor and popping materials into the proper places, practicing basketball shots accurately with other items. They had changed from "fresh boys" into almost friendly and cooperative ones, some leaving with the casual promise, "So long, see you next week."

Next week some of them came immediately to the clay room. The teacher wondered where their interest would now take them. They were rather quiet, in comparison with their usual behavior; they got their clay on their own, and the tools they needed. The teacher placed as much clay as possible at their disposal, well wedged and in the best condition for use. She had taken out her collection of photographs of sculpture mounted on sturdy boards—Michelangelo, Bernini, Rodin, Moore, Marini, Segal, Trova—in an effort to stimulate subject matter. The reaction of the children was loud and clear: How about wrestlers and other sportsmen? How about acrobats? Horsemen?

The schedule had been arranged, by the way, so that one teacher could remain continuously with these boys while another took care of the rest of the class. This went on for several months. (No pains should be spared in arranging continuity of this sort. Flexibility of schedule is one of the keys to working with preadolescents.)

As the boys pounded the clay on the tables, pushing, building, destroying, laughing, and chewing gum, there was a good deal of conversation about why artists represented their figures doing things without their clothes on. The teacher would perch on a stool and give attention to their intermittent questions. Why did sculptors make their human figures nude? Well, maybe it began with the Greeks, who believed that a beautiful body and a beautiful mind had a relation to each other. They made their men in the image of their gods, and gods were universal, not bound by local costume, a special time or a special place. Sculpture was thought of as the depiction of supermen, representing eternal ideas. Immortality was tied up with it, too. The gods had eternity at their disposal; it would have been inappropriate to show them as ordinary men limited by a short life span and the fashion of their times. The Romans admired the Greek attitudes and philosophy and disseminated them throughout their vast empire. These concepts were revived during the Renaissance and have survived to this day.

The boys had a good deal of knowledge at their fingertips from their history and social study classes, and this discussion spread over many periods. Modern sculpture was looked at as well as the old, demonstrating that ordinary men and ordinary activities seem to have become the sculptor's concern nowadays.

After the exhilaration of experiencing great sculpture, the teacher tried to channel the boys into personal expressions. She suggested that they investigate and depict figures from a period of history that attracted them or pick some outstanding contemporary prototypes they admired. She asked them to be ambitious in their ventures. "Look at these enormous things. They were built by men with gigantic ambition and ability. Make your things large—create whole scenes—tell complicated stories."

As it turned out, their selections naturally involved subjects close to preadolescent hearts and knowledge of reality. One student did a whole orchestra, with figures 8 to 10 inches high. Another chose to make his people nude as they enjoyed the tunnel of love at Coney Island.

Grade six—boy

Another did a saloon scene laid in the Old West, with all the main characters—gamblers in the corner, the bar with its drunks, the gunman at the door, and, most amazing feat of all, a row of cancan girls. These he deftly cut out with a knife without any preliminary drawing, like someone cutting out paper dolls, carrying on all the while an animated conversation about ball games and star players. He swiftly stood them up, bending their legs to give them proper balance, and then, standing back, he loudly declared, "Hey, you guys, look at this!" The rest of the class banged their tables, whistled, cheered, stomped their feet, and gave catcalls in proper appreciation. The teacher's extreme satisfaction and pleasure went unnoticed in the midst of the debris, displaced equipment and general chaos in which these gems had been formed.

Grade six—Joe

Grade six—Joe

Grade six—Joe

The clay service   A "clay service" came into being in our school more or less accidentally, but it turned out to be a boon for the preadolescent boys, the teachers, the building superintendent and the principal. The big boys had been making trouble for some time by going down into the subbasement to smoke and play around. Our chief superintendent was obliged to report them, and there was a punishment involved. The art teachers had to go down there often to the chamber where our dry, used clay was broken down, put into bins, watered, set, and then reconditioned through wedging so that it could be used again. It was a very messy job, and the art teachers took turns with the cutting, pounding and wedging. One of the maintenance men helped us lift the heavy cans.

The boys hung around when we were pounding the clay, and were often asked to pound and wedge with us so that we could justify their presence if an official came along. They loved the work; with their young exuberance and strength they threw the clay against the plaster like maniacs. Soon the word got around that there was a great thing going on down there. They began to keep track of our hours, and often there were small groups waiting to come down with us to the subbasement.

Finally, of course, this fun had to be legalized in some way, and that is how the boys' clay service came into being. In exchange for some assigned time to play in the subbasement, under the supervision of one of the maintenance men, the boys offered to wedge clay and deliver it to the various classrooms of the younger children who needed it (Lucile F. Young, instructor).

The boys organized themselves under elected leaders and made decisions about admitting other boys to their group. They made emblems for their service, which they pinned to their clothes, and advertised through the school paper and by means of posters which they designed themselves. They devised a bulletin board where teachers signed up for clay and which they ornamented with sketches and drawings of their adventures in the subbasement.

It seems redundant to point out the advantages to all concerned. The superintendent and his men were no longer policemen, the boys no longer delinquents. In a school where males were so scarce, they no longer had to fight with each other. One of the maintenance men became their teacher, supervisor and sponsor. The boys loved the work as well as the play and were proud to be in charge of the clay supply for the younger children. They liked having a clique with emblems and a place where they could get away from the girls. A good deal of artwork resulted from their project, plus many illustrated stories and poems for their English class—stories that made them appear as heroes to the younger children as they exaggerated the delightful dangers of the subbasement. Nor did they tire of it quickly;

the clay service went on for years. Waiting boys replaced the ones who graduated. That remote and steaming underworld, with its earthy clay to be pummeled and hurled with such abandon, had a perennial appeal.

Assessment for clay work Often before the pieces are ready for firing, a teacher will gather together all the work of an individual child and review with him what has happened. Evaluation means looking for the following qualities in a work: total feeling and expression of the piece; soundness of structure; subordination of details and textures to overall concept; qualities of the volumes, voids, penetrating forms, and variety of shape and size; motion through continuing contours and the actual change of mobile forms; and light and dark effects. Teacher and child will discuss the different pieces in relation to these sculptural aspects and come to some conclusions as to where a given work has succeeded and where the attempt—to create a sense of unity, for instance—has been abortive because cluttering has hampered a linear rhythmic flow. The range of a child's subject matter may need attention from time to time. Has he explored enough possibilities in the fields of representational, nonobjective, organic and symbolic forms? Does he have to? Perhaps his feeling and drive for one or a few of these is sufficient.

WOOD

In the dense prehistoric forest, wood was undoubtedly more plentiful than any other workable material. As soon as he had some sort of sharp tool, early man must have been a whittler and a carver. But unprotected wood is perishable, and while some bone, stone, terra cotta and bronze sculpture survived, we have inherited very few wooden objects from those obscure millennia. By the same token, the only wood carving that remains from earliest recorded centuries comes from lands where the climate and the cultural environment were conducive to its survival.

From Egypt come relief panels and some portrait sculpture. Here wood was scarce and so precious that it was considered almost sacred. Much of it was imported from Lebanon and Syria to make statues, thrones, coffins, and furniture. Often the artist encased a carved wooden figure in sheets of gold, copper or bronze. In the Orient, where wood was more plentiful, the climate on the whole more favorable and the culture advanced, a long tradition of carving exists. In India, Burma, Indonesia, Japan and China, wood has always been a medium inspiring great artistry and sophisticated techniques.

Greece and Rome have left us their history in marble, terra cotta, metal and stone, but wood seems to have been used mainly for perishable dwellings and furniture. In the early Middle Ages, Christian art produced small wood reliefs and objects made by skilled monks and used by pilgrims as they made their way on religious pilgrimages. They were mostly nonfigurative and show a fusion of classical, Byzantine and rhythmic Eastern influence. The Byzantine ban on artistic representation of human beings affected sculpture until the eleventh century, when figure carving again appeared. At that point, the new confidence of the people seems to have imbued wood sculpture with feeling and spontaneous expression. The artists' ideas were drawn mostly from illuminated manuscripts, the works of preceding times in metal, ivory, and textiles, and some from classical ruins. From this period come the Crucifixions and Madonnas with Child, showing the ravages of time but distinguished not only because they are a thousand years old but because they are warm, clumsy, human, and simple in their message and execution. All too many of them, unfortunately, were deliberately destroyed or defaced during later religious wars.

Gothic wood carvers followed the lead of the stonecutters and in fact replaced the stone furnishings of the churches with wooden pews, screens, choir stalls, altars, organ lofts, and galleries. Gradually they liberated themselves from the stone-carving traditions and created objects more suitable to their medium. But work in wood, even sacred work, has always been vulnerable to human whim, ignorance, anger, and vandalism. As Freda Skinner says:

In the course of refurbishing the old churches in past centuries— "clearing out the clutter," as one bishop expressed it—much of the wood-work used to be taken out and destroyed. . . . Wood is not as easily defaced as stone; the heads and hands of a wood carving cannot be struck off with a blow. But it is comparatively light and easy to remove and carry away, and being dry and well-seasoned, must unfortunately have made good fuel for iconoclasts' bonfires [17: pp. 123–124].

Gothic wood carvers have left us many clues to medieval life. Since their work was relegated to the less sacred spots in the church, they were allowed to indulge their individual tastes and, in some cases, their genius. Here we see a man with a jaw swollen from toothache; there are people sowing, baking bread, reaping the grain, hunting, hawking, and wrestling in a tournament. Pets and fantastic animals from the bestiary abound. Biblical characters wear the clothes of the time and have plain hardy European peasant faces.

Relief sculptures in that era were skillfully executed in rich woods, sometimes carved so deep as to resemble stage sets. Free-standing figures, from small to over-life-size, are also found all over Europe, though the gothic style never really took root on the Italian peninsula.

By the thirteenth century, Renaissance ideas and life styles had transformed all the arts in the cultural rejuvenation that lasted 300 years. The Italians found clues and inspiration among the fragments of their great Roman period. Since wood is scarce in Italy, they used mostly marble and stone, but there are extraordinary interior furnishings left, and several wooden pieces by Donatello. Renaissance statues in wood were made, however, all over Europe, to be followed quickly by baroque sculpture, which emphasized movement, restless energy, gesture, and liked to depict real people in moments of intense emotion—revelation, suffering, ecstasy—intended to stir the viewer and involve him in the miracles and martyrdoms of the saints. These same wooden figures have survived to this day and are carried in religious processions.

Under the aegis of the French rococco style (1720–1780) wood carving became highly decorative, frivolous, elegant and delicate. Its scrolls, swags, festoons, fans, shells, vases in linear relief, hair in corkscrews, fluttering materials, feathers, and delicate spreading limbs were all meticulously executed.

In reaction, neoclassical and romantic periods for the next hundred years harked back to medieval wood carving as well as to certain classical modes. William Morris in England promoted an arts and crafts movement to revive wood carving in protest against the increasing factory production. Some folk art was preserved, including the carving of figureheads. And with archaeology in full swing, expeditions all over the globe turned up heretofore unknown objects, concepts, forms, and styles. The superb wood carvings of the Northwest American Indians and the Africans were brought to light, and the skill and imaginative variety of these newly discovered works in wood had a profound influence on the artists of the twentieth century.

The finest sculpture that we inherit from the last 200 years is African. Its quality stems partly from the fact that it grew out of a persistent tradition of superb workmanship maintained from generation to generation. Even more, since its objects were an outgrowth of religious beliefs, magical forms to be worshiped and/or worn as charms against death and disaster, they had the energy and presence of a meaningful living art.

This brief history of wood usage has been included to assist the teacher in preparing the visual aids which will orient the children to the association between mankind and this material. (For further reading, see Peggy Mills [17: pp. 110–156].)

Carving and whittling   Almost any machine-age preadolescent would enjoy carving on a large free-standing log. Unfortunately such a piece of wood does not easily find its way into our city or suburban schools. Rural schools in forested regions could probably manage it, if those in authority believed in the arts and their serious inclusion in the curriculum.

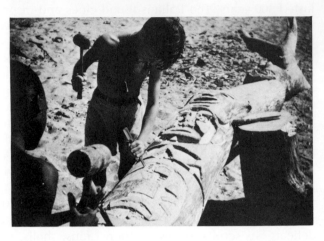

In America we have an extensive wood tradition to pass on to our children, beginning with the Indians in northwestern Canada and Alaska, who are excellent wood carvers; the Eskimos, who in Alaska carved the driftwood that floated in from the sea; the Hopis of our Southwest; and our Eastern seaboard founders, especially in New England, who were great shipbuilders, natural architects and wood craftsmen. They placed voluptuous figure-heads on the prows of their handsome wood vessels to bring luck on their journeys around the world. They made furniture and carved architectural details that have become collectors' items. Shaker wood craftsmanship is known for its elegant simplicity.

The expense of hardwood and carving tools, plus the time-consuming technical problem of sharpening these tools, seems to preclude any large preadolescent experience in carving in our schools. Softwood is much easier to come by—pine, bass-wood, balsa—but here again the upkeep of proper tools is hardly possible for either student or teacher. We have inevitably settled for the whittling of random wood scraps and the creation of interesting "constructions," many combining wood with other media.

One of the few essentials for the studio, apart from enough tools to go around, is a large bin for wood contributions. New wood, weathered wood, driftwood, bits of trim, spindles, spools, plywood veneers, knobs, coat hangers, remnants of wood furniture—everything and anything in wood is grist to the mill. If possible, some softwoods should be available. Dowels and rods are important items to stock, along with bamboo poles, cardboard, and plywood.

Tools should include simple knives, drills, wood-burning instruments, hammers, nails, coping saws, crosscut saws, a power saw if possible, pliers, screwdrivers, planes, vises, and steel wool. Adhesives should be plastic resin glues like epoxy, plus wood putty and plastic wood. Finishes can include wax, stains, oil, paints, shellac and lacquer.

Whittling in miniature and carving fruit pits, coconut shells, bamboo shoots, matchsticks, thick and thin sticks of all kinds, and small blocks of wood are activities that appeal to preadolescents. The resulting objects can stand, move, or be amalgamated into a more complex whole or embellished with other materials. For instance, a bird's body made from a block of wood can be given feathers for a tail, wires for chest and legs, etc. Children can whittle remarkable puppets from softwood. Boys who go fishing like to carve lures or lobster buoys. Chessmen and models of ships and planes are made from white pine, balsa, or basswood. These objects can be made kinetic in various ways as children learn the use of hinge and pivot. Thus, while children of this age may not have the patience or know-how to use or maintain carving tools, they can become happily and gainfully involved in whittling and finishing with care an endless number of small pieces.

Sawing, mounting and constructing   Children enjoy using both the hand and power saw and can be encouraged to cut out shapes, not only for three-dimensional structures but also for reliefs. The works of Arp can act as excellent inspiration for these projects. Children can use wood which they themselves have sawed into shapes or precut wood which they may or may

Girl, age ten
A Walk in the Park"

not be able to alter. They should be urged to handle and study the shapes for some time, and not decide too quickly which ones they want to change and how they will put them together. Until the child is satisfied with the arrangement, he may tape it together to see how it looks; later, glue, nails, brads, and rivets will permanently secure it. Wood scraps can often be combined into interesting geometric structures, as in the construction on page 299, called "A Walk in the Park."

Other kinds of constructions can be made with dowels, sticks or toothpicks. These structures can either be in relief or free-standing. Used with airplane model quick-drying cement, they make geometric shapes, cantilevered forms, and complex linear structures. The challenge of these materials is that they *are* linear. Usually a substantial number of similar units is required, and children must consider 1) the nature of the open structures, 2) succeeding levels of spatial penetration, and 3) the complicated movement caused by the multiplicity of directions assumed by the rods. The tempo may be rapid, slow, or staccato, according to the angles; the mood may be violent or calculated, heavy and complex, or buoyant, light and soaring.

Another challenge in rod and dowel and other linear structures lies in the area of color. Special considerations and problems of choice face the child as he attempts to achieve color unity to sustain a mood, communicate an emotion or make a social comment. The lack of planes and surfaces in such structures forces the child to use one overall neutralizing color, letting the linear action of the rods carry the meaning of the work. Otherwise he has to be extremely sensitive in his color selections.

Grade seven—boy

Children, like many adults, enjoy transforming a beaten-up, once elegant wood object into its original quality. They also like to do what modern artists are doing: giving old, used objects an exciting new existence as part of an assemblage. The wood assemblage shown is a collection of thread spools, rods and disks, and chest handles, among others. The children decided to make a series of persons and imaginary creatures. This sort of animism is very natural to children, who have no hesitation about turning objects into people and animals.

Finishing   Color can perform miracles on a wood structure. A strong example is the work of Louise Nevelson, which uses a coat of black paint to assimilate hundreds of dissimilar wooden objects into a new whole and to separate these familiar objects from their usual functional associations, giving them a new meaning. Her work projects a mood of dignity, urbanity, and sobriety. Monochromatic color gives unity to sculpture and sets it dramatically apart from its general environment, defining clearly the negative, or empty, spaces inside the construction.

Children should be constantly challenged to think of color because, like texture, it gives a special meaning to their work, expressing along with the shape the feeling they want to convey in their work. Grained wood, which of itself has so much beauty of texture and variety of color, may not be painted. Paint should be used to take care of some special aesthetic necessity, as in the case of the balsa airplane painted to simulate metal. In the sculpture entitled "Airplane Catapult" (see below), the artist has carefully assigned a special color to each function of the machine. Patterning and color communicate symbolically;

Boy   *Airplane catapult*

the striped sections emphasize the direction of flight, and the portions painted red and orange locate areas in which the energy will be produced. The painted cross might be used to indicate doors for entry into the machine.

It is possible that in spite of their love of radical color effects, children will find less appeal in painting wood than in waxing, oiling, staining, and shellacking in order to highlight texture, grain and subtle natural colors. Burning is another finishing process that appeals to them. A recent concept of finish —or "nonfinish," as one might call it—has emerged from the use of found objects. Instead of refurbishing old wood, it is left showing the signs of urban use it has suffered.

PAPER

The Orient has long been associated with artistic paper products, along with Poland and Mexico. Japan is often called a "paper country" because of its people's ingenious and original use of the medium for both practical and aesthetic creations. The Chinese invented the first paper about 200 B.C., and the Arabs took it to Europe, where it was used as writing paper to replace the ancient Egyptian papyrus. In the East, it was originally made by hand from bamboo, jute and other grasses, and leaves. In Europe it was made from rags until the idea of "using wood pulp occurred to a French naturalist named Reamer in 1719." By 1789, there was a paper-making machine in use (18: pp. 26–29).

Modern technology has made available an almost endless variety of papers for news and magazine printing, book printing, packaging, stationery, blotting, cleaning and cosmetic uses. Different textures, colors and weights expand these categories: shiny, opaque, transparent, flexible, and rigid paper comes in all colors, offering an enticing challenge to the artist. Found paper objects are also plentiful and can offer many opportunities for creative expression.

Paper can be worked in two or three dimensions; it can be stamped, painted, embossed, cut into, or folded. For school-children the expendability of paper makes it a delightful medium. They can experiment without fear or hesitation. Mistakes cost almost nothing. When the supply closet is empty, the children can turn to newspapers, magazines, etc., and still create objects of interest and meaning out of paper.

By the time they are ten or eleven, children bring to art class many techniques of paper work learned in earlier years. They are ready to explore every aesthetic possibility of the medium. They have strong motivation, too; this is the age of get-togethers, both formal and informal. They constantly need party hats, banners, decorations, and hanging objects. For their plays they use paper scenery, props and often costumes. There are special occasions—holiday and club celebrations—when a room will need a complete change of decor, and paper is the most effective and cheapest answer.

Basic techniques   Preadolescents can easily master some basic ways of turning flat paper into three-dimensional forms. These provide the springboard for flight into originality and invention.

Tools and materials consist of simple household scissors, knives, staplers, rulers, glues and adhesives of all kinds.

1. Folding and cutting are methods for gaining dimension. Children learn to pleat paper, to crease well, and to make accordian pleats for their complicated, ambitious projects.

Fold-cut designs are easy and quick to make. By simply folding a square or other shape of paper in half and cutting along the free edges but not through the fold, many beautiful symmetrical patterns can be produced. Polish and Mexican peasants have been famous for such designs, and children studying these cultures can be stimulated to try to make either representational or abstract repeating shapes. At celebration times, schools can come alive with paper art; the children may combine their fold-cut designs into layers to make them into three-dimensional objects to hang as mobiles.

Interlocking and lantern structures can be created by folding and cutting. Narrow rectangles folded along their creases provide other structural effects. Elaborate forms can result when strips of paper are woven in and out of the openings of a fold-cut design.

One of the things children want to know is how to get many identical shapes quickly. As a quick review, one that challenges ingenuity, the teacher asks every child to make a shape of firm paper to be used as a pattern. She also distributes a double sheet of the local newspaper or other thin paper. The challenge is: Which person in the room will come up with the greatest number of identical shapes? Figuring, folding, and cutting, techniques are ultimately taught by one or two of the group, and the point about conservation of material is made painlessly.

2. Paper strips provide the simplest means of achieving three-dimensionality and can result in a great variety of free-standing and relief constructions. Children take to this technique, since here they do not have to memorize the order of folds.

With paper strips on hand, there are so many potentialities that one does not know where to start. Before producing anything, however, children should practice certain techniques, such as stapling, folding and curling the strips. They can be taught to use the dull edge of a scissors to curl the strip in the direction of the grain. Cutting fringes is also important, and they are used for all sorts of details, such as hair, eyelashes, mustaches and beards, feathers, animal tails, wings, grass, and trees.

3. Scoring is a method of creasing papers so that they fold crisply along the crack. The pressure of a knife handle, blunt scissor edge or compass point will make a crack which does not cut the paper but permits it to fold easily. Learning to score is essential, for it permits the child to make all kinds of raised surfaces, three-dimensional forms, and reliefs.

4. Dimension can be given to a surface by cutting into a flat piece of drawing paper, metallic paper, or metal foil such as used in the kitchen, allowing the cut form to project, still attached, from the flat sheet. The cast shadows are very important here, as in all reliefs; attention must be given to the light source. The level of projection can be enormously subtle, depending on the skill of the maker. Or separate papers that have been folded into shapes can be pasted on a flat sheet to make reliefs.

If a sheet of paper is cut into strips which are held together by the margins, other strips can be inserted or woven through the slits to form projections in regular or random patterns.

Preadolescents will enjoy making such light-catching reliefs in themselves. They will also learn to utilize them for their textural and patterned effects when combined in free-standing, three-dimensional work. In this example, the surface is given depth by assembling and pasting a number of geometric forms to a surface.

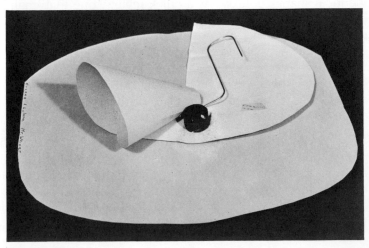

Boy, age twelve

Preadolescents as learners and teachers Many of the basic techniques and projects described here will have been learned by children when they were younger. To refresh the memories of some and to inspire good workmanship in all members of the class, a period or two during the early part of the semester should be devoted to review. This can be a very creative time for the children who remember accurately what they previously learned, either in or out of school, for they can be the demonstrators. Preparing teams of young instructors before the lesson usually stimulates interest, and if every member of the class is on some team or other, total involvement is assured.

There are some aesthetic warnings that the teacher can pass on to her young apprentice instructors. As they themselves know, one's first creations in paper are usually too fussy and unrelated in their parts. As one preadolescent said, they look like "garbage can sculpture," especially when shiny, polycolored papers are used. Tell students that there are some ways to counteract this. 1) Try to keep shapes, forms and strips of an equal size in a single structure, at least at first. 2) Vary them only after having had a number of successes with uniform shapes. For most projects, a single neutral color makes for the greatest clarity, catching the light in such a way as to give greatest contrast to the shadows (which is why white is so often preferred). All the attachments, such as staples, pins, and glue, should be kept unobtrusive.

Some children of this age become so expert that they want to spend most of their art periods working with paper. There should be enough flexibility in the program to allow this. Many others, however, will want to work on group paper projects only periodically and with a definite purpose in mind, such as a dramatic happening like a party or a play. Then they get together to accomplish ambitious group goals.

For these celebrations, many small similar items have to be produced for decoration. This is the moment for a happy and busy communal enterprise. The production line can come into great favor at such times. Several patterns are selected, and tables and materials are organized to take care of various stages of the operation. The children choose to perform various activities, and thus a massive project can get underway.

In connection with one particular project—decorations for a midwinter festival—when all kinds of leaves and birds had to be manufactured, the classroom teacher and the art teacher (whose husband was a production manager) discussed with the children how factory piece work was set up, with its progression of personnel—draftsmen, die makers, foremen, production managers, quality control men, etc.—and the children took on the various roles. A great deal of attention was given to economy, especially when the expensive papers where used. The leaves for the tree had to be laid out in a way that would get the most out of the paper, and leftover scraps were utilized. The children learned that at certain times a production line is not only a necessity but fun, and it thereafter became a regular method that they themselves could organize without the aid of adults.

Preadolescents are also capable of working in teams to teach younger children the skills they have developed. There was an impressive example of this in the Midtown Ethical Culture School in New York. A group of girls exhibited paper reliefs which so impressed a teacher in the lower grades that she asked them to demonstrate their techniques to her class. The art teacher agreed to supply the materials for their venture.

Once the word got around, other preadolescents thought they would like to become teachers, too. As time went on and more and more of them got involved, the whole procedure became better organized. Before going forth to their young pupils, they usually rehearsed their demonstration in front of the art class. This served as a good review for the rest of the class and an aid to the teacher. A demonstration van or cart was then devised to hold all the equipment the young teachers needed for their lessons so that they would be quickly available whenever and wherever they were needed in the school. At certain times of the year, such as Christmas and Easter, the cart was in daily use on a tight schedule. The younger children were actually taught all the basic techniques by preadolescents, and the art teacher spent her time working out new projects and ideas to be demonstrated by her pupils, along with devising more sophisticated objects for the older children to make for their own social functions. Below is one of the paper animals made by preadolescents to hang as decorations—the sort of thing they liked to teach the younger children to make.

Grade six—girl

Constructions with cylinders, angles, and flats Enormous as well as small structures, structures that emerge from a cooperative group effort, can be built with paper, oak tags, cardboard, or corrugated papers. Any of these materials in combination with armatures can expand a sculpture into a building feat. They can also be organized into modular units which again increase the variety of size and form attained. There are, moreover, many ways to combine all these types of paper once one becomes adventurous. They are all inexpensive, easy to work with, and useful in communicating important information to youngsters of this age about building, as they are manipulated with more or less the techniques used in that important trade.

1. Rolled tubes (cylinders) of newspaper (or other), cardboard tubes, or straws can be glued, tied, or taped together to make elaborate open structures or environments. The children can enter them. This is a good introduction to architecture and can be very exciting (19: p. 20).

2. Writing, tracing or drawing paper can be folded into strips lengthwise, forming a right angle. Constructing with angles, cleanly pasted and joined, provides structural elements which resemble metal angle irons, T bars, and steel joists. Elaborate abstract or figurative structures can be built with the help of these angles. Actual kinetic pieces can be made, too—pseudo-machines that can be made to move, depending on the skill of the child. Opaque or see-through papers can be fitted into the parts at will (19: p. 22).

3. Cardboard comes in large sheets, pretty much as metal does. Schools might go as far as supplying sheets of metal mesh or lighter gauges of metal, such as copper or zinc. This is easier today than it was in the past because of the relatively inexpensive rolls of fairly stiff aluminum available among our household products. It is too bad that we cannot give children an opportunity to construct and build in metal since they are living in the midst of a metal construction era. (Some of the most creative engineering minds of this century have concentrated on metal fabrication and use; it is the technological breakthrough on which America's prosperity is based. Children are not given any knowledge of this in the schools.

Papier-mâché Papier-mâché is an absolutely unbeatable medium for the ambitious preadolescent who needs scale and grandeur in his work to bolster his confidence in his ability to achieve. Every school, regardless of budget restrictions, can afford to let children work with papier-mâché. The wallpaper paste or paste made from flour and starch are very inexpensive, and newspaper is free.

Papier-mâché sculpture is made by soaking paper in paste and then applying it to an armature. Newspaper is most commonly used, but paper toweling, tissue and other papers are equally satisfactory. Armatures can include any object or structure which will retain its shape under moisture: wire, all kinds of wire meshes, wood and wood rods, plastic meshes and tubes, and cardboards. Ready-made natural or manufactured objects will do well: cans, boxes, balloons, bottles, utensils and tools. Fruits, vegetables, stones—even wadded, folded or crumpled paper—will serve as an armature.

There are a number of ways to use the paper. Paper pulp, handled like clay, can be molded into shapes which will harden with or without an armature. Paper strips can be laminated over armatures; thin layers of paper can be pressed into a mold to form a thin shell when dry. Paper can be laminated in large sheets, folded, and cut and put over a simple armature made of crumpled newspaper to give support to the structure until it dries.

When papier-mâché sculptures are dry, they may be finished in numerous fashions. They may be sandpapered to give smoothness, gesso-covered, and sandpapered for an even finer finish. Mosaic tesserie may be added; they can be covered with cloth and materials of all kinds (plastics, beans, furs, found objects). They can be painted, shellacked, varnished, lacquered, or waxed. Finishings for papier-mâché can fill a volume. The opportunity for original invention is staggering.

It is by no means a new medium. We have colorful and gay objects from China, Japan, India and Burma made in papier-mâché. On this continent, Mexico offers a delightful array of figures, animals and dishes made of this material. Papier-mâché figures are used profusely in department store window displays throughout Europe and the United States. Most recently, serious and dramatic sculptures have been created by such artists as Claes Oldenburg and Niki de Sainte Phalle. There are many examples in the art of the past and the present to use as illustration and motivation. In one school some fantastic fetish figures were made by children after some exposure to oceanic cultures. In another city school, a seventh-grade group started making papier-mâché jewelry which could be worn. From this they went on to the study of African costumes. Soon they had organized a fashion show in which they made and modeled their creations. The whole school was delighted. (Teacher: Ugo Hayes; student teacher: Pat Steiner.)

Pop objects are a natural for this medium. Papier-mâché strips can be placed over any machine or product of the machine, and a statement comes into being. Combining parts of objects of this kind into an assemblage or pop composition is enormous fun for children of this age, and adding light and sound and possibly movement presents enough challenge to absorb the preadolescent for hours at a time. The creating of life-sized environments with people and objects in them, in the manner of George Segal, for instance, is very much in the realm of possible achievement. Below we see two friends making a monster out of papier-mâché on a gigantic scale (Joan La Rocca, instructor).

WIRE AND METAL SCULPTURE

The preadolescent takes to wire immediately. Give him a strand of any thickness, and he begins immediately to explore its potentialities. First, he may admire it as a line in space; then he will look for its directional qualities.

Will it bend? Yes, and he finds next that it will also describe a form. The circle, simplest of forms, is usually hit upon first. If the preadolescent has as yet no other goal for the wire, you may see him peer through the circle he has made, or stick his tongue through, or even his head.

Soon he begins to make other shapes and to place them in juxtaposition. He thus finds that he can produce volume with his wire, and if he places wires over each other, he gets a transparent mesh in various patterns.

Will it twist? How will various lengths of wire combine? What other materials seem to go with wire? A teacher watching a child work in this medium for the first time will see him progress through all these explorative steps quickly or slowly, depending on his personality. She would do well to include these logical steps in her lesson planning, neither rushing nor overlooking them. Above all, she should not deprive the child of the pleasure of his own discoveries by overdoing her demonstrations of the possibilities of the medium (20).

Actions—people doing things, holding props, or engaging in

sports—are the best subjects for preadolescent wire sculpture. Following are illustrations of a project undertaken by a student teacher (Mrs. Shirley L. Pearman) at the New Lincoln School (director: Lois Lord; cooperating teacher: Tom Vega). Fifth-grade boys and girls were asked to think of some actions and gestures of interest to them and were shown photographs; they were then asked to reproduce, in wire, people doing things.

Girl, age eleven and a half

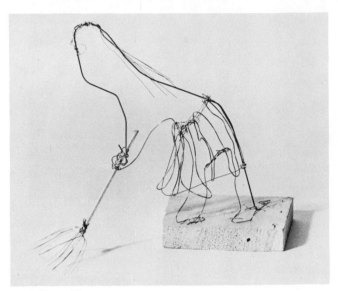

Grade five—girl

In wire, the special problem of making things stand up requires the child to give a good deal of attention to weight, stress, and balance. This requirement, of course, influences the form. As in the figure illustrated, the feet may have to be very big and the broom made in such a way that it will bear the weight of the body. For example, in the figure shown, the arms are outstretched and the figure leans on the hoop to gain stability.

In the wire construction of a lady in tears, carrying a handbag (page 311), the artist was evidently struggling with some personal problem, and though she tried to do the assigned project, the idea of an action pose was not as absorbing as her own hurts and anxieties.

Wire sculpture is also an excellent medium for the preadolescent because it leads him away from total realism. Emotional expressions come through forcefully because of the nature of the medium, which forces him to select and emphasize a limited number of symbols to communicate what he has in mind. The flexibility of the wire gives him many images with which to play. He can quickly move an arm into this or that position and discard a number of possibilities before he decides on one.

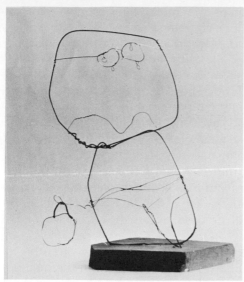

Grade five—girl
"*Lady in Tears Carrying a Bag*"

Materials and techniques   All that is needed for a beginning is several gauges of wire, a few tools, such as snub-nosed and needle-nosed pliers and wire cutters, and adhesives such as liquid solder, mastics, resins, white glue (which will hold nuts, bolts and washers) and airplane glue. Wire of different gauges is necessary to give the lineal quality variety and to fulfill certain constructional needs. Thin wire, for example, is excellent for securing parts together.

Wire is made in various metals, each having different color qualities. Coated wire in brilliant colors is also available in electrical supply and florist supply houses. Coat hangers, bailing wire, stovepipe wire, and aluminum clothesline wire are also useful. The most useful all-purpose wire is florist wire.

In addition to the cutting pliers, kitchen shears and metal shears that will cut thin-gauge sheet metal and screening are a help. There are a variety of adhesives: polyvinyl resin, white glue, contact cements, epoxies, library paste, and rubber cement.

Simple soldering has proven to be a safe process in the classroom. The author has taught this technique to large groups of preadolescents with no accident ever resulting. Soldering gives children an opportunity to make larger, more complicated structures.

Preadolescents are capable of discovering all kinds of scraps and bits of wire of all gauges to wrap around their figures for volume. They can also use steel wool, window screen, bits of tin, aluminum foil or other metals, cloth, plastic found forms, and glass. Children should be reminded that the color of all these additions must be considered and that the solid, semisolid and open forms should have a relationship. The same thing applies to the tactile range. Perhaps the most significant warning to make about the use of these combined forms is that they may lead to the loss of the fluid, linear quality of the wire.

What do these children make with wire? What are they capable of achieving? They will generally take as subject matter human activities, animals, or machines. They also make abstract constructions. Sometimes they create interior environment or landscapes with or without figures. The key words for children of this age are *action* and *props*. They take great pleasure in creating figures that are doing things and in adding the objects that go with the action— carrying books, holding a mirror, wearing skates, or putting on a hat. Because their figures often lack precision with regard to physical proportions, clothing, etc., they lavish much attention on some significant detail or prop, which helps communicate a story.

Flat drawing with wire, in two dimensions, may often be all they are at first able to achieve, until experience in the medium allows them to see more than line and outline. In the work of much younger children one usually does not see three-dimensional concepts operating except in an occasional piece. As they gain proficiency, they may achieve three-dimensionality in certain parts of the body while most often presenting the head or limbs in a two-dimensional statement.

To progress from two- to three-dimensional wire figures requires learning how to make the figures stand on their own. Because this is one of the hardest jumps for the preadolescent, it is wise to give attention to the problem at an early stage. A first project might be a series of quick nonobjective compositions which are designed to stand by whatever methods the children can devise. Using a group of wires, as shown in the photograph below, is another way of gaining stability. Note the device used in the figure to make it stand. Also, see the use of the base in the

Boy, age twelve

nonobjective work. When the children are working in wire human figures, animals or abstractions, have them use another material for the base. A rigid piece of cardboard or a paper box, for instance, can be perforated; the wires that form the legs are pushed through and knotted at the back. Other simple platforms can be made of plasticine, scrap wood, cork, sponges, Styrofoam or readymade plastic containers to which the wire figures can be tied, nailed, or stapled. These platforms increase the stability of the sculpture. They become the pedestals on which the sculpture stands, or they become environments for animals or persons.

To give volume to the figure is as difficult as finding devices by which figures stand without a base. Many preadolescents never abandon the base to make figures stand on their own. For many, the problem is too time-consuming and not worth the effort. Too frequently, insufficient time is allocated to the art period to allow for experimenting and building upon discoveries. Inventive teachers must find the means to interest children in investing their energies in the ensuing technical struggle.

Children can be motivated to make what might be called a cage (or outline), inside of which they can at intervals indicate a division of the interior space. They can also achieve bulk by using the outline of their form as an armature and wrapping lighter-weight wires around it until the outline is filled in. The sense of volume and dimension in this picture was achieved without any filling-in devices. Exercises pointing out how this can be accomplished through knowledge of drawing are useful. (Using a posed model helps enormously in aiding preadolescents to gain a sense of volume in wire sculpture.)

Girl, age twelve

Thin gauge sheet metals and screens Sheets of thin copper, pewter, lead, tin and other metals are available commercially. They can be tooled, embossed, and stamped to work into reliefs. Tin cans can be used to create sculptures. Tin snips, pliers, steel wool, and wooden mallets will cut, flatten, bend, scratch, and shape the tin into new forms. Some constructions will take advantage of the three-dimensionality of the can. A certain amount of soldering may be necessary to achieve the desired effect.

Wire screening holds great sculptural potential for children of this age. It is easy to form into shapes since the material has an intrinsic strength provided by the weaving of the wires; it combines a semblance of a third dimension with transparency. Also, children can make large objects since the material is relatively inexpensive, and comes in many gauges and colors. The objects seen on page 315 are held together by wires that have been used to sew the materials together. Bolting with brads, nailing, soldering, clipping and sewing were some of the techniques used by the boy in constructing the circus shown.

Size In the beginning, it is better to encourage the child to work quickly and on a small scale because of the variety of problems he is trying to solve and the numerous experiments he must make to discover the potentialities of different materials. Size may become important, however, and a child is capable of making very large objects if he has a strong enough urge to do so. He can also combine his figures and animals with those of other children to make large environments. In one of my classes, three boys working together made acrobatic pyramids with wires and then enlarged their project into a circus scene, with aerial artists reaching for ropes, nets to catch them, ladders and other paraphernalia. The small figures each child made gained scale

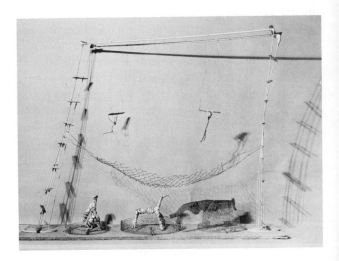

in combination with those of others and became valuable parts of a large expression. In the same mode, a group of girls who had been working individually decided to join their abstract wire constructions into a large intricate one. It grew and grew, as other students became interested. Finally, large clusters, with bits of mirror in them to make them glitter, were hung in various parts of the school.

Twine reinforced with wire will preserve the linear effect and at the same time increase the scale of the object. Some exciting sculpture can result. The use of an armature will allow for large structures. Liquid metal can be added to a screen wire armature, applied with a palette knife in successive layers to give bulk. Papier-mâché can be added to wire, mesh or plaster-soaked rags; enormous sculptures can be achieved by these and many other means. Inexpensive wadded aluminum foil over an armature of wire also makes possible large construction. The material also has bulk, and the wire armature allows for action. Older children interested in realistic proportions, such as thin ankles and small feet—difficult to achieve when the figure must support itself—will like this medium.

Open and semitransparent sculpture   Wire is especially suitable for open, space-spanning works. Wires in combination with string or plastics are highly successful in that they permit the trapping of air in exciting ways through changes in the gauge of the materials, through the density of the patterns, and through the directions indicated and inner spaces suggested.

Rods and reeds make fascinating nonobjective structures. By working in this medium, children become conscious of bending and twisting air, seeing air as a flat plane.

These simple techniques can be followed by more complicated ones, involving such concepts as multidimensional movement of planes in air, of either static or mobile forms. Intricate linear cages, webs, or boxes can also convey the sense of spaces intermingling in rhythmic patterns. It may interest those children who are fond of group projects to create, in cooperation with each other, large complicated stellar constructions which grow and change with each individual's contribution.

As in all art activities, it is important for youngsters to explore one medium over a long period of time and to become completely familiar with their materials and learn how to make the most of them. Victor D' Amico, Director of the People's Art Center of the Museum of Modern Art, was the first to lead art educators into explorations of three-dimensional media for young children. His books are recommended (21, 22).

REFERENCES

1. Jack Burnham, *Beyond Modern Sculpture,* George Braziller, Inc., New York, 1967.

2. David Mandel, *Changing Art, Changing Man,* Horizon Press, New York, 1967.

3. Wallace S. Baldinger, *The Visual Arts,* Holt, Rinehart and Winston, Inc., New York, 1960.

4. Albert E. Elsen, *Purposes of Art,* Holt, Rinehart and Winston, Inc., New York, 1962.

5. Bernard Myers, *Sculpture, Form and Method,* Reinhold Publishing Corporation, New York, 1965.

6. Udo Kultermann, *The New Sculpture,* Frederick A. Praeger, Inc., New York, 1968.

7. Edmund Burke Feldman, *Art as Image and Idea,* Prentice-Hall, Inc., Englewood Cliffs, N.J., 1967.

8. Ray Faulkner and Edwin Ziegfield, *Art Today,* Holt, Rinehart and Winston, Inc., New York, 1968.

9. Reid Hastie and Christian Schmidt, *Encounter with Art,* McGraw-Hill Book Company, New York, 1969.

10. Robert Gillam Scott, *Design Fundamentals,* McGraw-Hill Book Company, New York, 1951.

11. Lucy R. Lippard, "As Painting Is to Sculpture: A Changing Ratio," *American Sculpture of the Sixties,* ed. by Maurice Tuchman, Los Angeles County Museum of Art publication (New York Graphic Society, Ltd., distributors), 1967.

12. Irving Sandler, "Gesture and Non-Gesture in Recent Sculpture," *American Sculpture of the Sixties,* ed. by Maurice Tuchman, Los Angeles County Museum of Art publication (New York Graphic Society, Ltd., distributors), 1967.

13. Chandler Montgomery, *Art for Teachers of Children,* Charles E. Merrill Books, Inc., Columbus, Ohio, 1968.

14. Viktor Lowenfeld and W. Lambert Brittain, *Creative and Mental Growth,* The Macmillan Company, New York, 1964.

15. Ernst Rotter, *Creative Clay Design,* Reinhold Publishing Corporation, New York, 1963.

16. Henry Petterson, *Creative Teaching in Clay,* Reinhold Book Corporation, New York, 1968.

17. Freda Skinner, *Wood Carving,* Sterling Publishing Co., Inc., New York, 1963.

18. Spencer Moseley, Pauline Johnson, and Hazel Koenig, *Crafts Designs,* Wadsworth Publishing Company, Belmont, Calif., 1962.

19. Marjorie E. Doe (ed.), *New Ways in Art Education,* The Ealing Corporation, Cambridge, Mass., 1969.

20. Lois Lord, *Collage and Construction in the School: Preschool–Junior High School* (rev. ed.), Davis Press, Inc., Worcester, Mass., 1970.

21. Victor d'Amico, Marine Maser, and Frances Wilson, *Art for the Family,* Harper & Brothers, New York, 1958.

22. Victor d'Amico and Arlette Buchman, *Assemblage: A New Dimension in Creative Teaching in Action,* Museum of Modern Art, New York, 1971.

Our Assemblage Environment

10

In the early twentieth century, Picasso, Braque, and Gris began pasting "real" or "common" fragments of cloth, rope, newspaper, and random segments of words onto their canvases. The methods and concepts of collage set off a chain reaction, not only among painters but among sculptors, too, who began to conceive of new categories of expression derived from the vast reservoir of unrelated human experience. As disparate bits were put in satiric or sad or morbid or lighthearted juxtaposition, they became unified and transformed into new and unusual associations. The vitality of this genre has lasted throughout our century, channeled into three-dimensional constructions, assemblages, environments and "happenings."

It has survived because both the methods and results of the collage process are symptomatic of many ideas and issues that artists and philosophers of this century have believed to be important. Today all the arts employ the technique, including theater, dance and music, in what Kahler calls "the triumph of incoherence" (1: p. 49). He finds the tendency to create multi-sensory mixtures and simultaneous aesthetic events "a very frightening mode and degree of disintegration." Marshall McLuhan, on the other hand, finds the new art of heightened total experiences a sharpening of consciousness that will aid man in his survival.

Historically, the urge toward collage and assemblage at the turn of the century seized not only painters but also writers and philosophers who were making an onslaught on dogmatism, rigidity, sentimentality, materialism—in short, on the Establishment—using as their weapons irony, perversity, antireason and antiform. Literature, partly under the aegis of Freud, underwent a revolution involving disassociation and chaos, and a new regime of rule from the subconscious mind. A species of poetic collage developed. Mallarme, for instance, turning against the conventional declamatory style, envisioned a new role for words: They would be dynamically independent and alive through the quality of their sounds rather than tied strictly to meaning and consecutive thought (1: pp. 75–77).

The liberation from realistic representation accomplished by the early twentieth-century painters was a revolution along the same lines and is the basis of out present aesthetic concepts and creations. Cézanne willfully tore down and reconstructed objects and figures according to his own inspired geometrical vision, abstracting everyday forms into universal components. Proceeding from his work, the cubists created a spatial order in which objects existed no longer receded from the surface in an atmosphere of depth, as they had in paintings since the fifteenth century, but were brought to the foreground and occupied all of it. Gradually appreciation and desire for the sight of objects in this new plane spread from artists to the general audience. Everyone became involved in this exciting exercise of abstraction. Gradually, too, through the encroachment of collage, the sacrosanct medium of oil was invaded, and there was a blurring, then final disappearance, of the line between two- and three-dimensional assemblage.

The two world wars quickened the social and artistic revolution. The fight against authority, hypocrisy, and bourgeois philistinism vented itself in futurism, Dadaism, surrealism and later, abstract expressionism. The Italian futurists prophesied current modes of assemblage. It was they who first determinedly broke with the Renaissance forms, bringing art into intimate contact with urban living. With their experimental techniques— simultaneity by overlapping, transparent images, interpenetration of shapes—they expressed the kinetic, fast-paced continuity of modern life. The futurists, like birds, were harbingers of the immense complex of the speed, noise, vibration, and over-population in our cities that were soon to come.

The Dadaists made their collages, ready-mades, and photo-montages "antiart" objects to shock the complacent remnant of Victorian civilization. As Seitz says in *The Art of Assemblage,* the new method "is inconceivable without Dada's negativism, for the precondition of juxtaposition is a state of total random-ness and disassociation" (2: p. 38).

By this time, Freudian excavations below the surface of the conscious mind were in full flower; subjective associations began to be mined by all artists. Surrealism, with its interest in automatic expression centered on the unconscious—the mind turned in on itself—and irrational confrontations between the real and dream worlds. Assemblage has inherited its techniques and its iconoclasm. Abstract expressionism, born in New York City, has spread throughout the entire artistic world as a symbol of urban life. For America it represents the real break with the European tradition of aesthetic coherence. Seitz describes these painters as recording for us "the stress and strain and collisions of a million realities" (2: p. 74).

While sculptural assemblage owes much to all these antecedents, its manifestations are quite different. because it is a more extroverted medium, more oriented toward the immediate environmental scene than toward the subjective inner life of the mind. It concentrates on the reality of objects and their emotional potential. Though it deals with fragments, they are always fragments of the "real" material world, resulting in what Seitz appropriately calls "vernacular realism."

Yet, though anti-illusionistic, it has a poetry all its own. Ironic criticism of our culture can be as implicit (and explicit) in certain assemblages of today as it was in the Dada art at the turn of the century. But there seems to be a new energy pulsing through modern art which makes it less basically destructive than it was in the period of the demolition of formalisms.

TREASURIES FOR PRECIOUS JUNK

Box sculptures might be called modern icons. They are man-made, protected enclosures for precious objects. Objects are assembled within a private sanctuary. They gain symbolic associations and can become, according to Feldman, places for private communication with the spirit. Joseph Cornell's boxes, for instance, contain intimate fragments full of poetry and private dreams. Feldman calls them "surreal containers" with the "capacity of inducing dreams of old possessions and places, recollections of childhood, and images which seem to belong to the future" (3: p. 383).

For children, an initial project might be to make an autobiographical box sculpture, for private communication, with each child encouraged to create his own portrait by means of objects. Or he could make a symbolic box sculpture of his daily environment. One example may be seen in the work of children here, made from parts of furniture, something looking like a telephone dial, parts of cornices, etc. (instructor: Lee Anderson, Elizabeth, N.J.).

After providing motivation, with a Nevelson sculpture (see page 320), for example, suggest to the children that they attempt a huge box composite using orange crates and found wood parts. The contributions of thirty or forty children can set in motion quite a rich sculptural adventure. Actually it is a project of much appeal. First comes the search for things in basements and around the neighborhood, and then the selecting, hammering, gluing, painting, and final assembling—which requires a search into the best ways the composite can be assembled. The messages it should reveal will provoke much discussion and exchange of ideas—about personalities, environments, ecology, sculpture, etc. It is possible to decide on a theme beforehand and then work out individual interpretations.

Feel-boxes are interesting experiments for children. Vision is eliminated, and the tactile communication is paramount. Curiously enough, most of the principles of design which prevail in visual box sculpture also apply to feel-boxes. Gradation of size is important; repetition of shapes and textures is essential, producing rhythm. Unity is achieved through rhythm, balance and emphasis. One responds to geometric solids, to convex and concave shapes, penetrable forms, thick and thin forms, and flat forms. Lines in curves, zigzags, diagonals, verticals and horizontals are felt as edges of things, or independently if space is provided for them to be autonomous. The only basic art elements not included are the experiences of color and light and dark.

There are questions for the children to ponder: What is the effect as the probing hand goes deeper? How is the experience guided by the artist? How fast or slow should the hand proceed along the composition? The quality of the total experience must be considered; what is its mood, its theme? Are we afraid to proceed for fear of being hurt? Are the experiences choppy and unrelated, or is there a recognizable pattern? Is there an easy flow from one sensation to the other? Feel-boxes give ample proof that in the absence of vision, the other senses take on more life.

The peep show is a combination of boxes and light. If there

is a chink in the fence, what child can resist a look? The idea for a peep show came to this author when watching children peer eargerly through a hole in a box that had a few shiny papers inside. It was only a step from that revelation to the solution of a long-existing storage problem. There were twenty to thirty boxes insecurely stacked in the art room which had to be taken down and put back over and over again so that the children could take a look. The carpenter built for us, instead, a sturdy structure on wheels which had a removable plywood wall, and three levels, each of which was to contain cardboard boxes of various sizes. It was wired for electricity and had sockets for bulbs. It held approximately twenty-five boxes, and each had a peephole. Each child was assigned a box of his own and was asked to remove part of the back side of it to let light through.

POP ART

The pop trend, which began more or less in the early sixties, is still another assault on the public. Barely recovering from the adjustment to cubism, surrealism, and abstract expressionism and just beginning to find pleasure in objects they could associate—at least nostalgically—with the Parisian ateliers and cafés, the art audience has been barraged by the younger generation of artists with a whole new category of "repulsive" objects—the most energetic promulgation of nonart or antiart since the turn of the century. Pop art is produced by artists who suffered neither the Depression nor the world wars, but are veterans instead of the unending bomb threat and the vulgarity of American inflation. By not rejecting but embracing and glorifying in various media "the incredible proliferation of *kitsch* which provides the visual environment and probably most of the aesthetic experience for 99 percent of Americans," says Alan Solomon, these young artists have turned "with relish and excitement to what those of us who know better regard as the wastelands of television commercials, comic strips, hot dog stands, billboards, junkyards, hamburger joints, used-car lots, juke-boxes, slot machines and supermarkets." He doubts that they have done so "in the spirit of contempt or social criticism" (4: p. 72).

The fact that pop artists are participating with such gusto in this vulgar world does not mean, however, that there is not an implicit disgust, or at least a cynical spoof, in some of their burlesques. Ugo Kultermann sums up their general attitude:

The young artists of today are no longer concerned with the emphasis of social criticism, with aggression, but rather with a dispassionate statement of things as they are. Therefore an abundance of meanings and contents are offered, combined with one another and alternated in a merry, vicious, and ironic manner [5: p. 103].

Theirs is at any rate a boisterous, often entertaining, abnegation of aesthetic responsibility and rejection of all previous canons of art.

The sculpture below is an attempt at social criticism. It is made of several hundred boxes of a well-known brand of cigarettes into a construction that resembles a naval destroyer. The straws look like guns, and the composite is a floating armada of nicotine destruction.

Some subjects popular with the new realists and pop artists are food, clothing, furniture, transportation, and objects of magic.

It is interesting to watch pop art bring back the whole concept of "still life," which has not enjoyed popularity with the public since the seventeenth century, when Dutch artists painted with such éclat in this mode. The objections to the "vulgar" large still life, which irritates and shocks traditionalists today, are not too different from the arguments put forth in the past. Still life was then considered to lack dignity and nobility and to be unsuitable subject matter for art, especially for sculpture.

Although still-life sculpture began in the twentieth century with Picasso's absinthe glass and Boccioni's development of a bottle in place, only in comparatively recent years has it received considerable attention. Most apparent has been the furor created by Jasper John's beer cans, or Oldenberg's giant hamburgers, considered as pop. But Bourgeois' bowl of fruit treats the same kind of subject matter in as resolutely sculptural fashion . . . [6: p. 59].

The relevance of still-life art to daily existence makes it a mode especially appealing to children, and above all to preadolescents, who are in the process of adjusting to their environment. Unlike adults, they do not attach moral values to objects according to their uses and properties. They have no snobbery; their enjoyment of art is not conditioned by the bourgeois aesthetic scale determining what is proper for art to emphasize. A child will be far more interested in making a replica of an ice cream soda than in drawing a still life of fish, vegetables, fruit, and wine bottles. Given some paper plates, some Newark school children quickly made an assemblage representation of their favorite meals (instructor: Hedy Brash).

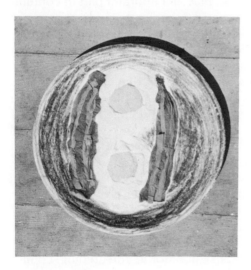

Pop sculpture appeals to youth all over the world. They have always done it; it is as natural for them to create a plastic roast beef as a pretty landscape. The contemporary scene, dotted by multitudinous machines, moved and ruled by machines, is the world they enjoy transforming into art. Former generations expressed the idea that our technological age was dangerous and the machine something to be feared. The younger generation may ridicule the machine age in order to debunk materialism, but they are not afraid of it. They use its objects and advertising idols to poke fun at items with which we are bombarded on subway signs, billboards, packaging, TV, in neon, newspapers, and magazines. Pop art and children's art remind us to look at the use mankind is making of the machine.

Still-life painters of the past have provided us with vicarious enjoyment of the beauty of the sea and field. Our artists today are showing us that a simple relationship between man and nature no longer exists. Most of our food is synthetically mass-produced, and most of us are not food growers but part of a vast complex of mass distribution and marketing. We are not entirely happy about this. The artists are registering our apprehension and pointing out what the world is really like in the twentieth century instead of fantasizing about the past.

Some of them make clothing a central theme. They may be preoccupied with clothes showing traces of human wear and tear, or sometimes they transform them into oversized symbols or decorate them with objects that abstract them into new meanings. The new sculpture also includes constructions of entire rooms, with all their furnishings. Kienholz sometimes uses objects bearing a depressing reminder of human use.

Images of transportation also play an important part in contemporary art. Airplanes, motorcycles, speedboats, and cars are not just status symbols; they have associations of sex, excitement, danger, disaster, and, above all for children, freedom from parental control. (They have actually become almost as vital to all of us as our limbs and muscles; they are mechanical appendages allowing us to become a part of the modern world.) In schools where children are allowed to indulge in their special interests, they are constantly making mock-ups of vehicles of transportation. These may or may not move. The themes and projects which can be developed around the automobile are innumerable. Preadolescents look forward with intense anticipation to the time when they, like their elder brothers and their neighborhood heroes, can drive cars and feel the exhilaration of escape from home pressures or from the ghetto; suburb, or farm. It is a symbol of growing up (5: pp. 64–94).

Pop artists have used the car symbol for its threatening, comic, erotic or elegant aspects. The works of Dine, Seley, Stankiewicz, Chamberlain and others can motivate preadolescents, already so involved in the theme, to look at the machine for its aesthetic qualities.

Children also make trains, buses and planes, and make-believe terminals, as well as automobiles. Teachers can cultivate more subtle responses to the age of transportation. Jasper Johns and others often use a medley of signs and directions common in gas stations and on highways as motifs in their works. The sculpture on page 325 is a highway item that reminds us of shapes seen on hydrants; it is painted red all over and has an aura of danger and death. Children are capable of understanding, more deeply than we often care to admit, the complications of our present civilization. This example, like those made by professional artists, demonstrate the contemporary need to create sculpture which interacts with the environment.

. . . the role of environment in today's art is no accident. We stand at the beginning of an epoch which, like the advances of the waning Middle Ages, explores not only the unfamiliar and distant regions, but also the unknown and unused areas of our immediate surroundings— the commonplace, technified and long-despised reality [5: p. 91].

With the population explosion and air pollution on us in earnest, we are becoming more and more aware of interior and exterior spaces, of the agonies of too much noise, too many people living and working in limited areas. Shaping and modifying our environment has become a vital interest, inspiring sculptors as well as architects.

Children are naturally aware of the problems of living space; they have always had an instinct to build structures into which they can crawl for protection and peace. Teachers can develop such a bent, by providing experiences both within the school and in the outside environment which will sharpen their desire to contribute to the comfort and sanity of human beings.

Preadolescents and younger children in suburbs, small towns or in the country have made such structures as tree houses and cave houses probably for as long as adults have made real dwellings. Khym has been building and rebuilding his tree house

for many years. His friends helped him weave twine into curtains for privacy and later on make sturdy ladders to the hideaway.

City children have less opportunity to satisfy this need, but they find their out-of-the-way places in cellars, backyards, under staircases, and in closets, using whatever comes to hand to build a private world.

In school they make miniature houses or more complicated structures, and, as we have seen earlier, they are fond of making interiors with innumerable details. In the Storefront Project in White Plains, the children made forts out of large crates in order to fight their Indian wars. On another occasion they piled them on top of each other and managed to make a huge wall of boxes, used sometimes to indicate an apartment house with many floor levels and at other times as their own version of a "Laugh-In Wall" from which they stuck their heads out and said "crazy" things.

In the inner cities, living together in close quarters in dwellings often far below minimum standards, many preadolescents have more incentive to become involved in environmental planning than previous American generations. A teacher can make them aware of the possibilities, or, on the other hand, make them feel it is hopeless to try to change the status quo.

In one school in New York City, the children were asked to design a playground they would enjoy using. Down the street from the school, a playground was actually being renovated, but the children were told nothing about it. They therefore embarked on their assignment with no enthusiasm and with no sense of how surroundings affect design. They were asked to produce in a vacuum, without any real reference to the neighborhood. The more dutiful and subdued among them produced miniature models of slides and swings which they had no hope would ever come into being. The rest of the children, who saw no sense in the project, made a general nuisance of themselves.

Two other educators set about deliberately to develop in their students an awareness of environment and architecture. They talked about what was happening on certain streets with which the children were familiar, and they evaluated the new structures that had already replaced the old. The children repeated comments made by their parents and discussed what was happening in general to the neighborhood. Together they listed the needs of the people who lived there and the activities in which they were interested. Items included better parking, a new library and a roller-skating rink for children. Then several lessons were devoted to what great architects has produced— qualities of light, comfort, beauty, and practicality. Which of these did the buildings express? How much had the architects achieved in combining pleasurable design with function? The slides and books presented a new world to the children, full of surprising possibilities (instructor: Jan McEvoy; student teacher: Joy Moser).

As the next step, the children made drawings, sketches, and house and apartment plans, discussing their efforts with each other and the teacher. Apartments without bathrooms and halls that led nowhere produced a lot of laughter. Ultimately, imaginative designs came into being. Some children continued in a

comic vein; others took their "designs for living" seriously. The children became convinced that their buildings were much more exciting than the ones that were being built in the neighborhood. And at an exhibit of the sketches and plans, the arts supervisor of the school agreed with them.

Forward-looking schools are involving children in these adventures. An energetic young man, Phillips Simkin, teaching in the Philadelphia school system, brought materials which gave children a new sense of the spaces they occupy and move in. One experience was to have the children get into individual boxes and experience a private world, listening to the sounds going on around them. The boxes were carried to various parts of the school so that they could be exposed to new sounds. They tolerated remaining in the box as long as possible, an isolated privacy many had not experienced before. In another experiment, the teacher inflated huge plastic tunnels. The children crawled into them and played. They heard different sounds and saw through the translucent material from different angles. They experienced its pliability and could push it and alter its shape and direction. At another time, the teacher produced balloons that stretched for yards, both indoors and outdoors, and the children lived among them. The material wrapped itself around them, and they pulled and pushed and changed it; it slipped away and twisted, and found its own directions. Through all the fun and laughter, the children were forming both aesthetic and kinesthetic realizations of what space is and how materials alter it and create new ways of existing within it (7).

In the past, the "landscape" was a lyrical part of the general human experience—subject matter for poets and painters.

America still has some untouched wilderness and countryside (and is now frantically trying to preserve them), but natural beauty has been considerably defaced by our machine and electronic culture. All of us have driven through the industrial wastelands surrounding our cities from ocean to ocean and know intimately the smells, the polluted waters, the smarting smog, and the metal debris in frightening forms and shapes that characterize the landscape. These brutal scenes make subject matter for artists, who are perhaps by definition more sensitive than others to ugliness and death, and for that reason more impelled to express such realities and encourage mankind to reform them.

Schoolchildren of Elizabeth, New Jersey, created the works shown below. Note the size of the human figures in contrast to the industrial shapes, and the chaotic and grotesque disassociation of the forms. Here are symbols the modern landscape evoked in the creative imaginations of schoolchildren.

What could be more exciting to a preadolescent, who is by definition a dynamic, changing being in constant physical motion, and who is also living in an electronic age, than to create objects that move, light up, and make sounds?

The idea of giving life to sculpture, or animating it through the use of devices, has been a challenge to sculptors in all ages. Both natural and man-made forces can be utilized to make sculptures come alive. Wind currents, magnets, and changes in temperature and gravity can produce movement. In ancient times, a man might have hidden within a sculpture in order to

**KINETICS:
MOVEMENT,
LIGHT AND
SOUND**

manipulate it. Smoke, streaming sacrifical blood, jets of water, showers of grain, fire and flickering lights—any of these might have issued from effigies of demons or gods to encourage the population to believe they were in the presence of a living deity or other supernatural creature.

We are more familiar with kinetic objects such as mechanical clocks, with toys and dolls and animals that walk with stiffened limbs, heads swiveling and making noises—replaced recently with dolls that eat and drink, and toys with complex electronic systems. The figures striking the hour in San Marco and the waterworks in the fountains of Tivoli have been superseded by such an array of sound and light machines and electrical displays that they are no longer marvels but commonplaces of science.

It is no wonder that in this moment of triumphant technology and such a sophisticated use of electric energy, many artists should devote themselves to the idea of simulating life in inanimate sculpture. Pellegrini says that "kinetic art tends to replace the preoccupation with space important to artists since the Renaissance" (8: p. 163), and Burnham's main thesis is that sculpture is not a "segregated endeavor" but "a vestigial biological activity closely related to the technological drive." He feels it is important "that we look upon sculpture as an indication of man's changing conception of biology, as an indication of his biological role, and especially as a form of biological activity itself" (9: p. 6).

The discovery of electricity was a giant change, but after that has come man's new consciousness of himself as a nervous as well as a fleshly entity, a receiving and broadcasting station for millions of tiny electrical impulses, and sometimes seeing himself as a cipher in a vast network of universal energy. One might speculate that this has changed the general human biological image and increased the impulse toward kinetic sculpture.

As early as the mid-eighteenth century and throughout the nineteenth, men experimented with objects that put light—first candles, then gas, then electricity—in conjunction with music. In 1919, Thomas Winifred began the experiments resulting in "Lumia," now housed in the Museum of Modern Art. By that time, whole groups of sculptors were exploring the aesthetics of the movement of light and sound and machines. It was the futurists who tried to incorporate the essence of movement itself. They were followed by the Constructivists, who were infatuated with industrial forms and products. Duchamps in 1925 experimented with a crystal sphere painted with concentric spirals and turning by means of a motor (rotative demi-sphere), and in 1935 he made optical disks which were called roto reliefs, to mention only two of his many inventions which were an inspiration to other artists.

In 1929, Moholy-Nagy constructed a light-space modulator, considered to be a prototype of modern light sculpture. In a letter to Kalimada Nagy he wrote: "Instead of painting with brushes and colors one could paint with light. I dreamed of apparatuses which, thanks to a manual or mechanical device, permitted the projection of luminous visions in the air, in vast halls, on screens of undreamed-of material: mists, gases, clouds . . ." (9: p. 163).

In 1930 Alexander Calder began working on his mobiles, creations that had a far-reaching influence on artists. Recently, Tinguely has at once charmed and shocked audiences with his pseudomachines, which are, according to Feldman, "mechanical poems about the absurdity of machines and, by implication, of a civilization which permits itself to be governed by them" (3: p. 39).

Today many artists are exploring the aesthetic potentialities of our latest technology. Antonakos, Rayess, Downey, Jeffries, and Roy, to mention just a few, are working with light and shadow, programmed in infinite variations, on and through both abstract and figurative sculpture. Von Schlegell has created a mechanical human figure controlled by radio; Harrison experiments with luminous gas and controlled heat. Len Lye's work incorporates sound, metallic glitter and movement.

Some modern sculptors are fascinated by the idea of utilizing natural elements like air, smoke, compressed earth, sand, water, growing matter and sound waves as sculptural media.

Preadolescents, who have been exposed to this new work and also motivated by an innate love of the machine in all its forms, will try to create robots and mechanical objects and bring sound and movement into their creations, according to how much they know about lighting systems and the help they can receive in working them out. Even if they cannot achieve a genuine mechanical device, they will settle for dials, wires, buttons and lights that do not go on but at least look like complex systems. In lieu of anything else, they may get inside them and make them come alive by their own physical presence.

Kinetic illusions in sculpture   An illusion of movement, sound or light can be created by static sculpture.

Movement and sound are communicated by the structure below. It seems to be able to perform a mechanical function, something like a teletype machine. If the finger should tap the button below, one feels, the carriage would move and a message would travel through the wires and also light up the electric bulb. This artist has achieved considerable audience involvement, all through static combinations of familiar objects common to our culture.

Boy, age eleven and a half

In the assemblage using eight bulbs of various sizes, the child gives us the sense of light without actual electricity. The use of irridescent paint was· highly successful.

Nature-driven sculpture   Flags and banners, kites, wind chimes, wind clocks, bells, marionettes and elements of theatrical design might be considered antecedents of the modern mobile. What they all have in common is suspension in air. They respond to the natural forces of wind and temperature; their movements are generally unprogrammed and more or less unpredictable.

In mobiles, sculpture moves to produce changing patterns. Clusters of shapes constructed from any material swing and turn freely to create constantly new relationships between voids, masses, lines, colors, etc. Balsa wood, cardboards or metal sheets, threads, wires, and rods provide some of the equipment a child needs to make a mobile. What can be emphasized is attention to balance, spatial arrangement, proportions and efficient attachments in order to achieve maximum movement and interesting visual qualities. Usually it is a good idea to have students work in wire on stabiles before attempting the mobile that is to hang in the air. This allows them to develop control.

After the child has worked for some time with wire, he can become involved in the idea of making parts that move on their own. By this time he has picked up some technical know-how regarding the joints that allow movement. He has also begun to notice how moving parts affect the design of the whole.

Kites are kinetic objects that children enjoy making and flying. They also are interested in studying about kites made by other children in other cultures.

Water-driven works have great appeal. All sorts of inventions can evolve out of catching water in receptacles which, when filled, spill their contents into other receptacles and, in turn, make objects move. Hoses, tubes and water locks make use of gravity. Hans Haacke, a modern sculptor, has created a group of structures in which bubbles of air are trapped in a body of water. They drift through a world of slow silence, pretty much as a man moves through the deep sea or in the atmosphere of the moon.

Jets of air propelled by hand or mechanized bellows, or by fans, can keep lightweight objects in the air indefinitely.

An amusing and inventive group of children made a box sculpture which in fact was a conglomeration of various cans and tin boxes fastened together to make a series of inner tunnels and apertures. Dampened paper towels were placed on a hot plate and the structure placed over them. The smoke from the damp towels eventually found its way through the maze of tunnels, and to the children's great delight the sculpture began to smoke. This project was used as an initial and motivating idea to inspire more permanent exploration and accomplishment.

Mechanically driven sculpture Mechanical devices used to animate sculpture can be powered by hand, by electricity or by fuel combustion motors. The resulting motion is predictable and repeats a performance in stable patterns.

Bicycle wheels, small wheels of metal, wood or cardboard, fan belts, chains, cranks, pulleys of all sorts, leftover parts of clocks, household gadgetry, cameras and radios, egg beaters, sieves, nuts, bolts, and tools of all kinds come in handy for the boys and girls who want to make their creations move, either by hand or by the use of a motor. Discarded turntables and hot plates can often be salvaged for aesthetic purposes.

In the relief below, a seventh-grade boy has assembled a group of objects which not only give the impression of movement but can actually be manipulated by hand. The free-standing sculpture below can also be set in motion by hand, but an extra dimension was added by placing it on a turntable.

Grade seven—boy

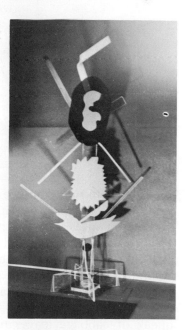

Another child utilized a spring, such as the one used in the familiar jack-in-the-box, and produced a sculpture with dozens of little doors, from which popped out all manner of fascinating objects: eyeballs, dolls, hands, etc. This piece had a remarkably surrealistic quality, making one feel that the motifs of art live on in a random stream from generation to generation.

Equipment used for the journeys into outer space intrigues children, especially boys. Now that the ideas expressed in comic strips and science fiction have become reality and man has gone to the moon, preadolescents are bound to be interested in creating symbolic objects expressing space travel. They may want to make mock capsules, experimenting with the aesthetics of the jet propulsion shape and trying to make them perform. Jerry Hochberg, art teacher in an Elizabeth, New Jersey, school, created the "sensory experience" helmet below, with the assistance of one of his students, who is displaying it.

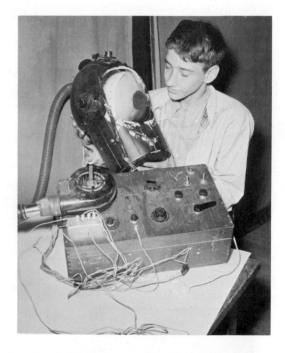

Sound in sculpture Len Lye's "The Storm King" and "Thundersheet" would make an exciting introduction to sound sculpture. Sheets of metal vibrate and make sounds which slowly increase in violence and motion and, after an agonizing climax, regain their tranquility. Sound has been added to mechanically driven sculpture to intensify the experience of the viewer.

Children can be encouraged to listen for the sounds of materials, for every material has its own distinctive sound—the squeak of cabbage leaves rubbing together, the squeak (very different) of Styrofoam, the rip of a banana peeling, the difference between a knock on plywood and a knock on solid oak, the whirrs of wire, string, elastic rubber, the snap of paper, or the rasp of corrugated metal. Have the class organize the sounds they hear into a structure that articulates them.

Wind and sound, of course, are natural companions. By forcing wind to go through various chambers or channeling it in other ways, we can create sound. Exploration of some of the methods used in musical instruments can produce ideas for sound sculpture.

One child built an elaborate structure entitled "Carnival" which was an intricate mixture of various wind-catching devices based on the pinwheel principle. When he turned a fan on his structure, it twirled and chirped like dozens of miniature hummingbirds.

Light sculpture The use of light as a sculptural element is still in its infancy; artists are still taking the initial exploratory steps. Some teacher training institutions, however, have set up courses in which their students experiment with the medium of light, along with other highly technical media. It must be admitted that most teachers already in the schools and even many prospective teachers will be poorly prepared to deal with structures featuring light, and that most schools are poorly equipped to handle it. Materials are not only expensive but dangerous. Interested science teachers are a great help. Collaboration between them and the art teachers is often necessary and very advantageous for the preadolescent.

A light sculpture can actually be created very simply. In the one below, a light bulb was placed in such a way that a mysterious and awful glow would shine from the eyes of the Egyptian head.

Grade seven—boy

A variation of this involves the use of background lighting for various wood, metal, or cardboard shapes. The edges of the piece will then disseminate light in an interesting way. Another method was developed by a boy who made a box in which he placed many incandescent bulbs and perforated the box into intricate panels to let the light shine through. (Transparent plastics could be used instead.)

A slightly more complicated structure might be created by programming light sequences in a very elementary way, perhaps by mounting miniature bulbs on masonite panels, in boxes, or in combination with transparent or translucent plastics. The life-sized structure below was lit with Christmas tree bulbs which flickered on and off at intervals.

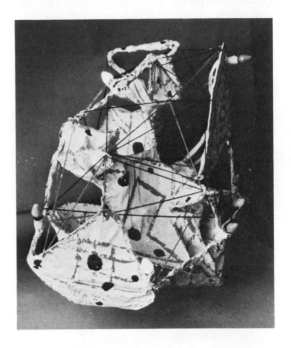

Adding motion to light opens up a whole new complex of images and adventures. Children can use old phonograph turntables or other low-power motors to give motion to the portion that holds the lights or to the sculptural forms themselves. (This kind of play can lead to the construction of a light organ.) Applying mirrors to the light machine adds yet another dimension.

Much can be learned about the play of light on color by making kaleidoscopes. They can be fashioned in uncomplicated ways and have universal appeal. The aesthetic qualities of light itself can be made real to children by setting up one light source in the room—a beam from a projector or spotlight—and giving each child a pocket mirror to catch the light and reflect it back to the mirrors of others or to a large mirror set up in the darkened room. The introduction of color jells makes the project more elaborate. After such a group session, the children will be interested enough to work on permanent sculptures utilizing mirrors and a light source.

To investigate shadows in their various intensities and forms, set up a spot or projector and a group of solid and transparent objects. By moving the light manually or mechanically, one can discover how shadows are born and how they behave. An additional experiment might involve using a screen with a light source behind it and projecting silhouettes into the light. Or one could string up a number of aluminum or aluminum foil shapes and activate them by the use of an electric fan in a darkened room, to see how the lights and shadows play through the room. The children may be inspired to conceive group shows, or each may experiment on his own to create elaborate structures.

In the picture below, we see children imaginatively projecting on the wall shapes and forms they made from colored transparencies, overlays, stencils and papers (instructor: George Trogler, Elizabeth, N. J.).

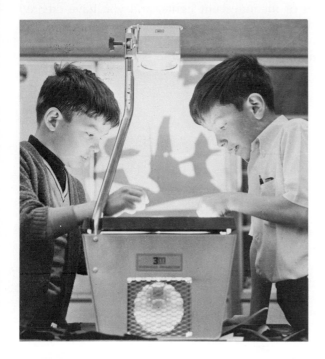

The kinetic wall   To stimulate children to think and feel in creative and inventive terms about kinetic art, it would be a good idea to put up a "kinetic wall" in a prominent and permanent position in the school where children can find it easily when they are in the mood. From time to time, parts of the wall should be changed to maintain their interest and to replace old inventions with new and better ones. The wall can contain all manner of simple and complicated devices, and it is desirable to have the science and shop teachers bring ideas, skills and objects basic to their own subject matter.

The wall should be built so that it can contain in a feasible way such things as large boxes with arm gloves in them into which the children can slip their arms and feel all kinds of strange and wonderful objects; areas into which children can stick their heads to hear extraordinary sounds or see unusual reflections made with mirrors or note the changes made by infrared light; strings and handles to pull, causing various forms to change position through the simple device of loose and taut string, sand bottles that can be upended to demonstrate the process of gravity; and some utilization of falling objects. Add a few cranks and wheels, and disks painted with spirals for interesting optical effects. There might be balls which sound horns or whistle when squeezed; wind chimes; or clanking devices. If possible, add a tape recorder for collected sound gems, spotlights and colored jells connected to a simple motor. Top it all off with a simple program of incandescent lights, and you have created a stimulating kinetic world which will bring children into direct contact with this new art form and will cause many to want to build a "better mouse trap" to add to the collection.

REFERENCES

1. Erich Kahler, *The Disintegration of Form in the Arts,* George Braziller, Inc., New York, 1968.

2. William C. Seitz, *The Art of Assemblage,* Museum of Modern Art, New York, 1961.

3. Edmund Burke Feldman, *Art as Image and Idea,* Prentice-Hall, Inc., Englewood Cliffs, N. J., 1967.

4. Alan Solomon, "The New Art," in *The New Art,* ed. by George Battcock, E. P. Dutton & Co., Inc., New York, 1966.

5. Udo Kultermann, *The New Sculpture,* Frederick A. Praeger, Inc., New York, 1968.

6. Daniel Robbins, "Recent Still-life," *Art in America,* vol. 54, no. 1, Art in America, Inc., New York, 1966.

7. Amalia Pearlman, "Art Education and Ekistics," unpublished doctoral dissertation, New York University, New York, 1970.

8. Aldo Pellegrini, *New Tendencies in Art,* Crown Publishers, Inc., New York, 1968.

9. Jack Burnham, *Beyond Modern Sculpture,* George Braziller, Inc., New York, 1967.

The Collaborative Arts

11

The emphasis on communication through multimedia is the primary aesthetic trend of our time. Since the turn of the century, the scope and objectives of differing art forms have altered in such a way that their isolation from each other has become more a matter of artificial verbal distinctions than of real cleavages. Painting and sculpture have claimed vast areas in common; boundaries have become blurred. Sculptural environments, static or kinetic, and happenings, wholly kinetic, are encroaching on the domain of the theater. Within each art, formalisms have broken down. We are challenged by atonal music, electronic music, prose-poetry, emotional journalism, journalistic novels, one-dimensional minimal novels, naked theater and soft, kinetic or light sculpture.

Artists move from medium to medium. Collaboration is the action, and new syntheses are in the offing. The arts, which have always shared a common language—line, color, emphasis, contrast, meaning, unity—are now sharing materials and techniques; the media are merging, with the blessing of electronics. The creations that result from these marriages are prophetic of the art that will confront, attract, and absorb the human beings who are now only nine, ten, and eleven years old. It behooves teachers to explore these communicating arts and use them wherever possible in our schools.

Nature of the medium   "Happenings" allow children to combine all that they are able to accomplish in the more deliberate graphic arts and sculpture with mimetic and verbal dramatic expression. A happening is a combination of environmental sculpture and actors, audience, light, color, smell, music, dance, movement of bodies and objects, and sounds of every description. Though a general plan for action and dialogue may be sketched out in advance by the organizers of the happening, improvisation is the key. In spite of the obvious relationship to

HAPPENINGS

theater art, the happening also has much in common with the jam session and with the ancient tribal dances that involved a high-pitched freedom of expression for one and all.

A happening is organized, like the "environment" that is assembled in a gallery and shown as a work of art, later to be disassembled and vanish forever. But it goes far beyond the passive spectacle of still-life assemblages or environments that a spectator can manipulate by pushing a few buttons, because of the inclusion of drama, dance, poetry, chance monologues, random movement, grunts, murmurs, laughter, and kinesthetic action of all kinds. It can be a vehicle of expression allowing both actors and audience to release unconscious springs of feeling and physical movement.

The urge to level distinctions and discard formalisms is a modern compulsion. As Seitz (1: p. 90) quotes from Allen Kaprow, who creates and also writes about happenings, they are born out of "a quite clear-headed decision to abandon craftsmanship" (2: p. 12a). An important feature is "the use of quite perishable media such as newspaper, string, adhesive tape, growing grass or real food" so that "no one can mistake the fact that the work will pass into dust or garbage quickly." Some painters and sculptors have been active in staging and scoring happenings— Robert Whitman, Claes Oldenburg, Red Grooms, and Jim Dine, among others. Their purpose seems to be to create a new awareness not possible in the realm of the traditional arts. By breaking away from the much-rehearsed, tight patterns to which our senses are accustomed, we begin to respond more intensely to what others are doing and, at the same time, to what we are doing, to what is happening, either solo or as a group.

It is perhaps the group energy involved that makes this active form so appealing to children. Here they have a chance to break through the repressive social barriers beginning to plague them in preadolescence and to reduce feelings of loneliness and awkwardness.

If teachers are sincerely exploring new avenues in educational methods, and if they want to bring to their prospective students experiences that arise from their own times, they would do well to experiment with art forms such as happenings. Following are experiences planned by Professor Richard Ruben (painter, teacher) of New York University for my class of prospective teachers in a course devoted to theory and practice in art education. The description given here is my personal response, and I have given each session an arbitrary title. The students saw the experience of these lessons as clues to teaching, and some of them who were working as student teachers in city schools tried them with sixth- and seventh-grade children and were impressed by the quality of the results.

"Four experiments" The materials used were intentionally extremely simple. They were kept that way to forestall the usual defenses against new methods: "If we had these materials, we would do it too"; "You had small classes and plenty of space, but we don't". There were thirty to thirty-five people in a studio which accommodates twenty to twenty-five, along with the usual paraphernalia of easels and stools, a model stand, two large tables, and paintings and drawing boards all over the room. Nor did we have any advantages of time and continuity. We met only once a week for about an hour and fifteen minutes. The class ahead of us left the place late and in a messy condition, and the class that came after us liked to arrive early.

I am not suggesting that these are conditions that should be accepted, merely that one must not be discouraged and wait to experiment until the time and place are exactly right. The ideal situation will never arrive until one begins to create it.

Session one: What is environment? We pushed all the objects in the studio against the walls and sat down together on the floor and contemplated the room—a large, dirty barn of a place with furniture stacked in the corners. Light came from fluorescents 18 feet above, and natural light came through an open door. What did we notice first about the room? Light was the answer. Could this quality be altered? One student turned out the fluorescents, and another closed the door. Immediately the room was drastically changed. The light that filtered in from the skylight was much softer and more diffused than the electric light, and another atmosphere pervaded the room.

The instructor rummaged in a big bag and brought out rolls of toilet paper in four solid-colored but muted hues. He rolled one of these across the floor; others imitated him, and soon the entire floor was covered with criss-cross patterns. As each roll streamed over the surface, it was as if a streak of light had flashed across the floor. The floor began to glow with them; the light permeated the room, and again the quality of the environment was changed.

In preparation for the next event, strings were installed in a network in square frets across the room as a false ceiling, within reach of our arms. Now he took from his bag many rolls of twine, and students began to attach the string wherever they could and to throw the balls of twine to each other. We made separations, screens, passages, cages—whatever we wanted—and we began to feel the space in the room and how it was changing, and also how our existence in it was changing. There were thirty-five of us weaving webs like spiders, each in spontaneous fashion and sometimes in unison, and finally we found ourselves canopied by a woven ceiling which cut at least 10 feet of the ceiling height and diminished considerably the light source from the skylight. Each of us felt and looked enlarged in relation to the chamber we had created around us.

We listened to the sounds the strings made when we moved, and to our own breathing. We swayed to create new sounds; we plucked the strings like harps; we sang and chuckled and clicked our fingers, and in a rising crescendo beat on every available surface. Then a roll of aluminum foil was produced from the sack. We passed it from hand to hand, unrolling a silver band into our string nest. We heard the swishing, slightly metallic sound it made. We saw how it changed the quality of the light again. In the cocoons it made around us we sat silent, removed from all other noises and motions. Someone began to take apart the silver foil. Then we all took pieces and created masks; one girl turned herself into Minerva in a complete coat of mail. Some made serpents to weave around necks and limbs, others hats, crowns, and jewels. We literally took from our environment to adorn our persons. We wore the environment. We and it became part of each other.

The time was almost up. As we began to take our nest apart, we created small skits involving the material, objects and people. Using several stools, we lifted the now sagging roof, and, taking hold of the ends of strings, some of us danced round and round, as with a maypole. Then when all that had been our world for an hour and a quarter lay as rubble in the middle of the room, we sat in a circle on the floor around it and remembered the magic we had made. The room returned to its former state, but we ourselves had been significantly altered.

Session two: Whom am I? Who is the other? We sat in groups of four and gazed into each other's eyes. The usual qualities by which we recognize a person—shape, movement, gesture, the way one stands or walks, clothes, hair color—all these characteristic clues melted completely away. Suddenly a whole new person was there. A new experience confronted all of us. Through our eyes we entered an inner landscape, and the outer qualities were forgotten. We changed places, passing from person to person. We experienced a kaleidoscope of visions, glances, revelations, tenderness, fear, evasion.

Later, in small groups, we patted one individual—gently, roughly—and in final exhilaration lifted that person high above our heads and carried him or her swiftly to all parts of the room. To be cherished and carried around by a group gives you a feeling of giving yourself wholly, trusting yourself into many hands, sure these hands will not be hurtful or disrespectful. The excitement and drama of the lifting and carrying, the gentle return to the darkness of the floor, means a flight and then a return to a reality where nothing has changed but you. For the lifters and for the lifted, it is an unusual and graphic revelation of human solidarity. The final half hour was spent sitting on the floor in unbroken silence. No one felt the need to talk; each had been included; all belonged. We were happy and content and had no desire to break away from each other.

What had happened? As visual artists, we had experienced in the first exercise (the eyes) the disappearance of the outer shape of the individual. In all our teaching we emphasize the contour, shape, silhouette, gesture, structure (stress and strain of weight distribution), and proportions of the individual. This is the *outside* look, the impression of the individual. In the exercise of the eyes, all these things were disregarded in a search for deeper aspects of the individual, for the psychological contour, the structure (gesture, too) of the spirit.

In the second exercise, we understood the vulnerability and extreme value of each human being; we lent ourselves to glorify another; we entrusted ourselves to others. Had we had the opportunity then to draw, paint, or sculpt, it is certain that reverence and care for fragile human sensibilities would have shown through.

Session three: What happens when we draw? We sat in a circle on the floor in alternating positions; one person faced out toward the wall and the next person faced inward toward the others, and so on. Then we were asked to make all manner of sounds with our mouths closed. In unison, we made a loud noise, but each person's sound was muffled inside his or her body. Sometimes the effect was like water dripping, sometimes like a stream murmuring. It was a group of sounds that merged soothingly together. Then we chose single words and said them in patterns, in slow tempo changing to rapid, and listened to their composition. Then those of us facing out spoke to the wall, and those facing in spoke across the room. The sounds, meanings, and fleeting associations created a loud or soft verbal assemblage. We were given crisp raw carrots and created counterpoint with the noises we made eating them. Then we filled our mouths with hard candy and talked in distorted, lopsided sounds and words. After that, we let soft chocolate candy melt down our throats and listened.

We were asked to draw the inner landscape of our mouths— not any dental charts we had seen, or even images remembered from looking in the mirror, but rather the images that had arisen during our experience of mouthing sounds and food. We tried to recall in images all the alterations of the vocal cavity during humming, speaking, shouting, chewing, and swallowing.

When it was over, we thought about what it meant to make

visible something that has not been seen by the eyes but rather felt through other senses. We realized that this is what artists and young children making art are doing, and that their gift is to broaden our sensibilities. As we looked at the strange drawings of landscapes involving images of our own mouths in action, we saw that making a drawing surely involves uniqueness—expression of a personal experience never witnessed by others. It also has to do with a rounded exploration of all aspects of an event. We had tasted, we had felt the action of our tongues making sound as well as the sensation of humming from the caverns of our closed mouths. We had sensed the texture of skin, teeth, rough tongue, wet salivation, dry throat, and the contour of our teeth. Senses other than the visual had been sharpened. Our drawings reflected this increased awareness, and each was highly individualized. We asked ourselves whether this experiment did not demonstrate that drawing has little to do with "learning" or "teaching" techniques but everything to do with finding and discovering the proper techniques to make each new individual awareness clear.

Session four: The splendor of art. The room was divided into diagonal tunnels created by fastening strings or cords across the room and hanging from them both clear and translucent plastics (inexpensive and reusable plastic cover cloths used by professional house painters). Projectors were placed at various points in the room, and an enormous variety of slides was available, covering subjects from nature to the fine art and architecture of all ages. From the record player came a continuous chant, of Tibetan origin. Groups of students gravitated to the projectors and began creating images on the wall and ceiling through the hanging plastic curtains. Other students wandered through the maze of plastic. Images from the projectors projected these as imaginary beings. Some students were content to watch or take turns participating. A set of huge mirrors reflected the bizarre and changing episodes. Several fans were started later to add a complex billowing out of the plastic sheets, making them look like the sails of a phantom ship. Tableaus were created by groups who wanted to express in common an image, feeling, or idea. At the end, the ceiling took on great fascination, and many in the company lay on the floor looking through the plastics, which had now become slow-moving psychedelic clouds, to the vibrant, changing imagery above them. The world of the everyday city was forgotten as we fed on this magnificent environment. Even as we dimly realized that our hour and a half was coming to a close, we still fashioned new images; we were reluctant to give up our experience.

As can be seen, throughout these sessions the teacher had some definite objectives in mind. The materials were chosen by him and, of course, limited what could be done. However, he assured us that he could never predict what would result under identical conditions and using the same materials. The people involved differed, and therefore each outcome was unique. Such open-ended activity allows freedom to each individual but also merges this individual, his actions and creations, into those of others. In this living art, each action begins to relate and adjust sensitively to other actions.

Happenings as educational vehicles To use the happening in art education means departing from conventional practice. Usually a selected idea is presented for study—an idea the experts consider "worthy"—and then related subject matter is brought in to supplement it. The ultimate application to life will, theoretically, be made by the student. Dependence on academic conditions and sanctions seems to result from exclusive use of this method.

In learning conditions provided by a happening, the teacher does not isolate what is to be studied. Education becomes person-centered. Each person learns from the event whatever he is ready to consider and confront. Students are not acted upon; they act. At certain times, a collection of these personal reactions, their rich complexity paralleling real-life situations, comes into a focus or synthesis, realized by the whole group and dealt with at that moment. The impact of the variety of personal ideas, purposes, and responses brings a sense of the necessity to work toward liberating yet interdependent ways of learning together, a sound exploratory beginning to a semester.

THEATER

The nature of the medium Consider what happens when we watch a play. For a brief time we exist within the lives of the characters, feeling conflict, climax, and resolution along with them, vicariously suffering, loving, and dying. Many experts have written about the emotional purge involved in such participation with actors onstage or in a film. For the actors, immersing themselves in roles created by others becomes a way of life. For children of all ages, the periodic performance of spontaneous skits or more elaborate plays can bring valuable release— of longings for utterance, expression of wild, crazy notions, passionate hates and joys. In role playing they can be cruel to adults in their mimicry, let off feelings about a drunken father or a cold mother; they can be heroes, bad guys, sobbing or intrepid heroines.

For teachers, the dramatic communal effort of a group of children can mean the momentary, exciting gathering up of all the strands of make-believe, dressing up, dramatic play, stories invented, and environments created in two or three dimensions. Words, paper constructions, paint, collage, and assemblage naturally find their way into either the spontaneous dramas children make up themselves or into the less frequent production of a formal play chosen by the class and the teacher to present before an audience.

Creative dramatics often socialize a too-retiring boy or girl. They can be dynamic vehicles for learning about human beings — their problems, satisfactions, behavior in times of stress, what ethics they live by, what tragedies destroy them. Sometimes, too, for a variety of reasons, they may turn out to be static and educationally negative. They involve a mingling of several arts and crafts, as well as collaboration between teachers in several fields. Because cooperation is an essential factor in their success, they are vulnerable and unpredictable, subject to all kinds of error but also capable of high-level communication.

Theater is a world of make-believe, but it is held together by human realities and traditional techniques. Children engaged in a dramatic project will be exposed to some aspects of play-writing, scene designing and constructing, costuming, makeup techniques, lighting, dancing, acting, directing, and inter-preting, cooperating in a group to make a whole out of many parts. Preadolescents are confronted in school with a confusing array of new ideas and skills to be mastered. The correlation in theater work of facts and techniques they have learned in various areas of study, such as social studies, English, art, and shop, can give them a sense of order and reinforcement.

A philosophy for preadolescent theater In the traditional dramatic activity in our schools, several basic concepts have often militated against the children, undermining their creativity and self-confidence.

One was the idea that the Broadway variety show production was the model to emulate. Parents, teachers and children cut and sewed costumes, and children paraded in and out of rehearsals for months before the day of the performance. In these schoolwide productions a loose-knit plan was made around a theme, and what finally evolved was a hodgepodge in which each grade level made a separate contribution, theoretically amalgamated into the general theme. Each class, dressed from head to toe in intricate costumes, came on to perform a skit or song and dance, straitjacketed in body and mind.

During the several weeks of rehearsals, with groups waiting their turn for use of the rehearsal hall and parents, teachers, and children all competing, a good deal of shouting went on. Nerves became frayed, and some permanent schisms developed between individuals and groups. The production, intended to provide the exhilaration of artistic expression, to teach people to cooperate, and to utilize all talents became a jumble of clichés, a bad copy of a variety show of the nineteen-fifties — out of date, out of keeping with the children's enthusiasms, and structured to a point where nothing spontaneous could occur.

The second destructive concept, ruling another type of production, involved what we might call "stars and flunkies." The privileged few — individual children chosen for the leads — received a great deal of acting experience and praise. The majority lived vicariously; their lot was to do supervised labor, fill in the minor parts or watch enviously from the audience. The "attractive" (according to rigid cultural standards) child was encouraged to strut onstage and show off, which was psychologically damaging to him or her as well as to those children in the wings. The ideal beauty chosen may have been one that excluded the type of features possessed by most of the children in the school. Such a procedure was detrimental to all concerned, bad education, and might even be called immoral.

The third mistake was the authoritarian setup. Teachers chose the play with minimum participation of the children. The director, one of the teachers, was also the stage designer and had the last word on the costumes. Little effort was made to involve the children in designing or in any of the decisions about the interpretation of the play, the allotting of parts, or the general atmosphere and style of the production. Naturalism, realism and simplified realism were the three modes used almost exclusively. The symbolic, expressionistic elements so much a part of modern theater were not represented (3). Directors concentrated on producing a letter-perfect, smooth-running spectacle; achieving this involved not a little heartache and deprivation. Drilling, rehearsals, long waits during which the children in minor parts had nothing to do — all this could turn young actors into little more than marionettes and, eventually, into discipline problems. Those in the lead parts became over-stimulated (sometimes spoiled) by the fuss made over them and their costumes and by the oversized audience. The production had been conceived and carried out by adults, placing the children beyond their ordinary world and without any control of the medium into which they were suddenly plunged. For them the whole thing was apt to become irritating and chaotic. Many of us noticed how children screamed out at each other even the most tender lines in a play. Was this their frustration and confusion coming through?

A fourth mistaken concept, which nowadays operates more rarely in our schools, involves the choice of plays. The teacher-director was often apt to select a nineteenth-century drama, set in a genteel English background and carrying a strongly moralistic message. Or a prejudiced version of a historic event was chosen, with little consideration for minority groups. Often both children and audience suffered through half-understood sentimental passages delivered haltingly or with artificial elocution developed through long hours of practice with the classroom teacher. Fortunately the new generation of teachers is bringing the range of plays chosen at least into the twentieth century, though schools still abound with watered-down versions of the classics, meaningless festivals and small moralistic skits with unreal dialogue based on social studies.

What all of these disturbing concepts have in common is a set of bygone values: the star system; the ambitious "spectacle" based on visual and verbal clichés; the regimenting of children instead of bringing them out creatively and giving some thought to individual psychological problems and the use of solely naturalistic or realistic theater design and acting. "The Method," for instance, has been a technique of actors for several decades. Is it not time that children were exposed to at least the rudiments of its theory and practice?

Children's theater should concentrate on styles of production other than the realistic. Symbolism, impressionism and expressionism draw more on the imagination, require personal interpretations, and involve the students more deeply in the meaning of what they are doing. For instance, when symbols are used, the child is stimulated to understand them in relation to the story. The expressionistic style calls into play the entire subconscious and emotional life of the child. Distortion in design elements and in acting out the characters results from a strong subjective response to the dramatic material. Impressionistic theater, in a lighter vein, fosters atmospheric mood and exposes children to lyricism. A combination of all three seems to work best for preadolescents, since there are so many personalities participating in one production. They merge well and reinforce each other, often creating a rich amalgam of personal sensibilities and talent (3).

Certain formal aspects can be presented to children as they venture into theater experiences ranging from small, quick skits to larger ventures. Viktor Lowenfeld has some pertinent thoughts on the subject of stage design for children. His suggestions include studying the effects of horizontal and vertical lines; different levels; light in relation to shadow and the importance of the illuminated parts; large and small spaces, background, foreground, center of interest; and the emotional content, the social atmosphere, period and style (4: p. 248). These phases by themselves will mean nothing to children, but when pointed out in a moment of crucial necessity and applied in the midst of a theatrical production, they can remain embedded in the mind.

The more elaborate productions of preadolescent groups will be much more inventive and integrated if they have behind them a long history of spontaneous skits and casual clowning, mimicry, dancing, happenings, light shows, and musical events. Dennison, working with children in New York's Lower East Side, cites many instances of natural theater. He has a set of stories about Maxine, whose mother was pregnant.

Maxine sat in the wastebasket and then tilted herself out on the floor and crawled like a baby. I asked her to get back in the basket and said I should deliver her like a regular baby. She complied immediately. The kids were very interested. I asked Maxine to make baby sounds in the basket. She did. I said, "Oh, look at the new baby! How are you, new baby?" She said, "Gooby, gooky, gobbledy kackie." So I called her Baby Kackie and we played baby games awhile . . . After a few minutes of this, the frenzy melted away from her and her eyes became clear. This is a good line to take with her, since she's imaginative and bright [5: p. 45].

Maxine and José are up on their feet every two minutes, doing dance steps. José expands his chest and makes like a wrestler, Maxine flaunts her fanny [5: p. 49].

Now Maxine has become inspired. She jumps into the center of the ring and brings on gales of laughter by her stylization. She puts one hand on her hip, looks utterly bored, turns her head from side to side and speaks the words, "Glory, glory" abruptly and dryly, like a store clerk reading an inventory: then grinning wildly and waving her arms, she jumps up and down and yells "Hallelujah". Then abruptly bored again, "Glory, glory," and jumping again, "Hallelujah!" The teachers, especially, are howling with laughter [5: p. 52].

Today's preadolescents have much more exposure to the theater than ever before because of long hours watching TV, the protest theaters in the streets of big cities, and participation in band groups for younger and younger children. Mimicry sprouts forth like wild flowers from them. It is their response to visual materials of all kinds—shows, souped-up dramatic advertisements, etc.—that fill their lives. The result is that they see the drama of themselves, their families and their neighbors in different imaginative terms.

If the teacher sees theater as beginning with spontaneous response, and if preadolescents are enough at ease in the atmosphere to respond with body movement, they can easily be led into more complicated group experiences, still based on spontaneity, talent for mimicry (at a peak at this age), and love of make-believe, a carry-over from childhood.

The preadolescent as costume designer Like stage sets, costumes can be realistic, symbolic, stylized, impressionistic, or expressionalistically exaggerated. They are extensions of both body and personality. In one sense of the word, they are always symbols—tokens of everything from sex to social status. We put on a "costume" every day, and for many, a change of clothes can mean a change of mood. Preadolescents, whose personalities are still in a state of flux, are passionate about dressing up. In the White Plains Store Front Art Project, during the hottest days of summer, children come in the morning and make immediately for the costume box to find a familiar article or rummage for a new disguise to wear that day. Mirrors are placed near the storage area, and there is much strutting back and forth and nudging others to get a better view as they try this and that one, add a sash, scarf, turban, train, or veil. They spend all the hot day in their costumes. Even the preadolescent boys remove their club shirts covered with prized insignia and adorn themselves with native African *dashikis*. One thirteen-year-old girl wore a magnificent red velvet floorlength gown through days of 100-degree heat.

Primitive man wore parts of animals—mane, wings, fangs, feathers, tails—hoping to appropriate the admired animal's attributes by adorning himself with the special part that gives the animal its advantage. Many psychologists say that protection against cold, heat and wetness is the least of our reasons for dressing; the true purposes are to attract the opposite sex and denote socioeconomic position and status. Every new subculture, every serious political upheaval, symbolizes itself by dress as well as social behavior. After the French Revolution women threw out their corsets and wore tiny red ribbons around their throats. Members of the Woman's Liberation movement are burning their brassieres. The young men and women of today have such startling new ways of dressing that they are often not allowed in restaurants, motels, and bourgeois sections of town. In their tattered jeans and long hair, headbands and beads, they are expressing a desire to return to a less artificial life, a more natural state in which life was simpler and more earthy. Their new symbolic costume, to which thousands conform, has supplanted the bourgeois costume—business suit, clean dress in the latest fashion, etc. Other less extreme young men are dressing up in wilder colors, flowered shirts, and flowing ties denoting perhaps the general loosening of rigid sex inhibitions and the orgy of new colors coming out of our technology to costume a less "uptight" way of existence.

Preadolescents throw themselves passionately into their own changing moods. Personalities appear and disappear. They may want to be some character they saw in a movie. They may want to feel grand, or be secure in a role out of their own past when they were loved and protected intensely. They pick up adult syndromes intuitively and put them into costume. They are quick-change artists, with an innate theatricality which will be toned down later by sobering experiences and ego integration.

There is no reason in the world to dampen preadolescents' enthusiastic, chameleonlike tendencies in school. In fact, they are far less apt to become discipline problems if they can play out their fantasies through dressing up. Furthermore, their own natural and impulsive costume ideas may be more successful in a dramatic production than the less flexible approach of adults.

The case of Susan's wig is a good example of putting cold water on the creative enthusiasm of a whole class. Susan was a shouter; the class called her "loud mouth." She was a hefty child of eleven and a half, aggressive, bossy and belligerent, who took on many a boy twice her size) in combat and yelled for attention at every turn. Her teachers and the guidance counselor were cooperating in an attempt to get at the root of her trouble.

The other children saw Susan immediately in the role of Queen Bess when their teacher picked the play, *Queen Elizabeth of England,* for the class to put on in relation to social studies. They elected her unanimously, and she was riding on the crest of the wave of happy success when she and the others came to the art studio to create their costumes. Susan whirled from drawer to drawer like a tornado, looking for one special, all-important item: her red wig. She felt the wig was her most important symbolic identification as the queen. Nothing suited her until she saw a piece of red flannel among the mass of materials. She held her breath and felt its softness; the color was just right, according to her—a fiery red. She tugged and tugged to get it out of the mess she had made during her rummaging. Finally, fully revealed, it turned out to be a suit of red woolen underwear, one of the many articles donated by parents. This did not discourage Susan. In a moment, it was a turban wrapped around her head, and she was strutting regally before the full-length mirror and shouting for the other children to come and see. They loved the whole scene, clapped and laughed, and made suggestions about getting some curls by clipping the material here and there.

All the costumes had to be approved by the classroom teacher, who was directing the play. The art teacher sent up a prayer: "God, let Susan have her wig!" But it was not to be. The children came back crushed. Wearing underwear on the head was not suitable or respectful. The Queen had to be played straight and the play done in the conventional way. What an opportunity was lost!

When the art teachers in the school were given more leeway and more responsibility in guiding the design of dramatic productions, they inherited a whole assortment of dress-up clothes stored in the attic, contributions of parents and leftovers from previous plays and festivals—all in various stages of cleanliness and repair. Every time a play was planned, the old closet was opened, and the job of an art teacher was to be a seamstress and fit the right item to the child. The role of the child in costume making was simply to stand still and be fitted. When the art teachers tried to stimulate a group putting on a play to design and make costumes of their own, the youngsters were never satisfied with what they did in comparison to the more finished-looking works made by adults. The other teachers, too, could not seem to see beyond this ready-made supply.

One summer the art teachers decided to do a little cleaning out, and in the fall the cupboards were bare. Traumatic reactions of the older teachers would theoretically be softened by presentation of a new plan and a description of the educational advantages the change entailed. But there was resentment, of course, not to be alleviated until the new program began to bear fruit during the school year.

The idea was that children should use their bodies to express ideas, characters, emotion, and action. The simpler the costumes, the freer and more spontaneous the make-believe.

Studio work on a play now began with the decoration of the face, using albaline as a base and theatrical paints and makeup. The children became symbolic rather than realistic characters. In their leotards and bathing caps they felt free to move their bodies in expressive ways. They never missed the old costumes.

To encourage spontaneous dressing up and to spur on the new concept of theater in each classroom, the art teachers set up costume boxes containing lengths of material in various textures —opaque and transparent, soft, rough, and smooth, along with filmy veils precut into various geometric shapes for transformation into dramatic cloaks, trains, bustles, and flowing scarves. A little pinning here and there, a bow and sash or veil, and the costume of any period appeared. Designs were quickly painted on any fabric that appealed to a child actor. Huge jewels were make from egg cartons, papier-maché, and other materials glued together and decorated to shine and sparkle. By making these and seeing them later on the stage, the children grasped firsthand the exaggeration necessary in the theater to make costumes, props, and actors take on life when seen from a distance, with colored lights on them. The whole notion of the effect on the audience of simplicity and scale dawned on them.

The props in school dramatics are best kept at a minimum. They present real problems, and pantomime can, for the most part, more creatively represent them. Everyone can remember, in the naturalistic children's productions of the past (still presented in many schools), a table being set for twelve while the audience shifted with impatience for about 15 minutes. Then there was always the child who saw that the forks were in the wrong place and proceeded to correct the mistake as the audience silently groaned. Eating can be indicated without utensils. Sets are easily devised that eliminate the necessity of realistic props.

Machine-made items should be completely eliminated. They are usually out of scale with the things the children make themselves. Also, they do not fit in aesthetically; they spoil the make-believe. A teacher who describes and shows illustrations of some historical item to be made into a prop limits the child's natural expression and, moreover, frustrates him since he is not familiar with the way of making it. It is far better to allow time for each child to experiment with a group of illustrations and visit a museum to see the object, to which he can refer to and perhaps find some symbolic item that will satisfy him as being representative of the period. To keep a unified atmosphere of make-believe in the tradition of expressionism, the materials should be unrelated to those used for a realistic object.

Size is an important consideration; children need to work with props in conjunction with the lighting, costumes and the action of the play. In this way they will see 1) how necessary the props really are, or if they hamper the action, confusing and cluttering the stage; 2) how large they must be to be seen; and 3) what the lights will do to them. Special lighting effects can destroy the volume and mass of an object. An item can be so strong in color and so active in design that it overpowers the characters. Some items fight each other on the stage, destroying continuity.

The preadolescent as stage designer   Teachers often sincerely fool themselves into believing that they are providing opportunities for youngsters to think creatively about theater design, when in fact it is they who are the stage designers, with some suggestions from the students. This is not intentional. It happens because we have neither the tools nor the time to give every child a chance to create a set on his own. We have to settle for second best. Usually the following arrangement is made: two or three committees of students are elected to work out several design solutions; these are presented to the whole group, which then votes on the one they want. This way every child learns something, if only by responding to the various aspects of designing a stage set and choosing between solutions. The children on the committees may have a deeper experience in this area.

But is this the best we should aim for and expect? To shoulder the creative responsibility, to think it through, to listen to others and discuss with them and then come up with a solution of one's own—that is the true way of learning something about stage designing. This ultimate and full experience, involving responsibility, thoughtful study, cooperation with others, and personal decision is what we should try to give each student. To find a method of achieving this is difficult, but worth every minute of the effort.

As a solution, in one school a unit or module stage, designed by the art teacher, Lucile F. Young, was built by the school carpenters. We had been struggling for years with a stage in a borrowed hall used by religious organizations for services, funerals, and other occasions. A special stage had to be added at considerable expense; because of fear of damage to the hall, all spontaneous or casual activities had to be prohibited. The module stage could be easily assembled in any large empty space such as the gym, the social hall in the basement, the music room, a classroom, or even the lunch room.

The units were built as hollow blocks, the largest dimension being 6 feet and most were 1 foot thick. These could be walked on and items pinned on to the vertical surfaces. Boys and girls were able to move the various pieces—columns, rounds, blocks, flats—easily. A young designer could change them into as

many arrangements as he wished until he arrived at a satisfactory solution with regard to flow of action, change of scene, and passage of time. These units could be nested together and stored compactly in the basement, to be brought up as needed on a dolly and moved on location. They were painted each time with liquid soap, plus whatever tempera colors were chosen for a specific production. Before storage, the janitors washed them off with a hose, and they were ready for the next performance. The units were in constant demand for cake sales, and fashion shows, as counters and platforms, etc. The sign-up list was never empty.

In addition to these large units, we had built three experimental miniature replica sets made to one-twelfth scale. Using one of these, each child could, if interested, decide how a set was to be designed by moving the pieces around. The more the children worked with their modules, the more simple, dramatic and unique their results. When ready to rehearse, they asked for the appropriate parts to be brought to their room from storage, thus getting an opportunity to iron out the kinks and see if the design really worked. In this way individual children, and not the teacher, became the stage designers.

One of the important features of these sets was that their scale was right for children. Most stages are too big, and a child feels lost and without control. Another advantage was the ease of changing scenes. Furthermore, time need not be wasted painting flats which, in the end, might not work well. If the children were dissatisfied with a color, they merely sponged the unit down and tried again. The result was that they could give a number of plays in the time it formerly took to give one. From such a quick, continuing sequence of work, they gained sophistication, sensibility and an understanding of the aesthetics of stage design.

Since there was no curtain, lighting had to play a greater role in the change of scene, to create passage of time and mood. Theater in the round was often used. Action arising in all parts of the given space became natural to the children. There was greater spontaneous flow; there were fewer long, stiff speeches. The children, who were full of exuberant energy, could indulge in wildly active scenes—battles, chases, jumping, and running. Whenever they needed more space, a column was pushed out here or a block there, without great difficulty.

As their theatrical experiences multiplied, two tendencies were noticeable: they began to discard the superficial plays in preference for plays of great quality exploring universal issues and to find greater satisfaction in writing and producing their own original dramas.

A play in production   In the Ethical Culture schools (Midtown), fifth-grade classroom teacher John Darr and ethics teacher Eddie Hirabayasha were searching for a vehicle to make ethics more meaningful to the class. Staging a play was one answer. A production of this sort requires the cooperation of everyone; ethical considerations on a real-life basis are bound to crop up. Correlated historical and social subjects can be woven into the project, depending on the nature of the play. The art of play-writing is made especially visible to children who study and take parts and actually live in its unified structure during its few hours on the stage.

The class was receptive to the idea. After some searching, the children and teachers chose Aristophanes' comedy *Peace*. It had special qualities appealing to preadolescent humor and imagination.

From the teacher's point of view, Aristophanes provided something meaty and cryptic enough to give the children a challenge and difficulty in its deciphering and understanding. The play is set in a period of Greek history when the Athenians were exasperated after ten years of war, yet unable to make peace. The play provided an active way of learning ancient history and mythology. The comedies of Aristophanes are masterpieces, and any contact with them is enlightening and provocative. They dramatize many ethical problems common to all humanity under a coat of slapstick and satirical humor.

Correlating the play with history and ethics was important, but the teachers planned to emphasize exploration of the children's talents in the areas of acting, diction, musical expression, and stage and costume design. An art teacher in the school was asked to join in the discussions and contribute her aesthetic ideas as well as help the children with costumes and scenery.

The classroom teacher, a specialist in literary and social studies, led the dialogue on the meaning of the play, the circumstances in which it was written, the theatrical form it represented, the characters, and the many symbols. The children were easily motivated to write out their ideas about the characters, both as symbols and as real people to be represented on the stage by color, materials, line and shape. The classroom teacher also helped them formulate and chart the action of the play; he gave directing hints on speech, gesture, body movement, and poise. Under his guidance, the class learned something about structure: how economical a playwright must be, making every line relevant to theme and plot in order to compress a great deal into a short time period of performance. He helped them become aware of pace as an element not to be neglected. It was part of the actor's job, for instance, to keep things rolling even when faced with his own or others' mistakes. The ethics teacher made important contributions to the analysis of the play and was invaluable when personal problems arose during stages of the production, such as the slotting of parts and the avoidance of power groups who would mar the democratic system of decision making and working committees that the children had established with his help. One of the main conflicts in the play involved the destructive warmongers, who had been profiting from the war for ten years, and those who wanted to return to peace and agriculture.

The music teacher developed the sound sequences, and the art teacher created conditions in her studio to motivate these fifth-grade children to express visually the way they wanted their stage set, lighting and costumes to look and function.

The teachers met informally a few times, to arrange scheduling or movement of materials. But the children themselves were in charge of all the decision-making meetings. They had set up a miniature government, with a class chairman who ran the meetings. Teachers could speak from the floor, like all the other members of the group. The classroom teacher took over only when it was time to end the discussion because of some outside commitment. The parliamentary procedure worked well; it was an open forum with equable reception of all ideas. Responsibilities for carrying out decisions were given to the committees, which chose their own chairman. Complaints of any kind, by child or teacher, were brought to the class chairman, who called the whole group together to discuss them if necessary.

The art teacher's role At the start, the children asked the art teacher to talk to them about the relation between writing a play and conceiving it in nonverbal, visual terms. Their work with the classroom teacher on dramatic structure—emphasis, climax, resolutions—had given them many ideas. They had come to conclusions about the structure, mood and meaning of this play. Could they carry out their ideas in costumes and sets?

The art teacher organized her presentation into three parts. The first dealt with the interrelation of the arts, all of them possessing certain elements in common, each with its own media and special concerns. All the arts are involved with line, color, texture, depth, shape, and the ways of creating through the use of rhythm, balance, variety, and emphasis a completely unified symbolic statement. The work of art makes its statement through symbols. Aristophanes had provided the literary and dramatic symbols of the play. Now it was up to the stage designers and the costume and prop makers to provide the visual symbols—in color, shape, texture, direction, light and dark, space illusions —which would bear out the author's intention kinesthetically and unify their production.

The second part of her presentation consisted of illustrations and slides showing how a professional theater designer organizes a production. Symbolic color may be used to clarify the plot or to call forth associations for the audience; static and moving shapes produce their different impacts; colors and shapes are repeated throughout the play for their rhythmic effect and power to unify; a repertoire of horizontals, diagonals, verticals, sub-ordination, and emphasis is fully realized by the stage designer. Light and shadow are used symbolically and to create illusions of depth and mass.

The art teacher then conferred with the children about organization and process. How would decisions be made on stage design, props, costumes? The children were unanimously firm in their desire to make the main decisions themselves, after gleaning all the advice they could from their teachers.

To include all the children to some extent in the decision making and eliminate any overall director to make the final choices appeared to be an idealistic, difficult task. Many possible ways of organizing were thrashed out. Finally the class chairman asked the art teacher to propose a method for producing the visual aspect of the play, one including suggestions made by the children. Later this overall plan was to be carefully weighed and accepted or rejected by the group.

The next step was the real beginning of process. The art teacher proposed that the entire class involve itself in a series of brainstorming—or rather, feeling-storming—sessions, experimenting in pastels, paint or collage in order to get down on paper their separate ideas about the visual presentation of the play. Such a process revealed each person's sensibility with regard to the colors, shapes, spatial aspects and textures the set might contain, and how he visualized the characters.

Step one: The children got down to work, making preliminary sketches on large pieces of paper of each of the main characters and the minor characters supporting or relating to him. At the end, every character had been suggested in abstract terms—color, shape, directional lines—by every boy and girl in the class.

Step two: The scenes of the play were represented in the same way, with color used for mood and symbol, and lines to indicate the flow of action and the structural weight of certain passages. Horizontal levels, vertical planes, and techniques of depth and diagonal action were used to visualize the different scenic effects needed for various types of action—for rough, ribald humor, for instance, or for the more poetic passages about the earth's abundance.

Step three: Now it was time to pin up the work and see if consistencies were occurring in terms of color and images among the members of the class and, if there were many glaring inconsistencies, to deal with them. All were fascinated to see how many points of agreement there were on the shapes, colors, values, and sizes associated with each personage in the play. The impact of the few leading characters and the general atmosphere of chorus, farmers, and war profiteers came through consistently in the majority of the children's responses.

With this evidence of unanimity before them, the children then settled on specific colors, lines, and contrasts for each important character in the play, to give each actor a distinct sense of who he was in terms of personality traits. The costume also had to relate to what the character symbolized in society, his dramatic importance, and his personality changes in the course of the play. (In Greek satire there is little or no development of character, but it was important for the children to understand the concept of psychological transformation so important in modern drama.) The minor characters received the same treatment, with the additional consideration that their costumes had to be symbolically related to those of the main characters with whom they were connected.

The children having made basic decisions on each costume, a volunteer committee was charged with the task of assembling the proper materials and dummying-up several models to be reviewed by the class later.

The same analyzing and filtering process was applied to the children's original sketches for different scenes—on earth, on Olympus, in front of the Senate, and so on. At that point the designs decided on for the major characters were applied to various scene designs, to see how they would work together. This resulted in modifications and new emphases—another round of decisions to be made. Committees were formed to present different combinations of set-costumes-lighting derived from selections made from the sketches.

Step four: These committees made their presentation. In preparation, the teacher and some of the children made a color-shape-line chart, with some verbal information added, of the previous decisions and the responsibilities assigned. Cartons large enough to house refrigerators were prepared for this next step. In them, all sort of materials were grouped in color families. The committees chose from these and made mock-ups of certain costumes. Care was taken not to be literal in the choice of materials. If necessary, papier-mâché or pulp were used to retain the symbolic effect. A veil, for instance, was made not from the usual gauze but from loosely woven paper, string or pleated tissue paper. The class reviewed each presentation, made suggestions, and decided when a material should be used exclusively for one character or in what proportion distributed among others. Qualities of sheen or dullness, saturation or density of color became important as children and teacher estimated how the materials would hold up when seen from the back of the hall. Finally, after experimentation with lights on colors and textures, choices were made, the working committees instructed, and the refinements of the ideas recorded on charts for future reference.

Step five: During the assigned art periods or whenever they had time, the committee members came to the studio to work on costumes, props or sets. The art teacher was available for consultation. While executing the work, each child developed an idea in his own manner, though within the bounds set by the group. There was speculation and argument about this point. An artist is given a commission to fill certain specifications, but his personal interpretation is bound to modify them.

The most serious problem which arose was the interpretation of the costume for Peace, a glamorous female to the three young girls working on her costume. They were at a stage in their art expression in which they used many clichés and stereotypes, the most significant being that of the "pretty girl." Their idea was to make a filmy bridal-type costume out of tulle, entirely out of keeping with the total symbolic interpretation. When the art teacher pointed out that this characterization of Peace would work against the specifications set by group decision and destroy the design unity of the play, they accused her of interfering, of injecting her own ideas and of dominating. The teacher took the issue to the class council. They called a meeting. After hearing all sides of the question, it was decided to call in the ethics teacher to help decide the following issues:

1. When a decision has been made by the group, is it proper for someone to deviate so far in interpreting it that the decision is virtually countermanded?

2. If a person was absent when the decision about this costume was made, does that mean he is not bound by it?

3. Should children carry over some prejudices against authority (perhaps justified) to a specific teacher who, in this instance, is not guilty of being authoritarian?

One of the impressive things to turn up during the meeting, and duly noted by the children, was the statement by the classroom teacher that he may have influenced the girls to design Peace's costume in the conventional cliché of a young girl in a white filmy gown, holding a dove, with olive leaves in her hair — probably flowing blond hair. The point was made that blondes were rare in Greece. Dark hair and a warm olive complexion were more appropriate, especially with the rich earth tones chosen for the rest of the costumes. In fact, all the materials chosen emphasized a sense of roughness without actually being burlap or similar cloth. The realistic conventional symbols for certain kinds of characters had also been ruled out in favor of a more abstract interpretation. The filmy net or tulle bridal or beauty queen dress for Peace struck a jarring note.

It was voted finally that anyone with ideas about Peace's costume could join the committee of three girls and add his or her ideas. The girls were joined promptly by a group of energetic boys who devised a strange and vigorous version of Peace, conceiving of her as a force combining beauty and strength, perhaps something like an earth mother, very different from the twentieth-century commercial advertisement the girls had created. She now represented an apex, a point of climax perfectly in spirit with the rest of the play.

Step six: Finalizing all the parts in terms of the whole: trying out costumes and props in combination with the action of the play. At this point, as at all the other stages, alterations and adjustments had to be made to solidify the unity of the production.
Evaluation of the project In summarizing what they got out of the project, the children said that they had gained insight into the meaning and artistic structure of a great work of art and that it took group solidarity to interpret it as a unified, cohesive statement. They also felt that what they learned about group life, the adjustment of each person to the group goal after he or she had had a chance to express ideas and creative talent,

was an impressive lesson in the democratic ethic. They also learned a lot about each other; class tensions were reduced, friendships made, and rivalries lessened.

The art teacher felt that the children had made great strides in recognizing the value of experimentation and the rewards of making decisions with care—spontaneity and intuition followed by judgment and perseverance. Many of the children tried to explain to the impatient ones why it was necessary to take time deciding such matters as color and design. And when, two days before the performance, the questions of makeup was raised for final decision, the children showed they had grasped the idea of sticking to basic principles in order to strengthen the unity of a work of art, rather than indulging in personal whims.

Above all, they felt the deep satisfaction of joining with others to carry through a unified, artistic production. This is especially significant for preadolescent children, who tend to divide into cliques, with the weaker egos suffering in the constant power struggle.

The class grew up a little in the process because they and not adults were responsible for the selection, interpretation, and visual illumination of this great play. It was an adult's, not a child's, play, and it gave them prestige in their own eyes to be able to understand it.

For the teachers, rare opportunities arose when they decided to cooperate and integrate their special skills and knowledge in a joint teaching and learning vehicle and to produce cooperatively a unified work of art. Each invested time and effort to help clarify the project for the children; they were in total agreement that the children gained from working out their own methods and processes.

Each teacher's contribution reinforced those of the other teachers. The in-depth discussions concerning the meaning of the play and of its different characters, led by the classroom and ethics teachers' bore fruit as the children started to draw and paint their conceptions of sets and costumes. With some direction from the art teacher, they also displayed an unusual willingness to experiment with complicated methods, using nonobjective forms to arrive at an original and cohesive visual interpretation of the play.

PUPPETRY

Puppetry is a collaboration of theater skills (voice, gesture, narrative talent) and sculptural techniques (carving, assemblage, construction). The voice might be considered the most important factor, though the hands, too, play a major role in the original construction and in the manipulation of the puppet.

Controlling a miniature body with strings or hands is a substitute for using one's own body on the stage. Strong identifications are possible. A piece of wood or other material carved into human shape has a deeply primitive ambience, a little frightening to some with its ancient undertones of fetishes, burial figurines, voodoo spells. As the puppet is conceived and as it moves, it can become a projection of the psyche of its master. An imaginative child identifies with the manikin, acting out wish fulfillments and traveling by means of the puppet into many environments, predicaments, and heroic deeds. Anxieties are released by means of this deputy, this "other," who plays many roles. Like all children's dramatic play, a puppet show is very revealing of personality and can give observant teachers many insights into the real problems of their students. The child puppeteer is alone with his *Doppelgänger* when he pulls the strings. He can make his actor perform more extravagantly, be freer in gesture than he could while using his own body. Self-consciousness can be almost completely eliminated. A comparison can be made with the acting children sometimes do when concealed by a theatrical mask.

Personalities other than the child's can be explored. A new human being, animal or some other image devised from found objects may arise from the preadolescent's curiosity regarding life, loves, hates, sentiments, or disgust for certain behavior. Mimicry can be ruthless here.

Factors of idea, color, line and shape selected by the child determine the visual quality of the character created. But sometimes a face and body accidentally appearing during the carving, assembling or painting will surprise the child with a brand new personality of which he never dreamed. The inanimate material comes to life, inspiring its master to give it a role and speak for it.

To make dramatic action on the puppet stage, children are required to observe carefully how people walk, run, swing their arms, toss their heads, shift their weight, and so on. Thus puppetry skills feed back to sculpture, and possibly to the children's own acting and dancing skills the more they become identified kinesthetically with their miniature performers.

Dr. Frank Lerch was such a prodigious devotee of puppetry that his art room in the school was a veritable heaven for his seventh-grade students. The room had been turned into a puppet theater; while some children huddled in groups, discussing skits and developing characters, others worked with lights, sounds and dialogue later to be organized into plays. The stage itself was a permanent feature of the room. Students were constantly climbing the stairs at the back to work with their small actors. On the occasion of my visit, a number of children were presenting a series of skits—trial runs. One was a short spoof on soap opera. Another was a robbery worked out comically by four boys. Still another was a very serious scene from *Romeo and Juliet.* Some were only sketches, others carefully worked out. After the presentation, the children thought how a thread might be woven through all three—by adding scenes, deleting, expanding—to unify the presentation. Later I saw the project, still in an experimental stage, the weather man had been made a lighthearted linking element. Time-space, weather, and travel were the concepts providing a skeletal frame. The personalities of several puppets had been expanded and deepened, and some new characters had been developed. The staging included some inventive props; a number of sketches had been arranged in tentative sequence. New ideas and new music were being tested. The children were discussing pacing, deciding that some parts of the action should move faster, others slower. Eventually a play emerged from the energies and interests of individuals and the group. At this age level, many plays can come into being in like manner.

Another remarkable puppet studio and a joy to preadolescents is pictured here. Puppets hang poised on their strings as if engaged in long conversations with each other. Others lie in heaps, their energies exhausted. Some are still pieces in various stages of construction. There is an electric sense

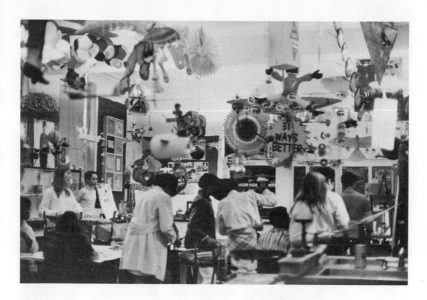

of something going on, as if many voices or the memory of voices and movement still linger. The teacher in the studio, Ronald Gaschke, has built a van to house all his marvels, and the puppeteers, like traveling artists of other days, move from school to school in Elizabeth, New Jersey, to give their shows.

Inanimate materials come alive   A fine experience in puppetry for youngsters is to pile materials on a table and let discoveries take place.

During the lesson José cut up the bulb of a syringe. With the split in it, it looked exactly like a woman's hip and ass. He showed it to me, saying only, "Look." I said, "It looks like a woman's ass." He roared with laughter, in which there was a ringing note of release. He widened the split so that he could make alternately a fat woman and a skinny one [5: pp. 47–48].

Using the qualities implicit in the material is one way to make a puppet. Will the material snap, curl, bounce? Will it roll, twist, or loop? Can it be made to flutter or vibrate? Does it inflate and deflate like an accordion? Does it have spring? What sounds can it make? Test it for rattle, click, clang, tinkle, rumble, hollow echo, squeal, knock, bang, squish, hum. How does it feel? Is it silky, smooth, grainy, slick, furry, gravelly, bumpy, stiff, sleazy, hard, beady? Any one of these qualities of a material will suffice for the creation for a puppet.

Once they have begun, preadolescents will discover innumerable materials from which to make puppets, ranging from wood, paper, papier-mâché, sawdust, collage, and cloth to a variety of found objects—natural or man-made in various materials—used for their associative values or completely transformed through inventive use. The simplest puppets made by children are sock, stick, vegetable, paper bag, hand and finger puppets, rod, shadow, collage puppets and puppets made of found materials.

Out of inanimate materials a puppet is born, a kinetic sculpture given life by human rather than mechanical energy. *Who is it?* Who do you have here? It may be a couple of peanut shells, plus some lengths of rope, plus some plastic odds and ends and a strip of cotton cloth. But it is a person emerging, a character is born through the merging of conscious concept with inert

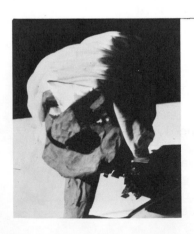

material. The state of mind of the maker may come through strong, something he is experiencing, or a would-be glamorous image of self, or a satire of a hated person. Grotesque puppet personalities generally reflect deep concerns and acute observations. Caricatures on the surface, these puppets on closer observation become individual personalities.

Physical traits Even as the puppet emerges from the material, its personality begins to show. Is it a he or a she? Do the teeth show? Are the ears prominent? Is the mouth thin or thick? Are the eyes round or slitted? Does she have a hat on, or is her hair luxuriously carved? Is her dress dowdy, or is she a modern swinger? Is she young or old?

Experimentations and discussions help the child make decisions about the shape of the face, the voids within it, and the size and proportions of the parts of the face that change as a result of emotions, especially the mouth and chin. Studying one's own face with a hand mirror and making sketches of features and lines that interest them for their puppets is a good exercise for the children. Another aid is for the teacher to demonstrate on a puppet head that is still blank and featureless how the personality can be created, changed, and re-created by adding (using pins) various combination of nose, ears, mustache, eyeglasses, eyebrows, beard, jowls, and cheekbones. This exercise dramatizes to the students the fact that a puppet will be seen from all sides. The teacher might also demonstrate the effect of strong lights on features—how the shadows flatten out masses.

Personality traits When the puppet is given distinctive traits of speech and behavior that set him apart from other puppets, when he can be recognized by name as soon as he opens his mouth or walks across the stage, then he becomes a character and remains one until accident, neglect or old age put him out of circulation.

If children are particulary interested in detail and the expression of emotion, it is a good idea to have them model the head in clay, a material so responsive to touch that they can experiment with many types of personalities quickly. Passages from novels, play introductions by the author describing his characters (Shaw's prefaces, Arthur Miller's preface to *Death of a Salesman*), and descriptive dialogue can be read to the children for hints on deepening the purely physical aspects of character as well as for the quirks and mannerisms that distinguish human beings from each other.

Ask the children to do some outside observation in connection with their puppet making: to watch a person in conversation for at least 3 minutes, noticing what he does with his face, hands and body. Have them jot down what they noticed and try to remember the details in order to describe them to the class. This exercise will demonstrate how many little actions a person goes through when in conversation. A student may be inspired by his observation of human quirks to utilize some of them when he is ready to perform with his puppet. A valuable connection between literature, art and real life will be made.

To stimulate the imagination, bring in an assortment of large stones; have each child choose one he or she likes. Tell them to pretend that inside each is the face of a puppet. Then they can cover the rocks with papier-mâché and use them as armatures. The shapes of the rocks, no two the same, will be good beginnings for puppet heads.

Puppets made out of collage, paper bags or found objects involve the choice of material things that can be transformed into something new. Children will learn how to avoid banal and too literal choices if the teacher shows them using slides, some excellent inventive use of materials, in assemblages and box sculptures.

Functional traits The puppet maker must think beyond the head. Even as the puppet is being made, the figure must be designed in terms of what he is expected to perform. If the puppet is expected to mount a horse, he will have to have separated legs and possibly special kinds of hands. Will he always ride the horse, or will he sometimes get off? If the puppet is to do something special, such as getting into a missile during the performance, the act must be carefully practiced so that the audience will understand it. The props have to be made at the same time as the puppet. If a marionette is going to comb her hair, she must have a comb. Musical puppets will need their guitars or drums. The puppet maker might practice on a drum himself, analyzing his poses as he works the drumsticks up into a frenzy of action, slouches over the drum, taps with his feet, and moves his head up and down as if in a trance.

Speech characteristics A voice with a quality of its own is an important characteristic of a convincing puppet personality. The puppeteer should talk to his puppet while he is being made, to learn where he comes from and what he has done. What will be his slang, his special phrases? Will he slur or have a nasal twang? Is she sincere, affected and pretentious, does she "talk down" to other puppets? Gradually the puppeteer learns who his character is and finds out his name. Perhaps he is poor. His father disappeared one day, and his mother brought him up; he has two older sisters who go out to work. The better the puppeteer knows his puppet, the closer they become, and the more there is to tell others about him.

Teachers arrange to have the children work in pairs so that puppets can converse together. As they talk, their makers can enlarge on their backgrounds. Perhaps the puppeteer is not satisfied with the story he told the first time. Then he can have his puppet chat with another child's marionette and approach the conversation from another angle. Thus through many practice sessions and dialogues, he discovers what is the most convincing characterization in relation to the design and details of his new friend.

A tape recorder is essential in a puppet-making room. Listening to himself, the child can hear objectively exactly where he is failing or succeeding. The tape recorder is also useful in developing a written script.

Staging, producing, writing   Many fine books and manuals are readily available to teachers on all aspects of puppetry: creating puppets, building puppet theaters, writing plays and handling publicity (6). The puppet stage, in addition to hiding the puppeteer, frames the puppets in relation to their scale, making them more visible, dramatically focused in their setting (7). A puppet theater can be as simple or complicated as one desires. Scenery, sound effects and properties all add punch and verve to the production but should never clutter or obstruct.

Learning by performing followed by analysis is the best method for preadolescents. Their first experience with puppets should be to make them quickly and in great numbers. Pair the children off to work with two puppet characters. Talking at random and doing a minimum of planning, they will discover episodes and situations natural for their puppets to perform.

A puppet show coalesces in many different ways. Sometimes a pair or small group of children come upon something they want to show to the class. Their skit is presented in a simple way, perhaps followed by those of other groups who have also been inspired to show their conceptions. Individual skits can be connected by some recurring element and an overall theme. Or one or two of the skits may be so fascinating that the whole group will decide to develop them and build a whole play around them. Song and dance acts are good practice: each puppet comes on in turn and does his thing, including the telling of jokes so popular with preadolescents. Audience participation provides wonderful excitement for preadolescents. All sorts of inventive back-and-forth banter, in keeping with the ancient puppet show traditions, can result. For example, clumsy insults, so characteristic of the age level, will certainly take place. This technique may even turn into a play as more and more appropriate dialogues are developed to draw the audience into the plot.

Making use of phonographic records as dialogue for pantomime teaches preadolescents timing, suspense, plot development, dialogue and other aspects of a play. Altering the words of a song they already know or adapting popular stories, comics or movies provide many inspirations for plots. Children can easily write rhyming poems and play with word gimmicks. All these bits and pieces of plots and dialogue can be jotted down and may provide a first step in script writing. The scenario is created from the contributions of many; a description of a scene by one child, ideas for music by another, and soon the outline of action from scene to scene is developed. But the writing and improvisations continue even while the play progresses. Each child will modify and grow as he gains more understanding of the part his puppet plays in clarifying the meaning of the total play. Language arts are also used for the creation of posters, programs, and advertisements. If the author of some bit of publicity cannot spell too well, give him cutouts from magazines and newspapers. He can make an interesting collage ad for the performance, adding drawings of the various puppets if he wishes (9).

Few classroom teachers have utilized completely the opportunities for developing their children's language skills by carrying puppetry into the classroom and using some of the time spent on spelling, grammar, and literature for writing characterizations, plot outlines, dialogue, and songs and poems for puppet production.

It is amazing to discover how much puppetry can help minority-group children to master the English language. Puerto Rican children often make a tremendous effort to have their marionettes communicate in English rather than in the Spanish they normally use when talking with each other. Probably they feel protected by the stage and their own hidden position behind it and are willing to take a chance on a bad accent or clumsy elocution. Evidently when they are in the personas of their puppets, they lose self-consciousness. The fear of losing face by making mistakes is a common trait. If the puppet makes a mistake in grammar or talks with an accent and if people laugh at him, that is all right; a puppet is meant to make people laugh. Immigrant and minority-group children can experiment freely with learning a language in a way not provided elsewhere. It is surprising that teachers who work with non-English-speaking children fail to capitalize fully on puppetry as a major learning tool, relying instead on such devices as spelling bees, with the possibility for humiliation which can turn children permanently away from spelling, grammar, and writing of all kinds.

Teachers learn through puppetry   An experiment was done with art student teachers in the use of puppetry as an exciting teaching method. Each person was asked to bring a small bag containing various found objects or materials he thought would make an interesting puppet. The bags were traded among the participants, who were then asked to create a puppet quickly from the contents of the bags they received. As a final step, they gathered in groups to put together skits and perform them.

Later, during analysis of the experiment, we noted the revelation of personality implicit in the activity. But our important discovery had to do with the subject matter chosen, and concepts and values that cropped up in the skits. These aspects of personality were bound to affect our relationships with the preadolescents we taught.

A look at the skits presented by the four groups is illuminating: 1) A Hollywood party hostessed by Elsa Maxwell. Guests were Zsa Zsa Gabor, the Duke of Windsor (represented by a fish smoking a cigarette), and Groucho Marx. 2) A magician at a ladies' club luncheon changes a pretty dancer into a bug, then a head without a body, and finally a monster. The monster devours all the ladies at the end of the skit. 3) A PTA meeting at which weird teachers of special subjects are introduced to tell parents what they teach their children. 4) A beauty contest in which a hippie from Greenwich Village is chosen to be queen.

The PTA skit was most edifying—a humorous and yet serious view of our teaching fetishes and our real feelings about community involvement in the schools. It stimulated us to probe further the issues involved and how we could adjust to them. It gave us a chance to laugh at ourselves. It was set in the present. The other skits showed us to be hopelessly out-of-date. Monsters, magicians, beauty queens and the Duke of Windsor have no meaning for most preadolescents today. Their monsters are probably drug pushers who devour children, not ladies (who is a lady?). Groucho Marx is a piece of celluloid brought out late at night on TV.

How can teachers get involved in the very different world of the children they teach? Accusations, made by minority groups and most children in America, that teachers fail to understand, even to guess, what is actually going on—demolition derbies, sex for the sake of sex—became startlingly true. These realities had come through to us from the make-believe of our puppets.

Nature and values of the medium   For the last ten or fifteen years, each generation of preadolescents has been a film-minded generation. They have had film before their eyes practically with their baby milk. Fond parents' home movies and TV start them off early; going to the movies is as popular a sport and entertainment as viewing a baseball game. Furthermore, on the more creative side, according to Annette Michelson, "ten-year-

FILMS

olds are now filming eight millimeter serials . . . in their own back-yards . . . perhaps . . . the *single most interesting fact* about cinema in our time. Given this new accessibility of the medium, anything can happen" (10: p. 101).

The art of the film should be included in every school curriculum. It is one of the most stimulating ways to interest preadolescents in aesthetics because of its immediacy, its relevance to the realities of life around them which they are trying so hard to correlate and understand, and because of necessary technical skills which they are old enough to master and thoroughly enjoy.

A film may combine the arts of motion (dance), acting, music of all kinds (including the preadolescents' own passion of the moment, shouting electronic rock), dramatic comedy, tragedy, and reportage. It also can include drawing, painting (animation), and three-dimensional construction. Writing and the study of literature correlates with the making of a film, as well as history and social studies. This is a machine art, or rather, an art growing out of and transcending a machine: the camera, the extension of the eye. It may be a focused, sharpened, edited documentation of reality; it may also be fluid impressionism or expressionism, symbolism or fantasy—all styles it shares with the theater, the big differences being the static quality of a theater set, the limitations of the human body onstage as compared with what can be done to it with film effects, and enormous disparities in the time-space relationship between the two media.

The materials of the film maker are light, color, space, time, and sound. These materials express natural or human phenomena, simple or deep themes of human consciousness. Time and space synthesize uniquely in the film medium: "We perceive space in large part by observing movement in it, and it takes time. We comprehend time by the action that takes place in space, such as the expansion and contraction of lungs" (11: p. 278). Susanne Langer likens the sensation produced in films to the time-space feeling of dreams. The viewer is moved out of his own space and placed in another; he can travel fast in any direction; he has the sensation of flying, or of being in a moving train, or walking in the snow—all impossible to experience in live theater.

Cinema is "like" dream in the mode of presentation: it creates a virtual present, an order of direct apparition. That is the mode, the dream. . . . But the camera is not a dreamer. We are usually agents in a dream. The camera (and its complement, the sound track) is not itself in the picture. It is the mind's eye and nothing more. Neither is the picture (if it is art) likely to be dreamlike in its structure. It is a poetic composition, coherent, organic, governed by a definitely conceived feeling, not dictated by actual emotional pressures [12: pp. 412–13].

When a child makes a film, he is forced into an act of coherent communication, applying the usual aesthetic discipline of ordering a chaotic group of impressions, selecting, discarding, and adding beginnings, endings, transitions or whatever to pull together a piece of work.

While viewing or making a film, a child applies previous learning or receives new knowledge about the society in which he lives. Learning by films has become commonplace in education. But the actual making of a movie (or still film) increases one's discrimination about the mass of film material thrown at one, day and night; the process, involving taste, develops standards of criticism and increases rejection of the banal, the vulgar, the vapid.

Above all, children's imaginations are enlarged. New sensations and perceptions of environment and human behavior are stimulated (just as a vivid dream life brings the dreamer original revelations). Through the process of doing, the child may increase his power of receiving, which in turn inspires to more creative performance. It is the musician who experiences most acutely (often painfully) concerts given by others, deriving practical learning from them.

A movie, like a play, must communicate immediately and strikingly. Unlike a play, more like pantomime, it is not dependent on verbal associations, vocabulary, or elocution. Dialogue and speech enrich a film, but they are not the be-all of the performance. The original impulse is to see and graphically record; the heart of the communication is visual. This means that a child with a language block or who, for emotional reasons, such as fright or hate or both, is inarticulate, can perhaps with a camera find a way to express himself. He may choose music to accompany his film and thus avoid a little longer the perils of language. Or he may find others to perform verbally on a tape recorder in order to point up his ideas or make his story more clear. Preferably he will be led through excelling in perceiving, photographing, splicing, coordinating his images, and adding the words of others to find his own voice eventually and either speak himself or formulate some kind of script.

Taking their cameras into the streets, into gang life, even into the intimacy of their homes, and bringing back the film to cut, unify and show in the studio gives these youngsters intense communications with their peers and teachers. Youngsters can become reporters, sociologists or writers of one-act plays. The impediment of words has been removed. They may probe the social structure of their neighborhoods, finding meaning in it as they can. Or, looking into their range finders, they may isolate episodes—happy or fierce moments, feats, failures, tortures, joyful discoveries of group solidarity—and record them. Such images do not become lost in the welter of visual experience superimposed on them, as normally happens in our lives. A child can take a certain moment back into the studio, relive it, and discuss it with his peers. Perhaps it will be useful only as a talk-it-out tool, but it might be the nucleus of a group plan for a short film with a definite plot or a documentary using the unifying reportage techniques of commentator and interviews.

Creative photography is especially conducive to the development of objectivity in preadolescents. It raises their standards vis-à-vis the second-rate photographs and movies deluging their environment.

Pictures in motion Students might learn film making by engaging in projects in which they learn movie principles and techniques by manipulating materials and ideas already familiar to them. Paintings, drawings, prints and collages, in which the main point is to tell a story by use of the *image alone,* provide a good starting medium. Photography experiences with both a still and a movie camera can be used in conjunction with them. In other words, here is a merging of graphic arts with film. The films consist of a series of pictures in planned sequence. As the pictures are ordered and reproduced on film, the students learn to think in terms of sequence—the beginning, the development of supporting materials, and the making of the point of the idea, story or event. While the main purpose will be to develop facility in using the *image,* words can be advantageously woven in. Once the child has caught on to the idea of pictures telling a story, he will feel free to experiment with the written message. Many examples of stories told by use of the image alone exist in art history; the teacher should refer to them whenever it will enrich the situation. There might also be a brief historical résumé, at significant moments, of how the film came into being. The original concepts and the devices used can be woven into these preliminary experiments to correlate the educational objectives of film study.

In advertisements and on TV, there are many excellent instances of story telling through the image; these can be visual aids and material for discussions.

Projects

1. Create books in paint or collage in which abstract forms change from page to page in ways to hold the viewer's interest and reveal in nonobjective terms a series of events in a story involving colors, shapes, lines.

2. Using light and several objects, record many arrangements of these objects on different sheets of photographic paper. Later, organize these prints into a picture story.

3. Tell a story with shapes, using either a two- or three-dimen-

sional overall pattern. Cut out numerous replicas of one shape (or several); then film a drama using them in various sequences. This project can be worked out with printing techniques. It can also be done three-dimensionally, using, for example, egg boxes or fruit containers with uniform concavities. Drop into them objects such as marbles, ping pong balls—any kind of object with the same shape—and photograph them with a still or moving picture camera in interesting sequences.

4. Make flip books. On each page repeat a selected image of someone or something in action. Images are brought in and removed at intervals. The technique is to make the image get smaller and smaller until it is gone, or bigger and bigger as it comes toward the viewer. It may come right out of the frame. On the other hand, the movement may be a natural evolutionary one, such as hen-egg-chicks or cocoon-worm-butterfly, or simply growing, bearing fruit and dying. The real movement comes when the story has been drawn on every page and the child flips the pages. A hand-manipulated moving picture is born.

5. The comic strip is an excellent way of demonstrating animation and the making of films. The device of frames echoes the frames (there are many more) on the strip of cellulose, which becomes a motion picture. Comic strips do not portray the infinitesimal changes of position registered on the movie film which our eyes then translate into motion, but they do use some movie devices, such as the close-up, repetition, and angle shots.

Many preadolescents are enthusiastic about comic strips; this enthusiasm often calls forth original work. They invent their own characters, select a story that can be told in visual images, and highlight it with written "asides" or bubbles containing exclama-

tions and conversations. Many teachers find they are very useful in motivating a child to draw, especially if he likes detail and working small.

Film production follows easily from these graphically told stories, since so many of the techniques can be translated to animation, such as representing characters in conversation from many points of view in their locale so that there is something interesting to look at while they talk, or showing the same character in different positions and in various sizes to indicate movement in space. (Instructor: Betty Thompson.)

6. Relating sequence to image can be a simple affair that preadolescents catch on to quickly. Often they have already been using these devices in their own drawings (as in the comic strips). The student teacher working with the children who made these paintings simply asked the children to paint a sequence—brushing teeth. One pictures the water pic at work, and the other the toothbrush. These initial statements could be elaborated into animated films (student teacher: Gail Miller; teacher: Walter Kendra).

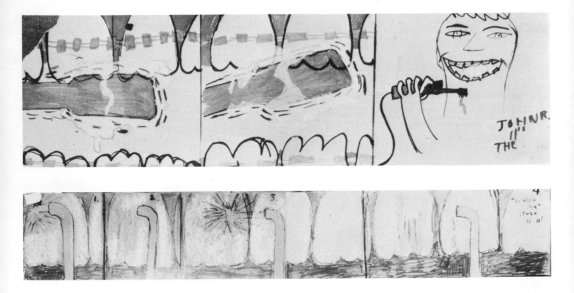

7. Most preadolescents tell stories when they make their individual paintings. Therefore, the idea of painting a series of pictures to tell a tale comes naturally to them. It can be an easy group project, developing skills for eventual movie making and, moreover, engaging many children who have been unwilling to paint and draw, especially if the group has decided on a thrilling story of interest to both boys and girls, coming out of their own real or fantasy life.

"This is the story of two boys and a girl who stow away in an airplane and travel all over the world" or "This is the story of a boy who goes to steal from an old man. While he is in the apartment, two men come in. The boy hides, and the men kill the old man, so the boy becomes mixed up in a big murder mystery. . . ."

The stories can be told into the tape recorder in a round-robin style with each student adding his version. As it is replayed, the children decide what is to be left in, taken out or made longer, an easy accomplishment since the tape can be stopped at any point for discussion. During this process, the teacher and some interested children can take notes, type the story, and read it to the class, at which point other adjustments may be made. With the story finalized, the children would divide into groups to develop certain sequences into rough sketches, returning later for larger group presentations. Good film-making techniques may be developed, such as showing close-ups of objects and people which dramatize a moment or emphasize certain plot hints; a close-up of a person to show the emotion in the face; a close-up and a long shot both in one frame; showing the reactions of two persons at the same time; or interesting angle shots of scenes, people, and objects—under a table, through a net curtain, through a window, from above in the hayloft, for instance. The paintings are finally photographed in sequence on movie film or a film strip.

Sometimes the children may want to add words to their series of pictures. These can be photographed in single frames of their own or superimposed on the picture as in the old silent films; or words in balloons can be used as in the comic strips. There is no end to the variations children will discover and add to their films as they work.

8. A simple type of animated movie can be made by photographing one figure, several figures, or objects against a background. The figures' limbs will not be articulated, but a series of them placed and photographed in different positions in relation to the background will appear to be moving. Having been first drawn and then cut out, they are placed against as many different backgrounds as it takes to tell the story. The use of whole drawings combines well with this technique, as does the addition of written, painted or cut-out words.

9. Cutouts from magazines make excellent material for an animated film. Set up a camera in a permanent place for photographing. Have each child or several working together go on a scavenger hunt through piles of magazines to clip items and work out any little sequence of interest to them, and then take their turn photographing them. They do not have to paste anything down, but can put the pieces in place with their hands between the shots. In an hour or so, a film can be made. If the children are ambitious and have sustaining power, they may do an experi-

mental film first and a more carefully planned one next. The second will usually have a more interesting beginning, and perhaps some good repetition of images to unify it, and it will certainly have a strong end. Individual children participating in such group efforts may become so interested that they will decide to do an entire film by themselves or with a friend.

10. Simple animated films can be made by posing and photographing three-dimensional materials, found objects, structures, or toys with kinetic possibilities. A movie camera can be set up in a permanent position and a sequence of images shot of the movements (set off by hand between shots) made by these objects. Stress should be placed on learning about light effects, which can make or destroy mass. Shadows should be noted. With the right sounds added, the whole adventure can be very provocative.

Here are two examples which may stimulate some to think up projects of their own. Two girls working directly under the camera told lyrical stories, oddly full of suspense, simply by manipulating two different pieces of string in contrasting colors. Several boys, working with clay and filming directly as they worked, manipulated the clay in its various stages of construction to create images of monsters who gobbled up the vegetation and every smaller animal in sight, including humans, and then ate each other.

11. Continuous animation in a simplified version can be easy for preadolescents, provided a few rudimentary steps are mastered. The project requires typewriter-sized paper that can be seen through to some degree. Working at a desk or table, make a right-angled holder (register) of the right size so that each piece of paper can be slipped into exactly the same position. The identical image or images must be drawn for twenty-four frames, showing some part of the sequential progression of movement. The drawings are then photographed with a movie camera (use the register for accuracy). At least two frames are required for each drawing in order to give continuous movement in the film and prevent jerkiness. The movie camera should be mounted on a tripod or copy stand; the lighting also is to be firmly mounted. Additional movement can be introduced by shifting the drawing or the camera between shots, or using the zoom lens on the camera.

At left is one example of animated drawings made by a class teacher in the Alaska school system. The photographer, Tom Cresap, was responsible for its success. Many distinctly different approaches were taken. Several featured simple transformations of geometric or amorphous shapes; some employed cartoon techniques & others realistic drawings. Here, the artist overcame the tedium of repeating the same drawing many times by

Xeroxing the stable portions of the sequence and drawing in only the moving element. Teachers might use this duplication technique to advantage. Color can be added by hand to give extra clarification to the story. (Artist: Elaine Borden.)

Stories through stills   The still camera can be utilized as an aid to develop discriminatory viewing. The photographer does more than portray the literal. He selects, intensifies and makes clear those aspects of the real world he wants the observer to contemplate. Children should study the works of such great artists as Ernest Hass, René Burri, and Henri Cartier-Bresson to discover how, through the arresting arrangements of sizes, shapes, texture, space and other elements, these men have achieved their expressive statements.

For the purpose of eventual film making, there are many activities in which the children can engage. The primary aims of the projects suggested here are 1) to identify the significant aspects of a subject, noting the pertinent stages of an event or emotional experience and 2) to improve their sense of composition in arrangements of single frames. The following projects should stress the process of following an event in space, time and thought.

1. Ask the children to photograph a series of stills of one object, such as a garbage truck, a printing press, or a juke box. They are to take note of the various parts and their functions, significant details of the construction, dramatic and suggestive aspects of the machine's performance, and to amalgamate all of these into a significant statement about the machine.

2. To separate and put into significant new form the stages of an episode or event is the theme here. Choose any simple, ordinary process—baking a cake, fixing a faulty lock, getting up in the morning, wrapping a package, a bicycle trip—for the children to photograph with a 35-millimeter camera, using thirty-six shots. Some of these can be done in the studio, or a group of children might record a trip they take together. One child might persuade a parent to let him photograph the process of getting up. After all the pictures are in, the final stage of the project involves cutting the images from the contact print and rearranging selected ones into a logical but visually stimulating story of the event (13).

3. The significant traits of a character are as important in film making as they are in puppetry or playwriting. Ask the students to shoot thirty-six exposures of a face, preferably of someone they know, such as a classmate or a relative. The idea is to identify the essence of personality and communicate it. Throughout the project, emphasize that the camera is objective; it often captures things never imagined about the person. The inner

realities of the subject being photographed can be caught only if he is communicating. One of the functions of the photographer is to be sensitive to moods and gestures, to catch the expression on his subject's face when he is talking, reacting to the words of others, or perhaps hard bent on some private work and unconsciously showing resolution, despair, pride, etc. Later the child will select from the thirty-six shots a group that relate to each other and can be joined to build a total impression. This exercise not only sharpens a child's camera work, it also provokes thoughts on self, appearance, and relation of face to mind, and often helps children to see other members of the peer group in a new light.

Experimenting with visual phenomena   Visual exploration with slide projectors and slides, making film strips and slide tapes, is another route for experimentation with film. They discover new forms and patterns in found objects, natural or man-made. They may organize these into slide strips or slide tapes.

Experienced teachers will agree that it is rare to find commercial movies and slides which fit the special, immediate needs that arise out of class investigations. Even excellent commercially made visual aids may not deal with the point being developed by the group. It is absolutely necessary, therefore, that the teacher, independently or in collaboration with her children and/or peers, develop her own teaching materials.

The Silverman and Hoepfner study, *Developing and Evaluating Art Curricula specifically Designed for Disadvantaged Youth,* strongly recommends this practice. "Teachers who are most effective in bringing about improvements in their students tend to rely less upon media and information which they have not developed" (14: p. 65). Children, too, should be encouraged to do reports, to discover materials, arrange them on tapes with music or voices, and present them to the class. This practically guarantees relevance. In a way, they will be writing their own textbooks, which may communicate better than the ones adults write for them. The teacher can assist them in integrating all aspects of their learning as they edit and organize the materials.

1. Remove the slide carrier from a slide projector and insert found objects, such as leaves, interesting plastics, broken bits of glass, gelatins, see-through materials of all kinds, and small bottles filled with liquid and fragments (providing movement). The magnifying glass in the projector will reveal fascinating shapes and textures on the screen (13: p. 76).

2. Making transparencies for a slide projector of any size can expand the vision, turning the miniature life of materials into a remarkable world of shape, texture and line, structures and color. Use acetate sandwiches, commercial "ready-mounts" or

glass, and have the children draw, paint, scratch, pierce holes, and paste all manner of things on them. These blow up on the screen in exciting ways. As an independent project in social studies, one girl made a series of drawings of period costumes for a play which the class later produced. A teacher made a complete series of slides dealing with design principles, using cardboard and paper jells. These were utilized over and over again as teaching aids.

3. Producing slide tapes is another rewarding process. A slide tape is a 35-millimeter arrangement of slides in connection with a tape recorder sound track. The two are synchronized so that on a signal from the tape the slide changes in the projector. To make and replay a slide tape, three machines are necessary: a tape recorder, a projector for 35-millimeter slides, and an automatic synchronizer. (It is possible to eliminate the synchonizer and move the slides with a manual changer.)

Kodak has numerous helpful pamphlets on slide production which a teacher can profitably study. Copying slides from material in books, magazines, charts, and maps can be enriching for both teacher and child.

A group of student teachers prepared 3-minute motivating slide tapes on numerous subjects to be used in their teaching. One dealt with examining one's neighborhood for things to paint and referred to artists who had painted their surroundings.

4. Making films without a camera has been popular for years. It is a simple way to get adults and children excited about the potentiality of films. Use a clear leader or an old film which has been cleared of the image by the use of household bleach. Stretch the leader out (taping it down at intervals) over tables, desks, and other objects as far as you wish. Let each child have at least 3 or 4 feet. On each frame, indicated by sprockets, he draws an image, making an animation sequence as he goes. Felt-tipped pens, India ink, and scratching and piercing tools produce the most interesting results. Thirty to thirty-five children can produce a film in about an hour and review it immediately after it is made. It is almost essential to have some rock 'n' roll music to accompany the film. Another film should be made soon after by the same method, since everyone will be brimming with ideas.

Sounds, words, and images Sound in films influences imagery and unifies and reinforces meaning, style, and mood. Music can improve or spoil a movie. Voices in speech or in song, bird sounds, machine sounds, sounds of wind, water and storm, abstract electronic sounds—all these lift us from the mute to the vibrating aspects of the living world. It would be disappointing and anachronistic for many children, exposed for years to the combination of sound and visual image, to make wholly silent movies. The tape recorder is an indispensable item in the studio. (Lowndes, in *Film Making in Schools* [13], provides some excellent exercises with sound, words and use of the tape recorder.)

1. Each student is to bring in an article that has the potentiality of producing a sound, to be recorded. He should also select a word or group of words to be recorded. Then he will make a drawing and a still photograph of each sound he chose. Slides are taken of each. Later he will show them in groups of drawings related to one sound, with the tape recorder making that sound as accompaniment. (The same projects can be done with graphic arts media instead of photography.) These same sounds can later be used in film making.

2. As an experiment with movie camera and tape recorder, ask the children to do a film series of things that make sounds, such as a dripping water faucet, banging on the table, gurgling bottles, tapping foot, ticking clock, or flushing toilet. Follow by taping a suitable sound or music to go with the film, or create musical or sound backgrounds for films made by others, perhaps bought or borrowed: a train going by, a flowing stream or water-fall, or someone running or walking. Be sure that the students see each other's interpretations as a source of learning.

3. Children can explore the possibilities of sound by making their own sound effects, by playing musical scores in their own instruments, by using choral speech, by conducting interviews, by extending sound (on some tape recorders) with echo chambers and tone controls, and by deliberately using discord and atonality (15: p. 74).

4. Encourage free, spontaneous associations to create a mixed-media work. A film can be constructed out of a mixture of words—prose, poetry, or merely spoken, still photographs, and short pieces of film action, montages and collages made of advertisement cutouts consisting of images and words. Photograph the whole thing with a movie camera. Matching sound to image can be relatively easy. When the film is projected, children using a microphone, erasing the tapes, stopping and starting both recorder and projector when necessary, can experiment dubbing in noises, silences, music and conversations.

Making movies Many teachers in schools and many more in inner-city storefronts, centers, and clubs are making films with children and finding it one of the most rewarding of all media. Some teachers have engaged in it so deeply that parents and administrators have instituted film making on a regular basis. They are now convinced that all subject matter can be correlated with it, and that children will bend their energies to learn anything when motivated by the prospect of making a film. They improve their math so that they can help with the camera work; they concentrate on reading and writing so that they can create more interesting scripts and dialogues.

A usual first film, very popular with preadolescents, is a conglomeration of wild antics and pop art, accompanied by rock music. The film consists of many unrelated cuts juxtaposed to create humorous, shocking, ambiguous statements—in other words, preadolescent rebellion. Probably preadolescents will experiment with every possible showy trick: flashback, dream sequences and advertising gimmicks seen on TV. They are pleased with the chaos they create, sometimes miraculously held together by the beat of the music. From these typical frenetic experiments, children move independently or in groups to making films of a more subjective nature, frequently using a story line.

As an example, in one school there were many disturbed children with personal difficulties and antagonisms, incapable of cooperating or relating to each other. Film brought them together in an extraordinary manner. They produced an old-fashioned melodrama divided into skits, as in a variety or vaudeville show. There was a spoof on TV medical programs: in a beautifully antiseptic operating room, the anesthetic is applied in rhythmic motion. The operation begins. Knife and scalpel are passed with a loud slap into the doctor's hands; the sweat is wiped off his brow; other doctors look on worriedly. Suddenly in all this whiteness, great spurts of blood squirt into the doctor's eyes; the operating room goes berserk; bloody prints appear on walls and uniforms. Bloody rags appear, too. The audience is reeling with nausea when the camera is lowered to focus on the operating table, revealing the patient—a large, smiling toy rabbit. (Instructors: Carol Reilly and Patrick Kirmer.)

Teachers can include some instructive exercises in these spontaneous adventures. For example, some pointers on lighting are in order. Show the children that by changing the lighting, texture, shapes of shadows, sense of depth, and masses can be altered by the camera. What happens when the object is lighted from the front? From the rear? What if the background is lit up instead of the subject itself? Will a key light eliminate harsh shadows? Will they intensify when the key light is moved to the side? The teacher can provide technical knowledge about splicing, synchronizing sound to film, potentialities of the camera, and managing the camera and lighting. The children will pick up know-how from each other and from books.

Each teacher uses a film program in a different way. In an inner-city school, for instance, the class had divided into cliques along racial lines. Steven Greenbaum, a teacher there has written an interesting report on what film making did for his students (40 percent Puerto Rican, 40 percent Chinese, 10 percent black, 10 percent white). First, he presented a weekly film festival, including fantasies, and documentaries, some with a moral theme that were "later picked up in composition and discussion." Second, he gave a number of lessons in the use of still and movie cameras, projector and lighting. He brought in some of his own equipment and showed some of his own films. He taught the students how to make flip books as they studied the animation process together.

The class wrote compositions on what sort of film they wanted to make, and in the end they decided on the circus as a theme. Some became actors; others took on the roles of clowns, set designers, cameramen, director, etc. At the same time this large project was being planned, smaller skitlike films were being shot by groups of two to seven children. When these films came back from the lab, no additional motivation was needed. The teacher and class stayed after school two nights each week; discipline problems disappeared. The films were shown to all grades during assembly periods, and other classes were invited into the classroom for previews. The circus film "succeeded on all levels," wrote Greenbaum, "but the most important thing was that by the end of the term, I had a class."

Correlating academic studies with art A group of fourth-grade boys, in a temporary state of social rebellion, wanted to do a dramatic art project on their own. The old movie *King Kong,* just revived on TV, appealed to them, and they wanted to act it out. Other boys and girls listened in, and soon the whole class joined in the plans. The art teacher pointed out that what really seemed to interest them was dramatizing the things that frightened people. This led the children to consider what had made people afraid in the past: the Sphinx, witches, dragons, or the edge of the world where sailors were sure they would fall into the abyss and be lost forever. As third graders, this same class had been fascinated by the primeval world and its strange animals. From this evolved an interest in the human culture that followed the dinosaurs, so that in the fourth grade the culture of the Stone Age became the central theme of their social studies. They were ripe for the suggestion that they dramatize the spirit-haunted world of primitive man. (Class teacher: Letitia Gudell.)

At one point in the process of making their film, the children wrote this charming résumé of their slender plot.

Early man did not live alone with the animals, the birds and the fish. There were many spirits living on the land, in the sea and in the air. Each spirit had a different job. . . . Some spirits were good. Some spirits were evil. . . . One cold and stormy night primitive man came back to his cave after a day of hunting. He had had bad luck that day. There was little to eat. So tired and hungry he lay down and went to sleep. Even his sleep was not undisturbed. The spirits he was aware of came to visit him in his dreams.

The film was conceived as a combination of assemblage and theater, to be enriched with the material from the books the students read in their classroom. The art and classroom teachers collaborated intensively and successfully during the months that followed.

The children began with discussions, followed by experiments with materials. They created small-group skits about some fears of early man which interested them as possible film subjects. These sequences, involving some costuming and props, were photographed in black-and-white film. When the children saw the rushes, they were horrified. They saw that there were too many people in the shots and that they moved awkwardly and self-consciously. They saw that the realism of their own bodies, combined with the symbolic objects they had made, destroyed the sense of fantasy and mystery. The characters had too little to do because the story was not developed. After this first viewing, the students decided that the girls should wear leotards

to give their bodies uniformity and that all faces should be covered with masks. They also wanted fantastic objects to predominate in any one sequence.

They then split into groups again and made masks, imps, gods and demons. The teacher helped them. Each child was asked to sketch the mask or prop he had in mind, dummy it up and select materials so that the whole group could see and think about his idea. The many rain and fire demons had to be clearly distinguished from each other, perhaps unified only by a color or colors. The children were hard put to find enough materials different from each other for representing the same quality, such as rain or fire. Dullness, shine, and texture affecting reflection or absorption of light became major concerns. During the rushes, a relatively unimportant item made of metallic paper was found to be distracting; it stole the show from a leading character. Also, certain colors thought to be brilliant lost their potency in black and white. Everyone was asked to analyze his piece intently during the showings and to request help from the teacher if changes seemed necessary.

Soon the class had worked up another group of objects to be used in new, more developed sequences, again in black and white. They noticed the greater sophistication immediately. They discussed fitting the different sequences into each other. Transitions were discussed. Certain parts of the films were ruled out as banal.

The most disturbing thing about the second showing was that there was not enough motion. Everyone's interest was turned in this direction, and soon electric fans came from homes, to be

used with objects that could blow and flutter in the wind. A series of bars on pulleys, part of the art studio equipment for work with mobiles, was utilized to lower and raise the gods of the sky. One of the most exciting parts of the film was a rain storm painstakingly arranged by the children. Hundreds of strips of transparent celluloid or plastic ticker tape were attached to the bars, and the "rain" descended in shimmering sheets. When the fan was turned on them, a magnificent storm appeared. Blowing confetti created snow. Lights, spots and projectors created a play of shadows cast by flickering lights which represented fires, the rising sun and the changing moon. All these effects were filmed to see how they looked before being used. Finally, the teachers and children were confident enough to film the production in color.

There was a shooting script noting how the film would be shot, sequence by sequence: from what angles, at what distance, medium or close-up, how many minutes it would take to shoot, when the zoom lens would be used, and many more.

The search for an interesting opening led from one unsatisfactory trial to another until the class hit upon the idea of using a mural which synthesized various portions of the film. Pastels, a usually unsuitable medium for murals, produced a highly satisfactory product in a few hours. Eight feet high, thirty-six feet long, the finished mural pictured activity in the night: planets wheeling, luminous imps haunting, men blindly creeping, and lightning splitting trees. At the start of the film a primitive flute played as the moon (a large spot) traveled slowly over the surface of the mural.

Some objects from the movie are shown. In a tremendous mask and matching robe is the god of nature who makes things grow. In the film, girls in green leotards with green-painted faces, carrying leafy stalks symbolizing the rise of vegetation in spring after the god has caused rain to fall on earth, swayed and danced.

Below are rain masks. The god of thunder had a little bag of "hail" and two large bags of "rain" that fluttered furiously when the fan was turned on. Wind issued from his mouth and lightning from his many hands.

One of the best sequences was filmed with the children wearing these 4-foot-high masks in a night scene, with firelight flickering on them.

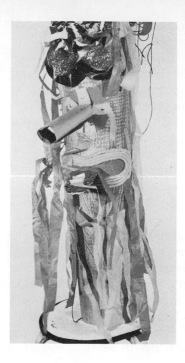

The idol was large enough to hide two boys. Its eyes rolled, its tongue moved in and out, and its arms lifted. The mask represents the planets in the sky.

The final filming was a glorious madhouse. The two art teachers and the children locked themselves in the studio for three straight days during school hours. Of course, the overall schedule was disrupted, but that was one of the qualities of the school; everyone had an opportunity to embark on an art adventure whenever feasible. An open studio was set up for classes working on projects other than this film, which they carried on by themselves and with the help of student teachers, parents, and friends.

The film makers, locked in the studio, sat down to make plans. Space was set aside for the numerous costumes and properties; a repair center was established and manned. Children took turns as filming crew (we had only one camera); an area for filming was cleared. Each tool—lights, fans, spots, record players, tape recorders—had a person in charge of it. A master chart indicated all the job changes, since each child wanted to try different jobs.

Rest periods were introduced. There were breaks for lunch and an hour for gym or outdoor play if the children wanted it. For many of the group, the intensity, the working together, the group dependency, and the newfound friendships made it one of the most memorable experiences of their lives.

This experimental movie represents the essence of several

months' intensive work and study in the areas of the arts, social studies and language. A belief in the importance of form in all creative activities—in writing or discussion or in making something with one's hands—motivated both the teachers who collaborated on this project. The academic program was as rich, exciting and challenging as any other part of the project.

William Chapman's film *Cradle of Man's Art,* which shows the prehistoric cave paintings at Lascaux, France, brought the children face to face with the people they were studying. It meant more to them because they had read Hans Bauman's "Caves of the Great Hunters," a story about the discovery of the paintings by boys their own age. Books like May Edel's *The Story of People,* Peter Lum's *Fabulous Beasts,* and *First Men,* by Irving and Hannah Goldman, also helped the class to relate anthropological studies to their own project.

The classroom teacher supplemented the children's reading by reporting and reading to the group from such books as Ralph Linton's *Tree of Culture* and James Frazer's *Golden Bough.* Some of this material might seem beyond the scope of a nine-year-old's comprehension, but the children's urge to find out what they needed for their film gave them the drive to understand and utilize it.

Viewing films as a way of learning This is as important as experimenting with one's own work and criticizing that of one's peers. Standards of criticism are built up by exposure to a variety of materials.

An organized viewing program, set up as part of the activities every afternoon in the White Plains Storefront Arts Projects, inspired the children to perform remarkable feats of imagination in a film of their own. They had been shown many movies on African life (most of the children were blacks) and had heard and handled African musical instruments; they had become familiar with social customs, animals, and some of the history of African tribes. They were fascinated by the terrain as it unfolded before them in films. They decided to make their own African film.

They used the lots next to the storefront—expanses of city blocks and areas of rubble left by demolition gangs—as African savannahs, deserts and plains. They wove a story about two tribes that were at war because one had stolen women from the other. The raid and theft were followed by dances and incantations building up the warlike spirit. Then on to the field of battle.

Even though the camera jiggled and jumped and was sometimes out of focus, it was a movie to be remembered for a long time. The poses and the shots reflected acute observation and learning on the part of these youngsters who had been viewing the African films every afternoon. I cannot forget the young warriors standing in groups with their arrows raised, poised to spring, their robes falling in fluted arrangements emphasizing the thrust of their leaning bodies.

Study of self and other selves Films of a serious and intensely personal nature can come into being as young people begin to look at their own moods, motivations, and hangups and those of their family, neighbors, and friends. A good technique for getting them started in this vein is to make a list of all the subjects they would like to put into a movie. They may come up with a list like this.

Being rejected by your gang

Pollution—drug abuse

What can I do in the world?

Not having enough money

Fear that war, plus the atomic bomb, will wipe out everybody

Stories about disasters to family and friends

Hating one's parents and not wanting to

Terrible dreams

Being in love with someone

Having a dog or cat and losing it

Getting in trouble in school or with the law

The unfairness of the principal and some teachers

Of course, the list will vary enormously with the cultural background of the children. Help them gain a little objectivity about their personal problems before embarking on an extensive film project. Send them out with a 35-millimeter camera on "looking exercises." Give them a theme such as the supermarket, the penny arcade, people buying shoes, those who eat hot dogs, different ways people read newspapers, laughing people, drug store clerks, construction workers, or different ways of pushing a baby carriage. Vary the themes from the lighthearted to the tragic. On a given excursion, suggest that everyone take the same theme. See what whole statement emerges when the films come back.

It may be premature for preadolescents to study the documentary film. However, they are very often sensitive to social conditions. From TV and from older brothers and sisters, they have learned about the war on poverty, exploitation of migrant workers, minority-group problems, and water and air pollution; they might be interested in handling such themes. Preadolescents must be guided, however, to deal with these complex concerns in a way that is true to the range of their experience and observation. In documentaries, as in their films about personal joys and despairs, clichés must be avoided. They must be taught, too, that observation is not enough. A documentary is held together and given force only when it is a strong statement of a point of view. The mind as well as the camera must bear on the material subjectively. This does not mean distortion or inaccuracy. "One of the documentary's most important problems must be faced. Clearly a full and real expression of modern scene and modern experience cannot be achieved unless people are observed in accurate relationship to their surroundings" (15: p. 242). It is far better to help the children of today face the issues of great concern in modern life than to have them live by a set of empty, idealistic canons having questionable relation to what is really happening.

The making of films and slide tapes brings the outside world into the school world. Boys and girls today no longer have to rely entirely on words, books, random reproductions, stereotyped drawings and the teacher's special bias for their knowledge. They have a new visual tool which they can wield themselves, often more skillfully than they can read or write. The resulting confidence and increase in their knowledge in many cases steps up their verbal proficiency—a nonvicious cycle.

Teachers, too, have a distinct advantage here, if they are sufficiently aware of what is happening. They no longer have the responsibility of being the major provider of knowledge, with books as their bank accounts and set lessons as insurance. The children they teach have more access to information; they have more realization of what there is to know and what they want to investigate. The preadolescent especially is less dependent. He has been exposed earlier than his peers in previous times, and he is at a stage when he is ready to absorb.

Yet teachers have other and urgent responsibilities. Vast numbers of children thrown into our many-faceted society are more sophisticated than their predecessors. To meet their needs, creative, sophisticated, and humanistic teachers are called for today as never before, particularly at this age level.

REFERENCES

1. William C. Seitz, *The Art of Assemblage*, The Museum of Modern Art, New York, 1962.

2. Allen Kaprow, "Paintings, Environments and Happenings," unpublished manuscript, 1962.

3. Jed Horace Davis and Mary Jane Watkins, *Children's Theatre,* Harper & Brothers, New York, 1960.

4. Viktor Lowenfeld, *Creative and Mental Growth,* The Macmillan Company, New York, 1947.

5. George Dennison, *The Lives of Children,* Random House, Inc., New York, 1969.

6. Majorie Batchelder and Virginia Lee Comer, *Puppets and Plays: A Creative Approach,* Harper & Brothers, 1956.

7. John Bodor, *Creating and Presenting Hand Puppets,* Rinehold Publishing Corporation, New York, 1967.

8. Marjorie Batchelder, *The Puppet Theatre Handbook,* Harper & Brothers, New York, 1947.

9. A. D. Smith, *The Puppet Book: A Practical Guide to Puppetry,* ed. by L. V. Wall et al., Plays, Inc., Boston, 1965.

10. Annette Michelson, "Film and the Radical Aspiration," in *The New American Cinema,* ed. by Gregory Battcock, E. P. Dutton & Co., Inc., New York, 1969.

11. Ray Falkner and Edwin Ziegfeld, *Art Today,* Holt, Rinehart and Winston, Inc., New York, 1969.

12. Susanne K. Langer, *Feeling and Form,* Charles Scribner's Sons, New York, 1953.

13. Douglas Lowndes, *Film Making in Schools,* Watson-Guptill, New York, 1968.

14. Ronald H. Silverman and Ralph Hoepfner, *Developing and Evaluating Art Curricula Specifically Designed for Disadvantaged Youth,* U. S. Department of Health, Education, and Welfare, Office of Education, Bureau of Research, Washington, D.C., 1969.

15. Paul Rotha, "Some Principles of Documentary," from *Film: An Anthology,* ed. by Daniel Talbot, University of California Press, Berkeley, Calif., 1967.

Summary:
A Time for Liberation

Now is the time to liberate all teachers from their traditional roles and traditional isolation. They have long suffered the tyranny of rigid time schedules, uniform lesson plans, generalized teaching guides, and the lowest position in the public school hierarchy. Insecurity and a sense of inferiority, perpetuated by a repressive bureaucracy, have kept the majority of teachers from changing their methods with the changing times. They have not known the pleasure of noncompetitive sharing of mental resources with peers. Nor have they worked in an ambience where their needs, growth, and potentialities were nurtured with consideration. These conditions have hampered them in their efforts to reach the modern educational goals centered on the idea that children should be allowed to think and choose for themselves. For both teacher and child, dependency, joylessness and boredom have been the result.

The pressure to change now is as great as the resistance to change. New educational perspectives are being developed that take cognizance of the social and economic facts of the lives of the children we are teaching. Each teacher has to come to grips with these facts. As Dennison says, "It is no longer feasible to repeat past successes with past techniques" (1: p. 258). Teachers who consciously or unconsciously apply outdated norms of expected behavior will find that they are not reaching their students, or, if they are, may be handicapping them in their adjustment to the outside world and their future. It is time for a twofold liberation " . . . we must rescue the individuals from their present obscurity in the bureaucratic heap: the students, because they are what the activity is all about; the teachers, because they are the ones who must act" (1: p. 247).

What has been the schoolteacher's traditional role? To be an expert in one or many subjects, a clerk, part-time policeman, psychologist and counselor—these duties all to be performed in relative isolation from the rest of the staff. Teachers have never been truly free to act as they think best. Their supervisors may not have time to watch them at work in the classroom, but they control them by means of a slipshod, often inconsistent bureaucratic operation, a set of rules for their conduct (authoritarian), and statewide curricula and textbooks that may or may not apply to the students in any particular locale. The bureaucracy tests teachers' competency and "worth" by how well their students pass standardized achievement tests, which are all too often meaningless. Administrators, by virtue of their position, set the conditions in each school. This is an antiquated method of education, an antihumanistic situation. The direct and dire result is that the majority of students feel trapped, powerless, and unable to identify with either the school or their teachers (2).

The administrators themselves are caught within this moribund concept of education. They are afraid that without strict order, undeviating routine and a paternalistic system of passing knowledge down to children on an assembly line, they would become victims of chaos and informality. Excessive formality is a protective device; only the strong can dare to be informal. New teachers and many of those who are veterans of the system can be taught that there are other ways besides the authoritarian to work with students, that being a leader does not have to mean being a dictator, nineteenth-century father, infallible wise man, or prison warden. The Guskins define the "informal" leader as one who has knowledge, possibly charisma, and certainly an ability to "fill the social or emotional needs of others." The "formal" leader uses fear of punishment and hope of reward as means of power. "Informal leadership achieves influence because the follower wants to be influenced. . . . If the teacher wants to avoid being a policeman he must in some way relate to the students so that they begin to enjoy learning" (2: pp. 69–71).

Today a teacher cannot assume that he is a legitimate leader merely because he has been hired. He must prove it by making an honest attempt to understand his students. What is happening to them outside of school? How and why are they different from the children in a different school or in some other city or town? What is their exposure to the cultural revolution that has involved their brothers and sisters? What is poetry to them? Morality? What drummer are they following? It is not easy for middle-class teachers to capture the confidence and the following of children from a lower socioeconomic level. There are fears and uncertainties, possibly racial barriers involved. However, teaching conditions in depressed areas are no longer much more uncomfortable emotionally than those in many middle-class public schools where children are feverishly impatient with the old stereotyped teaching methods, caught in the life-style gap between them and their parents, or neurotically (drug-oriented) apathetic.

Whether he is hired by dogmatic or enlightened administrators, the success of the formal leader depends upon his "ability to become an informal leader at the same time" (2: p. 69). Systematic repression, a hard shell of dignity, and assumption of superior knowledge no longer work with these youngsters. Such tactics are the cause of many of the discipline problems today. Teachers, children, and parents all agree on the need for more stimulating, creative public education. Two distinct transformations are in order if this need is to be met. First, teacher training and the continuing education of in-service teachers must be modernized. Second, the curriculum must continue to be revised and realistically oriented to the needs of the children. Without the second, the most creative teacher in the world will remain hamstrung. Without the first, any reform on the planning level will be hollow and ineffective.

How can one liberate instructors, novice or experienced, to use the new, more informal methods that have already been well substantiated in many child-centered schools? One of the first steps is to make it clear how unrealistic it is for today's teachers to set themselves up as infallible dispensers of knowledge. Culkin has an interesting story about McLuhan's startling a few hundred teachers at a lecture by denying the whole concept of the generation gap. According to Culkin, McLuhan meant that "because of the information that is available through the media . . . for the first time in history both the kids and their parents and their teachers are living in exactly the same information world . . . the kids are no longer . . . in the dark, to be programmed and brought along step by step according to the dictates of the adult culture, and that has created a new situation" (3: pp. 23–24).

NEW ROLES AND RESPONSIBILITIES

Only by becoming familiar with the "new situation," with all its ramifications, horrors, challenges, potentialities and dead ends can a teacher perform with empathy and force of character. Knowledge of the past and in-depth knowledge of subjects to be taught are as important as ever—in fact, more so, since modern methods preclude falling back on uniform textbooks and the crutch of infallibility. Informal teaching is possible only when a teacher is well grounded academically, sure of the philosophy behind the curriculum, and able to enrich the learning process of individual students in a number of ways. Teachers, however, more than other scholars, need to have a sharp personal orientation to the present. As Culkin says, "if you have a kind of school system, which we do have, which ignores the realities of the kids' world, the pop music . . . if we ignore the poetry of Simon and Garfunkel, they will be quite right in ignoring the poetry of any old boy that we talk to them about" (3: p. 23). Intellectual study and direct experience of our present culture are vitally important in the making of a good teacher. Sometimes this takes the unblinking courage of facing facts.

POPULAR CULTURE AND EDUCATIONAL REFORM

PHENOMENON	ARTISTS' REACTION
Mass media (publications, film, television)	Feelings of alienation, dislocation, helplessness
Worldwide communication	Anger against:
Confrontation of races and cultures	wars
	technology
Continuing wars	standardization
Violence of communism and fascism	stagnant institutions
Inept bureaucracy of socialism and democracy	Withdrawal into subjective art divorced from society
Technological marvels:	Shock tactics: emphasis on
computer	grotesque
nuclear bombs	obscene
other weapons	sour
space travel	satirical
Overpopulation	Withdrawal into pure form
Overcrowding	Back-to-nature movements
Pollution	
Inflation	
Advertising	
Drug invasion	

The chart on pp. 400–401 summarizes some of the influential phenomena of our day and the reactions to them which only artists and young people are free and direct enough to express.

Modern art is mainly a protest art. In the present crisis, artists are fighting to save the individual, and, in the long run, the human race. They feel that a tidal wave of cultural mediocrity is in danger of swamping the creative, humanistic instincts which have spurred our evolution so far. They are also apprehensive about the proliferation of processes and objects—over-extensions (as with the dinosaurs) of growth in certain directions. They are not against science per se; it is a creative discipline like their own. What they fear is the use to which it is put: destruction, self-indulgence, alienation, deracination.

Since art is at the forefront of the struggle, what justification

ART FORM	YOUTHS' REACTION	POSSIBLE EDUCATIONAL REFORM

Mixed-media works, performances, happenings	Need for:
	  firm self-image
	  reassuring image of man
	  acceptance
		Children planning their own curriculum

Group identification sessions, rock music festivals	human contacts
	  physical release from
	    overcrowding
		Flexible scheduling
		Mixing of age and intelligence levels

Pop art	variety and color in the environment	No marks
Assemblage	Desire to:	New teaching methods (teams): student teachers

Soft sculpture	express native intelligence
	  master machines
		college students
		  class teachers

Electronic music	rediscover nature use the body	artists
Kinetic art	Anger against:	parents community specialists
Luminaries	exclusion	children themselves
Underground cinema	class and race snobbery suppression	Interrelated learning
Naked theater	indifference rigid scheduling	Correlation of arts with humanities and with all correlations of

Concrete art	teaching not related to the
	    student or the modern
	    world
		arts with other
		  subject areas

Earth art	brutal or insecure teachers	and daily life
Modular art	dull textbooks outdated values and ideas	Art studio to be a large, adjustable loftlike or basement space
Environments	Passion for new lyric music	Studio to be open continuously, available to the community
City Planning—ekistics street art	Drug addiction	Textbook and art materials adjusted to student background and cultural origins
		Teachers and students producing their own visual aids and teaching material

can educators find in refusing art education any real place in the curriculum? The answer is, of course, that modern art and modern artists offer, as they always have, a threat to the Establishment. But for teachers sincerely anxious to make contact with their young pupils, contemporary art, like contemporary music and dance, can help them learn the emotional realities they face when meeting children in the classroom. These children are far deeper (sometimes fatally) immersed in the tide of mass helplessness than their elders. As we have shown, children and artists reflect each other's needs and frustrations; both are sensitively attuned to the world's weather. It is up to teachers to try to develop some sensitivity in this direction, even to the extent of engaging in some form of artistic activity themselves—in a graphic, verbal, scientific or mixed medium.

For art teachers, all their emphasis on perception and feeling should have developed in them not only the gift of informality and sympathy but also more rapid understanding of their students. This is not true, however, of art teachers who reject modern art, youth cults, long hair, outlandish dress, and, unconsciously, any ethnic group but their own. This same rigidity may make them afraid of collaboration with other teachers, and they will be unable to allow children a voice in planning programs. These teachers are trapped in the old role. They may be older individuals (and thus more understandable), or they may be student teachers who have decided, because of personal insecurity, to flee from involvement in the new, disturbing currents and find a private island where they can try to evoke past order and serene art. These negative reactions can be countered only by providing positive modern values and methods which make teachers feel secure as well as creative.

Many established teachers, inexperienced with informal instruction, will be horrified with what seems to them to be chaos. They will also be sincerely concerned that learning is not taking place. For them, to give credence to the concept that children are best motivated to learn when allowed to follow their own bents, in an environment rich with resources to be explored, may be a difficult leap to make. Dewey and Piaget, among others, have prepared the ground. Research has verified what most teachers fail to recognize and trust—a child's strong instinct for self-determination. Giving the child the possibility of choice does not preclude making sure that true learning is taking place. The informal method puts teachers in the role of helping children evaluate their activities, providing well-articulated choices for them to make, and broadening and enriching the scope of the studies they have undertaken with correlated ideas from other disciplines. Let the children do, and let the teacher supplement and guide. It could also be pointed out, by those of us who have worked with the new methods and by numerous examples throughout this book, that order, rather than chaos, results when students are allowed to cooperate in the detailed planning of their days. In fact, it has been found that manners, ethics, generosity and self-control are much more likely to bloom in an atmosphere of informality and individual choices than in the repressive joylessness of many classrooms.

The advantages of a freer schedule are not all slanted in the direction of the children. For countless years the classroom teacher has been operating under the nervous strain of contact with the same group of children during most of the hours of a school day. In more liberal systems of scheduling, worked out together by teachers, administrators and children, teachers would spend a limited number of the prime hours of their day with the children (except for special occasions, when both teacher and class elect to work around the clock on some project).

What would teachers do the rest of the time? Part of their job would be allocated to working with other teachers, evaluating and improving methods and curriculum; clarifying for each other the educational significance of what is going on; and analyzing programs to decide if they are indeed philosophy in action. There would be time for conferences with parents, for private research projects, and for study groups. Above all, clarifying curriculum objectives, observing how the children learn, and conducting research studies related to teaching should be the concern of all art educators. At the present time the teaching profession is making extensive efforts to evaluate and modify curriculum content and to refine its methods of research into learning theories, perception, and other areas (4). As more and more teachers are released from grueling, long hours confined in one classroom to take part in these explorations, their lives should indeed take on a different tone. Their voices will be heard, and they will have a part in bringing about the curriculum changes that they themselves will try out. This is a creative role and a highly responsible one.

If schools were reorganized into smaller units, the nature of the physical plant itself would allow the staff to come together more frequently. (Even in our present enormous schools, significant separations could be made.) Teachers could identify more humanly and effectively. It is important that they work together more than they have in the past. It is one way of keeping abreast of the times and the changing student body, of examining themselves and the curriculum, of avoiding the ever present pitfalls — either the intimidation or overprotection of children. The airing of opinion, discussion and eventual teacher solidarity on important issues provide a profound lesson to children; an example of cooperation in action. A demonstration of how one voice, even a child's, among many — is fortified by group intent.

With such a system of schools within a school, more could be accomplished in the realm of educational philosophy, not to mention the advantage of pooling techniques and increasing the number of approaches to a child or a group of children in trouble. Research would be stimulated and shared more extensively. As it is today, research is accumulated with difficulty. Isolated individuals are often shunted away from the schools that could provide them with information; questionnaires go unanswered. Doctoral students find it difficult to identify significant problems. Active teachers in the school seldom find time for advanced study, since it takes superhuman energy to work full time with children and also do graduate work. The liberation of teachers will allow us to approach this problem in a new way. Teachers in the schools will make important contributions to research investigations, individually and in teams. They are in a natural position to accumulate evidence and verify theories of teaching. Colleges would undoubtedly come to admit such arrangements whereby both the teacher (receiving a degree) and the educational community would benefit. When teachers are learning as well as teaching, all their powers are alive. Much of school life should be devoted to their continuing education. Ultimately, the investment of time away from the children will benefit the children a hundredfold.

Personal work in one of the arts is another vitalizing activity for art teachers, especially when combined with a fresh look at contemporary art. Such ventures can raise morale and energy and make the transition from authoritarian to permissive teaching conditions more feasible. By doing, by themselves exploring, they give nerve and blood to their thinking and increase their ability to communicate ideas and enthusiasms. With the subject matter lit up in their minds, teachers who have previously relied on a shoddy and banal set of lesson plans will have the courage to experiment and explore with their pupils: "exploration is not a sign of inefficiency or incompetence or ignorance, but rather a sign of sophistication and deep understanding of the realities of human experience" (5: p. 300).

THE STUDENT TEACHER

Students who are training to become teachers have for more than five years been clamoring for participation in city life with all its traumas and challenges. They have a new perception of the place of the city in American life and the university in the life of the city—its role, as they see it, being to give substance and guidance to reform and opportunity to the disadvantaged. College students in rural areas have the same urge. They all want to prove that they can do significant teaching even while they are training. They find many of the methods they are taught unsatisfactory in relation to new concepts of personal relations. They are discontented with the standard art education literature. In fact, they try to write their own, in the form of films, slide tapes, and descriptive lesson plans with photographs, which they circulate among themselves.

Their instinct is right. In our training schools it is essential that student teachers be provided with opportunities to analyze and discover their abilities, bents, personal problems, and reactions to bureaucracy, poverty and danger. In every aspect of teacher training, they need to have direct contact with children of various kinds and ages, to test methods and materials, and to see exactly what they will meet in their chosen profession. Much of the content of methods courses merely serves to frighten and confuse the students with superficial details and numerous dos and don'ts having little relation to life in the schools today. A student trained on theory alone is apt to feel that he has lost his identity. Without personal experience in the field, these young people tend to become indoctrinated robots, dependent on other people's ideas. Then the first years in the school bureaucracy complete the tragedy. Having been sent in cold and asked to adjust to existing conditions, they are crushed by the weight of many depressing realities; their initiative is killed, and they become so confused that they often never find their own way.

It is possible to conceive and organize education courses and student teaching experiences innovatively. Teams of prospective teachers can set up programs of their own in informal places— storefronts, settlement houses, or even within school systems that will have them—to run as they see fit. With their college professors, in seminars, they can discuss and justify their procedures in terms of research and learning theories, evaluating and analyzing their activities. Students who have initiated such programs have found the experience the most vital and meaningful method of learning how to educate children. The trainees preserve their independence and develop self-confidence as teachers. They are saved from blind resentment against the school bureaucracy before they know what teaching involves. They are also saved from passive submission; the knowledge and ego strength they have gained through actual experience makes them strong enough to pursue reforms.

Training in human relations must go hand in hand with the deepening of art background and the exploration of teaching methods. Today there are many techniques, growing originally out of psychiatric research, whereby experienced and student teachers discover their individual personalities and explore group relations. As Sharp says, "probably no factor clogs the functioning of human relations more than the lack of understanding of emotional, aggressive, hostile behavior and how to deal with it" (6: p. 61).

Psychologists and others have been focusing on the middle-class teacher's dilemma—his changing role, his understandable fear of the growing violence, his alienation from both the militant inner-city students and the administrators who block new methods of teaching. Teachers are often alienated from each other as well. In the past few years, sensitivity training and confrontation groups have been tried with considerable success (2: pp. 167–70). Administrators on both grade school and college level often lack the courage and faith to trust their staff to arrive eventually at rational, mature behavior by these new, direct methods. Usually they shrink back from even recognizing the hostile emotions that are bound to occur in any teaching community. This avoidance merely intensifies the situation, producing more irrationality.

As we embark on needed social reforms, sound group dynamics techniques can be taught to experienced and prospective teachers. Important, emotion-laden debates are now being held in the schools. Committees from minority groups and groups of the poor are asking for communication; our whole democratic ethos of civil rights is being tested; it is a time for cool heads and prodigious feats of understanding.

AN INTEGRATED CURRICULUM

Changes in our school curricula have been proceeding at snail's pace. This lag deters progress toward a form of public education which might help save our children in their present perils of nihilism, rejection of society, and drug addiction. If we lag much longer, we may be too late.

Curriculum development has many divisions. A curriculum is devised on a schoolwide basis and includes all the subject areas. It is then broken down into subject areas and finally into the various activities which take place in the classroom. The teacher evolves these activities, adjusting them to the educational interests of the children. The curriculum also has ramifications outside the school community; it becomes part of the national philosophy of education.

In order to handle the complexities of curriculum reform with objectivity and scientific method, Eisner suggests the establishment of various research and development centers. Their functions would be pre- and post-testing of programs; designing means of evaluating activities; assisting in the formulation of objectives for schoolwide areas (which he calls "academic curricula") and subject areas; and carrying out some of the studies necessary before establishing innovative programs in a community (7: pp. 222–34).

The young people, who are the ones primarily at stake in any curriculum change, have much to offer in terms of proposals and experimentation. Their impatience for reform and their energies and ideas constitute a vital and inextricable force in the evolution of a more humanistic curriculum. Harold Taylor writes eloquently of these young people:

They are writing their own poems, building their own curriculum for Negro children, composing and playing their own music, organizing their own theater to play before audiences in the south who have never seen live theater, mimeographing their own literary magazines, writing their own research on social and political problems. I see no reason why, with the variety and wealth of talent in the arts displayed by the younger generation, we cannot do them the honor of including these vital aspects of their present lives in the curricula of our schools and colleges. They should not be forced to give up art and creative thinking simply because they enter an institution of education. . . . The only place in which a fundamental attitude to the arts and the humanities in America can be created and long-run support can be developed lies in the educational system [8: p. 5].

Slow as it may seem in terms of progress, there is a definite tendency in the schools today to bring together the arts and humanities in meaningful ways. In spite of dread, stubborn roadblocks, and downright ignorance, some interesting programs have been started. They are backed up by a growing conviction that the arts can bring deeper significance to all areas of thought and fields of learning, since they are based primarily on the senses and involve the total being of an individual. The visual arts in a humanities program have an important role, one that was not possible in the pioneering days of America, when the conquest of nature and achievement of material security were the main preoccupations. Now, as Francis Villemain predicted for the latter part of the twentieth century, we are perhaps "on the threshold of a cultural renaissance and have achieved the social and physical foundations upon which we can build an artistic-educational expression of the highest order" (9: p. 419).

This text has tried to show the potential relationships between the visual arts and other subjects in the average curriculum. Correlations have been slow in coming because of conditions and attitudes in our schools. But just as democracy implies and demands that every individual have an opportunity to acquire the tools of reading and writing, it also implies and demands that every individual be given a chance to develop his aesthetic perception and creativity—equally important tools of communication (10: p. 63). The need for correlation between the academic and aesthetic disciplines is corroborated by the research of Rudolf Arnheim, who is convinced that visual training is fundamental to concept formation and intellectual growth: "once it is recognized that productive thinking in any area of cognition is perceptual thinking, the central function of art in general education will become evident" (11: p. 296).

Because of the specialization and fragmentation in our society, it is important that we integrate all aspects of education in order to strengthen the underlying unifying elements and ensure communication. No discipline can any longer afford to be insular, although this does not imply that its special quality will be sacrificed and lost in a vague amalgam of learning. Gradually—one hopes not too gradually—concepts new and unfamiliar to many educators—informality, new roles for teachers, shared power with children and the community, the necessity for creative expression—will be absorbed into our institutions and lead public education out of its present impasse. There is now a climate for change which is encouraging, for it turns into possibilities the innovations which heretofore we had relegated to the world of dreams.

REFERENCES

1. George Dennison, *The Lives of Children,* Random House, Inc., New York, 1969.

2. Alan Edward Guskin and Samuel Louis Guskin, *A Psychology of Education,* Addison-Wesley Publishing Company, Reading, Mass., 1970.

3. Father John Culkin, S. J., "Films that Delight the Eye," in *The Arts in Education,* Seventh National Conference on Education, sponsored by The National Council on the Arts in Education, Sarah Lawrence College, Bronxville, N.Y., 1968.

4. Edward L. Mattil (ed.), *A Seminar in Art Education for Research and Curriculum Development,* Cooperative Research Project No. V-002, Pennsylvania State University, University Park, Pa., 1966.

5. Herbert Thelen, *Dynamics of Groups at Work,* University of Chicago Press, Chicago, Ill., 1955.

6. George Sharp, *Curriculum Development as Re-education of the Teacher,* Teachers College, Columbia University, New York, 1951.

7. Elliot M. Eisner, "Concepts, Issues, and Problems in the Field of Curriculum" in *A Seminar in Art Education for Research and Curriculum Development,* Cooperative Research Project No. V-002, Pennsylvania State University, University Park, Pa., 1966.

8. Harold Taylor, *Humanities and the Schools,* A Symposium on the Humanities and the Secondary Schools, University of Kentucky, Lexington, Ky., 1965.

9. Francis T. Villemain, "Democracy, Education and Art," in *Readings in Art Education,* ed. by Elliot W. Eisner and David W. Ecker, Blaisdell Publishing Company, Waltham, Mass., 1966.

10. Philip H. Phenix, *Education and the Common Good: A Moral Philosophy of Curriculum,* Harper & Brothers, New York, 1961.

11. Rudolf Arnheim, *Visual Thinking,* University of California Press, Berkeley and Los Angeles, Calif., 1969.

Tools for Teaching: Visual Aids

The teacher today is aided in her work with the preadolescent as never before by having at her disposal recent technological developments which have provided new teaching materials. The alert teacher is constantly aware of the new audiovisual materials being developed, notices of which appear in the many publications provided by the educational organizations to which she may belong. In addition, a variety of materials useful in audiovisual collections is being made available through the many industrial and commercial concerns which have in recent years produced educational materials pertinent to the field of art.

THE ART STUDIO

No modern art room should be without the full range of equipment our technological development has made possible. Architects and school boards have the responsibility to make available audiovisual equipment as well as a room that has stackable chairs, stools, and tables. The furniture should be out of the way when not used or arranged in the numerous patterns an active and changing program requires. The ceiling of the art studio should have the look of a television studio, with lights, spots, and gadgets that let articles and screens move up and down. Files and storage bins should line some of the walls, while other walls should be of material which will permit the teacher to display artwork on them. Motivational materials should be housed in the studio or in a nearby art office, so that the teacher and children can use them as needed.

COMPILING ART REFERENCE FILES

The student of art has, through his years of study, accumulated a collection of resource materials consisting of clippings, reproductions, and articles pertaining to the field. These can be useful to him in teaching if he organizes and labels them so as to provide the greatest possible facility and practicability in their use. Children can take their own photographs of animals, objects, and places and put them in the file on temporary or permanent loan. Also, some children may have photographs they or their families have taken on trips or during vacations. Files which serve various functions may be considered.

Picture file — photographs   One type of file is especially useful to the child himself: high-quality photographs. Useful categories of photographs are:

Animal life: Insects, sea life, mammals.

The land: Rock formations, scenes of jungles, deserts, mountains, seashores.

Waterways: Streams, rivers, lakes, seas.

Uniforms: Various occupations.

The figure in action: Tennis, swimming, diving.

Details: Eyes, nose, mouth.

Transportation: Boats (docks), locomotives and trains, train stations, automobiles, buses, trucks, carriages.

Plant life: Flowers, vegetables, fruits, trees, leaves.

Building and structures: Bridges of all kinds.

Miscellaneous: Crown jewels, thrones, costumes of different areas, houses through the ages, gardens.

Drawings or illustrations drawn by professional artists should *not* be included in this file, as these will influence the child's own expression. The photographs, many of which will be clipped from magazines and mounted, and others from museum collections (such as a museum of natural history), National Geographic magazine, and others, are to be used by the children only as references, not for copying.

Example: One child does not remember the exact construction of a horse's leg; reference to a photograph may help him. Children should be encouraged to study the photographs in the files without carrying them away. That is, they should look at the photograph, replace it, and return to work, retaining the memory of the photograph. This method will be a safeguard against copying.

Example: The class is doing a project involving jungle animals. The children have thought about all the popular varieties, but more and different kinds are needed. Let them look at the files to see if there are some animals not yet considered. Following this, a visit to a museum of natural history or a film borrowed from such an institution may give the children an opportunity to observe and become more familiar with the animals. Talking about how the animals walk or run, how they capture their food, and possibly acting out these functions will also increase vitality.

Example: Some of the children are interested in snakes. They know a great deal about them; they want to know more. They incorporate this new knowledge into their work. The teacher points out, too, that nature is certainly inventive. Their next work might be one in which they invent a new variety. A follow-up activity could be a trip to the snake house at the zoo.

Example: A child is painting an old-fashioned town. She does not know too much about Victorian houses. The files can give much more information on which to base her work.

Example: A boy is painting a factory scene. He once visited a factory and has some idea of a conveyer belt, but needs more details. The files can provide them.

There is no doubt that direct observation of nature and actual objects is far superior to reference to a picture file. This file is to be considered only as an *aid* to bolster a felt response to something already begun. Overdependence on the photograph file should be definitely discouraged. Injudicious use of the file can be a threat to the art expression of children. Also, it must be understood that only certain types of individuals may feel the need for it at all (see Chapter 8).

Small reproductions file A well-rounded art reference file, accumulated from magazines and consisting of reproductions of artwork in all media, is an invaluable resource for teaching. Arrangement of these files should serve the individual teacher's methods. In addition, a regular file organized by historical period, subdivided into four categories (painting, sculpture, architecture, crafts) and classified by subject matter, serves well. Such an arrangement might be: 1) portraits through the ages (double, full face); 2) sea; 3) land; 4) landscapes; 5) animals; 6) games, parades, circuses, and others. Reproductions of this size are not useful for motivating an entire class, as they cannot be seen from a distance. However, they can be used successfully by the individual child wishing to research a special theme or by a teacher motivating an individual child.

Example: The teacher wishes to make a point to an individual child while the rest of the class is working on various painting subjects or is otherwise engaged. She pulls out the portrait file and says, "Last time you tried a face. Have you thought of a full-figure portrait? What does the artist do in several of these examples? He shows the hobbies or feats or professional position of the sitter. Would such an idea interest you?"

Example: Students are doing a play set in the past. They can do some research in the picture file on architecture, furniture, and decorations of the period.

Large reproductions file   A file of large reproductions, mounted in rigid, light, and durable fashion, is a must for study and enjoyment and for integrating the disciplines in any school.[1] Large reproductions are useful to a class for exhibitions in the hall and for individual study. Unlike the slide, which he can observe only briefly, the child can live with the reproduction, absorbing its message at various times when he chooses to look at it. Reproductions should be of the best quality. An effort should be made to obtain only those prints which are considered to be as close in color to the original as possible. Poor color prints can give a false image and thereby mislead the child in his understanding and appreciation of the original. (This file can be organized like the small reproductions file.)

Slides file   The slides file can be of several types: 1) the *art history* file, which supplements the large reproductions file (often large reproductions are not published for every work of art desired); 2) the *motivational file,* consisting of landscapes, historic places, objects, city scenes, and people, which can be used to recall personal experience (see Chapter 5); and 3) the *children's record file,* in which a record of the children's work is kept (see Chapter 7).

An exciting device used by some teachers is that of providing, in a quiet, dark corner of the room, an automatic and continuous showing of selected slides, where children go to contemplate and study, singly or in groups of varying size, while other activities are taking place in the studio.

Audio file   A collection of tapes and records can be inspiring motivational material (children can help make the tapes): sounds of trains, boats and harbors, fairgrounds, rain and storm, running water, airport sounds; crowds; pure sounds; poetry; and music old and new. One teacher made a sound tape which proved very useful for Halloween. Every time the sound of a creaking door painfully inched open was heard, there was a pause in which the listener waited for the sound inside. Behind one door was the full blast of a carousel; behind the next, the

[1]Such a tool has been devised by Co-Ord Associates, Inc., Blauvelt, New York. Angiola Churchill: Educational Director.

roar of lions; then a brass band in grand form, followed by
tinkling water and so on (Tad Krumeich, tape).

Texture and the rubbings bank The author had a bank of rubbings and visual textures to which children contributed when
they wished.

Example: A child who did not feel like working one day, perhaps because of a cold, he worked on the rubbings bank.

Example: A child wanted an idea for a visual texture to fit a
specific problem; he searched and found an ideal one. (The
child who borrowed was expected to replace one or several as
soon as he could.)

Book and poetry collections A collection of poetry books
should be available, as well as many books on art that children
can read and browse through. Poems and nonsense verses written
by the children also serve as motivational materials.

Collections of children's paintings Another tool for teaching
consists of original works by other children—younger, older,
peers, in other lands. Through these works the teacher can under-
score the universality of subject matter. She can also give confidence to individual children as they compare their technical
abilities and ideas with the works of others, inspire them to try
other ways of doing things, and encourage them to find a
kindred spirit.

Example: Children have been working on a subject; the color
is uninspired. Showing works by their peers that possess the
desired qualities will awaken them to new possibilities. For
example, the work of Japanese children stresses the beauty of
detail and love of texture. Other children will respond immediately to these qualities. This method is valuable because it
works by implication. The teacher need not refer to the children's
need of being more conscious of these qualities in their own
work. She is spared the necessity of preaching.

Showing works or reproductions of the works of artists in
combination with children's works, sensitively selected, can also
instruct and motivate. (This is more fully discussed in Chapter
7 in the section "Assessment.")

Pick-a-card file This file was started by sixth-grade children
and provided much fun and pleasure. Symbols or suggestive
ideas are cut out of magazines. When children do not have
ideas of subjects to paint or wish to play a game with their

friends, they can turn to this collection, which grows year by year.

Teacher's professional file The files described thus far are generally used freely by the children as well as the teacher. However, the teacher will also need her own file, in addition to her lesson and curriculum plans and her records of the children's progress. This file is composed essentially of materials to keep her abreast of new developments in her profession. Some of the subjects could be as follows:

Art media (related study areas)

Art fields

Design: Elements and principles

Aesthetics and criticism

Museology

Art education: Developmental levels, lesson plans, unit ideas

Sources of supplies and visual aids

Records of children's development (see Chapter 7)

Film banks An alert teacher should be familiar with films available and useful in her field. These she can order if her budget allows. She should keep a record of her reactions to them: how they were used; what they cost; where they were ordered. There is one source of films that can be used as motivational material which involves little or no cost. This is the film libraries which supply film that may be rejected or dated but still are in good condition. Biology films and films on games, for example, can be used to study action, body movements, kinds of terrain, new forms, and animal life, thereby motivating the student in his projects.

Teachers and children can make their own motivational films. Children could be asked to research a certain subject about which they wish to paint. Or they can do as the student teacher did in the project described in Chapter 8 (see pp. 233), who made a film to motivate the class. Such films eventually build an invaluable bank for use in subsequent lessons.

EVALUATING TYPES OF RESOURCES

The teacher today is presented with a wide array of aids, making it imperative that she select wisely. Among the more popular forms are:

Motion pictures	Recordings
Slides	Models
Photographs	Radio
Reproductions	Television
Charts	Tapes
Art collections	Film Strips

Resources should be regarded and used as integral parts of the motivation-stimulation process in teaching. They can be used to pinpoint ideas and techniques, to stress those aspects of art that have been identified as important, and to evoke responses to the processes and manifestations of art. Overuse or unrelated use limits their effectiveness. The teacher must constantly evaluate their appropriateness to the activity at hand, ascertaining whether they meet the following standards: extending experience, knowledge, and understanding; clarifying the material to be learned; arousing the interest of the age level and stimulating creative responses; having high artistic worth; avoiding indoctrination and the perpetuation of stereotypes.

Tools for Teaching: Self-appraisal Forms

HOW I FELT WHILE WORKING TODAY

Getting Started

I started out feeling enthusiastic____normally inspired____not very inspired____without much idea of what I was going to do____.

I had a hard time getting started because I had other things on my mind____. I was distracted by noise____watching what others were doing____interested in a conversation about_____.

I was tired____because_____.

I was bored____because_____.

I didn't have any ideas____I was in a mood that could be described as_____.

*Comments:*_____
_____

I started out well because I had seen something I might like to do ____. I could almost see the object exactly as I was going to do it____. I had a sort of feeling which I was trying to put down____. I didn't know what I was going to do but felt sure I would get an idea as I worked____.

*Comments:*_____
_____

During the Lesson

My mood changed from_____to_____.

My mood did not change____.
My feelings about my work changed from_____
to_____. My feelings about my work did not change____.

Frustrating things happened with regard to color____line____space____ mistakes____values____technical things____textures____sizes____ mood____other_____. I felt inadequate____.

People said and did things to upset me_____ . I made destructive comments to others, such as_____ .
I made constructive comments, such as_____ .

Good things happened in the painting (sculpture, collage, assemblage) with regard to color_____ line_____ space_____ values_____ mood_____ total impact_____ sizes_____ textures_____ other_____ .

I had problems with_____
but felt adequate to handle them. I asked the teacher's help with_____
_____ . I knew I needed help but did not ask for it because_____ .

End of Lesson

What I learned about myself and my work:

I should try to settle on one idea before I get started_____ . I should ask for the teacher's help when I get started_____ , when I get frustrated_____ , when others upset me_____ , when I'm in a poor mood_____ .

I seem to do well when I have no set idea and look for it as I go along_____ .

During this period, working next to_____did not seem helpful to me because_____ .

Working next to_____ was helpful because_____ .

Conclusions

Next period I shall work next to_____ not work next to_____ .

I shall think about coming prepared to work with an idea_____ .

I am going to ask for help when I need it from the teacher with regard to_____ .

Comments: _____
_____

I AM FINISHED WITH THIS PROJECT

I am no longer interested in this project because I thought of a better way to express my idea_____ because I want a fresh start_____ because I feel that altering the object I am working on will do no good_____ .

I just cannot handle_____ ; the way I handle_____ spoils it_____ .

I was distracted by people ____ things ____ situations ____ and lost track of my original idea and the enthusiasm I felt for it.

I had a poor start to begin with____. I didn't have a good idea____.

I had too many ideas at once____. I had no enthusiasm for the idea____.

I was influenced by someone else's idea____style____subject matter____mood____and then discovered I was not really interested in it for myself.

I made some sloppy mistakes and wanted to make a fresh start____.

I don't like this painting (collage, sculpture, assemblage) because_____
_____.

I could improve this painting by_____
_____. I don't choose to do these things because_____
_____. In my next project I shall_____
_____. I have a wonderful new idea____. I shall____
I shall not____return to this one later.

I am finished with this project because it gives me a sense of completion____because I have done a satisfactory job____because I can't think of ways to improve it____.

I still have problems with_____
_____
_____

but don't know what to do about them in this work____.

The following qualities please me in this work_____
_____.

I have made the following discoveries (describe):
  How I handle materials _____
  How to render people _____
  How to use color _____
  My ability to concentrate _____
  My ability to tolerate setbacks _____
  Time requirement _____
  Best conditions for working _____
  Other _____
_____
_____
_____
_____
_____
_____
_____
_____

Guidance and Evaluation in Art Education Literature

In most current texts on art education, evaluation of children's creative expression is divided into two major areas: 1) teacher evaluation of the child's relationship to his own work (some texts give special attention to self-evaluation) and 2) teacher effectiveness in communicating ideas, motivating children, and planning the program. According to the literature, educators conceive of and practice evaluation in terms of informal, intuitive judgments about the pupil's behavior and growth as a way of identifying what constitutes desirable activity for him. Few, if any, educators have utilized or expressed confidence in formal measuring by standardized aptitude tests, although recent research has increasingly employed these means. Vincent Lanier has expressed the general sentiments of the profession: "Most art educators will agree unequivocally that there are as yet no significant valid or reliable objective tests or scales of measurement of art" (1: p. 141).

All of us engaged in education are concerned that evaluation should not, as Erdt points out, destroy the "quality of child art." She continues: "The delicate situation that arises for the teacher is to maintain the quality that is intrinsic to child art and not let it be overshadowed by an emerging concern for technique which is natural as children mature" (2: p. 212). Maturation rates differ with each child. Therefore, each child's level of achievement should vary from a theoretical norm. Blanche Jefferson states: "It is the standard of each child that is important. This emphasis on individuality and on each child's standards as right for him is a thread that runs through the art education of all children in every grade" (3: p. 210). John Michael and others (4) agree that older children should have the opportunity to appraise their own work and draw their own conclusions. This can be done through group discussion and the display of their work. Carl Reed warns that most early adolescents are easily discouraged and sensitive to criticism, and that their interests change easily. Enormous upsets occur when insensitive, rigid measurement is applied to their work. However, they are interested in improving and achieving. Therefore, properly handled, they can benefit greatly from discussions about their work.

The development of a desire for technical proficiency grows as the student matures and is motivated by the urge for better self-expression in areas in which he is most interested. Evaluation helps to determine these interests and to keep a check on developmental stages [5: p. 195].

The teacher's self-assessment is seen by many authors as important in the evaluation process. Randall and Halvorsen (6: pp. 99–100) present guidelines for this purpose which emphasize helping the child emerge from art experiences as an independent personality rather than a dependent one, confident of his own techniques and of his own view of his surroundings and experiences. A similar but more extensively amplified list is provided in The Visual Arts in General Education (7: pp. 104–16).

Most art educators feel that only a very general and flexible scale can be devised for evaluating creative growth and product in children. Many have devised such criteria in the forms of lists, charts, and questions, which they use merely as reminders of what it is possible to achieve in a specific activity or area of art. Recent research has become more active in this area simply because it is difficult to do research without it, and also because the establishment of art education as a firm discipline requires it. Tests intended to measure or determine art aptitude, judgment, and vocabulary are increasingly being devised.

Over the last twenty years many art educators have disputed what they regard as disproportionate emphasis on judgment of the art *product* in evaluating pupil growth. While the value of the product is not denied, many educators wish to have it considered as only one of the many ways of inducing and judging growth. The *process,* they argue, holds equal potentiality for ascertaining development. Indeed, several authors have advised emphasizing the child's growing consciousness of art rather than his skill and performance as revealed by the product (8: pp. 51–63).

A number of authors support the view that during the transitional years of preadolescence the skilled teacher is more important than in the lower grades. During these years, the child's need for highly skilled guidance in creative expression is probably greater than at any other phase of life (8: p. 66). Miriam Lindstrom says: "Children of this age left to themselves without guidance of their proclivities seldom improve their drawing skill relative to their advanced mental powers" (9: p. 54).

There is a general belief that teachers of art should practice art and, in general, keep abreast of what is happening in the world of art. Blanche Jefferson says: "Children's attention should constantly be called to the qualities of many different kinds of art products. Art products change, and our view of color, design and style change" (3: pp. 173–74). Helen Merritt focuses on the influence that the teacher's attitude toward his own skill has on children's attitude and development in art. She believes that in order for children to visualize themselves as makers of art, they need the example of a creative adult. This does not mean that all teachers must be accomplished artists. But they must have the confidence to feel relaxed, unafraid of art, and to have faith in their ability to grow and improve. Only with this belief in themselves as artists can they believe in the children's possibility for expression and growth.

If a teacher is fearful that others will discover his limited drawing skill, he communicates fearfulness to the children. But his fear is really a bond he shares with the children. They too are afraid of ridicule. But if a teacher can feel at ease at trying to draw, even though his actual skill is limited, he can communicate confidence to his children. If the teacher is willing to exercise his own potential, having the attitude that with practice he will improve, his attitude leads children to think in the same way about their efforts [10: p. 36].

Robert C. Burkhart and others believe that the struggle in which the student is involved when he faces the demands of creative action in the arts is far more complex than that of merely learning a skill. To appreciate their plight, the teacher should be capable of and accustomed to facing the rigors of creative action: "To inspire this form of response in another, a teacher must have experienced within himself the courage, in spite of self doubt, to face and struggle fully with the issues of discovery in the fearful hope that some new accomplishment may emerge as the result of this effort" (11: p. 1).

David Ecker raises interesting questions regarding current objectives for art education, confronting us with some additional or alternative objectives. He points out that current educational objectives can be stated to be as follows: engendering an understanding of the arts, acquiring the skill for artistic production, and developing the skills for the analysis and evaluation of art. He asks, " . . . how *understandings* are related to *skills* . . . how *knowing about* art is related to *knowing how* to produce art. . . . Is one ability a necessary condition for the achievement of the other ability?" (12: p. 3).

Art instruction, he claims, has been carried out in the public schools "with the images of the creative studio artist . . . acting as models of behavior for both student and teacher" (12: p. 4). Yet to fulfill this aim various important factors seem to be neglected or altogether missing.

. . . the task of building a curriculum which has pretensions beyond the training of skills in artistic production and performance (to include, for example, teaching for understanding and appreciation of the arts), must necessarily include a consideration of many more possible kinds of models [12: p. 4].

He asks us to consider that the art critic, the curator, the anthropologists, the aesthetician become relevant models requiring scrutiny and inclusion. Such a consideration would broaden the path which leads to enjoyment and appreciation of the arts since we are presented with the alternates to the single concept that the only way or supreme way to understanding is through the making of art.

REFERENCES

1. Vincent Lanier, *Teaching Secondary Art,* International Textbook Company, Scranton, Pa., 1958.

2. Margaret Hamilton Erdt, *Teaching Art in the Elementary School,* Holt, Rinehart and Winston, Inc., New York, 1964.

3. Blanche Jefferson, *Teaching Art to Children: The Values of Creative Expression,* Allyn and Bacon, Inc., Boston, 1960.

4. John A. Michael (ed.), *Art Education in the Junior High School,* National Art Education Association, Washington, D.C., 1964.

5. Carl Reed, *Early Adolescent Art Education,* Chas. A. Bennett Co., Inc., Peoria, Ill., 1957.

6. Arne W. Randall and Ruth Elsie Halvorsen, *Painting in the Classroom: A Key to Child Growth,* Davis Publications, Inc., Worcester, Mass., 1962.

7. *The Visual Arts In General Education,* Progressive Education Association, Commission on the Secondary School Curriculum, D. Appleton-Century Company, Inc., New York, 1940.

8. Paul Edmonston, "Overview: Product and Evaluation," Eastert Art Association *Research Bulletin,* vol. 18, no. 4, 1961.

9. Miriam Lindstrom, *Children's Art: A Study of Normal Development in Children's Modes of Visualization,* University of California Press, Berkeley, Calif., 1957.

10. Helen Merritt, *Guiding Free Expression in Children's Art,* Holt, Rinehart and Winston, Inc., New York, 1964.

11. Robert C. Burkhart, *Spontaneous and Immediate Ways of Learning,* International Textbook Company, Scranton, Pa., 1962

12. David W. Ecker, *How to Think in Other Categories: The Problem of Alternative Conceptions of Aesthetic Education,* Central Midwestern Regional Educational Laboratory, Inc., St. Ann, Missouri, 1969.

Bibliography

Today's art teacher must realize that the teaching of art cannot take place in a vacuum but, rather, must become an interdisciplinary endeavor. In recognition of this principle, this bibliography cuts across subject-area lines.

ART, ART CRITICISM, ART HISTORY

Alloway, Lawrence, "Notes on Art," in Gregory Battcock (ed.), *The New Art: A Critical Anthology*, E. P. Dutton & Co., Inc., New York, 1966.

Appolonio, Umbro, et al., *Art Since 1945*, Washington Square Press, New York, 1962.

Arnheim, Rudolf, *Film as Art*, University of California Press, Berkeley and Los Angeles, Calif., 1967.

Ashton, Dore, *Modern American Sculpture*, Harry N. Abrams, Inc., New York, 1969.

——, *A Reading of Modern Art*, The Press of Case Western Reserve University, Cleveland, Ohio, 1969.

Baldinger, Wallace S., and H. B. Green, *The Visual Arts*, Holt, Rinehart and Winston, Inc., New York, 1960.

Ballinger, Louise Bowen, and Thomas F. Vroman, *Sources and Responses*, Reinhold Publishing Corporation, New York, 1965.

Bates, Lowry, *The Visual Experience: An Introduction to Art*, Harry N. Abrams, Inc., New York, 1961.

Battcock, Gregory (ed.), *The New Art: A Critical Anthology*, E. P. Dutton & Co., New York, 1966.

—— (ed.), *The New American Cinema: A Critical Anthology*, E. P. Dutton & Co., Inc., New York, 1967.

Baur, John I., *Revolution and Tradition in Modern Art*, Frederick A. Praeger, Inc., New York, 1951.

Bornstein, Eli (ed.), *The Structurists* (annual), University of Saskatoon, Saskatoon, Canada, 1966, 1967.

Burnham, Jack, *Beyond Modern Sculpture*, George Braziller, Inc., New York, 1968.

Capers, Roberta M., and Jerrold Maddox, *Images and Imagination: An Introduction to Art*, The Ronald Press Company, New York, 1965.

Carraher, Ronald G., and Jacqueline B. Thurston, *Optical Illusions and the Visual Arts*, Reinhold Publishing Corporation, New York, 1966.

Christensen, Edwin O., *Primitive Art*, Crowell-Collier Publishing Co., New York, 1955.

Clark, Kenneth, *The Nude: A Study of Ideal Form*, Pantheon Books, New York, 1953.

Collier, Graham, *Form, Space and Vision*, Prentice-Hall, Inc., Englewood Cliffs, N.J., 1963.

Contemporary American Painting and Sculpture, University of Illinois Press, Urbana, Ill., 1963.

De Sausmarey, Maurice, *Basic Design: The Dynamics of Visual Form*, Reinhold Publishing Corporation, New York, 1964.

Dickerman, George, "The Strange Eye and Art of De Kooning," *The Saturday Evening Post*, Nov. 21, 1964.

Eitner, Lorenz, *Introduction to Art*, Burgess Publishing Company, Minneapolis, Minn., 1961.

Elliot, Alexander, *Sight and Insight*, E. P. Dutton & Co., New York, 1960.

Elsen, Albert E., *Purposes of Art: An Introduction to the History and Appreciation of Art*, Holt, Rinehart and Winston, Inc., New York, 1962.

Feldman, Edmund Burke, *Art as Image and Idea*, Prentice-Hall, Inc., Englewood Cliffs, N.J., 1967.

Fleming, William, *Art and Ideas*, Holt, Rinehart and Winston, Inc., New York, 1968.

Gilson, Etienne, *Painting and Reality*, Meridian Books, Inc., New York, 1959.

Goldwater, Robert, *Sculpture from Africa in the Museum of Primitive Art*, Museum of Primitive Art, New York, 1963.

Goosen, E. C., "The Big Canvas," *The New Art: A Critical Anthology*, ed. by Gregory Battcock, E. P. Dutton & Co., Inc., New York, 1966.

Gore, Frederick, *Painting: Some Basic Principles*, Reinhold Publishing Corporation, New York, 1965.

Grosser, Maurice, *The Painter's Eye*, Mentor Books, New York, 1966.

Guggenheimer, Richard, *Creative Vision for Art and for Life*, Harper & Brothers, New York, 1960.

Haftmann, Werner, *Painting of the Twentieth Century*, Frederick A. Praeger, Inc., New York, 1960.

Hansen, Al, *A Primer of Happenings and Time/*

Space Art, Something Else Press, Inc., New York, 1965.

Hauser, Arnold, *Naturalism to the Film Age,* vol. 4, *The Social History of Art,* Vintage Books, Inc., New York, 1958.

Hodin, J. P., *The Dilemma of Being Modern,* Routledge & Kegan Paul, Ltd., London, 1956.

Hofmann, Hans, *Search for the Real,* Addison Gallery of American Art, Andover, Mass., 1948.

Hunter, Samuel (ed.), *Modern American Painting and Sculpture,* Dell Publishing Co., Inc., New York, 1959.

Hurwitz, Elizabeth Adams, *Design: A Search for Essentials,* International Textbook Company, Scranton, Pa., 1964.

Huyghe, René, *Art and the Spirit of Man,* Harry N. Abrams, Inc., New York, 1962.

Irwin, Edman, *Arts and the Man,* W. W. Norton & Company, Inc., New York, 1939.

Kahler, Erich, *The Disintegration of Form in the Arts,* George Braziller, Inc., New York, 1968.

Kaprow, Allen, "Paintings, Environments and Happenings" unpublished manuscript, 1960.

Kepes, Gyorgy (ed.), *Education of Vision,* George Braziller, Inc., New York, 1950.

———, *Structure in Art and Science,* George Braziller, Inc., New York, 1965.

———, *The Nature and Art of Motion,* George Braziller, Inc., New York, 1965.

Kirby, Michael (ed.), *The Art of Time: Essays on the Avant-Garde,* E. P. Dutton & Co., Inc., New York, 1960.

———, *Happenings: An Illustrated Anthology,* E. P. Dutton & Co., Inc., New York, 1965.

Kouwenhoven, John A., *Made in America,* Anchor Books, New York, 1962.

Krutch, Joseph Wood, *Experience and Art,* P. F. Collier & Son Corporation, New York, 1962.

Kultermann, Udo, *The New Sculpture,* Frederick A. Praeger, Inc., New York, 1968.

Kulver, Billy, *Some More Beginnings,* Experiments in Art and Technology, Inc., New York, 1968.

Langer, Susanne K., *Feeling and Form,* Charles Scribner's Sons, New York, 1953.

———, *Problems of Art,* Charles Scribner's Sons, New York, 1957.

Lawson, John Howard, *Film: The Creative Process,* Hill and Wang, Inc., New York, 1967.

Leepa, Allen, *The Challenge of Modern Art,* A. S. Barnes and Co., Inc., Cranbury, N.Y., 1949.

Lippard, Lucy R., *Pop Art,* Frederick A. Praeger, Inc., New York, 1966.

———, "As Painting Is to Sculpture: A Changing Ratio," in *American Sculpture of the Sixties,* ed. by Maurice Tuchman, Los Angeles County Museum of Art publication, Los Angeles, Calif., (New York Graphic Society, Ltd., distributors), 1967.

Malraux, André, *The Creative Art,* Pantheon Books, Inc., New York, 1949.

———, *Voices of Silence,* Doubleday & Company, Inc., Garden City, N.Y., 1953.

Mandel, David, *Changing Art, Changing Man,* Horizon Press, New York, 1967.

McDarrah, Fred W., *The Artist's World in Pictures,* E. P. Dutton & Co., Inc., New York, 1961.

Michelson, Annette, "Film and the Radical Aspiration," in *The New American Cinema: A Critical Anthology,* ed. by Gregory Battcock, E. P. Dutton & Co., Inc., New York, 1967.

Monte, James, *Anti-Illusion: Procedures/Materials,* Museum of American Art, New York, 1969.

Moseley, Spencer, Pauline Johnson, and Hazel Koening, *Crafts Design: An Illustrated Guide,* Wadsworth Publishing Company, Inc., Belmont, Calif., 1962.

Mumford, Lewis, et al., *The Arts in Renewal,* A. S. Barnes and Co., Inc., Cranbury, N.J., 1961.

Munro, Thomas, *The Arts and Their Interrelations,* The Liberal Arts Press, Inc., New York, 1956.

Myers, Bernard, *Sculpture, Form and Method,* Reinhold Publishing Corporation, New York, 1965.

Myers, Bernard S., *Understanding the Arts,* Holt, Rinehart and Winston, Inc., New York, 1958.

Ocvirk, Otto G., et al., *Art Fundamentals: Theory and Practice,* Wm. C. Brown Company, Publishers, Dubuque, Iowa, 1960.

Ortega y Gasset, José, *The Dehumanization of Art and Other Writings on Art Culture,* Anchor Books, New York, 1948.

Pellegrini, Aldo, *New Tendencies in Art,* Crown Publishers, Inc., New York, 1966.

Popper, Frank, *Origins and Development of Kinetic Art,* New York Graphic Society, New York, 1968.

Read, Herbert, *The Meaning of Art,* Penguin Books, Inc., Baltimore, Md., 1949.

———, *A Concise History of Modern Painting,* Frederick A. Praeger, Inc., New York, 1959.

———, *A Concise History of Modern Sculpture,* Frederick A. Praeger, Inc., New York, 1964.

Richardson, Edgar P., *A Short History of Painting in America,* Thomas Y. Crowell Company, New York, 1956.

Ritchie, Andrew Carnduff, *Sculpture of the Twentieth Century,* The Museum of Modern Art, New York, 1952.

Robbins, Daniel, "Recent Still-Life," in *Art in America,* ed. by Jean Lipman, vol. 54, no. 1, Art in America, Inc., New York, January–February, 1966.

Rodman, Selden, *Conversations with Artists,* Capricorn Books, New York, 1961.

Rose, Barbara, *American Art Since 1900: A Critical History,* Frederick A. Praeger, Inc., New York, 1967.

——— (ed.), *Readings in American Art Since 1900: A Documentary Survey,* Frederick A. Praeger, Inc., New York, 1968.

Rotha, Paul, "Some Principles of Documentary," *Film: An Anthology,* ed. by David Talbot, University of California Press, Berkeley, Calif., 1967.

Rothchild, Lincoln, *Style in Art: The Dynamics of Art as Cultural Expression,* A. S. Barnes & Co., Inc., Cranbury, N.J., 1962.

Sandler, Irving, "Gesture and Non-Gesture in Recent Sculpture," *American Sculpture of the Sixties,* ed. by Maurice Tuchman, Los Angeles County Museum of Art Publication, Los Angeles,

Calif., (New York Graphic Society, Ltd., distributors), 1967.

Schinneller, James A., *Art: Search and Self-Discovery*, International Textbook Company, Scranton, Pa., 1961.

Schorr, Justin, *Aspects of Art*, A. S. Barnes & Co., Inc., Cranbury, N.J., 1967.

Scott, Robert Gilliam, *Design Fundamentals*, McGraw-Hill Book Company, New York, 1951.

Seiberling, Frank, *Looking Into Art*, Holt, Rinehart and Winston, Inc., New York, 1959.

Seitz, William C., *The Art of Assemblage*, copyright The Museum of Modern Art, New York, printed by the Case-Hoyt Corp. (Rochester, N.Y.) and Plantin Press (N.Y.), 1965.

——, *The Responsive Eye*, copyright The Museum of Modern Art, New York, printed by the Case-Hoyt Corp., Rochester, N.Y., 1965.

Seuphor, Michael, *Abstract Painting*, Dell Publishing Co., Inc., New York, 1964.

Shahn, Ben, *The Shape of Content*, Random House, Inc., New York, 1957.

Shapiro, Meyer, "The Liberating Quality of Avant-Garde Art," *Art News*, vol. 56, no. 4, Summer, 1956.

Sloan, Patricia, *Color: Basic Principles and New Directions*, Reinhold Book Corporation, New York, 1968.

Solomon, Alan, "The New Art," *The New Art: A Critical Anthology*, ed. by Gregory Battcock, E. P. Dutton & Co., Inc., New York, 1966.

Sourian, Etienne, "Time in the Plastic Arts," *Reflections of Art*, ed. by Susanne K. Langer, Oxford University Press, New York, 1961.

Steinberg, Leo, "Contemporary Art and the Plight of Its Public," *The New Art: A Critical Anthology*, ed. by Gregory Battcock, E. P. Dutton & Co., Inc., New York, 1966.

Sweeney, James Johnson, "Miro," *Art News Annual*, vol. XXIII, 1954.

Talbot, Daniel (ed.), *Film: An Anthology*, University of California Press, Berkeley and Los Angeles, Calif., 1967.

Tuchman, Maurice (ed.), *American Sculpture of the Sixties*, Los Angeles County Museum of Art publication, Los Angeles, Calif. (New York Graphic Society, Ltd., distributors), 1967.

Voglstein, Julie Braun, *Art: The Image of the West*, Pantheon Books, Inc., New York, 1952.

Weller, Allen S., *Contemporary American Painting and Sculpture*, University of Illinois Press, Urbana, Ill., 1963.

Whyte, Lancelot Law, *Aspects of Form*, Indiana University Press, Bloomington, Ind., 1961.

Wilenski, R. H., *The Meaning of Modern Sculpture*, Beacon Press, Boston, 1932.

Williams, Hiram, *Notes for a Young Painter*, Prentice-Hall, Inc., Englewood Cliffs, N.J., 1963.

Ziegfeld, Edwin, and Ray Faulkner, *Art Today*, Holt, Rinehart and Winston, Inc., New York, 1968.

Zucker, Paul, *Styles in Painting*, The Viking Press, Inc., New York, 1950.

ART EDUCATION

Anderson, Harold H. (ed.), *Creativity and Its Cultivation*, Harper & Brothers, New York, 1959.

Andrews, Michael F. (ed.), *Aesthetic Form and Education*, Syracuse University Press, Syracuse, N.Y., 1958.

—— (ed.), *Creativity and Psychological Health*, Syracuse University Press, Syracuse, N.Y., 1961.

Arnheim, Rudolf, "Growth," *Art and Visual Perception*, University of California Press, Berkeley, Calif., 1954.

——, *Art and Visual Perception*, University of California Press, Berkeley and Los Angeles, Calif., 1966.

——, *Toward A Psychology of Art: Collected Essays*, University of California Press, Berkeley and Los Angeles, Calif., 1967.

——, *Visual Thinking*, University of California Press, Berkeley and Los Angeles, Calif., 1969.

Arnstine, Donald, "Needed Research and the Role of Definitions in Art Education," *Studies in Art Education*, vol. 7, no. 1, National Art Education Association, Washington, D.C., Autumn, 1965, pp. 2–17.

——, "The Aesthetic as a Context for General Education," *Studies in Art Education*, vol. 8, no. 1, National Art Education Association, Washington, D.C., Autumn, 1966, pp. 13–21.

Barkan, Manuel, *A Foundation for Art Education*, The Ronald Press Company, New York, 1955.

——, *Through Art to Creativity, Art in the Elementary School Program*, Allyn and Bacon, Inc., Boston, 1960.

Biettal, Kenneth R., "The Creativity Complex in the Visual Arts," *Studies in Art Education*, vol. 1, no. 1, National Art Education Association, Washington, D.C., Autumn, 1959, pp. 26–37.

——, "Art: A Review of Research in Art and Art Education, 1948–58," *Encyclopedia of Educational Research*, ed. by C. W. Harris, The Macmillan Company, New York, 1960, pp. 77–87.

—— and Robert C. Burkhardt, "Strategies of Spontaneous, Divergent and Academic Art Students," *Studies in Art Education*, vol. 5, no. 1, National Art Education Association, Washington, D.C., Fall, 1963.

——, "Curriculum Experimentation in Art Education as Seen through Recent Research," *Modern Viewpoints in the Curriculum*, ed. by Paul C. Rosenbloom, McGraw-Hill Book Company, New York, 1964.

Berheim, Gloria D., "The Dimensionality of Differentiated Criteria in the Visual Art Product," *Studies in Art Education*, vol. 5, no. 1, National Art Education Association, Washington, D.C., Autumn, 1964.

Brittain, W. Lambert, "An Exploratory Investigation

of Early Adolescent Expression in Art," *Studies in Art Education,* vol. 9, Winter, 1968, pp. 5–12.

Brittain, W. Lambert, and Kenneth R. Beittal, "Analysis of Creative Performance in the Visual Arts," *Journal of Aesthetics and Art Criticism,* vol. 19, no. 1, Fall, 1960, pp. 83–90.

——, "A Study of Some Tests of Creativity in Relationship to Performances in the Visual Arts," *Studies in Art Education,* vol. 2, no. 2, National Art Education Association, Washington, D.C., Spring, 1961, pp. 54–55.

Brittain, W. Lambert, Robert H. Johnson, and Harlan E. Hoffa, "Some Studies Relating to Product and Evaluation," *Art Education Bulletin,* The Eastern Art Association, vol. 18, no. 4, Bureau of Publications, Teachers College, Columbia University, New York, April, 1961, pp. 51–64.

——, *Creativity and Art Education,* National Art Education Association, Washington, D.C., 1964.

—— (eds.), *Report of the Commission of Art Education,* National Art Education, Washington, D.C., 1965.

Burkhart, Robert C., *Spontaneous and Deliberate Ways of Learning,* International Textbook Company, Scranton, Pa., 1962.

——, "Progress in Art as Self-Reflective Learning for the Student," *Western Arts Bulletin,* National Art Education Association, Washington, D.C., Fall, 1962.

——, "Conditions Increasing Self-Reflective Learning in Art," *School Arts,* October, 1964, pp. 23–30.

Burns, Robert, "Some Correlations of Design with Personality," *Research in Art Education,* Ninth Yearbook of the National Art Education Association, State Teachers College, Kutztown, Pa., 1959, pp. 125–130.

Carr, Pete J., and Robert D. Clements, "The Relation of Art Work to Two Socio-Economic Variables (Culturally-Advantaged and Culturally-Deprived) to Motivational Variables (Fantasy and Realism), and to Budget Variables (Found and Expensive Materials)," U.S. Department of Health, Education and Welfare, Office of Education, Bureau of Research, Washington, D.C., 1967.

Churchill, Angiola, and Lera Beth Lumbley (eds.), *Art Education for the Urban Black Child,* Report of a Greater New York Metropolitan Area Conference, Sponsored by the Office of Educational Research Services, New York University, New York, 1968.

Clements, Robert D., "The Junior High Art Teacher's Guide to Research," *Art Education,* vol. 22, no. 81, 1969, pp. 12–15.

Conant, Howard, *Art Education,* The Center for Applied Research in Education, Inc., Washington, D.C., 1964.

—— (ed.), *Seminar on Elementary and Secondary School Education in the Visual Arts,* New York University, New York, 1965.

Corcoran, Ambrose L., "Children's Responses to Color Stimuli," *Research in Art Education,* Seventh Yearbook of the National Art Education

Association, Washington, D.C., 1956, pp. 83–95.

Crespi, David Emanuel, "A Study of the Role of Early Adolescent Reality for Art Education in the Junior High School," doctoral dissertation, Bureau of Publications, Columbia University, New York, 1959.

Crowmartie, Sue W., "Criteria for Evaluation of Children's Art," *Arts and Activities,* April, 1964, p. 38.

Culkin, Father John, S. J., "Films that Delight the Eye," *The Arts in Education,* Seventh National Conference on Education, sponsored by The National Council on the Arts in Education, Sarah Lawrence College, Bronxville, N.Y., Sept. 3–6, 1968, pp. 21–29.

Czurles, Stanley, "Aims and Objectives of Junior High School Art Activities," The Related Arts Service, vol. 14, no. 1, 1960.

D'Amico, Victor, *Experiment in Creative Art Teaching,* Museum of Modern Art, New York, 1960.

—— and Arlette Buchman, *Assemblage: A New Dimension in Creative Teaching in Art,* Museum of Modern Art, New York, 1971.

Davis, Carol Anne, "A Study of Controlled Attention to Aesthetic Qualities in Works of Art by Ninth-Grade Students of Differing Socioeconomic Environments," *Studies in Art Education,* vol. 10, no. 3, Spring, 1969, pp. 49–62.

De Francesco, Italio, *Art Education: Its Means and Ends,* Harper & Brothers, New York, 1958.

Dewey, John, *Art as Experience,* Minton, Balch & Co., New York, 1934.

Diamond, Florence Rand, "The Effectiveness of a Children's Workshop in the Creative Arts in Forwarding Personal and Intellectual Development," *Studies In Art Education,* vol. 11, no. 1, Fall, 1969, pp. 52–59.

Doe, Marjorie (ed.), *Participating Teacher's Guide: New Ways in Art Education,* The Ealing Corp., Cambridge, Mass., 1969.

Drainer, Barbara Adeline, "A Study of Children's Self-Feelings through Drawing; A Family Technique and Spontaneous Paintings," unpublished doctoral dissertation, Bureau of Publications, Teachers College, Columbia University, New York, 1963.

Ecker, David W., "The Artistic Process as Qualitative Problem Solving," *Journal of Aesthetics and Art Criticism,* vol. XXI, no. 3, Spring 1963.

—— (project director), *Improving the Teaching of Art Appreciation,* U.S. Department of Health, Education and Welfare, Research and Development Team for Improvement of Teaching Art in the Secondary Schools, Washington, D.C., 1966.

Edmonston, Paul, "Overview: Product and Evaluation," *Art Education Bulletin,* vol. 18, no. 4, The Eastern Art Association, State Teachers College, Kutztown, Pa., 1961, pp. 51–65.

Eisner, Elliott, "Initiating Art Experiences for Delinquent Students," *Art Education,* vol. 13, no. 2, National Art Education Association, Washington, D.C., Feb., 1960, pp. 8–9.

——, "A Typology of Creativity in the Visual Arts," *Studies in Art Education,* vol. 4, no. 2, National Art Education Association, Washington, D.C., Autumn, 1962, pp. 11–22.

——, *Think with Me About Creativity,* F. A. Owen, Publishing Co., New York, 1964.

——, "American Education and the Future of Art Education," *Art Education,* Sixty-fourth Yearbook of the National Society for the Study of Education Part II, National Art Education Association, Washington, D.C., 1965, pp. 299–325.

—— and D. Ecker, *Readings in Art Education,* Blaidsell Publishing Company, Waltham, Mass., 1966.

——, "The Drawings of the Disadvantaged: A Comparative Study," *Studies in Art Education,* vol. 11, no. 1, Fall, 1969, 5–19.

"Factor Analysis of Three Dimensions of the Art Judgment Complex: Criteria, Art Objects, and Judges," *The Journal of Experimental Education,* vol. 32, no. 2, Winter, 1963, pp. 167–174.

Feldman, Edward B., "Process," *Art Education Bulletin,* The Eastern Art Association, vol. 18, no. 4, State Teachers College, Kutztown, Pa., April, 1961, pp. 44–45.

——, *Becoming Human through Art,* Prentice-Hall, Inc., Englewood Cliffs, N.J., 1970.

Fine Arts Staff, Teachers College, Columbia University, *Art Education Today,* Yearbook, Bureau of Publications, Teachers College, Columbia University, New York, 1935–1943, 1948, 1949–1950, 1951–1952.

Force, Lorrain Stewart, "An Experimental Study to Examine the Response of Sixth-grade Students to Programmed Instruction in Art Design to Correspond to Selected Ability Trait Variables," *Studies in Art Education,* vol. 10, no. 3, Spring, 1969, pp. 37–50.

Fortress, Lillian, "A Suggested Guide to the Use of Paintings as Resources in the Social Studies for the Middle Grades," unpublished doctoral dissertation, New York University, 1960.

Fortieth Yearbook of the National Society of the Study of Education, *Art in American Life and Education,* Public School Publishing Co., Bloomington, Ill., 1941.

Frank, Lawrence, "The Integrative Role of the Arts in Personality," *The Integrative Function of Art Education, Art Education Bulletin,* 1950 Yearbook, The Eastern Arts Association, State Teachers College, Kutztown, Pa., 1950, pp. 17–30.

Frankston, Leon, "Effects of Two Programs and Two Methods of Teaching upon the Quality of Art Products of Adolescents," Cooperative Research Project, Eric Document 003 451, Pennsylvania State University, University Park, Pa., 1965.

Frederick, Ard Saradell, "An Analysis of Two Dimensional Representation with Relevance for Art Teaching in Alaska," unpublished doctoral dissertation, Teachers College, Columbia University, New York, 1970.

Freyberger, Ruth M., "Differences in the Creative Drawings of Children of Varying Ethnic and Socio-Economic Backgrounds in Pennsylvania Based on Samplings of Grades One Through Six," *Research in Art Education,* Seventh Yearbook of the National Art Education Association, Washington, D.C., 1956, pp. 115–125.

Gaitskell, Charles D., and Margaret R. Gaitskell, *Art Education During Adolescence,* Harcourt, Brace and Company, Inc., New York, 1954.

—— and Al Hurwitz, *Children and Their Art: Methods for the Elementary School,* Harcourt Brace Jovanovich, Inc., New York, 1970.

Getzels, Jacob W., and Philip Jackson, *Creativity and Intelligence,* John Wiley & Sons, Inc., New York, 1962.

Gezari, Temina F., *Footprints and New Worlds: Experiences in Art with Child and Adult,* Reconstructionist Press, New York, 1957.

Ghiselin, Brewster, "Cultivating Imagination," *Education and Imagination,* ed. by Irving Kaufman, University of Michigan Press, Ann Arbor, Mich., 1958.

—— (ed.), *The Creative Process,* Mentor Books, New York, 1955.

Gordon, Donald A., "Individual Differences in the Evaluation of Art and the Nature of Art Standards," *Journal of Educational Research,* vol. 50, no. 7, 1956, pp. 19–30.

Guilford, J. P., "The Psychology of Creativity," *Creative Crafts Magazine,* Los Angeles, 1964.

Haberer, Robert, and John Hill, "Children and Artificial Incentives," *School Arts,* March, 1960, p. 11.

Hastie, W. Reid (ed.), *National Society for the Study of Education Yearbook,* Part II, University of Chicago Press, Chicago, 1965.

—— and Christian Schmidt, *Encounter with Art,* McGraw-Hill Book Company, New York, 1969.

Hausman, Jerome J. (ed.), *Report of the Commission on Art Education,* National Art Education Association, Washington, D.C., 1965.

Henrickson, Paul R., and Paul R. Torance, "Some Implications for Art Education from the Minnesota Studies of Creative Thinking," *Studies in Art Education,* vol. 2, no. 2, National Art Education Association, State Teachers College, Kutztown, Pa., 1961, pp. 36–43.

Henry, Edith M., "Evaluation of Children's Growth Through Art Experiences," National Art Education Association, Washington, D.C., October, 1959.

Herberholtz, Donald and Barbara, *A Child's Pursuit of Art,* Wm. C. Brown Company, Publishers, Dubuque, Iowa, 1967.

Hoffa, Harlan E., "Overview: Outcome and Effect," *Art Education Bulletin,* vol. 18, no. 4, The Eastern Art Association, State Teachers College, Kutztown, Pa., April, 1961, pp. 66–67.

Jefferson, Blanche, and McGeary, Clyde, *My World of Art,* Allyn and Bacon, Boston, 1964.

Johnson, Robert H., "Some Selected Studies," *Art Education Bulletin,* vol. 18, no. 4, The Eastern Art Association, State Teachers College, Kutztown, Pa., April, 1961.

Junior High Art Teachers Guide, 1963, Division

of Fine and Applied Art, Cleveland Public Schools, Cleveland, Ohio, 1963.

Kaelin, Eugene F., "Aesthetics and the Teaching of Art," *Studies in Art Education,* vol. 5, no. 2, National Art Education Association, Washington, D.C., Spring, 1964, pp. 42–56.

Kaufman, Irving, *Art and Education in Contemporary Culture,* The Macmillan Company, New York, 1966.

Kaupelis, Robert, *Learning to Draw,* Watson-Guptill Publications, New York, 1966.

Keel, John S., "Art Education, 1940–64," *Art Education,* Sixty-fourth Yearbook of the National Society for the Study of Education, Part II, National Art Education Association, Washington, D.C., 1965, pp. 35–50.

Kellogg, Rhoda, *Analyzing Children's Art,* National Press Books, Palo Alto, Calif., 1969.

Kenseler, Gordon L., "The Effects of Perceptual Training and Modes of Perceiving upon Individual Differences in Ability to Learn Perspective Drawing," *Studies in Art Education,* vol. 7, no. 1, National Art Education Association, Washington, D.C., Autumn, 1965, pp. 34–41.

Kincaid, Clarence E., "The Determination and Description of Various Creative Attributes of Children," *Studies in Art Education,* vol. 2, no. 2, National Art Education Association, State Teachers College, Kutztown, Pa., 1961, pp. 45–53.

Knee, Sidney Max, "Art Appreciation for 5th and 6th Grades," unpublished doctoral dissertation, New York University, New York, 1961.

Kramer, Edith, *Art Therapy in a Children's Community,* Charles C Thomas, Publisher, Springfield, Ill., 1958.

Lanier, Vincent, *Teaching Secondary Art,* International Textbook Company, Scranton, Pa., 1958.

Lansing, Kenneth, "The Effect of Class Size and Room Size upon the Creative Drawings of Fifth Grade Children," *Research in Art Education,* Ninth Yearbook of the National Art Education Association, State Teachers College, Kutztown, Pa., 1959, pp. 70–74.

——, *Art, Artist, and Art Education,* McGraw-Hill Book Company, New York, 1969.

Lark-Horovitz, Betty, Hilda Present Lewis, and Mark Luca, *Understanding Children's Art for Better Teaching,* Charles E. Merrill Publishing Company, Columbus, Ohio, 1967.

Linderman, Earl W., and Donald W. Herberholz, *Developing Artistic and Perceptual Awareness,* 2d ed., Wm. C. Brown Company, Publishers, Dubuque, Iowa, 1969.

Lindstrom, Miriam, *Children's Art: A Study of Normal Development in Children's Modes of Visualization,* University of California Press, Berkeley, Calif., 1957.

Logan, Frederick M., *Growth of Art in American Schools,* Harper & Brothers, New York, 1955.

Lord, Lois, *Constructions and Mobiles: Preschool-Junior High School,* rev. ed., Davis Press, Inc., Worcester, Mass., 1970.

Lowenfeld, Viktor, *Creative and Mental Growth,* The Macmillan Company, New York, 1957.

—— and W. Lambert Brittain, *Creative and Mental Growth,* The Macmillan Company, New York, 1964.

—— and Kenneth Beittel, "Interdisciplinary Criteria of Creativity in the Arts and Sciences: A Progress Report," *Research in Art Education,* Ninth Yearbook of the National Art Education Association, State Teachers College, Kutztown, Pa., 1959, pp. 35–43.

Mattil, Edward L. (project director), *A Seminar in Art Education for Research and Curriculum Development,* Cooperative Research Project V-002, Pennsylvania State University, University Park, Pa., 1966.

McFee, June King, *Preparation for Art,* Wadsworth Publishing Co., San Francisco, Calif., 1961.

——, "Art for the Economically and Socially Deprived," *Art Education,* Sixty-fourth Yearbook of the National Society for the Study of Education, Part II, National Art Education Association, Washington, D.C., 1965, pp. 153–174.

——, "Urbanism and Art Education in the U.S.A.," *Art Education,* vol. 22, no. 6, 1969, 16–18.

McVitty, Lawrence F., "An Experimental Study on Various Methods in Art Motivations at the Fifth Grade Level," *Research in Art Education,* Seventh Yearbook of the National Art Education Association, Washington, D.C., 1956, pp. 74–83.

Merritt, Helen, *Guiding Free Expression in Children's Art,* Holt, Rinehart and Winston, Inc., New York, 1964.

Michael, John A., "The Effect of Award, Adult Standards and Peer Standards upon the Creativeness in Art of High School Pupils," *Research in Art Education,* Eighth Yearbook of the National Art Education Association, Washington, D.C., 1959, pp. 98–105.

—— (ed.), *Art Education in the Junior High School,* National Art Education Association, Washington, D.C., 1964.

——, "Art Experience During Early Adolescence," *Art Education,* 64th Yearbook of the National Society for the Study of Education, Part II, University of Chicago Press, Chicago, 1965, pp. 86–144.

Mitchell, Coretta, "A Study of Relationships Between Attitudes about Art Experience and Behavior in Art Activity," *Research in Art Education,* Seventh Yearbook of the National Art Education Association, Washington, D.C., 1956, pp. 105–111.

Montgomery, Chandler, *Art for Teachers of Children,* Charles E. Merrill Publishing Company, Columbus, Ohio, 1968.

Munro, Thomas, *Art Education: Its Philosophy and Psychology,* The Liberal Arts Press, Inc., New York, 1956.

Murphy, Judith, and Ronald Gross, *The Arts and the Poor,* U.S. Department of Health, Education and Welfare, U.S. Government Printing Office, Washington, D.C., 1968.

New York City Board of Education, *Major Art,*

Board of Education 1960–1961 Series, Curriculum Bulletin No. 11, Brooklyn, N.Y., 1960–1961.

——, *Art for the Intermediate Schools (Grades 5, 6, 7, 8)*, Bureau of Art—Bureau of Curriculum Development, Brooklyn, N.Y., 1972.

Nuss, Eugene M., "An Exploration of the Relationship between Creativity and Certain Personal-Social Variables among Eighth Grade Pupils," unpublished doctoral dissertation, University of Maryland, 1961.

Pappas, George, "An Analysis of the Process of Beginning and Developing Works of Art," *Research in Art Education*, Ninth Yearbook of the National Art Education Association, State Teachers College, Kutztown, Pa., 1959, pp. 119–124.

Pearlman, Amalia, "The Development and Testing Instructional Strategy Which Provides for Participation of Art Students in Urban Planning," U.S. Department of Health, Education and Welfare, Washington, D.C., 1969.

——, "Art Education and Ekistics," unpublished doctoral dissertation, New York University, 1970.

Perry, Kenneth F., *An Experiment with a Diversified Art Program*, Bureau of Publications, Teachers College, Columbia University, New York, 1943.

Petterson, Henry, and Ray Gerring, *Exploring with Paint*, Reinhold Publishing Corporation, New York, 1964.

Progressive Education Association, Commission on the Secondary School Curriculum, *The Visual Arts in General Education*, D. Appleton-Century Company, New York, 1940.

Raleigh, Henry P., "The Image of the Art Teacher," *Art Education*, vol. 18, no. 7, 1965, pp. 13–15.

Randall, Arne W., and Ruth Elsie Halvorsen, *Painting in the Classroom: A Key to Child Growth*, Davis Publications, Inc., Worcester, Mass., 1962.

Read, Herbert, *Education through Art*, Pantheon Books, New York, 1943.

——, "Culture and Education in World Order," an address delivered before the Annual Convention of the Committee on Art Education, Museum of Modern Art, New York, 1948.

——, *Education through Art*, 2d ed., Pantheon Books, Inc., New York, 1949.

——, *A Concise History of Modern Painting*, Frederick A. Praeger, Inc., New York, 1959.

——, "The Third Realm of Education," *The Creative Arts in American Education*, Cambridge University Press, Cambridge, Mass., 1960.

Reed, Carl, *Early Adolescent Art Education*, Chas. A. Bennett Co., Inc., Peoria, Ill., 1957.

Rose, Helen C., "Directions in Junior High School Art Education: A Pilot Survey of City Junior High School Programs," *Research in Art Education*, Ninth Yearbook of the National Art Education Association, State Teachers College, Kutztown, Pa., 1959, pp. 131–136.

Rouse, Mary J., "A New Look at an Old Theory: A Comparison of Lowenfeld's 'Haptic-Visual' Theory with Witkin's Perceptual Theory," *Studies in Art Education*, vol. 7, no. 1, National Art Education Association, Washington, D.C., Autumn, 1965, pp. 42–55.

Rowan, Herman Thomas, "A Survey of Junior High School Art Education," *Eastern Art Association Research Bulletin*, vol. 4, State Teachers College, Kutztown, Pa., April, 1953, pp. 16–17.

Russell, A. Barklay, "Art and the Adolescent," *Education in Art*, ed. by Edwin Ziegfeld, UNESCO, Paris, 1953, pp. 46–49.

Salome, R. A., "The Effects of Perceptual Training upon the Two-Dimensional Drawings of Children," *Studies in Art Education*, vol. 7, no. 1, National Art Education Association, Washington, D.C., Autumn, 1965, pp. 18–33.

Saunders, Robert J., "The Contributions of Viktor Lowenfeld to Art Education," Part I, "Early Influences on His Thoughts," *Studies in Art Education*, vol. 2, no. 1, National Art Education Association, Washington, D.C., Fall, 1960.

Schaefer-Simmern, Henry, *The Unfolding of Artistic Activity*, University of California Press, Los Angeles, Calif., 1948.

Schwartz, Fred R., *Structure and Potential in Art Education*, Ginn and Company, Waltham, Mass., 1970.

Shroff, Piroja D., "Seventh Grade Art Curriculum and Instruction in the Public Schools of Los Angeles County," unpublished doctoral dissertation, University of Southern California, 1961.

Silverman, Ronald H., "Watts, the Disadvantaged, and Art Education," *Art Education*, vol. 19, no. 3, March, 1966.

—— and Ralph Hoepfner, *Developing and Evaluating Art Curricula Specifically Designed for Disadvantaged Youth*, U.S. Department of Health, Education and Welfare, Los Angeles, Calif., 1969.

Smith, Ralph A., "The Structure of Art—Historical Knowledge and Art Education," *Art Education*, Sixty-fourth Yearbook of the National Society for the Study of Education, Part II, The National Education Association, Washington, D.C., 1965, pp. 23–33.

——, "Images of Art Education," *Studies in Art Education*, vol. 7, no. 1, National Art Education Association, Washington, D.C., Autumn, 1965, pp. 56–61.

Stuart, William, "Painting, A Fundamental Experience for Children," *School Arts*, vol. 63, no. 3, November, 1963, pp. 21–23.

Taylor, Calvin W. (ed.), *Creativity, Progress and Potential*, McGraw-Hill Book Company, New York, 1964.

Taylor, Harold, *Art and Intellect*, Museum of Modern Art, New York, 1960.

Teachers College, Bureau of Publications, *Art Education Today*, Yearbooks, Columbia University, New York, 1935, 1943, 1948, 1949, 1952.

The Arts in Education, Seventh National Conference on the Arts in Education, sponsored by the National Council of the Arts in Education, Sarah Lawrence College, Bronxville, N.Y., Sept. 3–6, 1968.

"The Symposium of the Uses of Newer Media in

Art Education Projects," from a transcript of selected portions of a conference sponsored by the National Art Education Association and the U.S. Office of Education (Vincent Lanier: project director), Dec. 12–17, 1965.

The Visual Arts in General Education, a Report of the Committee on the Foundation of Art in General Education for the Commission on Secondary School Curriculum Progressive Education Association, D. Appleton & Company, Inc., New York, 1940.

Torrance, Paul R., and Paul R. Henrickson, "Some Implications for Art Education from the Minnesota Studies of Creative Thinking," *Studies in Art Education,* National Art Education Association, vol. 2, no. 2, Washington, D.C., Spring, 1961.

✓Tritten, Gottfried, *Art Techniques for Children,* Reinhold Publishing Corporation, New York, 1964.

Tumin, Melvin, "Art Education and Creative Social Life," *Art Education: A Frontier for Freedom,* Sixth Yearbook of National Art Education Association, State Teachers College, Kutztown, Pa., 1955.

UNESCO, *Education and Art: A Symposium,* ed. by Edwin Ziegfeld, Paris, 1953.

U.S. Department of Health, Education and Welfare, *The Arts and the Poor,* Washington, D.C., 1968.

Villemain, Francis T., "Democracy, Education, and Art," in *Readings in Art Education,* ed. by Elliot W. Eisner and David W. Ecker, Blaisdell Publishing Company, Waltham, Mass., 1966.

Wachowiak, Frank, and Theodore Ramsy, *Emphasis: Art,* International Textbook Company, Scranton, Pa., 1965.

—— and David Hodge, *Art in Depth: A Qualitative Program for the Young Adolescent,* International Textbook Company, Scranton, Pa., 1970.

Wilson, Brent G., "An Experimental Study Designed to Alter Fifth and Sixth Grade Students' Perception of Paintings," *Studies in Art Education,* National Art Education Association, Washington, D.C., vol. 6, no. 1, Fall, 1966, pp. 33–42.

CHILD DEVELOPMENT AND PSYCHOLOGY

Bernard, Harold, *Human Development in Western Culture,* Allyn and Bacon, Inc., Boston, 1962.

Biemenstok, Theodore, "The Peer Culture of Youth and School," *Readings in the Psychology of Human Growth and Development,* Holt, Rinehart and Winston, Inc., New York, 1962.

Blair, Arthur Witt, and William H. Burton, *Growth and Development of the Pre-Adolescent,* Appleton Century Crofts, Inc., New York, 1951.

Boll, Eleanor Stoker, and James Herbert Bosard, *The Sociology of Child Development,* Harper & Row, Publishers, Incorporated, 1966.

Campbell, Elise Hatt, "The Social-Sex Development of Children," *Genetic Psychology Monographs,* vol. XXI, The Journal Press, Provincetown, Mass., 1939.

Children's Bureau, *Your Child from Six to Twelve,* Publication No. 324, U.S. Government Printing Office, Washington, D.C., 1949.

Combs, Arthur W., "A Perceptual View of the Adequate Personality," *Perceiving, Behaving, Becoming,* Yearbook of the Association for Supervision and Curriculum Development, National Education Association, Washington, D.C., 1962.

Corey, Stephen M., and Virgil E. Herrick, "The Developmental Task of Children and Young People," *Readings in the Psychology of Human Growth and Development,* ed. by Warren R. Baller, Holt, Rinehart and Winston, Inc., New York, 1962.

Coser, R. L., "Laughter Among Colleagues," *Psychiatry,* vol. 23, no. 1, 1960, 81–89.

Dennis, Wayne (ed.), *Readings in Child Psychology,* 2d ed., Prentice-Hall, Inc., Englewood Cliffs, N.J., 1963.

Erikson, Erik H., *Childhood and Society,* W. W. Norton & Company, Inc., New York, 1963.

Flavell, John H., *The Development Psychology of Jean Piaget,* D. Van Nostrand Co., Inc., Princeton, N.J., 1963.

Frenkel-Brunswick, Else, "A Study of Prejudice in Children," *Human Relations,* University of California Press, Berkeley, Calif.,

Gesell, Arnold, et al., *Youth, the Years from Ten to Sixteen,* Harper & Brothers, New York, 1956.

Haimowitz, Morris L., and Natalie R. Haimowitz (eds.), *Human Development: Selected Readings.* Thomas Y. Crowell Company, New York, 1960.

Harris, Dale E., *Children's Drawing as Measures of Intellectual Maturity,* Harcourt, Brace & World, Inc., New York, 1966.

Hatfield, J. A., *Childhood and Adolescence,* Penguin Books, Inc., Baltimore, Md., 1965.

Havighurst, Robert J., *Human Development and Education,* Longmans, Green & Co., Ltd., London, 1953.

Hawkes, Glenn R., and Damaris Pease, *Behavior and Development from 5 to 12,* Harper & Brothers, New York, 1962.

Hurlock, Elizabeth, Frances Ilge, and Louise Bates, *Child Development,* McGraw-Hill Book Company, New York, 1950.

Jersild, Arthur T., Frances U. Markey, and Catherine L. Jersild, "Children's Fears, Dreams, Wishes, Daydreams, Likes, Dislikes, Pleasant and Unpleasant Memories," *Child Development Monograph,* No. 12, 1933.

—— and Ruth J. Tasch, *Children's Interests,* Bureau of Publications, Teachers College, Columbia University, New York, 1949.

Jung, Carl, "Archetypes and the Collective Unconscious," *Collected Works*, vol. 9, part 1, Bollingen series, ed. by Phelin Adler, Princeton University Press, Princeton, N.J., 1968.

Knoles, Gerald, "Teacher-Pupil Relationships as Related to Self-Concept Needs," unpublished doctoral dissertation, University of Illinois, Urbana, Ill., 1966.

Laughlin, Frances, *The Peer Status of Sixth and Seventh Grade Children*, Bureau of Publications, Teachers College, Columbia University, New York, 1954.

Lehman, M. C., and P. A. Witty, *The Psychology of Play Activities*, Barnes & Noble, Inc., New York, 1927.

Lewis, Gertrude K. (Chairman), *Educating Children in Grades Four, Five and Six*, a report prepared by five staff members in the Elementary School Section of the U.S. Office of Education, Department of Health, Education and Welfare, Bulletin No. 3, U.S. Government Printing Office, Washington, D.C., 1960 reprint.

Lindgren, Henry Clay, *Educational Psychology in the Classroom*, 2d ed., John Wiley & Sons, Inc., New York, 1962.

Loomis, Mary Jane, *The Preadolescent*, Appleton Century Crofts, New York, 1959.

Maslow, Abraham H., "A Theory of Human Motivation," *Psychological Review*, vol. 50, 1943, pp. 370–96.

——, "Some Theoretical Consequences of Basic Need Gratification," *Journal of Personality*, no. 16, 1946, pp. 404–416.

——, "The Creative Attitude," Address to the Canadian Society for Education through Art, Annual Conference, Saskatoon, Canada, Oct., 1962.

McCandless, Boyd R., *Children and Adolescents: Behavior and Development*, Holt, Rinehart and Winston, Inc., New York, 1961.

McDonald, Frederick J., *Educational Psychology*, Wadsworth Publishing Company, Inc., San Francisco, Calif., 1961.

Meyer, W. J., "Relationship Between Social Need Strivings and the Development of Heterosexual Affiliation," *Journal of Abnormal Psychology*, vol. 59, no. 1, 1959.

Moreno, J. L., "Changes in Sex Groupings of School Children," *Readings in Social Psychology*, ed. by G. E. Swanson et al., Henry Holt and Company, Inc., New York, 1952.

Mussen, Paul Henry, *The Psychological Development of the Child, Foundations of Modern Psychology Series*, Prentice-Hall, Inc., Englewood Cliffs, N.J., 1963.

——, John Janeway Conger, and Jerome Kagan, *Child Development and Personality*, 2d ed., Harper & Row, Publishers, Incorporated, New York, 1963.

Perceiving, Behaving, Becoming, A Yearbook prepared by the Association for Supervision and Curriculum, 1962 Yearbook Committee, Arthur W. Combs, chairman, National Education Association, Washington, D.C., 1962.

Piston, Frederick, "How Time Concepts Are Acquired by Children," *Educational Method*, vol. 20, Nov. 20, 1940.

Pope, B., "Socio-economic Contrasts in Children's Peer Culture Prestige Values," *Genetic Psychological Monographs*, vol. 48, 1953.

Rabban, M., "Sex-Role Identification of Younger Children in Two Diverse Social Groups," *Genetic Psychological Monographs*, vol. 48, 1953.

Rand, Paul, "Design and the Play Instinct," *Education of Vision*, ed. by Gyorgy Kepes, George Braziller, Inc., New York, 1965.

Redl, Fritz, "Preadolescents: What Makes Them Tick?", reprint from *Child Study*, vol. 21, Winter, 1943/44, 44–48, 58–59.

——, *What Do Children Think of Teachers?* Reinhold Publishing Corporation, New York, 1968.

Rosenblith, Judy F., and Wesley Allinsmith, *Causes of Behavior: Readings in Child Development and Educational Psychology*, Allyn and Bacon, Inc., Boston, 1964.

Stone, Lawrence Joseph, and Joseph Church, *Childhood and Adolescence: A Psychology of the Growing Person*, Random House, Inc., New York, 1957.

Sullivan, Harry Stack, *Conceptions of Modern Psychiatry*, William Alanson White Psychiatric Foundation, Washington, D.C., 1940.

Tyler, L. H., "The Development of Vocational Interests," in "Observation of Likes and Dislikes in Ten-Year-Old Children," *Journal of Genetic Psychology*, vol. 86–87, March, 1955.

Wolfenstein, Martha, "Riddles and the Legend of the Moron," in *Causes of Behavior: Readings in Child Development and Educational Psychology*, ed. by Judy Rosenblith, Allyn and Bacon, Inc., Boston, 1964.

THE DISADVANTAGED

Barclay, Doris L., "Dissemination and Implementation of Research on Art Education for the Disadvantaged Child" (Summary Statement to the series on Art Education for the Disadvantaged Child), *Art Education*, vol. 22, no. 5, May, 1969, pp. 23–24.

Bigart, Homer, "A New-Mexican-American Militancy," New York *Times*, Apr. 20, 1968.

Bloom, Benjamin, Allison Davis, and Robert Hess, *Compensatory Education For Cultural Deprivation*, Holt, Rinehart and Winston, Inc., New York, 1965.

Brody, William A., and Sophie D. Aberle (compilers), *The Indian: America's Unfinished Business*, University of Oklahoma Press, Norman, Okla., 1966.

——, *The Indian, America's Unfinished Business,* Report of the Commission on the Rights, Liberties and Responsibilities of the American Indian, University of Oklahoma Press, Norman, Okla., 1966.

Cahill, Imogen D., "Child Rearing Practices in Lower Socio-Economic Ethnic Groups," *The Urban R's: Race Relations as the Problem in Urban Education,* ed. by Robert A. Dentler, Bernard Mackler, and Mary Ellen Warshauer, Frederick A. Praeger, Inc., New York, 1967.

Chance, Norman A., *The Eskimo of North Alaska,* Holt, Rinehart and Winston, Inc., New York, 1966.

Clark, Kenneth B., *Prejudice and Your Child,* Beacon Press, Boston, 1963.

——, "Alternatives to Urban Public Schools," *The Schoolhouse In the City,* ed. by Alvin Toffler, Frederick A. Praeger, Inc., New York, 1968.

Cleaver, Eldridge, *Soul on Ice,* McGraw-Hill Book Company, New York, 1968.

Cohen, Harold L. "Learning Stimulation" (Art Education for the Disadvantaged Child: Part 5), *Art Education,* vol. 22, no. 3, March, 1969, pp. 2–8.

Collier, John, *Indians of the Americas,* New American Library, Inc., New York, 1946. Reprinted in *The Indian in America's Past,* ed. by Jack D. Forbes, Prentice-Hall, Inc., Englewood Cliffs, N.J., 1964.

Coombs, Madison L., Ralf E. Kron, E. Gordon Collier, and Kenneth Anderson, *The Indian Child Goes to School, A Study of Interracial Differences,* Bureau of Indian Affairs, Department of the Interior, distributed by the Haskell Institute, Lawrence, Kans.

Daedalus, Journal of the Academy of Arts and Sciences, Boston, Fall, 1965, and Winter, 1966.

Dawson, Helaine S., *On the Outskirts of Hope,* McGraw-Hill Book Company, New York, 1968.

Dennison, George, *The Lives of Children,* Random House, Inc., New York, 1969.

Dentler, Robert A., Bernard Mackler and Mary Ellen Warshauer (ed.), *The Urban R's: Race Relations as the Problem in Urban Education,* Frederick A. Praeger, Inc., New York, 1967.

Deutsch, Martin, Irinn Kates, and Arthur R. Jensen (eds.), *Social Class, Race and Psychological Development,* Holt, Rinehart and Winston, Inc., New York, 1968.

Eisenberg, Leon, "Strengths of the Inner City Child," *Disadvantaged Minority Groups,* ed. by A. Harry Passow, Miriam Goldberg, and Abraham Tannenbaum, Holt, Rinehart and Winston, Inc., New York, 1967.

Fantini, Mario, *The Disadvantaged: Challenge to Education,* Harper & Row, Publishers, Incorporated, New York, 1968.

—— and Gerald Weinstein, *Making Urban Schools Work: Social Realities and the Urban School,* Holt, Rinehart and Winston, Inc., New York, 1968.

Frazier, Franklin E., *The Negro Family in the United States,* University of Chicago Press, Chicago, 1966.

Gaps, Herbert J., *The Urban Villagers,* The Macmillan Company, New York, 1962.

Glazer, Nathan, "The Peoples of America," *Minorities in a Changing World,* ed. by Milton T. Barron, Alfred A. Knopf, Inc., 1967.

—— and Patrick Moynihan, *Beyond the Melting Pot,* The M.I.T. Press, Cambridge, Mass., 1963.

Greenberg, Norman, and Gilda Greenberg, *Education of the American Indian in Today's World,* Wm. C. Brown Company, Publishers, Dubuque, Iowa, 1964.

Greenwalt, Crawford M., "To Balance Our Talent," *Teachers College Record,* January, 1964, pp. 373–379.

King, A. Richard, *The School at Mopass: A Problem of Identity,* Holt, Rinehart and Winston, Inc., 1967.

Kohl, Herbert, *36 Children,* New American Library, Inc., 1967.

Landis, Margaret, *Eskimo Childhood and Interpersonal Relationships,* University of Washington Press, Seattle, Wash., 1960.

Moe, Edward O., *The Changing Rural Scene,* Conference on Solving Educational Problems in Sparsely Populated Areas, Denver, Colo., March, 1969.

Mohr, George J., and Marian A. Despres, *A Stormy Decade: Adolescence,* Random House, Inc., New York, 1958.

Nearine, Robert J., "Hope in Our Time: Some Explorations into Compensatory Education" (Art Education for the Disadvantaged Child: Part 6 [conclusion], *Art Education,* vol. 22, no. 5, May, 1969, pp. 7–8.

Passow, A. Harry (ed.), *Education in Depressed Areas,* Teachers College, Columbia University New York, 1963.

——, Miriam Goldberg, and J. Tannenbaum (eds.), *Education of the Disadvantaged: A Book of Readings,* Holt, Rinehart and Winston, Inc., 1967.

Powledge, Fred, *To Change a Child,* A Report on the Institute for Developmental Studies, Quadrangle Books and Anti-Defamation, League of B'nai Brith, Chicago, 1967.

Reichard, Gladys, "The Navajo and Christianity," *American Anthropologist,* Jan.–March, 1949.

Riessman, Frank, *The Culturally Deprived Child,* Harper & Brothers, New York, 1962.

Roman, Melvin, "The Arts as Agents of Social Change: A Psychologist's Viewpoint," *Art Education* (Art Education for the Disadvantaged Child: Part 3), vol. 21, no. 9, 1968, 23–27.

Roseman, Tena, "Relationship of Northern Born and Reared Negro Children and Southern Born and Reared Negro Children in Terms of Self-Concept," unpublished doctoral dissertation, New York University, New York, 1962.

Segall, Marshall H., Donald T. Campbell, and Melville J. Herskonits, *The Influence of Culture on Visual Perception,* The Bobbs-Merrill Company, Inc., New York, 1966.

Sexton, Patricia Cayo, *Education and Income,* The Viking Press, Inc., New York, 1964.

———, *Spanish Harlem,* Harper & Row, Publishers, Incorporated, New York, 1965.

Skeel, Dorothy, "Determining the Compatibility of Student Teachers of Culturally Deprived Schools by Means of a Cultural Attitude Inventory," unpublished doctoral dissertation, Pennsylvania State University, University Park, Pa., 1962.

Skinner, Vincent, "Why Many Appalachian Children are Problem Readers—We Create the Problem," *Journal of Reading,* Nov., 1967.

Snyder, Eldon E., "Self-Concept Theory," *Clearing House,* vol. 40, Dec., 1965, pp. 242–246.

Special Report, Rockefeller Foundation, New York, Winter, 1965.

Steiner, Stan, *The New Indians,* Harper & Row, Publishers, Incorporated, New York, 1968.

Studies in Art Education, A Journal of Issues and Research in Art Education, National Art Education Association, Washington, D.C., vol. 11,

no. 1, Fall, 1969.

The Use of Art in Compensatory Education Projects: An Inventory, prepared by the staff of the Urban Child Center, School of Education, University of Chicago, 1966.

Toffler, Alvin, *The Schoolhouse in the City,* Frederick A. Praeger, Inc., New York, 1968.

Wax, Rosalie H., and Robert K. Thomas, "American Indians and White People," *Phylon,* vol. 22, no. 4, 1961.

Westby-Gibson, Dorothy, "New Perspectives for Art Education: Teaching the Disadvantaged" (Art Education for the Disadvantaged Child: Part 2), *Art Education,* vol. 1, no. 8, November, 1968, pp. 22–24.

Wolcott, Harry F., *A Kwakiutl Village and School,* Holt, Rinehart and Winston, Inc., New York, 1967.

Zintz, Miles V., *Education Across Cultures,* Wm. C. Brown Book Co., Dubuque, Iowa, 1963.

ART TECHNIQUES

Anderson, Patricia E., *Creative Activities with Clay,* San Diego Public Schools, San Diego, Calif., 1961.

Beaumont, Cyril, *Puppets and Puppetry,* The Studio Publications, New York, 1958.

Bethers, Ray, *Composition in Pictures,* 2d ed., Pitman Publishing Corporation, New York, 1956.

Brow, Francis, *Collage,* Pitman Publishing Corporation, New York, 1963.

Buerki, Frederick A., *Stagecraft For Nonprofessionals,* University of Wisconsin Press, Madison, Wis., 1955.

Carry, P., *Lighting the Stage,* Sir Isaac Pitman & Sons, Ltd., London, 1954.

Chast, Bernard, *Artist at Work,* Webb Books, Inc., Cambridge, Mass., 1960.

Durland, Francis Caldwell, *Creative Dramatics for Children,* The Antioch Press, Yellow Springs, Ohio, 1952.

Ford, Betty Davenport, *Ceramic Sculpture,* Reinhold Publishing Corporation, New York, 1964.

Fraser, John H., and Willard J. Friedrich, *Scenery Design For the Amateur Stage,* The Macmillan Company, New York, 1960.

Green, Peter, *Introducing Surface Printing,* Watson-Guptill, New York, 1967.

Hankes, Robert, *Orientation to Drawing and Painting,* Kalamazoo Public Schools and the Institute of Arts Press, Kalamazoo, Mich., 1965.

Jensen, Lawrence N., *Synthetic Painting Media,* Prentice-Hall, Inc., Englewood Cliffs, N.J., 1964.

Karasq, Mariska, *Adventures in Stitches,* Funk & Wagnalls, New York, 1949.

Krenitsky, Nik, *Stitchery,* Reinhold Publishing Corporation, New York, 1966.

———, *Batik: Art & Craft,* Reinhold Publishing Corporation, New York, 1964.

Lidstone, John, *Building with Cardboard,* Reinhold Publishing Corporation, New York, 1968.

——— and Don McIntosh, *Children as Film Makers,* Van Nostrand Reinhold Company, New York, 1970.

——— and Lewis Brody, *Reinhold Visuals Aids,* Reinhold Publishing Corp., New York, 1968.

McDarrah, Fred W., *The Artist's World in Pictures,* E. P. Dutton & Co., Inc., New York, 1961.

Meilach, Dona, and Elvie Ten Hoor, *Collage and Found Art,* Reinhold Publishing Corporation, New York, 1964.

Miller, Helen L., *Pointers on Producing the School Play,* Plays, Inc., Boston, 1960.

Newman, Thelma R., *Plastics as an Art Form,* Chilton Books, Philadelphia, 1964.

Petterson, Henry, *Creating from Clay,* Reinhold Publishing Corporation, New York, 1968.

——— and Ray Gerring, *Exploring with Paint,* Reinhold Publishing Corporation, New York, 1964.

Proctor, Richard M., *The Principles of Pattern,* Van Nostrand Reinhold Company, New York, 1969.

Rausmusen, Henry, and Art Grant, *Sculpture from Junk,* Reinhold Publishing Corporation, New York, 1967.

Riley, Olive L., *Drawing and Painting,* Capitol Publishing Co., Inc., New York, 1958.

——— and Louise C. Kainz, *Exploring Art,* Harcourt, Brace & World, Inc., New York, 1951.

Rotter, Ernst, *Creative Paper Design,* Reinhold Publishing Corporation, New York, 1959.

———, *Creative Clay Design,* Reinhold Publishing Corporation, New York, 1963.

Skinner, Freda, *Wood Carving,* Sterling Publishing Co., Inc., New York, 1963.

Snoum, Gunnar, *Teaching Design and Form,* Reinhold Publishing Corporation, New York, 1965.

Watson, Ernest W., *Perspective for Sketchers,* Reinhold Publishing Corporation, New York, 1964.

Waxtheimer, Bodo W., *Drawing and Painting Book,* Reinhold Publishing Corporation, New York, 1961.

Wittick, Walter A., and Charles F. Schuller, *Audio-Visual Materials: Their Use and Nature,* Harper & Row, Publishers, Incorporated, New York, 1962.

ADDITIONAL SOURCES

Allstrom, Elizabeth, *Let's Play a Story,* Friendship Press, New York, 1957.

Brod, Pearl, "The Middle School: Trends towards Its Adoption," *The Clearing House,* vol. 40, no. 6, February, 1966, pp. 331–333.

Bruner, Jerome S., *On Knowing,* Harvard University Press, Cambridge, Mass., 1963.

——, *The Process of Education,* Random House, Inc., New York, 1963.

Chiver, Peter, *Staging a School Play,* Harper & Row, Publishers, Incorporated, New York, 1967.

Communication: A Creative Approach to Teaching English and the Arts, Pennsylvania Advancement School, Inc., Philadelphia, Pa., 1968.

Dunphy, Dexter C., "The Social Structure of Urban Adolescent Peer Groups," *Sociometry,* vol. 26, June, 1963, pp. 230–246.

Godfrey, Barbara B., and Newell C. Kephart, *Movement Patterns and Motor Education,* Appleton Century Crofts, New York, 1969.

Goodman, Paul, *Growing Up Absurd,* Vintage Books, New York, 1966.

Gunn, Richard, "Effectiveness of Art Teachers in Meeting Needs of Adolescents," unpublished doctoral dissertation, Stanford University, 1955.

Guskin, Edward Allen, and Samuel Louis Guskin, *A Social Psychology of Education,* Addison-Wesley Publishing Co., Reading, Mass., 1970.

Hecksher, William S., *Art and Literature: Art Treasures of the World,* Harry N. Abrams, Inc., New York, 1954.

Holt, John, *How Children Fail,* Dell Publishing Co., Inc., New York, 1964.

Leonard, George B., *Education and Ecstasy,* Delacorte Press, New York, 1968.

Madon, Constant A., "The Middle School: Its Philosophy and Purpose," *The Clearing House,* vol. 40, no. 6, February, 1966, pp. 329–330.

Mead, Margaret, "The Role of Art in a Culture," *Art Education Bulletin,* Yearbook of the Eastern Art Association, State Teachers College, Kutztown, Pa., 1950.

——, *Cultural Patterns and Technical Change,* A Manual Prepared by the World Federation for Mental Health, Mentor Books, New York, 1955.

McLuhan, Marshall, *Understanding Media: The Extensions of Man,* The New American Library, Signet Books, New York, 1964.

——, *The Medium is the Message,* Bantam Books, New York, 1967.

—— and Harley Parker, *Through the Vanishing Point: Space in Poetry and Painting,* Harper & Row, Publishers, Incorporated, New York, 1968.

Muller, Richard J. (conference coordinator), *Humanities in The Schools: A Symposium on Humanities,* University of Kentucky, Lexington, Ky., Dec. 9–10, 1965.

Murphy, Judith, *Middle Schools,* Educational Facilities Laboratories, New York, 1965.

Parker, Cecil J., and Lois J. Rubin, *Process as Content: Curriculum Design and the Application of Knowledge,* Rand McNally & Company, Chicago, 1966.

Phenin, Philip H., *Education for the Common Good, A Moral Philosophy of the Curriculum,* Harper & Brothers, Inc., New York, 1961.

——, *Realms of Meaning,* McGraw-Hill Book Company, New York, 1964.

Rowen, Betty, *Learning through Movement,* Teachers College, Columbia University, New York, 1963.

Rugg, Harold, *Imagination,* Harper & Row, Publishers, Incorporated, New York, 1963.

School Arts Magazine, "Fourth Grade Puppets Aid Learning," Davis Publications, Inc., Worcester, Mass., December, 1958, pp. 27–28.

——, "Designing through Slide Projections," Davis Publications, Inc., Worcester, Mass., November, 1960, pp. 23–24.

Schurr, Evelyn L., *Movement Experiences for Children,* Appleton Century Crofts, New York, 1967.

Schwartz, Gary, and Don Merten, "The Language of Adolescence: An Anthropological Approach to the Youth Culture," *The American Journal of Sociology,* vol. 72, no. 5, 1967, 453–468.

Selden, Samuel, *Man in His Theatre,* University of North Carolina Press, Chapel Hill, N.C., 1957.

Sharp, George, *Curriculum Development as Reeducation of the Teacher,* Teachers College, Columbia University, New York, 1951.

Van Hooft, Gordon E., *The Humanities: A Planning Guide for Teachers,* N.Y. State Education Department, Bureau of Secondary Curriculum, Albany, N.Y., 1966.

Vernon, Howard, *The Complete Book of Children's Theatre,* Doubleday & Company, Garden City, N.Y., 1969.

Yochim, Louise D., *Perceptual Growth in Creativity,* International Textbook Company, Scranton, Pa., 1967.

Index

Index

439